WARSHIP 2000-2001

WARSHIP 2000-2001

Edited by Antony Preston

CONWAY

MARITIME PRESS

Frontispiece
*Included in this year's Warship Gallery are photographs of the US landings at Casablanca harbour on 8 November 1942. This strik-
ing image was taken from USS* Wilkes *and shows two of the three other destroyers* (Swanson, Ludlow *and* Murphy) *involved in the
operation.* (Robert P. Largesse).

First published in Great Britain in 2000 by
Conway Maritime Press,
9 Blenheim Court, Brewery Road,
London N7 9NT

A member of the Chrysalis Group plc

British Library Cataloguing in Publication Data
A record of this title is available on request from the British Library.

ISBN 0 85177 791 0

Conway editorial team: Daniel Mersey and Martin Robson
Typesetting and layout by Stephen Dent
Printed and bound in Spain.

CONTENTS

EDITORIAL

Readers of *Warship* will, we hope, be cheered by the appearance of the latest volume, which is back on schedule, roughly a year after its predecessor.

The pace of warship-design continues to advance at frightening speed. With a bit of imagination we can guess at the feeling of headlong change which must have affected naval observers in the middle of the nineteenth century and again fifty years later. The new ships were not only faster and better-armed; they *looked* different, even outlandish to the traditionalists.

Today we shudder at the 'bald' uncluttered appearance of ships like the US Navy's new *Zumwalt* (DD-21) class destroyers or the Royal Swedish Navy's *Visby* class corvettes, but a previous generation was appalled at the 'underarmed' appearance of post-1945 ships. 'Stealth' is not only transforming naval warfare, but also the way ships are built. Materials are changing, with composites used for superstructures in a number of designs, and advances in technology now permit all-electric drive to replace traditional shaftlines. It is all too easy to wallow in nostalgia and regret the passing of veterans who would stand no chance of surviving modern battle. Late Victorian public opinion prevented the Admiralty from getting rid of 'coffin ships', and vast sums were spent on refitting doughty veterans. The basic laws of economics do not change; money spent on extending the lives of over-age warships is better spent on new construction. The folly of the Reagan administration's obsession with maintaining a '600 Ship Navy' (a figure plucked from the air by Secretary of the Navy John Lehman, incidentally) resulted in refits of 50-year old auxiliaries, and finally left the US Navy with fewer than 300 ships.

It would be a pointless exercise to list all the 'theories and certainties' of self-appointed prophets of naval trends. In my own lifetime I have read endless theories about the future, starting with the impotence of navies in the face of air power, the 'four-minute war' of mutual nuclear destruction, the supremacy of the anti-ship missile, the 'undefeatable' fast attack craft, and the omnipotence of the submarine. As a university student I was told by an older friend who 'knew all about military strategy' that if navies had any future at all, they would be under the command of the air force. With such infallible guidance at my disposal, I learned to avoid prophecy, and two maxims: never say 'never again', and never say, 'it will be over by Christmas'.

One of the purposes of *Warship* is to take note of bygone theories of warfare, and to trace their impact on ship-design, and to examine the behaviour of ships in action. Battle experience remains the acid test of the validity of all theories, and even if contemporary analysis was poor, we ought to try to match the conflicting evidence and produce credible answers to important questions. Another aim is to bridge the generations by illustrating the basic problems of matching ship-technology to operational requirements, contemporary politics and, ultimately, money. Naval architecture has always been a series of trade-offs, and the 'perfect ship' has yet to be invented.

Within that loose editorial framework, Peter Brook looks at the relatively obscure Battle of Ulsan in the Russo-Japanese War, one of only two occasions when armoured cruiser fought each other. The First Class cruiser (nowadays often confused with the armoured cruiser) marked another phase in theoretical warfare, this time to hunt down French and Russian commerce-raiding cruisers. These ships ranged from medium displacement to huge 11,000-ton ships, equivalent in some respects to Second Class battleships. Chris Ware has completed the work started by the late David Topliss, but it was intended to be published as a book, and has had to be divided into three sections.

Stephen McLaughlin describes the *Retvizan*, the only American-designed and built battleship to serve in the Imperial Russian Navy, while Keith McBride does another excellent job on HMS *Nile* and HMS *Trafalgar*, famous for being described by the First Sea Lord as 'possibly the last such ships to be built for the Royal Navy', shortly before a series of much larger designs was built. Their imposing appearance endeared them to the public, and foreshadowed William White's *Royal Sovereign* class, but they were soon overtaken by superior designs.

The navy built for the Australian State of Victoria was the first colonial adjunct to the Royal Navy, and it too was predicated on a fear of Russian cruisers raiding shipping in the South West Pacific. Although limited to a role of coast defence, Colin Jones shows that it included some of the most advanced warships available, including the turret ship *Cerberus* and torpedo boats.

In the years after the Russian War and the American Civil War, the Royal Swedish Navy embraced the latest theories of coast defence, using pare torpedoes, 'automobile' torpedoes and mines. Daniel Harris shows how this translated into extensive programmes of torpedo boat construction, culminating in the first destroyers. It could be argued that the Swedish taxpayers' money was wasted, but equally, can we rule out the possibility that the Swedish naval policy deterred the Russians?

David Brown has provided another biographical sketch, this time of Sir William White, the great Victorian Director of Naval Construction who gave the Royal Navy a magnificent set of some forty homogenous battleships. White was not only a brilliant naval architect but also a superb administrator. His reorganisation of the Royal Dockyards to cope with Naval Defence Act made them competitive with the best private shipyards.

Peter Kelly describes the German U-boats' war against Allied hospital ships in the First World War, a tale of heroism, decency among some U-boat captains, and ruthlessness interpretation of official policy by others. Although not warships in the technical sense, hospital ships play a vital part in naval warfare, and it entirely appropriate that we should know more about their activities in the First World War.

Between the two world wars the French Navy produced a series of large destroyers, of which the ultra-fast *Fantasque* class *contre-torpilleurs* were the only ones to see serious action in wartime. John Jordan assesses the performance and fighting power of these controversial ships.

Pierre Hervieux examines the achievements of the *Kriegsmarine*'s Type II coastal U-boats which formed the core of the U-boat Arm in the early months of the war. Despite their small displacement they saw service in a number of theatres, right to the end in 1945. George Moore examines the complex story of Royal Navy destroyer-development at the end of the Second World War. The 'Weapon' class saw post-war service, but the enlarged *Gallant* class never got beyond the drawing-board.

As a short epilogue, the Editor has provided a short history of air-independent propulsion (AIP) for Russian and Soviet submarines. AIP experiments go back much further than previously thought, underlining the formidable ingenuity of Russian engineers. If only the political system had been less murderously inefficient these ideas might have given the Soviet Navy a vital advantage over its adversaries. This edition is concluded by the usual round-up of important naval developments, it has been a particularly busy year for the world's navies, with new programmes and policy initiatives.

As always, comments and criticisms are welcomed, and we look forward to receiving submissions for next year's *Warship*. My personal thanks go to the Conway team for their invaluable support in getting this volume completed, particularly Daniel Mersey and Martin Robson, and designer Steve Dent, and of course the patient contributors who have to wait while the production process grinds on.

Antony Preston

FIRST CLASS CRUISERS

Part One

This first article by **David Topliss** and **Chris Ware** outlines the reason for the development of the true First Class cruisers for the Royal Navy. It looks at the debates fuelled inside and out of the Navy by the introduction of this type of vessel. Part two will look at later classes of protected and Armoured Cruisers as well as some more detailed discussion of their armament and armour and their performance in action.

Orlando Class

The *Orlandos* were the Royal Navy's first true large cruisers. Unlike previous ships, the *Orlandos* were true cruising ships with high speed, good armament, reasonable protection and a good radius of action. But although they were always regarded as cruisers, and fulfilled the duties of cruisers, this was not the purpose for which there were designed.

The class grew out of the Northbrook programme of 1884 and were conceived in something of a panic. In the July of that year Lord Northbrook had declared that, considering the uncertain state of naval architecture: 'The great difficulty the Admiralty would have to contend with if they were granted £3,000.000 or £4,000,000 would be to decide how to spend the money'. In September the consequences of this rather rash statement came home to roost when the Pall Mall Gazette published the first of a series of articles called 'What is the Truth about the Navy?'. Written by W T Stead, the paper's editor, with information supplied by Captain J A Fisher (later Admiral of the Fleet Lord Fisher) the articles caused a panic in Britain that only subsided when the Government undertook to order two first class ironclads, five first class cruisers, six torpedo cruisers and fourteen torpedo boats in addition to the normal yearly programme.

The *Orlandos* emerged out of this programme, as a development of the *Mersey* class of second class cruisers. The *Merseys* were the best British cruiser design to date, and marked the definitive break from the masted cruisers that had preceded them. But at the same time as they were laid down Armstrongs were building a cruiser for Chile, the *Esmeralda*. The Chilean ship, which was over a thousand tons lighter, was faster, and carried two 10in guns compared to the two 8in of the *Mersey's*, had been designed by George Rendel of Armstrongs. Rendel and Lord Armstrong both believed that in the struggle between the gun and armour the balance had swung decisively in favour of the former and that the battleship was an obsolescent type, which would be replaced by swift, well armed vessels which would be able to destroy the slow and now vulnerable battleships of the day. The *Esmeralda* was the product of this thinking and although the Chileans regarded her as a cruiser, Rendel had conceived her as a battleship destroyer.

In 1881 Rendel had been appointed to the Admiralty as an additional Civil Lord, largely to help sort out the navy's problems with its ordnance, and he soon expressed his ideas on ship design. The *Mersey's* had a designed armament of two 8in guns: it was suggested that one of these should be replaced by four 6in guns. Rendel disagreed fiercely with the proposed move and explained his thinking to Sir Astley Cooper Key in October 1882. 'These ships were especially designed to accompany the ironclad fleet and to form with it a composite force which it has been agreed, value for value, will have more fighting efficiency than a fleet composed of ironclads alone. Unless they are to engage ironclads their value to a fleet, would be simply that of scouts and they must hold aloft from any action'. Sir Nathaniel Barnaby, the Director of Naval Construction (DNC) had been looking at the possibility of building a more powerful version of the *Mersey* class at least since 1883, but the combination of the Northbrook programme and pressure from Rendel for ships that could act with the battlefleet was the force behind the design of the *Orlando*.

Barnaby was never really happy with ships that did not clearly fall either into the small cruising ship type or large ironclads, so it is not surprising that it was hard for him to decide what function he wanted the ships to fulfil. Rendel had earlier argued that the torpedo cruiser was misconceived, since the range of contemporary torpedoes was so much less than that of modern guns and that the ship would be fatally crippled before it got into a position where it could fire its torpedoes. Barnaby on the other hand thought that the rate of fire of heavy guns was so slow as to allow either a torpedo or ramming attack to succeed. Indeed he proposed that it should be made possible for officers to fire the guns from the conning tower, while withdrawing the gun crews themselves undercover during an attack, since presumably he thought it unlikely that the guns could be reloaded in time to fire again. The first drawing for an enlarged *Mersey* shows what is clearly a torpedo vessel, armed with no less than 8 torpedo tubes, six forward and aft and two amidships. The design studies show differing armament, either a uniform 6in battery or a mixture of 9.2 and 6in guns. By June 1884 the displacement was beginning to rise, largely due to doubling the number of 6in guns from six to 12 and

Orlando. *First ship of the first class cruisers built under the 1884 Naval Defence Act.* (NMM).

increasing the thickness of the armour deck slopes from 2 to 6in. But it is possible that these were no more than exploratory studies? The Protection for designs up to June 1884 was formed by a protective deck, horizontal above the water line, then sloping at an angle of 30 degrees to below the water line. From August 1884 this protective deck was replaced as the main form of protection by an armour belt 10in thick, reaching from one foot above the water line to four below, covering the magazines and machinery spaces. Beyond the ends of the belt fore and aft there was to be a further protective deck. Amidships the protective deck was to be horizontal and to be at the level of the upper edge of the armour belt. There had been a debate as to whether the protective deck should be above or below the waterline. It was felt that the main objection to the underwater deck was that there was a risk of water coming down through the openings into the hold if the hull was extensively damaged above the water line. The design of 30 October received the Board stamp of approval on the 18th of November 1884. Rendel wrote: 'The ship is transformed and is brought up to something like the rank of a second class ironclad in point of protection at the water line while preserving much of the special qualities of the unarmoured cruiser'.

The design continued to be developed, reaching its definitive form in early 1885, when invitations to tender were sent out to the major shipbuilders. The beam had grown to 56ft, there were to be two less 6in guns, and the torpedo armament was reduced from 14 tubes to eight. Almost immediately the lack of control over shipbuild-

ing that was the hallmark of Barnaby's last years as DNC became apparent. Even before the tendering process was complete, the shipbuilders had suggested the substitution of horizontal triple expansion engines for the compound machinery specified in the design. The new machinery did indeed promise higher efficiency and more power but at the cost of greater weight and space. To counter this the coal supply was reduced by 60 tons. The designers seemed to accept any increase in weight without regard for cost, and certainly until the appointment of William White as DNC, without reference to higher authority. The weight of the new 9.2 gun came out at 22 tons each rather than the 18 allowed. Electric light and the machinery involved was installed, when none had been allowed for in the design, at a cost of 15 tons. The armament, alterations in ammunition supply, and armour ammunition tubes for the 9.2in guns cost another 80 tons; increasing the complement from 350 to 421, another 60 tons. In all, the alterations added an extra 186 tons on the legend displacement, or 7in extra draught at the load water line. The ships had been designed to have an armoured freeboard of 18in at load displacement, the alterations reduced this to 11in. At deep load the condition was much worse, if the full load of coal were carried the draught would increase by 17in, and the top of the armour belt would be six inches below the waterline.

White found himself in the unenviable position of trying to find a condition that would allow the ship to have some measure of protection, and to defend the Admiralty to an angry House of Commons. The first was the easier of the two. The adoption of triple expansion engines meant that the ships could achieve the designed radius of action, with much less coal. White recommended that the coal allowance should be set at 750 tons. In that condition the top of the armour belt would be about level with the waterline. With all bunkers empty the upper edge of the belt would be 2ft 3in above the water line.

Defending the ships to the House was more difficult. Sir Edward Reed, a former DNC, had, since resigning in 1870, been a constant thorn in the side. Reed's criticism was almost totally centered upon the position and extent of the armoured belt. He believed that armoured ships should always be provided with adequate armoured freeboard: for this reason he would like White's design no more than he had approved of Barnaby's. The Admiralty's defence of the ships was led by White and involved a good deal of doublespeak. Like many others he had favoured the system of protection using a curved steel deck and the careful positioning of coal bunkers rather than an armoured belt: vessels using this system were known as protected cruisers. White argued that the effect of the overloading of the *Orlando's* was to convert them from belted to protected cruisers, and that they shared all the advantages of the later type. White stressed that the coal bunkers above the protective deck added to the safety of the ship, even though this had been no part of the original scheme of protection. He also laid great stress on the fact that the extra weight had all come from measures to increase the offensive power of the design.

Within the Admiralty, however, the result of the fiasco was a major shake up in the design procedure, the First Lord wrote a damming critique of the process. As a result in February 1887 new rules were laid down which were intended to ensure that much tighter control would be exercised in warship design. The Controller was to consult with the First Naval Lord as to the required speed, armament and complement, and then pass these requirements to the DNC. The DNC would then work with the Engineer in Chief the Director of Naval Ordnance to prepare the design. After the design had received the Board stamp no alterations were to be made without the approval of the Board. These regulations were added to in September when the Board laid down that when the ship's requirements had been met and the displacement calculated, the displacement should be increased by 4.5 per cent as a margin against which alteration could be made.

Blake *and* Edgar

William Whites return as DNC in 1885 carried with it an expectation of radical change in cruiser design. At Armstrong's White had earned a reputation for designing fast heavily armed cruisers for Japan, as well as smaller cruisers for Austria and Spain. His first cruiser design for the Royal Navy, were 2nd class *Medeas* class under the 1886-87 programme. But the next year's programme saw a requirement for two 1st class cruisers, which were to become the *Blake* and the *Blenheim*. These were followed by the *Edgar* class of the 1889 programme. It is sometimes thought, quite naturally, that the *Edgar* class was a straightforward development of the *Blake* design. The new ships were to be somewhat smaller, to reflect a proper regard for economy when a large number of ships were to be built under the Naval Defence Act of 1889. But the relationship between the two classes is more complicated: it would be more accurate to say that the design of the *Edgar* retrospectively influenced that of the *Blake*. Equally modifications made to the *Blake* were later applied to the *Edgar*.

The design work for two first class cruisers to be included in the 1888 programme had begun in August 1887. The new ships, like the *Medea* design of the previous year, were to replace the armour belt of the *Orlando* with a curved protected deck. White's reason for the new scheme of protection lay in the need to obtain high speed coupled with a large radius of action while keeping the size of the ship within reasonable limits. Even so, when completed the *Blake* was the largest cruiser yet built. White stressed the need for high speed from the very beginning, intending that the new ships would have a 2kt superiority over any existing cruiser. White instructed that the design work was to be carried out by Assistant Constructor Benton, under the supervision of William Smith. The first sketch shows a ship with an armament of four 9.2in guns carried in single mountings, two abreast fore and aft, but this was quickly changed to two 9.2in guns, one each fore and aft. The secondary armament, was to be a new 70pdr quick firing gun under development by Armstrong. But hardly had the design work started when the repercussions of the *Orlando* being overweight were felt in the form of the Board Minute of 21 September 1887 which required that an allowance of 4½ per cent over the design displacement should be added for growth. In the cruiser the result of this was that the displacement had to grow by 1000 tons and power increase from 18,000 to 20,000ihp if the basic features of the design were to be attained. These alterations added an estimated £25,000 to the cost of each ship.

The need for high sustained speed, coupled with a large radius of action, resulted in an unusual machinery arrangement, which in turn determined the length of the ship. Four, rather than the normal two, triple expansion engines were fitted in separate engine rooms, with two engines connected to each shaft. The forward engines could be disconnected for normal cruising, only being put in gear when the need came to make full speed. This alone would allow the ship to make between 15 and 16kts, while at the normal cruising speed of 10kts she would use only 7 per cent of her total power. This arrangement was never again used by the Royal Navy and it was only copied by the US Navy in the cruiser *Brooklyn* and by the Russian Navy in the cruiser *Rurik*, both of which were intended as high-speed commerce raiders. The main disadvantage of the arrangement was that it was more expensive, both in engine and hull costs, than simply installing larger engines. It was also necessary to stop the engines in order to connect the front set, not something desirable when chasing an enemy, and even less when trying to escape. It also seems that it proved extremely difficult to ensure that the two engines lined up perfectly on the propeller shafts and this caused excessive wear on the shaft and engine bearings. White acknowledged that the increased length caused by the machinery arrangement would result in a loss of handiness but thought that this was of small concern in vessels of high speed.

Equally important to the nature of the design was the size of the coal supply, which was set at 1500 tons to provide a range of 10,400nm at normal cruising speed. Since the ships were specifically designed for continuous high, speed steaming, great attention was paid to the ease of working of the coal: each of the four stokeholds was given its own cross bunker and White reported that the transport of coal to these had been specially studied. But while the designed bunkerage allowed for up to seven days' steaming at 20kts and ten weeks at 10kts, White did not consider that this really represented the design's full capabilities. The wing compartments of both the engine and boiler rooms formed additional bunker space, which would bring the total fuel capacity to nearly 1800 tons. The extra capacity would in terms of weight be nearly equal to the 4½ per cent of the Board Margin. Alterations and additions during building absorbed almost all of the Margin and in the end it was only possible to carry the projected fuel supply by using the machinery wing compartments. To some extent this represented a reduction in coal capacity, since it was intended that the wing bunkers next to the engine rooms would only be used in wartime, and that the coal there, like much of that carried above the protective deck, was primarily intended as protection.

The most controversial aspect of the design was the abandonment of the armour belt in favour of a protective deck. The use of a curved protective deck had found favour with naval architects since its introduction by the Italian constructor Benedetto Brin in the battleship *Italia* of 1880. The main advantage of the system over the armour belt was that it offered equal, or better, real protection to the ship's vitals for a much lower weight. The weight thus saved could be used to gain greater speed from more powerful engines, or greater endurance from larger coal bunkerage. Yet many officers of the Royal Navy remained unconvinced and in both the *Blake* and the *Edgar* classes White had to make provision for their views. Armament was originally set at two 9in guns carried fore and aft, ten 70pdr on the main deck and eighteen, 8½pdrs distributed between the main and upper decks. The 70pdrs which were to be fitted to a new Vavasseur mounting, were regarded with some unease from the beginning and White asked Vavasseur if the mounting could take both a 6in BL and a 6in QF gun as well as the 70pdr. Although the 70pdr was at the time the largest QF gun in existence, neither White nor the DNO favoured the introduction of a new calibre between 5in and 6in. It was with some relief therefore that news was received from Armstrong that development work on the 70pdr gun was not going well but that they had high hopes for a 6in QF gun and the substitution of the 6in QF gun was authorised. To help compensate for extra weight 3pdrs were fitted. There were to be four torpedo tubes, two above water and two in submerged torpedo rooms.

The design was approved by the Board at the end of January 1888 and for the first time the names *Blake* and *Blenheim* were mentioned. *Blake* was to be built at the Royal Dockyard at Chatham and, even though there remained some items in the design to be decided by the Board, the yard was sent a copy of the lines plan and a midship section so that laying off could begin. The contract for the second ship, *Blenheim*, was put out to tender and was eventually awarded to the Thames Ironworks Company at Blackwall.

The *Blake* was laid down at Chatham in July 1888 and almost immediately design work began on what would become the *Edgar* class for the next year's programme. At the same time as the design for the *Blake* was being developed, another design team was working on a torpedo/boat carrier, which was laid down as the *Vulcan* in June of 1888 at Portsmouth, like the *Blake* the *Vulcan* had a protective deck. She had a high speed of 20kts and a respectable armament of eight 4.7in QF guns. It was the design of the *Vulcan* that was chosen as the starting point for the *Edgar* class. Approval for the development of the new design was given at a Board meeting held in mid-August 1888. It seems likely that White originally proposed a direct development of the *Blake*, there are two sketch designs with the *Blake*'s engine arrangement but with an extra boiler room, a speed of 23kts and four 9.2in guns on a displacement of 8900 tons. This proposal was quickly rejected, almost certainly on account of cost, since no less than nine vessels were to be provided under the 1889 Naval Defence Act. The new cruisers were to have the same dimensions and engines as the *Vulcan*, with a protective deck 5in thick. The armament was to be the same as that of the *Blake*, but with the 6in QF guns arranged with four in casemates on the main deck and six on the upper deck.

This arrangement of the 6in battery was as a result of the experiments on the old ironclad *Resistance*. These showed that guns in unarmoured positions should have the widest possible degree of separation. This could be achieved by placing three of the guns on the upper deck, and increasing the spacing of those left on the main deck. This would also allow for the main deck guns to be carried in armoured casemates. White estimated the cost of the new ships would be £275,000 each as against £440,000 for the *Blake*'s.

In October White suggested that the *Blake*'s armament arrangements should be modified to match those of the *Edgar*. This would present no problems for the ship building by contract, the *Blenheim*, but the construction of the *Blake* was well advanced at Chatham, and alteration of the design at this stage would seriously affect progress on the ship. White suggested that the yard should complete the framing and plating of the hull, then the four casemate openings on the main deck could be cut out at a later stage. The revised layout of the guns led to alterations in the system of ammunition supply: the casemate guns were to have ready-use magazines holding 30 rounds of 6in shell, set into the coal bunkers above the protective deck. The cost in weight terms of these alterations was 300 tons, or about 7.5in on the draught, and White suggested that rather than increase the legend displacement there should be a corresponding reduction in coal carried. This also meant that the engine room wing bunkers would have to be used as normal bunkerage space if the coal supply was to be kept at 1500 tons.

Blake, *developed from the* Orlando, *with old pattern 9.2in and 6in breechloaders not yet the QFs to overwhelm the enemy.* (NMM).

Meanwhile the design team was working on the task of turning the *Vulcan* into a first class cruiser. Crew size was set the same as for the *Blake*, but with the *Vulcan's* engine room complement. Range with 850 tons of coal was 10,000nm at 10kts, 40 per cent greater than the *Orlando*, while at 18kts range would be about 2600nm. Trial speed was 20kts with forced draft, but continuous sea speed would be 18kts. Total bunker capacity was to be 1000 tons, only two thirds that of the *Blake*, the extra 150 tons over the legend would increase the draught by 4-5in and reduce the speed by ¼kt.

So that the ship could maintain prolonged cruising at high speed, additional cross bunkers were fitted. These would also mean that when in action the bunkers above the protective deck would not be required for the stoke holds. The cross bunkers alone could hold 600 tons of coal and would provide for four days steaming at 18kts.

This resulted in a ship ten feet longer and two feet broader than *Vulcan* with a displacement 400 tons greater at 7000 tons. However compared with the *Blake* there was no provision for ready-use magazines or for armoured tubes for the ammunition hoists, except for the 9.2in guns. Only 100 tons had been allowed for the casemate armour, which would limit the casemate protection to 4in faces and 2in sides, against 6in thick fronts in the *Blake*. White suggested that these differences compared to the *Blake* could be overcome by using 160 to 180 tons of the Board Margin. There would be a need to add 6in to the beam, and speed at the legend draught would be reduced by ¼kt to 19¾kts at forced draft. However the financial secretary suggested that it would make more

sense to simply make the ships bigger rather than use any of the Board Margin; this must be one of the few times in history when an accountant took a long term view.

Compared with the *Vulcan*, the *Edgar* was to have the thickness of her protective decks increased, in both ships the thickness was 5in over the engine and boiler spaces, but in the *Vulcan* this thinned to 2.5in over the magazines. In the *Edgar* the thickness over the magazines was to be raised to 4in and there were to be improvements too in the protection of the ends of the ship. Outside of the main protected deck the *Vulcan* was fitted with a flat armoured deck 1 to 1.5in thick forward and 2in aft over the steering gear. In the *Edgar* this was replaced by a 2in thick curved deck. These alterations to the protective deck absorbed an extra 100 tons of weight.

The *Resistance* experiments raised again the question of protection. There was a very vocal body that had never accepted the arguments put forward by the supporters of the protective deck and the tests seemed to prove the value of side armour over protective decks. White responded to these arguments in a long minute in March 1889 entitled 'On the use of side armour and casemate protection'. First White reiterated the advantages of using protective decks and coal bunkers as the major means of protection. Coal closely packed into the bunkers above the protective deck would smother the effects of high explosive shell, and restrict the entry of water into the hull. Damage control parties working behind the watertight cofferdams at the rear of the coal-bunkers would be able to deal with any leaks while under cover from enemy fire.

Edgar. The next stage in the development of the first class cruisers, pictured here in mid career. (NMM).

White then examined the possibility of fitting an armour belt to the *Edgar* design. It would be possible to fit a 3in thick belt, bolted to 1in thick plating. If this belt were to extend along the length of the engine and boiler rooms, and to cover the depth from the lower edge of the protective deck up to the main deck it would absorb almost 280 tons, or the entire Board Margin allowed for the ship. The *Resistance* experiments had shown that a 4in belt was freely penetrated by both 4.7 and 6in shell, and that the effects of the explosion behind the armour were worse than if there had been no armour there. White pointed out that the power of shells and explosives were increasing, reducing still further the effectiveness of thin armour belts. He then put forward a skilful compromise, intended no doubt to mollify the supporters of armour belts while leaving the protective decks system unchanged. It would be possible, he wrote, to provide the necessary support for an armour belt, 3in thick, if it should become desirable to fit one at a later stage.

The support would be in the form of an extra 1in thick hull plating, rivetted flush, for a length of 150 feet in the *Blakes* and 130 feet in the *Edgars*. The cost in terms of weight would be about 55 and 45 tons respectively. If, however, the Board did decide to order the fitting of armour belts, then White strongly felt that these should run for the whole length of the ships, or at a minimum all the way to the bows. This would involve an additional 700 tons in weight in the *Blake*, which could only by found by reducing the thickness of the protective deck, the plating for which had already been ordered. In the *Edgars* the armour belt would weigh 650 tons, which

could only be found by a complete re-casting of the design. Faced with such consequences the Board approved White's compromise proposal and instructions were issued to double the plating amidships in both classes.

In late April 1889 the *Edgar*'s design team realised that the ships would be under-powered. The power specified was for 8000ihp at natural draft to give a speed of 18kts, with 12,000ihp forced draft for 20kts. However White had become convinced that forced draft, while giving impressive results on trials, was impracticable in service conditions. He persuaded the Board that from now on Royal Navy ships should have their speed and machinery performance specified at natural draft. It was realised that if the *Edgar*'s were to be able to steam continuously at 18kts with two thirds power then the boilers would have to be able to deliver 12,000ihp at natural rather than at forced draft.

This increase in horse power could not be supplied with four boilers of the standard pattern, while six would mean enlarging the ship. An alternative would be to increase the size of the boilers and it was suggested that by increasing the boiler diameter by 18in to 16ft that 10,000ihp could be obtained for an extra 90 tons. Installation of the larger boilers would mean some loss of bunker capacity if ease of access was to be maintained, but this would be minimal.

It was not simply a matter of installing bigger boilers, the proposed change threw into question the Navy's whole policy on machinery, and a meeting was held between the First Lord, Durston (the Engineer in Chief) and White. There was a fear, shared by both White and

Durston, that increasing the size of the boilers would produce more steam than the engines could handle, with an attendant risk of damage to both. Durston was often the butt of public criticism over the performance of the Navy's machinery and was worried that increasing the machinery weight without an increase in trial performance would be grounds for still more attacks from the press. White argued that the real point was not whether the ships should have sufficient boiler power at natural draft, but whether the size of ships in general should be increased to allow it. Even though the new boilers would eat up 90 tons of the Board Margin and cost an extra £4000, the change was approved.

The *Edgar* class were all laid down between June 1889 and July 1890, five to be built by contract and four in the Royal Dockyards. In early April 1890 it was suggested that the two ships being built in Portsmouth, *Crescent* and *Centaur* (renamed *Royal Arthur* before launch), should have their design modified by having the forecastle raised one deck level. This would provide for extra accommodation for ships intended to act as flagships on foreign stations, as well has giving improved sea going performance. There was, as always, a penalty to be paid for any alteration of the design and it was decided that it would be necessary to replace the forward 9.2in gun with two 6in QFs if sufficient stability was to be maintained. Both White and the Board viewed the reduction in gun power forward with equanimity, White in particular believing that it was more important to have heavy gun power aft rather than forward. His reason for this was the rational observation that since any design would be outclassed by newer, more powerful, vessels in time, the ships could well have to run away and heavy armament aft would stand a ship in good stead when trying to slow down a pursuer. Having only 6in guns forward would be no real disadvantage since the ships would only be likely to chase protected or unarmoured ships, and the increased rate of fire in these circumstances would be a positive advantage. However the high forecastle brought such an improvement in seakeeping that it became a permanent feature of White's designs. Five of the ships, including *Crescent* and *Royal Arthur*, were sheathed in wood and copper for overseas service.

Powerful

The cruiser programme for 1893-94 was to be dominated by the Royal Navy's response to the construction by Russia of a cruiser designed for commerce raiding, the *Rurik*. Designed to combine high speed, heavy armament, good protection and with the ability to steam from the Baltic to Vladivostock without coaling, the Russian ship appeared on paper to be a threat to which the British had to reply. The result of what can only be described as a naval panic was two of the largest and least useful vessels yet built for the Royal Navy.

The *Rurik* had been laid down in May 1890, but the need to complete the ships ordered under the Naval Defence Act meant that the British response would be delayed until 1893. Even so the DNC was discussing the Royal Navy's counter to the Russian ship by November 1891. Based on reports that the *Rurik* would have a machinery weight of 2050 tons, White argued that her published sea speed of 18kts must be a deliberate underestimate, and that in all probability the true sea speed would be 19kts. To obtain a 1kt superiority over the *Rurik*, 20kts sea speed, the new British ship would have to have a trial speed of 22kts. White also estimated the endurance of the Russian ship not as the published figure of 16,000nm but as half that, 8500nm. White therefore saw the design requirements for the new cruisers as

Blenheim shows the incremental development of the type before the next leap to the Powerful *and her sister the* Terrible. (NMM).

having a speed and radius of action superior to the *Rurik*, with a more powerful armament, and protection at least equal to her, all of which would mean a ship larger than its Russian rival. The demands of speed and range would dominate the design. The *Blake*, the Royal Navy's largest cruiser, had a range at 10kts of 1200nm less than the *Rurik*, while the *Edgar's* could steam only 5300nm. In a ship designed to counter the *Rurik*, fuel consumption would be greater by a factor of 8 to 7 compared to the *Edgar*, once again pushing up the displacement.

The dimensions of the new ships were largely determined by the size of the available dry docks. There were few docks in Britain or the Empire which could accommodate ships as long as the new cruiser would have to be, and even fewer that could cope with the combination of great length and the beam necessary if the required stability was to be obtained. These restrictions set the length at 500ft pp and the beam at 70.5ft. Compared to both *Blake* and *Edgar*, the *Powerfuls* were to be much longer ships for their beam, the beam to length ratio rising from an average of 5.6 to 7.04. There were some on the Board who were unhappy at the building of such a huge vessel, and suggested that the length be reduced to 450ft. White's reply to this was threefold, firstly that the machinery spaces required would remain the same in a ship 450ft long, and that the reduction in length could only be obtained by giving up a submerged torpedo room; secondly, that shortening the ship would so alter the form of the hull that a sea speed of 20kts could not be guaranteed unless the size and power of the machinery plant were increased; and thirdly, that a length of 450ft would not improve the situation as regards the availability of dry docks.

Within the set length, the size of the machinery plant was crucial. It was evident from the beginning that the Royal Navy's machinery types could not supply enough power within the constraints of weight and space, and that the only solution would be to adopt the water tube boilers developed by the Frenchman Julian Belleville. These boilers promised much higher working pressures, against those of the *Edgar* class. The Belleville boiler also required less water to produce steam, reducing their overall weight and increasing the speed at which steam can be raised. That these improvements were necessary is shown by the fact that compared to the *Edgar* the *Powerful* required 60 per cent more power at all speeds up to 16kts. It was originally proposed to carry a mixture of water tube and cylindrical boilers, with two out of six boiler rooms having the cylindrical type, but the finalised design had a uniform steam plant of 48 Belleville boilers. The decision to install a uniform type of boiler was taken to avoid having to have stokers trained in handling both cylindrical and water tube boilers. The ships were unusual in that they were to be able to steam at their maximum cruising speed continuously. Normal practice was to provide enough stokers to supply steam for only 60 per cent of the natural draft (ND) power. The *Powerful* was to have the boiler room complements increased so that 100 per cent ND power would always be available without calling the off watch hands.

The boilers were to be arranged with their backs to a longitudinal bulkhead on the middle line of the ship. This removed the need for cross bunkers and helped to reduce the overall length of the machinery compartments: of the proposed 500ft length of the ship 240ft was taken up by the machinery. If the machinery spaces were ignored the *Powerfuls* were only 40ft longer than the *Edgars*, and this difference was largely the result of a second submerged torpedo room.

Protection was to be in the form of a curved protective deck. Unlike the two previous classes the deck was to be of uniform thickness, 4in on both the flat and the slopes. In this class White, for the first time, adopted what was to become normal practice in almost all warships, two ammunition passages ran the full length of the machinery compartments underneath the protective deck. This not only gave greater protection to the ammunition supply, but ensured that, even if the magazines at one end of the ship were put out of action, all the guns could be supplied from the other magazines. The DNO suggested that the ammunition passages should be used for the storage of ready use ammunition, rather than storing it in the casemates to reduce the danger of explosions in action.

The original proposal for armament was for a uniform battery of 20-6in QF guns. These were to be arranged with one on the centre line forward and aft, eight in two storeyed casemates, two forward and aft, giving a theoretical bow and stern fire of 5-6in guns, and five more guns on each broadside in casemates on the main deck. There were 10-25pdrs in open shields on the upper deck. The uniform armament was probably a reflection of the views of Fisher who, even at this stage, was a firm believer in the value of a single calibre armament. White stated that the object was to maximise the number of guns that could be carried and supplied, while protecting as many of the gun crews as possible in casemates. Also the use of the 6in gun would avoid the use of power handling and loading machinery. This was an important consideration since the total weight allowed for armament was 1500 tons.

But the DNO took great exception to the proposed armament, which he saw as being fundamentally faulty in both its composition and its disposition, and so provoked a heated exchange of papers. The DNO's view was that the most valuable gun positions in the ship were those forward and aft on the forecasfle and poop, and that in these positions a 6in gun was clearly inadequate. He pointed out that the disposition of 6in guns forward in the *Royal Arthur* and *Crescent* was adopted to secure better seakeeping and accommodation, and not as a change in tactical doctrine. For the DNO the primary function of cruisers was to chase and destroy other ships, and for this purpose it was vital that there should be heavy guns forward and aft. In these positions the destructive power of the shell counted for far more than rapidity of fire. Nor did the DNO perceive high rates of fire, an advantage during a chase in which the range would change slowly, as would the rate of change of range. In these circumstance a slow and deliberate fire would be the most suitable. He compared the new design's armament unfavourably with that of the American cruiser *Brooklyn* with its 8-8in guns in four turrets. The *Brooklyn's* disposition of armament would allow her to concentrate almost all her heavy guns on any target. Assuming that the *Brooklyn* was being chased by the *Powerful*, which was to have a one knot advantage in speed, it would take an hour to reduce the distance between the ships from 3000 to 2000yds, during which the *Powerful* would be under fire from heavy guns, while her own 6in guns could do no damage to the vital parts of the *Brooklyn*. The DNO therefore advocated that a new 8in 40cal gun should be developed. He was sure that Armstrongs could develop both the gun and a twin mounting quickly, and that the new ship should be armed with 4-8in, 16 or 14-6in QF, 16-12pdr QF guns. The 8in guns were to be placed in twin mounts, protected only by light shields.

White's reply to these arguments bordered on the dismissive. The *Resistance* experiments had shown that the 6in shell could do all that was necessary in wrecking an enemy cruiser and destroying the lives of its crew. White seems to have felt that the DNO had misunderstood what the ships were meant to do: if the task of the new cruisers was to hunt down enemy commerce raiders then the 6in gun was more than adequate. If on the other hand they were intended to fight, rather than flee from, enemy battleships, then the 8in gun was completely inadequate and the minimum gun necessary would be the 9.2in. He saw no need to restrict the rate of fire against a fleeing enemy, especially since slow alterations in range made good, fast shooting comparatively easy. The DNO's advocacy of the 8in gun, rather than the established 9.2in, came from his belief that it could be hand loaded, White replied that the 8in shell would be just as difficult to handle in a seaway.

Fisher urged the Board to confirm its original decision for the uniform 6in armament. The issue was finally brought to the Board for a decision, with both White and the DNO being present, and resulted in an outcome that probably pleased neither. Lord Walter Kerr thought that the argument for a uniform 6in gun armament convincing, and would certainly not be prepared to see heavy guns in twin mountings protected only by light shields. Others thought that while the balance of the argument lay with Fisher and White, none the less the DNO's general point, that there should be heavy chase guns fore and aft, was valid, and that the ship should carry 9.2in guns well protected by armour even if some of the 6in gun casemates had to be given up. But it was agreed that the total weight of the armament should not exceed the 1500 tons laid down in the original legend.

The 9.2in guns were to be carried in shallow barbettes, protected by armour 6in thick. Like the 6in guns the 9.2in were to be of a new pattern and Armstrong, Whitworth and Woolwich Arsenal were all asked to submit designs for the new gun. The extra weight involved in the decision to carry 9.2in guns meant that sacrifices had to be made elsewhere: the number of 6in guns was reduced from 20 to 12 and the 25pdr guns replaced by 12pdrs.

With the final decision on the ship's armament made in July 1893 the detailed design work could finally begin ready for submission to the Board in October. The calculated weights required a displacement of 14,000 tons without any allowance for a Board margin. The size of the Board margin became a subject of serious debate: if the current rules were to be applied the margin would be 630 tons. But as experience with the *Blake* had shown the size of the ship would have to be increased by much more than the straight figure if the performance of the ship was not to be adversely affected. The course taken was to modify the rules for the size of the margin. From now on the margin for large vessels was to be fixed at 200 tons rather than as a percentage of the displacement.

For the *Powerful* the addition of the Board margin meant that the beam had to be increased by 6in and the draught by 3in. White explained that the critical point was that it was unknown where the extra weight would come from. Experience would suggest that it was most likely to be in the form of extra topweight, from additions to the guns and equipment. But the adoption of Bellevile boilers had meant that they could not be sure where the centre of gravity of the machinery would be, making necessary an increase of beam to ensure stability.

As the design neared completion White personally toured the major ship building yards to ensure that they could build a vessel 500ft long. Many would only be able to undertake the work if modifications were made to their building slips, while there were doubts as to the financial health of Palmers and Earles of Hull. In the end the order for the *Powerful* went to Vickers Barrow and the *Terrible* to Thompsons of Clydebank.

The design was heavily criticised almost from the beginning on account of the large size and apparently weak armament. To a particularly trenchant critic published in the magazine *Engineering*, the DNC's department felt it necessary to make a pointed rebuttal. In reply to the alleged underguning of the *Powerful* it was pointed out that the weight given over to armament represented a 27 per cent increase over that of the *Blake*, while the weight of armour used to protect the guns was 340 tons in the *Blake* as against 660 tons for the *Powerful*. White argued that there was no point in having large numbers of guns unless they could be supplied with adequate quantities of ammunition, and since it was impossible to increase the size of the magazines, the fitting of additional guns was pointless. Yet the general feeling that the ships were undergunned persisted, and during the ships' 1902-1904 refit four extra 6in guns were provided by turning the broadside casemates into two story positions, like those at bow and stern.

The Admiralty almost certainly regarded the type as an expensive mistake. Compared to the *Edgar*, the *Powerful* had a crew that was 64 per cent larger. Exclusive of armament they cost 61 per cent more, yet the ships only carried two more 6in guns. The size of the mistake seemed even greater when the true nature of the *Rurik* became clear. Far from being the great threat so much to be feared, she proved to be very much of a damp squib, so much so that the French thought that the guns had been put on as an afterthought.

[The second part of 'First Class Cruisers' will look at the subsequent development of the first class cruisers. It will also discuss how successful these cruisers were in action, in terms of the inevitable trade off between speed, armament and armour. It will appear in Warship 2001-2002]

GERMAN TYPE II
SUBMARINES AT WAR

In this study **Pierre Hervieux** considers an under-examined aspect of the German submarine campaign during the Second World War. With a limited operating radius Type II U-boats, nicknamed 'the canoes' by their crews, were designed for warfare in the littoral areas of the North Sea, Baltic and Black Sea. Engaged in successful operations throughout the war in this latter theatre the *Kriegsmarine* remained undefeated.

Fifty coastal submarines of this class were launched in Germany between June 1935 (*U-1*) and December 1940 (*U-152*), being commissioned respectively in June 1935 and January 1941. They were divided into: type IIA *U-1/U-6*, type IIB *U-7/U-24* and *U-120/U-121* (these last two were being built for the Royal Yugoslav Navy when acquired at the outbreak of the Second World War), type IIC *U-56/U-63*, type IID *U-137/U-152*. All types were first employed operationally and later for training, to prepare crews for bigger and more modern U-boats. They were used offensively in the North Sea, the Baltic, the Black Sea and even the Atlantic for the type IID. This latter model had much bigger bunkers (38 tons of fuel oil) compared to the types IIA (12 tons), IIB (21 tons) and IIC (23 tons). To give an idea, the types IA, VIIA and IXA were carrying respectively 96, 67 and 154 tons of fuel oil! Their respective radius of action was:

IIA 1050 miles }
IIB 1800 miles }
IIC 1900 miles } – surfaced at 12kts
IID 3450 miles }

All type II submarines could carry 8 mines.

On 22 November 1936, *U-18* sank after a collision with the submarine tender *T-156* (ex-torpedo boat) and was later salvaged.

1939

At 04:45 on 1 September 1939 the German attack on Poland began. In the Baltic, under the command of *Fregatten-Kapitän* Schomburg, Officer Commanding U-Boats in the East, *U-5, U-6, U-7, U-14, U-18, U-22, U-57* and three type VIIA submarines were included in the naval German forces. Submarine operations were quite limited against Polish warships, three of their four destroyers having sailed for Britain on 30 August, two days before the German attack. That measure of security

proves that the Poles knew the date of the impending invasion and were not, therefore, taken by surprise.

Before they were either interned in Sweden or sailed to Britain, two of the five Polish submarines escaped destruction because of premature German torpedo explosions. These two missed occasions were the first of a long series of torpedo faults which lasted for about a year. First, on 3 September, at 22:10 (all the times given are German, except when a ship was sunk on a mine), *U-14* (*Kapitänleutnant* Wellner) launched one torpedo at a Polish submarine off the Island of Aland and claimed to have sunk her. That submarine was the *Sep*, but the single torpedo, fired from a distance of less than 1100 metres, detonated prematurely and then *Sep* crash-dived. On 7 September at 23:09, *U-22* (*Kapitänleutnant* Winter) launched one torpedo at the Polish submarine *Zbik* and also claimed wrongly to have torpedoed and sunk her, in about the same position!

In the North Sea, *U-13* (*Kapitänleutnant* Daublesky Von Eichhain), *U-15* (*Kapitänleutnant* Buchholz), *U-16* (*Kapitänleutnant* Weingaertner) and *U-17* (*Kapitänleutnant* Von Reiche) sailed from the German Bight on 3 September and laid magnetic mines on the British east coast, off Orfordness, Flamborough, Hartlepool and the Downs. *U-13* laid her mines on 4 September, sinking the British cargo ship *Magdapur* (launched in 1921, 8641 tons) on 10 September, at 17:25, position 52° 11N/01°43E, damaging the British cargo ship *City of Paris* (1922, 10902 tons) on 16 September, at 52°14N/01°43E, and sinking the French cargo ship *Phryne* (1938, 2660 tons) on 24 September, at 01:00, 3 miles east of Aldeburgh. *U-15* laid her mines on 6 September, on which sank the British cargo ship *Goodwood* (1937, 2796 tons) on 10 September, at 06:10, one mile south-east of Flamborough Head and another British cargo ship, the *Orsa* (1925, 1478 tons) on 21 October, 15 miles from Flamborough Head.

Between 3 and 10 September, *U-12, U-56, U-58* and *U-59* were stationed in the North Sea, on Great Fisher Bank, and *U-9* and *U-19* off the Scottish east coast against British naval units. No result was obtained. *U-20* operated off Southern Norway. Off the Scottish east coast, on 22 September, at 14:18, *U-21* (*Kapitänleutnant*

U-58 *(type IIC) survived the war and was scuttled on 3 May 1945 in Kiel.* (Drüppel).

Frauenheim) missed a British destroyer because of torpedo defects. Between 15 September and 4 October, four type II and one type VIIA submarines operated off the Norwegian southern coast in mercantile warfare, in accordance with prize regulations. *U-3* (*Kapitänleutnant* Schepke) sank two ships: on 30 September, at 11:00, 35 miles north-west of Hanstolm, the Danish cargo ship *Vendia* (1924, 1150 tons) with gunfire and torpedo. On the same day, at 21:30, she boarded and sank, with scuttling charges, the Swedish cargo ship *Gun* (1891, 1198 tons), 30 miles north-west of Hanstholm. Following the British Admiralty's advice, the *Gun* tried to ram and sink *U-3* before her boarding party came on board, but the U-boat succeeded in avoiding damage with an emergency manoeuvre.

U-4 (*Kapitänleutnant* Von Klot-Heydenfeldt) sank three ships: on 22 September, at 23:00, she boarded and scuttled the Finnish cargo ship *Martti Ragnar* (1903, 2262 tons), 5 miles south of Arendal. On the following day, at 11:20, she boarded and scuttled another Finnish cargo ship, the *Walma* (1908, 1361 tons), at 58°4ON/09°52E. *U-7* (*Leutnant zur See* Heidel) sank three ships: on 22 September, at 14:30, she torpedoed and sank the British cargo ship *Akenside* (1917, 2694 tons), at 60°07N/04°37E. On 28 September, *U-7* torpedoed and sank the Norwegian cargo ship *Solaas* (1917, 1368 tons), 25 miles south-west of Lista light. On the same day, at 08:55, she torpedoed and sank the Norwegian cargo ship *Takstaas* (1916, 1830 tons), at 60°15N/04°41E. *U-16*, on 28 September at 00:30, torpedoed and sank the Swedish cargo ship *Nyland* (1909, 3378 tons), 45 miles south-west

of Stavanger. Because of torpedo defects, off the Scottish east coast, *U-14*, *U-24* (*Kapitänleutnant* Behrens) and *U-22* missed respectively a submarine, a destroyer and a submarine, all British, on 24, 24 and 29 September! The Royal Navy laid deep anti-U-Boat barrages in the Straits of Dover, with a total of 3636 mines, between Folkestone and Cap Gris Nez, from 25 September to 23 October. One of them was responsible for the loss of *U-12* (Von der Ropp) on 8 October.

In the North Sea, on 4 October, at 06:00, *U-23* (*Kapitänleutnant* Kretschmer) sank the British cargo ship *Glen Farg* (1937, 876 tons) with gunfire and torpedo, at 58°52N/01°31W. U-Boats laid magnetic mine barrages off the British east coast: *U-16* (*Kapitänleutnant* Wellner) in the Sraits of Dover on 22 October. The next day she was depth charged by the patrol sloop HMS *Puffin* and the armed trawler HMS *Cayton Wyke*. On 24 October, *U-16* ran on a British mine and sank at 51°09N/01°28E. *U-19* (*Kapitänleutnant* Meckel) laid her mines off Inner Dowsing on 17 October, *U-21* in the Firth of Forth on 3 and 4 November, *U-23* off Cromarty and *U-24* (*Kapitänleutnant* Jeppener-Haltenhoff) off Hartlepool on 27 October. The following losses occurred in these barrages: on 21 October, at 02:00, the French cargo ship *Capitaine Edmond Laborie* (1923, 3087 tons), 2 miles east of Inner Dowsing Light Vessel. On the same day, the Norwegian tanker ship *Deodata* (1897, 3295 tons), 1.5 miles from Inner Dowsing Light Vessel. On 24 October, at 09:00, the Greek cargo ship *Konstantinos Hadjipateras* (1913, 5962 tons) near the Inner Dowsing Light Vessel. These three vessels were sunk by mines laid by *U-19*. On

9 November, at 07:20, the British cargo ship *Carmarthen Coast* (1921, 961 tons) sank on a mine laid by *U-24*, 3 miles east of Seaham harbour. On 21 November, the French auxiliary minesweeper *Sainte Clair* (1906, 58 tons) sank, 10 miles south-east of Folkestone, on a mine laid by *U-16*. On the same day, in the Firth of Forth, the light cruiser HMS *Belfast* (1938, 10550 tons) was heavily damaged on a mine laid by *U-21* and, in addition, that submarine's mines sank two ships: as late as 21 December, the netlayer HMS *Bayonet* (1938, 605 tons) and on 24 February 1940 (!) the British cargo ship *Royal Archer* (1928, 2266 tons), at 56°06N/02°55W. HMS *Belfast's* damage was bad, for the mine exploded below the forward engine room, broke the ship's back and fractured all the machinery supports. She did not return to service until October 1942.

From 24 October to 13 November, four U-Boats operated against units of the Home Fleet, west of the Orkneys, and subsequently against merchant ships. On 30 October, at 10:00, *U-56* (*Kapitänleutnant* Zahn) attacked a British force comprising the battleships *Nelson*, *Rodney*, *Hood* and 6 destroyers. A full salvo of three torpedoes was launched at the *Nelson*, hit the battleship and did not explode! To have succeeded getting through the screen of destroyers for such a result was demoralising and, in addition, Churchill was on board! Zahn was so depressed that Admiral Dönitz sent him to a Submarine Training School to take care of future crews. On 23 October, at 03:05, U-59 (*Leutnant zur See* Jürst) sank, with gunfire and scuttling charges, the British trawler *St. Nidan* (1937, 565 tons) at 59°50N/04°20W. On the same day, at 06:55, in the same position, *U-59* sank, in the same way, the British trawler *Lynx II* (1906, 250 tons). Two days later, at 23:35, *U-59* torpedoed and sank the armed trawler HMS *Northern Rover* (1936, 655 tons), near Kirkwall in the Orkneys. On the same day too, at 22:50, *U-13* torpedoed and sank the British cargo ship *Cairn Mona* (1918, 4666 tons) from convoy HX.5B, at 57°38N/01°45W.

Magnetic mines were laid, on the British east coast, by *U-15* (*Kapitänleutnant* Frahm) off Lowestoft, on 17 November, and sank with one of them the British trawler *Resercho* (1917, 258 tons) 6 miles south-east of Flamborough Head, on 28 December at 22:53. *U-19* (*Kapitänleutnant* Müller-Arnecke) also laid hers on 17 November, off Orfordness, and was responsible for sinking the Yugoslavian cargo ship *Carica Milica* (1928, 6371 tons) on the following day at 11:55, 3.5 miles off Shipwash Light Vessel. Finally, *U-20* (*Kapitänleutnant* Moehle) laid her mines on 22 November near Newarp Light Vessel, two ships being sunk: on 29 November, at 01:30, the British cargo ship *Ionian* (1938, 3114 tons) from convoy FN.43, 1.5 miles from Newarp Light Vessel and, on 10 December, at 16:00, the British cargo ship *Willowpool* (1925, 4815 tons), 3 miles east of Newarp light Vessel.

In simultaneous operations on the east coast, *U-57* (*Kapitänleutnant* Korth) on 17 November, at 20:15, torpedoed and sank the Lithuanian cargo ship *Kaunas* (1931, 1566 tons), 6.5 miles west-north-west of Noordbinder Light Vessel. *U-18* (*Leutnant zur See*

Mengersen) torpedoed and sank the British trawler *Wigmore* (1928, 395 tons), on 18 November, at 21:16, by 57°59N/02°06W. The *Wigmore* belonged to an Iceland fishing convoy. *U-22* on the same day, at 23:10, torpedoed and sank the British cargo ship *Parkhill* (1915,500 tons), at 58°07N/02°18W. On 19 November, at 02:13, *U-57* torpedoed and sank the British cargo ship *Stanbrook* (1909, 1383 tons), near the Noordkinder Light Vessel, as she was sailing from Antwerp to the Tyne. On 20 November, at 01:00, near Rattray Head, *U-18* missed with torpedoes the destroyer HMS *Inglefield*.

Between 27 November and 7 December, U-Boats laid magnetic mines on the British east coast and attacked shipping with torpedoes: *U-58* (*Kapitänleutnant* Kuppisch) laid her mines off Lowestoft, obtaining no result. *U-59* laid hers off the Cockle Light Vessel on 5 December and, the following day, at 10:32, the armed trawler HMS *Washington* (1909, 209 tons) was sunk *en route* for Great Yarmouth. On 12 December, at 08:15, the British cargo ship *Marwick Head* (1920, 496 tons) was sunk by another *U-59* mine, 0.5 miles south of north Caister Bay. *U-61* (*Kapitänleutnant* Oesten) laid her mines on 2 December, off Newcastle, and on 22 December, at 13:40, the British cargo ship *Gryfevale* (1929, 4434 tons) was damaged, 3 miles east of the Tyne Piers. On 1 December, at 04:53, *U-21* torpedoed and sank the Norwegian cargo ship *Arcturus* (1910, 1277 tons), off the east Scottish coast. *Kapitänleutnant* Zahn, having recovered, and being back to operations with his *U-56*, succeeded in hitting two cargo ships, both of them at 22:40, on 2 December: the British *Eskedene* (1934, 3829 tons), who was damaged at 56°30N/01°40W, and the Swedish *Rudolf* (1922, 2119 tons) who sank at 56°15N/01°25W.

Between 7 and 22 December, the 'canoes', as the Type II submarines were nicknamed by their crews, laid magnetic mines on the British east coast and also attacked shipping with torpedoes in that area and in the southern part of the North Sea. On 12 December, *U-13* (*Kapitänleutnant* Scheringer) laid her mines off Dundee,

After the arrival of the U-61 (type IIC) in Wilhelmshaven, during winter 1939-40, Kapitänleutnant Oesten is welcomed by Admiral Dönitz. He was later in command of U-106 and U-861 and survived the war. (ECPA).

resulting in the sinking of the Estonian cargo ship *Anu* (1883, 1421 tons), on 6 February 1940, off the river Tay. *U-22* (*Kapitänleutnant* Jenisch) laid hers on 15, 20 and 22 December off Blyth, sinking four ships: on 20 December, at 14:30, the Swedish cargo ship *Mars* (1924, 1877 tons), 1 mile east of St.Mary's Light Vessel. On 25 December, at 07:45, the armed trawler HMS *Loch Doon* (1937, 534 tons). On 28 December, at 09:32, the Danish cargo ship *Hanne* (1905, 1080 tons), 1 mile east of Blyth. Finally, on 28 January 1940, the British cargo ship *Eston* (1919, 1487 tons) from convoy FN.81.

U-60 (*Kapitänleutnant* Schewe) laid her mines on 17 December, off Cross Sands, and sank the British cargo ship *City of Kobe* (1924, 4373 tons) from convoy FS.56, on 19 December, at 03:35, by 52°35N/01°59E. *U-61* laid her mines on 11 December, off the Firth of Forth, and sank the British cargo ship *Ferryhill* (1919, 1086 tons) on 21 January 1940, at 14:30, 1.5 miles north of St. Mary. In attacks against shipping, *U-20* torpedoed and sank the Danish cargo ship *Magnus* (1906, 1339 tons) on 9 December, at 18:41, at 57°48N/00°35W. *U-21* on 21 December, at 07:25, torpedoed and sank the Swedish cargo ship *Mars* (another of the same name, 1882, 1475 tons), east-north-east of May Island, and on the same day, ten minutes later, torpedoed and sank another Swedish cargo ship, the *Carl Henckel* (1882, 1352 tons) at 57°00N/00°17E. *U-23* on 7 December, at 23:26, torpedoed and sank the Danish cargo ship *Scotia* (1924, 2400 tons), at 57°31N/02°17E. *U-57* on 13 December, at 19:15, torpedoed and sank the Soviet cargo ship *Mina* (1899,1173 tons), near Cross Sands.

U-59 on 16 December, at 00:28, torpedoed and sank the Swedish cargo ship *Lister* (1928, 1366 tons), at 55°13N/01°33E. On the same day, at 12:49, *U-59* torpedoed and sank the Norwegian cargo ship *Glittrefjell* (1934, 1568 tons), 56°14N/01°04E. On 17 December, at 02:34, *U-59* torpedoed and sank the Danish cargo ship *Bogo* (1920, 1214 tons), 75 miles east of May Island. On the same day, at 05:36, *U-59* also claimed to have torpedoed and sunk an unknown cargo ship of about 3000 tons. To compare, it must be recalled that the *Bogo* had been also estimated 3000 tons. Kretschmer, with his *U-23*, also claimed to have torpedoed and sunk, on 9 December, an unknown cargo ship of about 2500 tons, in the area where the *Magnus* was sunk. Between 28 December 1939 and 12 January 1940, *U-56* and *U-58* operated in the North Sea. On 31 December, off the Scottish east coast, *U-58* missed a British destroyer, position being about 58°N02°W.

1940

On 1 January 1940, at 10:58, *U-58* torpedoed and sank the Swedish cargo ship *Lars Magnus Trozelli* (1920, 1951 tons) at 58°14N/01°36W. On 3 January, at 09:11, another Swedish cargo ship, the *Svarton* (1906, 2475 tons) from convoy HN.61, was torpedoed and sunk at 57°48N01°47W, by *U-58*. On 8 January, *U-56* laid mines on Cross Sands, sinking the Finnish cargo ship *Onto* (1918, 1333 tons), on 23 January, at 22:13, 2.7 miles from

Smith's Light Vessel. From 6 to 16 January, four U-Boats operated off the Scottish east coast. *U-19* (*Kapitänleutnant* Schepke) on 9 January, at 02:21, torpedoed and sank the Norwegian cargo ship *Manx* (1916, 1343 tons), 58°30N/01°33W. *U-23* on 11 January, at 16:32, torpedoed and sank the Norwegian cargo ship *Fredville* (1917, 1150 tons), at 58°25/01°10W and, on the following day, at 06:50, the Danish tanker ship *Danmark* (1931, 10517 tons) by 58°59N/02°53W. *U-20* on 13 January, at 04:30, torpedoed and sank the Swedish cargo ship *Sylvia* (1883, 1524 tons), north-east of Aberdeen.

Further successes by *U-24* were frustrated by torpedo failures. From 18 to 27 January, no fewer than twelve U-Boats operated on the British east coast and in the southern part of the North Sea. On 18 January, at 23:53, the Swedish cargo ship *Flandria* (1898, 1179 tons) was torpedoed and sunk by *U-9* (*Leutnant zur See* Lüth) at 54°00N/03°40E. On the following day, at 01:45, the Swedish cargo ship *Patria* (1915, 1188 tons) was also torpedoed and sunk by *U-9*, at 54°00N/03°30E. On 19 January, at 21:00, the French cargo ship *Quiberon* (1922, 1296 tons) was torpedoed and sunk by *U-59* off Great Yarmouth. On 21 January, at 05:35, *U-22* torpedoed and sank the destroyer HMS *Exmouth* (1934, 1519 tons), off Tarbett Ness in the Moray Firth; she sank with all her crew of about 200. At 07:11, U-22 torpedoed and sank the Norwegian cargo ship *Miranda* (1920, 1328 tons), at 5814N/0205W.

On 22 January, *U-57* laid mines off Cromarty and, in that barrage, the base ship HMS *Durham Castle* (1904, 8240 tons) sank on 26 January. On 22 January too, at 21:27, *U-61* torpedoed and sank the Norwegian cargo ship *Sydvold* (1918, 2434 tons), at 58°40N/00°30W. On 23 January, at 07:01, the Norwegian cargo ship *Bisp* (1889, 1000 tons), sailing from Sunderland to Andalsnes, was torpedoed and sunk by *U-18*. On the same day, at 08:40, *U-19* torpedoed and sank the British cargo ship *Baltanglia* (1921, 1523 tons), at 55°35N/01°27W. Eight minutes later *U-19* torpedoed and sank another cargo ship, the Norwegian *Pluto* (1918, 1598 tons) in the same position. On 24 January, at 19:08, *U-23* torpedoed and sank the Norwegian cargo ship *Varild* (1910, 1086 tons) as she was sailing from Horten to Sunderland. On 25 January, at 02:30, *U-14* (*Leutnant zur See* Wohlfarth) torpedoed and sank the Norwegian cargo ship *Biarritz* (1922, 1752 tons), at 52°39N/04°15E. On 25 January, at 21:12, *U-19* torpedoed and sank the Latvian cargo ship *Everene* (1906, 4434 tons) near Longstone L.T. Eighteen minutes later, *U-19* torpedoed and sank the Norwegian cargo ship *Gudveig* (1919, 1300 tons), 4.5 miles east of Longstone. On 27 January, at 20:03, *U-20* (*Kapitänleutnant* Von Klot-Heydenfeldt) torpedoed and sank the Norwegian cargo ship *Faro* (1918, 844 tons) 15 miles south-east of Copinsay, in the Orkneys. Later in the day, in the same place, *U-20* torpedoed and sank three other cargo ships: at 20:52, the Danish *Fredensburg* (1922, 2094 tons), 5825N/0153W; at 21:24, the Danish *England* (1930, 2319 tons) and at 23:13 the Norwegian *Hosanger* (1911, 1591 tons). *U-15* and *U-60* returned, without success, owing to torpedo failures.

Four views of U-9 (type IIB) coming back home, after the war patrol in which she sank the French submarine Doris on 9 May 1940. The U-9 was the only U-Boat to wear an Iron Cross on her conning-tower, to commemorate the sinkings of the large cruisers HMS Aboukir, Cressy and Hogue, by the the First World War U-9 on 22 September 1914. Leutnant zur See Lüth is wearing his white cap. (ECPA).

From 27 January to 10 Febuary, seven U-Boats operated on the British east coast and in the Scottish part of the North Sea. *U-13* (*Oberleutnant zur See* Schulte) claimed to have torpedoed and damaged a cargo ship of about 4000 tons, which so far has not been identified, early on 29 January, off the Northern East Scottish coast. On 30 January, in the North Sea, *U-15* was sunk on the return voyage in a collision with the torpedo boat *Iltis*. On 31 January, at 00:43, *U-13* torpedoed and sank the Norwegian cargo ship *Start* (1923, 1168 tons) as she was sailing from Sunderland to Oslo. On the same day, at 19:54, *U-21* (*Oberleutnant zur See* Stiebler) torpedoed and sank the Danish cargo ship *Vidar* (1925, 1353 tons) at 58°39N/02°00E. On 1 Febuary, at 01:43, *U-13* torpedoed and sank the Swedish cargo ship *Fram* (1897, 2491 tons) at 57°43N02°06W. On the same day, at 20:44, *U-59* torpedoed and sank the British cargo ship *Ellen M* (1938, 498 tons) at 52°33N/02°15E. On 2 February, at 06:24, *U-59* torpedoed and sank another British merchant ship, the tanker *Creofield* (1928, 838 tons) at 52°33N/02°25E. On the same day, at 20:40, *U-59* torpedoed and sank the British cargo ship *Portelet* (1918, 1064 tons) at 52°40N/02°13E. The same evening, at 22:41, in the same area, *U-59* claimed to have torpedoed and sunk an unidentified cargo ship of about 2000 tons. On 3 February, at 09:36, *U-58* torpedoed and sank the

Estonian cargo ship *Reet* (1904, 815 tons), in approximate position 58°N02°E, as she was sailing from Methil to Goteborg. On 4 February, at 21:04, *U-21* torpedoed and sank the Yugoslav cargo ship *Vid* (1910, 3547 tons) at 58°15N00°48W. *U-17* (*Kapitänleutnant* Behrens), *U-24* and *U-56* had no success.

During Operation 'Nordmark', against convoy traffic between Britain and Scandinavia, as well as in the southern part of the North Sea, nine U-boats were employed. On 11 February, at 18:20, *U-9* torpedoed and sank the Estonian cargo ship *Linda* (1899, 1213 tons) at 5851N/0154E. On 14 February, at 01:35, *U-57* torpedoed and sank the British tanker ship *Gretafield* (1928, 10191 tons) belonging to convoy HX.18, at 58°27N02°33W. On 15 February, at 23:55, *U-14* torpedoed and sank the Danish cargo ship *Sleipner* (1915, 1066 tons) at 58°18N/01°46W. Five minutes later, she torpedoed and sank another Danish cargo ship, the *Rhone* (1915, 1064 tons). On the same day, at 21:25, *U-14* torpedoed and sank the Swedish cargo ship *Osmed* (1903, 1526 tons), 20 miles north of Kinnaird Head. Ten minutes later, she torpedoed and sank another Swedish cargo ship, the *Liana* (1898, 1664 tons), 24 miles north of Kinnaird Head. On 17 February, at 02:05, *U-10* (*Oberleutnant zur See* Preuss) torpedoed and sank the Norwegian cargo ship *Kvernaas* (1918, 1819 tons) at 51°50N/03°19E. On 18 February, at

00:23, *U-61* torpedoed and sank the Panamanian cargo ship *El Sonador* (1897, 1406 tons), east of the Shetlands. On the same day, at 03:54, *U-23* torpedoed and sank the destroyer HMS *Daring* (1932, 1397 tons) from a Bergen-Methil HN convoy, at 58°40N/01°40E; there were only 15 survivors.

On 18 February too, at 06:09, *U-16* torpedoed and sank the Norwegian cargo ship *Sangstad* (1925, 4297 tons) at 59°00N/00°25E. Also on the same day, at 09:26, *U-10* torpedoed and sank the Dutch cargo ship *Ameland* (1930, 4537 tons) at 51°54N/03°01E. On 20 February, at 00:15, *U-19* missed the British oil tanker *Daghestan*, at 59°21N/01°48W, because of torpedo defect. On 21 February, at 06:26, *U-22* had the same problem with the British trawler *Strathclova* north of Fair Island. On the same day, at 18:09, *U-57* torpedoed and damaged the British cargo ship *Loch Maddy* (1934, 4996 tons) from convoy HX.19, 20 miles from Copinsay Lighthouse in the Orkneys. *U-23* finished her off with a torpedo, on 22 February, at 01:07. On 24 February, at 21:00 (British time), *U-63* (*Oberleutnant zur See* Lorentz) torpedoed and sank the Swedish cargo ship *Santos* (1925, 3840 tons) from the Britain-Norway convoy HN.14, 59°17N/00°42W. A few hours later, on 25 February, in trying to attack again the convoy, *U-63* was sighted by the submarine HMS *Narwhal* and sunk, south-east of the Shetlands, by the escorting destroyers HMS *Escort*, HMS *Imogen* and HMS *Inglefield*, the latter being herself sunk

on 25 February 1944 by a German glider bomb, four years later, to the day! *U-63* was the first type II U-boat sunk by surface forces after six months of operations. *U-63* was a brand new submarine, launched on 6 December 1939 and commissioned in January 1940. She was, in fact, taking part in her first operational sortie when sunk.

From 29 February to 9 March, three U-boats operated off Cross Sands and in the southern part of the North Sea. On 29 February, at 22:32, *U-20* (*Kapitänleutnant* Von Klot-Heydenfeldt) torpedoed and sank the Italian cargo ship *Maria Rosa* (1914, 4211 tons), at 52°24N/01°59E. On the next day, at 03:15, *U-20* torpedoed and sank a second Italian cargo ship, the *Mirella* (1918, 5340) at 52°24N/02°02E. It must be mentioned that, on 9 February, *U-9* laid mines in approximate position 58°N/0°E and, on 4 May 1940, the British tanker ship *San Tiburcio* (1921, 5995 tons) was sunk, 4 miles from Tarbet Ness, Moray Firth, by one of them. On 2 March, at 21:59, *U-17* torpedoed and sank the Dutch cargo ship *Rijnstroom* (1937, 695 tons) at 51°36N/02°54E. On 5 March, at 20:38, *U-17* torpedoed and sank the Dutch cargo ship *Grotto* (1925, 920 tons) at 51°41N/02°47E. On 7 March, at 04:30, *U-14* torpedoed and sank the Dutch cargo ship *Vecht* (1917, 19 65 tons) at 51°45N/03°05E. On 9 March, at 05:42, *U-14* torpedoed and sank the British cargo ship *Borthwick* (1920, 1097 tons) at 51°44N/03°22E. On the same day, at 23:30, *U-14* torpedoed and sank another British cargo ship, the

An unidentified type IIA or IIB, back from an operation, entering the harbour of Wilhelmshaven, like the U-9 on the same day. (ECPA).

The U-1 (type IIA) which was probably sunk in April 1940, by a mine laid by the submarine HMS Narwhal on 4 April 1940. (Drüppel).

Abbotsford (1924, 1585 tons), in the same area. Fifteen minutes later, *U-14* torpedoed and sank another British cargo ship, the *Akeld* (1922, 643 Tons) at 51°44N/03°22E.

From 14 March an unsuccessful operation took place to hunt down British and French submarines in the North Sea, by *U-7, U-9, U-19, U-20, U-23, U-24, U-56, U-57* and *U-59* and, off southern Norway by *U-1, U-2, U-3* and *U-4*. Then the U-Boats were ordered to the British East Coast. On 19 March, at 22:21, *U-19* sank with gun-fire and torpedo the Danish cargo ship *Minsk* (1911, 1229 tons) at 58°07N/02°39W. Sixteen minutes later, *U-19* torpedoed and sank another Danish cargo ship, the *Charkow* (1913, 1026 tons). On 20 March, at 04:57, *U-19* torpedoed and sank the Danish cargo ship *Viking* (1893, 1153 tons) at 58°21N/02°22W. Finally, twenty-one minutes later, *U-19* torpedoed and sank a fourth Danish cargo ship, the *Bothal* (1920, 2109 tons). On 21 March, *U-57* sighted a cargo ship, who had been bombed and damaged the day before by a German aircraft. She torpedoed and finished her off, 4.75 miles east of Copinsay Lighthouse, in the Orkneys. She was the Norwegian *Svinta* (1916, 1267 tons). *U-22* departed 20 march for the south of Lindesnes. On 24 March she was off Pentland Forth and she was lost, from unknown cause, about 31 March (probably the last date of her transmissions) whilst operating in the Moray Firth. On 25 March, at 20:11, *U-57*, specialising in the *coup de grace*, torpedoed and finished off another ship, the British tanker *Daghestan* (1921, 5742 tons), 9 miles east of Copinsay Lighthouse. This ship had also been damaged on 20

March by the bombing of a German aircraft, and had escaped destruction from *U-19* thanks to torpedo failure on 20 February! On 27 March, following a navigational error, *U-21* grounded in Norwegian waters on a reef, near Mandal, and was interned by Norwegian authorities; not for a long time!

On 6 April Operation 'Weserubung' started for the surface ships and U-Boats of the *Kriegsmarine* (the invasion of Norway). Thirty-one submarines were involved, among them 18 type II boats:

For the Bergen area, *U-9, U-14, U-56, U-60,* and *U-62*,
Stavanger, *U-1* and *U-4*,
Pentland Firth, *U-13, U-19, U-57, U-58* and *U-59*,
Tindesnes, *U-2, U-3, U-5* and *U-6*, Shetlands/Orkneys, *U-7* and *U-10*.

The U-boat operations ended with incomplete achievements, despite favourable firing opportunities, because of defects in the depth-keeping mechanisms and in the magnetic fusing of the torpedoes.

On 6 April, at 03:16, on outward trip, *U-59* torpedoed and sank the Norwegian cargo ship *Navarra* (1920, 2118 tons) at 59°N/04°W. On 10 April, at 02:13, *U-4* (*Kapitänleutnant* Hinsch) torpedoed and sank the submarine HMS *Thistle* (1938, 1326 tons), north-west of Stavanger, off Skudesnes. *U-1* (*Korvettenkapitän* Deccke) was recorded in every source available as having been torpedoed and sunk by the submarine HMS *Porpoise* on 16 April 1940. Research has indicated that the boat attacked by the *Porpoise* was *U-3*, which escaped undamaged. *U-1*

The U-4 (type IIA) who torpedoed and sank the submarine HMS Thistle on 10 April 1940. (Drüppel).

was probably lost on a mine laid on 4 April 1940 by the submarine HMS *Narwhal*, which laid 50 mines at a depth of eight feet within a five mile radius about position 54°37N/06°35E. *U-1* left Wilhelmshaven on 6 April with orders to patrol off Stavanger. She was never heard from after she sailed. On 16 April, at 15:19, *U-13* missed a British destroyer, off the Shetlands, because of torpedo defect. On the next day, at 17:33, *U-13* torpedoed and sank the British cargo ship *Swainby* (1917, 4935 tons), 25 miles north of Muckle Flugga, in the Shetlands. On 20 April, at 12:48, an attack by *U-9* on the Polish destroyer *Blyskawica* failed because of a premature torpedo fuze, in approximate position 61°N/02°E. On 26 April, at 01:17, *U-13* claimed to have torpedoed and sunk a so far unidentified cargo ship of about 4000 tons who sank in 45 seconds, in approximate position 59°N04°W. On 28 April, at 01:29, *U-13* torpedoed and damaged the British tanker *Scottish American* (1920, 6999 tons) at 58°41N/04°40W.

From 6 May, twelve Allied submarines operated unsuccessfully off the Dutch coast and in the southern part of

the North Sea, to cover the eastern entrance to the English Channel. The submarines HMS *Seawolf*, HMS *Shark*, HMS *Snapper*, HMS *Sturgeon* and HMS *Triad*, the French submarines *Antiope*, *Calypso*, *Circe*, *Doris*, *La Sibyile*, *Orphee* and *Thetis* were employed. The *Kriegsmarine* had sent two submarines to operate in the same area, *U-7* and *U-9*. On 9 May, at 00:14, *U-9* torpedoed and sank the French submarine *Doris* (1927, 615 tons) at 53°40N/04°E. On 11 May, at 00:49, *U-9* torpedoed and sank the Estonian cargo ship *Viiu* (1917, 1908 tons) near the Westhinder Buoy. On the same day, at 14:00, *U-9* torpedoed and sank the British cargo ship *Tringa* (1925, 1930 tons) at 51°21N/02°25E. In the southern North Sea too, *U-9* torpedoed and sank, on 23 May, at 12:54, the German cargo ship *Sigurds Faulbaums* (1913, 3256 tons) who, captured by the British, was sailing to England, at 51°29N/02°38E.

On 29 May, west of Dunkirk, *U-62* (*Oberleutnant zur See* Michalowski) torpedoed and sank the destroyer HMS *Grafton* (1935, 1355 tons) at 51°22N/02°45E. Attacks on the Polish destroyer *Blyskawica* and the destroyer HMS *Vimy* by *U-60* failed because of torpedo defects. Between 22 May and 12 June, *U-8*, *U-56* and *U-58* operated from Bergen, west of the Orkneys and in the North Minch. Torpedo defects prevented successes. For instance, on 30 May, at 05:17, *U-56* (*Kapitänleutnat* Harms) missed the British cargo ship *Ulster Prince*, at 59°32N/06°23W. On 31 May, in trying to attack the troop transport convoy FN.184, *U-13* was sunk by the sloop HMS *Weston*, off Lowestoft, at 52°27/02°02E. On 1 June, at 23:48, *U-58* torpedoed and sank the British cargo ship *Astronomer* (1917, 8401 tons) at 58°01N/02°12W. Between 16 June and 2 July, *U-61* and *U-62* operated from Bergen in the area of the Hebrides. On 26 June, at 07:19, *U-62* torpedoed and sank the British trawler *Castleton* (1904, 211 tons) in the vicinity of the Orkneys. *U-62* missed two ships and an attack by *U-61* on an auxiliary cruiser failed, in the three cases probably because of torpedo defects.

A type IIC submarine. In wartime numbers were not painted on the conning-tower. (ECPA).

The U-62 (type IIC) who torpedoed and sank the destroyer HMS Grafton, *off Dunkirk, on 29 May 1940. (Drüppel).*

Between 10 and 23 July, *U-56, U-57, U-58, U-61* and *U-62* operated from Bergen, between the North Minch and North channel. They attacked independents and convoys. On 10 July, at 13:06, *U-61* torpedoed and sank the Dutch passenger ship *Alwaki* (1922, 4533 tons) belonging to convoy OA.180, at 58°46N/04°46W. On 12 July, at 10:06, *U-56* missed the British cargo ship *Dunera*, in the North Channel. The *Dunera* had German and Italian civilian internees on board, but was unnotified. Torpedo defects frustrated this and some ten other attacks made by the five U-boats. On 15 July, at 20:35, *U-58* (*Oberleutnant zur See* Schonder) claimed to have torpedoed and sunk a tanker of about 9000 tons, in approximate position 58°N/05°W. On 16 July, at 12:23, *U-61* torpedoed and reduced to a wreck the British tanker ship *Scottish Minstrel* (1922, 6998 tons) belonging to an HX Convoy, at 56°10N/10°20W. The wreck sank on the next day. On 17 July, at 04:10, *U-57* (*Oberleutnant zur See* Topp) torpedoed and sank the Swedish cargo ship *O.A. Brodin* (1921, 1960 tons) at 59°22/03°40W. On the same day, at 22:22, *U-57* torpedoed and sank the British cargo ship *Manipur* (1920, 8652 tons) at 58°41N/05°14W. On 18 July, at 16:41, *U-58* torpedoed and sank the Norwegian cargo ship *Gyda* (1920, 1591 tons) at 56N/10W, and put into Lorient for replenishment. On 19 July, at 18:28, *U-62* torpedoed and sank the British cargo ship *Pearlmoor* (1923, 4581 tons) at 55°23/09°18W.

From 28 July, *U56, U-57* and *U-59* operated from Bergen off the North Channel. The operations again suffered from torpedo failures. On 1 August, at 03:45, *U-59* (*Kapitänleutnant* Matz) torpedoed and sank the Swedish cargo ship *Sigyn* (1897, 1981 tons) at 56°10N/09°25W.

On 3 August, at 08:10, *U-57* torpedoed and sank the Swedish cargo ship *Atos* (1902, 2161 tons) at 56N/07W. Operating from Lorient off the North Channel too, on 4 August, at 21:20, *U-58* attacked convoy HX.60, torpedoing and sinking the Greek cargo ship *Pindos* (1908, 4360 tons) at 55°20N/08°50W. Early on the next day, from the same convoy, *U-58* torpedoed and sank the British cargo ship *Boma* (1920, 5408 tons) at 55°44N/08°04W. On 10 August, north of Ireland, at 01:00 *U-56* (*Oberleutnant zur See* Harms) torpedoed and sank the auxiliary cruiser HMS *Transylvania* (1925, 16923 tons) at 55°50N/08°03W. *U-59* went to Bergen for replenishment, the others to Lorient. Then, during the first half of August, *U-59* and *U-60* operated from Bergen off the North Channel. On 13 August, at 21:47, *U-60* (*Oberleutnant zur See* Schnee) torpedoed and sank the Swedish cargo ship *Nils Gorthon* (1921, 1787 tons), 25 miles north-east of Malin Head. On the next day, at 21:23, *U-60* claimed to have torpedoed and sunk a cargo ship of about 7000 tons, in approximate position 55N/09W. A little more than an hour later, at 23:34, *U-59* torpedoed and sank the British cargo ship *Betty* (1918, 2339 tons), 35 miles north of Tory Island.

After setting out from Lorient, *U-56, U-57, U-59* and *U-60* operated against independents and convoys in the area between the Hebrides, the North Channel, Ireland and Rockall Bank. On 24 August, at 00:42, *U-57* attacked convoy OB.202, torpedoing and sinking the British cargo ship *Cumberland* (1919, 10939 tons) at 55°43N/0733°W. *U-57* torpedoed two more ships from the OB.202 convoy, at the same time: the British cargo ship *Saint Dunstan* (1919, 5681 tons), who sank in position 5543N/0810W,

Aboard the U-58, *near Lorient, on 2 September 1940. Leutnant zur See* Schonder *is wearing a white cap.* (ECPA).

and the brand new British cargo ship *Havildar* (1940, 5407 tons) who was only damaged. On 25 August, at 19:48, *U-57* torpedoed and sank the British tanker ship *Pecten* (1927, 7468 tons) at 56°22N/07°55W. On 30 August, at 21:34, *U-59* attacked convoy OB.205, torpedoing and damaging beyond repair the Greek cargo ship *San Gabriel* (1920, 4943 tons) at 5604N/0954W. Nineteen minutes later, *U-59* torpedoed and damaged the British tanker ship *Anadara* (1935, 8009 tons) from the same convoy, at 56°15N/09°10W. On 31 August, at midnight, *U-60* torpedoed and damaged the Dutch passenger ship *Volendam* (1922, 15434 tons) at 5604/0952W.[1] On the same day, at 02:06, *U-59* torpedoed and sank the British passenger ship *Har Zion* (1907, 2508 tons) at 56°20N/10°W. The last two ships belonged also to convoy OB.205. On 3 September, at 03:26. *U-60* torpedoed and sank the British cargo ship *Ulva* (1912, 1401 tons) at 55°45N/11°45W. On the same day, *U-57* (Kapitän Kühl) was sunk in a collision with the Norwegian steamer *Rona*, in Brunsbüttel on the Elbe. She was salved before the end of the year and re-commissioned. On 8 September, in the Atlantic, an attack by *U-56* on the heavy cruiser HMAS *Australia* was unsuccessful because of torpedo defects.

By the middle of September *U-58, U-59, U-61* and *U-138* were despatched and stationed west of the Hebrides and off the North Channel, operating individually. On 20 September, *U-138* (Oberleutnant zur See Lüth) attacked convoy OB.216 successfully, sinking no less than four merchant ships, three of them in six minutes! At 21:20, *U-138* torpedoed and sank the British tanker ship *New Sevilla* (1900, 13801 tons) at 55°48N/07°22W. Three minutes later she torpedoed and sank the Panamanian cargo ship *Boka* (1920, 5560 tons) at 55°54N/07°24W and, three more minutes later, the British cargo ship *Empire Adventure* (1921, 5145 tons) was torpedoed and sunk off Islay. On the next day, at 02:27, *U-138*, in a last attack (only six torpedoes were embarked in those tiny 'canoes'!) torpedoed and sank the British cargo ship *City Of Simla* (1921, 10138 tons) at 55°55N/08°20W.

At the end of September, *U-137* (Oberleutnant zur See Wohlfarth) arrived in the North Atlantic, in company of nine 'big brothers', between the North Channel and Rockall Bank, and operated individually. On 20 September, at 00:50, *U-137* torpedoed and sank the British cargo ship *Manchester Brigade* (1918, 6042 tons) at 54°53N/10°22W. One minute later, another British cargo ship, the *Ashantian* (1935, 4917 tons) was torpedoed and damaged by *U-137*. At 01:35 on the same day, *U-137* torpedoed and sank the British tanker *Stratford*

(1913, 4753 tons) at 54°50/10°40W. Still on 26 September, at 04:10, *U-137* torpedoed and sank the Norwegian cargo ship *Asgerd* (1924, 1308 tons) at 56°34N/09°10W. The missions undertaken by *U-60* off the Pentland Firth, and by *U-61* (*Kapitänleutnant* Stiebler) off the North Minch, had no success. The Dutch submarines *0-21* and *0-24* operated off Norway between 23 September and 6 October. *O-21* just missed *U-61* near Bergen. Between 5 and 16 October, in operations against independents and convoys, in and just off the North Channel, *U-58*, *U-59*, *U-137* and *U-138* had the following successes. On 7 October, at 16:01, *U-59* torpedoed and sank the Norwegian cargo ship *Touraine* (1925, 5811 tons) at 55°14N/10°34W. On 8 October, at 21:31, *U-58* torpedoed the brand new British cargo ship *Confield* (1940, 4956 tons) at 5648N/1017W, who sank on the next morning. On 12 October, at 18:03, *U-59* torpedoed and sank the British cargo ship *Pacific Ranger* (1929, 6895 tons) at 5620N/1143W.

On 13 October, at 15:32, *U-138* torpedoed and damaged the Norwegian cargo ship *Dagrun* (1928, 4562 tons) in approximate position 55°N/08°W. On the next day, at 21:28, *U-137* torpedoed and damaged the auxiliary cruiser HMS *Cheshire* (1927, 10552 tons), north-west of Ireland, at about 54°N/13°W. She was immobilised in Liverpool during six months for repairs. On 15 October, at 05:10, *U-138* torpedoed and sank the British cargo ship *Bonheur* (1920, 5327 tons) at 57°10N/08°36W. Five minutes later, *U-138* torpedoed and damaged the British tanker ship *British Glory* (1928, 6993 tons). Both ships belonged to the convoy OB.228. In November, *U-137* and *U-138* operated in the area west of the North Channel. On 13 November, at 21:08, *U-137* torpedoed and sank the British cargo ship *Cape St. Andrew* (1928, 5094 tons) at 5514N/1029W. Then, on 16 November, *U-137* attacked an outward-bound convoy and, at 20:15, torpedoed and sank the British cargo ship *Planter* (1927, 5887 tons) at 5538/0828W. On the next day, at 20:14, from the same convoy, *U-137* torpedoed and sank the Swedish cargo ship *Veronica* (1918, 1316 tons) at 55°20N/08°45W. That convoy lost a third vessel, at 20:50, when the British cargo ship *Saint Germain* (1924 1044 tons) was torpedoed and sunk, at 55°40N/08°40W. From the end of November, *U-140* (*Oberleutnant zur See* Hinsch) operated in the North Atlantic, west of the North Channel. On 2 December, at 21:43, she torpedoed and sank the British cargo ship *Victoria City* (1929, 4739 tons). On 8 December, at 12:26, *U-140* torpedoed and sank the Finnish sailing vessel *Lawhill* (1892, 2816 tons) at about 55°N/10°W. Later in the day, at 20:20, *U-140* torpedoed and sank the British cargo ship *Ashcrest* (1920, 5652 tons) at about 55°N/08°W.

1941

As there were more 'big brothers' available, from January 1941, the 'canoes' were much less employed in the North Atlantic. At the end of February, *U-147* (*Kapitänleutnant* Hardegen) operated between the North Minch and the Faeroes. On 2 March, at 22:12, she attacked convoy HX.109 and succeeded in torpedoing and sinking the Norwegian cargo ship *Augvald* (1920, 4811 tons), 150 miles north-west of Loch Ewe. In the second half of April, *U-147*, now under the command of *Oberleutnant* Wetjen, was again stationed off the Faeroes. On 27 April, at 02:42, she torpedoed and sank the Norwegian cargo ship *Rimfakse* (1921, 1334 tons) at 60°10N/08°54W. On 3 May, *U-143* sighted a south-bound convoy, south of the Faeroes, but *U-141* (*Oberleutnant zur See* Schüler) and *U-147* and Focke-Wulf FW.200 reconnaissance bombers did not come up on 3-4 May. On 20 May, operating off the Faeroes, at 21:24, *U-138* (*Oberleutnant zur See* Gramitzky) torpedoed and sank the British cargo ship *Javanese Prince* (1926, 8593 tons) at 59°46N/10°45W. Off the North Channel, on 31 May, *U-147* torpedoed and sank the British cargo ship *Gravelines* (1925, 2491 tons) at 56°10N/11°13W. On 2 June, north-west of Ireland, she torpedoed and damaged the Belgian cargo ship *Mokambo* (1938, 4996 tons) in a convoy, at 56°38N/10°24W, but was depth-charged and sunk by the destroyer HMS *Wanderer* and the corvette HMS *Periwinkle* of the escort.

In June *U-141* operated west of Ireland and, on 16 June, at 08:06, missed a passenger ship, evaluated at around 21000 tons, for the torpedoes did not explode. On 18 June, 100 miles west of Cape Trafalgar, *U-138*, the only U-Boat deployed in the area, was depth charged and sunk by the destroyers HMS *Faulknor*, HMS *Fearless*, HMS *Forester*, HMS *Foxhound* and HMS *Foresight*, who, after escorting Force 'H', had been sent to Gibraltar to refuel. On 22 June, at 03:29, *U-141* torpedoed and sank the Swedish cargo ship *Calabria* (1916, 1277 tons, evaluated around 4000 tons), 100 miles west of Inishtrabull. On 28 June, at 02:07, *U-146* (*Oberleutnant zur See* Ites), operating north-west of the Hebrides, torpedoed and sank the Finnish cargo ship *Pluto* (1907, 3496 tons), 100 miles north-north-west of the Butt of Lewis. *U-137* had no success.

In July, *U-143* operated in the North Channel without success. Off Northern Ireland, on 26 July, *U-141* attacked the outward-bound convoy OS.1 which was escorted by the 5th Escort Group with Captain Donald Macintyre in the destroyer HMS *Walker*. At 03:28, *U-141* torpedoed and sank the British cargo ship *Botwey* (1916, 5106 tons, estimated 6000 tons) at 55°42N/09°53W. Two minutes later *U-141* torpedoed and damaged the brand new British cargo ship *Atlantic City* (1941, 5133 tons) at 5542/0958W. *U-141*, at 03:35, claimed to have torpedoed and sunk a cargo ship estimated to be about 10,000 tons, which was not confirmed. *U-141* was then pursued for twenty hours with depth charges. *U-141* and *U-145* were stationed in the area west of the North Channel from 22 August to 30 August. On 23 august, at 23:47, *U-143* (*Oberleutnant zur See* Gelhaus) torpedoed and sank the Norwegian cargo ship *Inger* (1930 1418 tons) in a convoy, at 5858N/0750W. On 26 August, *U-141* sighted the outward-bound convoy OS.4 west of Ireland, but was forced to submerge by an aircraft. On 30 August, *U-143* sighted an outward-bound convoy, off the North Channel, but was forced to submerge. On 5 September, at 23:37, *U-141* claimed to have torpedoed and sunk an

A type IID submarine in Lorient. In the right background the old French light cruiser Strasbourg *(ex-German* Regensburg*) used as a pontoon. (ECPA).*

armed trawler, estimated to be about 800 tons, in the approximate position 58°N/11°W. The identity of that ship is unknown, and perhaps she was only heavily damaged. Was she HMS *Brora* (1940, 545 tons) which was grounded and became a total loss in the Hebrides on the next day? On 6 September, at 23:30, *U-141* torpedoed and sank an estimated 500-ton armed trawler in approximate position 61°N/12°W. That ship was the British trawler *King Erik* (1899, 228 tons).

After September 1941 the 'canoes' were never again employed operationally in the West, but with the invasion of the Soviet Union on 22 June 1941, it is necessary to look back at what happened in the Baltic from that date, where type II U-boats were active right from the start of the campaign. Between 22 and 30 June, *U-140*, *U-142*, *U-144*, *U-145* and *U-149* operated west of Memel, south of Gotland, west of Windau and west of Ösel-Dagö and off the Gulf of Finland. On the very first day of the war, 22 June, the Soviet submarines *M-77*, *M-78* and *S-9* were moved with a steamer to Dünamünde and, on the way, in the night of 22/23 June, *M-78* (1935, 161 tons) was torpedoed and sunk by *U-144* (*Kapitänleutnant* Von Mittelstaedt) west of Windau. On 24 June, *U-140* (*Oberleutnant zur See* Hellwegel) missed a large soviet submarine. On 26 June, *U-149* (*Kapitänleutnant* Höltring) torpedoed and sank the Soviet submarine *M-99* (1939, 210 tons) off the Gulf of Finland, at 59°20N/21°12E. On 21 July, at 06:55, off Dagö Island, *U-140* torpedoed and sank the Soviet submarine *M-94* (1937, 210 tons) at 58°51N/22°00E. That submarine was returning home after operating in the Baltic. On 28 July, off the Gulf of Finland, the Soviet submarine *Shch-307* (Lieutnant-Commander Petrov) torpedoed and sank *U-144*. For that loss, the U-Boats had sunk three Soviet submarines, *M-78*, *M-94* and *M-99*. The 'canoes' were then sent back to Germany where they joined other type II submarines, for training the crews to be used by the increasing number of brand new 'big brothers'.

1942/1943

When it became evident that the Russian campaign would last much longer than the German General Staff had foreseen the Supreme Command of the *Kriegsmarine* decided to send a number of warships to the Black Sea, in addition to the Danube Flotilla. Only small ships could be used, for they had to be carried overland from the Elbe River below Dresden to the Danube, below Regensburg. The largest were six 'canoes'! As much weight as possible, including the engines, was taken out before they were lifted by cranes onto special oversize trucks that could carry them only on the *autobahn*. The 'emigrants' were then sent to Constanza in the Black Sea through Galatz on the Danube with the aid of pontoons. The first three to arrive in October 1942 were *U-9*, *U-19* and *U-24*. By June 1943 they had been followed successively by *U-18*, *U-20* and *U-23*. It was a remarkable feat of improvisation and organisation by the Germans.

On 5 November 1942, at 21:37, *U-24* (*Kapitänleutnant* Petersen) missed a Soviet tanker (estimated at 2100 tons), because of a torpedo defect, by 4208N/4105E. In February 1943 there were Soviet movements with steamers and small craft along the Caucasus coast. *U-9*, *U-19* and *U-24* were deployed against these transports. On 14 February, south-west of Tuapse, *U-19* (*Oberleutnant zur See* Gaude) torpedoed and sank the Soviet cargo ship *Krasny Profintern* (1902, 4648 tons). From 17 to 31 March, *U-19* and *U-24* operated against Soviet supply traffic off the Caucasus coast near Sukhumi and Gagry. On 28 March, at 13:03, *U-19* torpedoed and damaged a passenger ship of about 2000 tons in Gagry Bay. On 31 March, at 12:30, *U-24* (*Kapitänleutnant* Schöler) claimed to have torpedoed and sunk the Soviet tanker *Sovietskaya Neft* (1929, 8228 tons), also in Gagry Bay. In reality, the tanker was only damaged and she was the *Kreml*. In the night of 30 April/1May, the Soviet destroyers *Boiki* and

Besposhchadny tried in vain to attack *U-19*, as they were on their way to shell Cape Meganon and Cape Claude. On 5 May, *U-9* (*Oberleutnant zur See* Schmidt-Weichert) torpedoed and sank (not damaged as previously stated in other sources) the Soviet tanker *Kreml* (1932, 7666 tons), 22 miles south of Cape Kodor.

In May too, *U-18* and *U-19* had no success off Sukhumi and Poti because of strong defence. Then *U-18*, *U-19*, *U-20*, *U-23* and *U-24* operated against the Soviet supply traffic off the Caucasus coast: on 15 June, *U-24* torpedoed and sank the Soviet minesweeper *Zashchitnik* (1940, 441 tons), off Tuapse. On 23 June, *U-18* (*Oberleutnant zur See* Fleige) torpedoed and sank the Soviet cargo ship *Leningrad* (1889, 1783 tons), near Sukhumi, at 43°50N39°15E. On the same day, *U-18* also claimed to have torpedoed and damaged a barge of 800 tons, near Cape Pizunda, and missed the Soviet tanker *Stalin* (estimated at 1000 tons), off Sukhumi. On 17 July, 20 miles south-east of Tuapse, *U-18* claimed to have torpedoed and sunk the Soviet cargo ship *Voroshilov* (1924, 3908 tons) from a convoy, but it is dubious. On 18 July, the Soviet dredger *Dunaj-2* was torpedoed and sunk by *U-20*. The *U-19*, and *U-24* operated again off the Caucasus coast against Soviet supply transports, from 30 July to 10 September. On 30 July, at 20:07, *U-24* torpedoed and damaged (not sunk as previously stated in other sources) the Soviet tanker ship *Emba* (1929, 7886 tons), in the harbour of Sukhumi.

On 22 August, *U-24* sank with 20mm gunfire a small Soviet tug (about 10 tons) and captured two Soviet motor boats (numbered 36 and 37, each of about 9 tons) and sank them with scuttling charges; all three south-

west of Gagry Bay. On 24 August, *U-23* (*Oberleutnant zur See* Wahlen) torpedoed and sank the Soviet survey vessel *Shkval* near Cape Kodor, 22 miles south of Sukhumi. On 29 August, at 21:58, *U-18* torpedoed and sank the Soviet decoy ship *Djalita* (1926, 470 tons), 34 miles south of Sukhumi. On 30 august, at 19:43, *U-18* damaged the Soviet patrol boat *SKA.0132* (50 tons), with 20mm gunfire, north-north-west of Poti. Off the Caucasus coast, on 18 September, at 05:40, *U-18* torpedoed and sank a small Soviet cargo ship of about 800 tons, 20 miles north-west of Tuapse. On 20 September, *U-20* (*Oberleutnant zur See* Schöler) laid mines off Sochi and, on 30 September, off Anapa torpedoed and sank a Soviet lighter of about 800 tons. On 15 October, at 21:31, off Poti, *U-23* torpedoed and damaged (not sunk as previously stated in other sources) the Soviet cargo ship *TSC-486 Sovietskaya Rossiya* (1880, 426 tons). On 23 October, 20 miles north-west of Poti, *U-23* claimed to have torpedoed and sunk a Soviet cargo ship of about 1000 tons and also to have sunk, with 20mm gunfire, a Soviet fishing cutter off Poti. In reality the Soviet ship was the dredger *Danais* which was only damaged. On 29 October, at 21:30, *U-9* (*Oberleutnant zur See* Klapdor) reported to have torpedoed and probably sunk a Soviet tanker of about 3000 tons, north-west of Sochi. On 31 October, at 01:50, *U-24* torpedoed and sank a Soviet motor minesweeper, 40 miles north-west of Sukhumi; it was in fact the Soviet patrol boat *SKA.088* (50 tons). On 8 November, at 11:16, *U-18* torpedoed and sank a Soviet tanker of about 2000 tons in the roadstead of Batum. On 18 November, at 17:15, 10 miles south of Tuapse, *U-18* claimed to have torpedoed and sunk a Soviet cargo ship of about 1500

The U-149 (type IID) which torpedoed and sank the Soviet submarine M-99, in the Baltic, on 26 June 1941. (Drüppel).

tons. She was the *I. Stalin* and was only damaged. On 29 November, *U-20* torpedoed and damaged the Soviet tanker *Peredovik* (1940, 1857 tons). *U-9* and *U-19*, also deployed off the Caucasus coast, had no success.

1944

From 5 January 1944, *U-19*, *U-20*, *U-23* and *U-24* operated against Soviet coastal traffic off the Caucasus. In January, *U-23* claimed to have torpedoed and sunk two Soviet merchant ships, off Sukhumi, one freighter of about 1500 tons and one tanker of about 2000 tons. On 16 January, at 16:35, off Poti, *U-20* (*Oberleutnant zur See* Grafen) torpedoed the Soviet tanker ship *Vayan Kuturie* (1930, 7596 tons), which sank the next day. On 17 February, *U-18*, finding the net-barrage opened, launched torpedoes into the harbour of Batum and claimed a Soviet cargo ship of about 1500 tons sunk. Another direct hit was observed on boats or a pier. In February too, *U-19* (*Oberleutnant zur See* Ohlenburg) and *U-20* operated off Batum and Poti, the latter submarine laying mines off Poti. At the beginning of March, *U-20* and *U-24* were deployed against Soviet traffic from Poti to Trapezunt. On 5 April, 10 miles north-west of Poti, *U-23* had a surface engagement with the Soviet patrol boat *SKA.099* (50 tons) who was damaged (not sunk as previously stated in other sources) by 20mm gunfire. On 7 April, *U-23* torpedoed and sank the Soviet dredger *Rion* (1928, 591 tons). On 24 April, 22 miles south-east of Gelerdzik, *U-18* attacked a Soviet towing convoy, launched three torpedoes and heard three explosions; the tug (about 500 tons) was sunk, a barge (about 600 tons) was probably sunk and another one was damaged.

On 5 May, near Tuapse, *U-9* (*Kapitänleutnant* Petersen) sank a Soviet fishing cutter (about 50 tons) with 20mm gunfire. On 11 May, at 16:30, 20 miles south-east of Tuapse, *U-9* attacked a small convoy, comprising one torpedo boat, one minesweeper and one tanker. She launched one torpedo and observed a large detonation after 2 minutes 31 seconds. A hit on the torpedo boat was assumed and there was a heavy oil smell the next day; effectively the torpedo boat *Shtorm* (1930, 478 tons) was damaged. On 12 May, in the evening, *U-24* (*Oberleutnant zur See* Landt-Hayen) torpedoed and sank the Soviet patrol boat *SKA-0376* (50 tons), near Poti. On 17 May, around midday, *U-9* torpedoed and damaged a Soviet tanker ship who was sailing with a patrol boat, 18 miles-east of Gelendzik. On 22 May, near Batum, *U-24* claimed to have torpedoed and sunk another patrol boat of about 50 tons. On 23 May, in the morning, *U-23* torpedoed and perhaps sank a Soviet cargo ship of about 1500 tons, eight miles south-east of Adler. In the morning of 25 May, *U-9* fired and missed a patrol boat, south of Tuapse. Early on 27 May, north of Poti, *U-24* damaged a patrol boat with gunfire. On 27 May, at 12:56, 10 miles south Sukhumi, *U-23* sighted a small Soviet tanker who was grounded and gave her the coup de grace with a torpedo hit; it was, in fact, the tug *Smelyi*. On 31 May, at 08:28, 12 miles south-east of Gelendzik, *U-18*

(*Oberleutnant zur See* Arendt) torpedoed and sank a Soviet tug of about 300 tons. On the next day, at 14:34, 14 miles north-west of Tuapse, *U-18* torpedoed and sank a Soviet gunboat of about 200 tons, with a GNAT acoustic homing torpedo.

On 2 June, at 10:06, *U-23* captured a Soviet fishing cutter, took off three prisoners, and sank her with hand grenades, 13 miles north-north-west of Poti. On the next day, at 21:19, *U-23* claimed to have torpedoed and sunk a Soviet motor gunboat with an acoustic torpedo, north-north-west of Tuapse. On 19 June, at 20:28, 8 miles north-east of Trapezunt, *U-20* torpedoed and damaged (not sunk as previously stated in other sources) the Soviet cargo ship *Pestel* (1890, 1850 tons), estimated at 2000 tons by *Oberleutnant zur See* Grafen. On 24 June, 13 miles south-south-east of Adler, *U-20* sank four small motor boats, representing about 15 tons together, with 20mm gunfire; one of them was the fishing boat *DB-26*. On 27 June, north-west of Tuapse, *U-19* torpedoed and did sink an unidentified tug and claimed to have sunk a barge. *U-9* and *U-24* operated off the Caucasus coast at the end of July. On 2 August, 10 miles north-west of Poti, *U-18* torpedoed and damaged a patrol boat and a cargo ship of about 1500 tons.

A very strange and important event then took place. 'With German authorization', the small Turkish motor sailing ships *Morina*, *Bulbul* and *Mefkure* set out from Constanza on 3 August, to proceed towards the Bosporos with 913 Jewish refugees. According to other sources they were 1016 on board. They were escorted by two Rumanian KFK submarine-chasers. Near the Rumanian-Bulgarian border, the submarine-chasers turned away and the sailing ships continued their journey alone. In the night of 4/5 August, the Soviet submarine *Shch-215* (3rd Rank Captain A I Strizhak), which was employed in the operational area off Burgas against German and Axis shipping, to and from the Bosphorous, encountered the *Mefkure* and sank her in a gun attack. Of the approximately 320 refugees on board, only five of them and some members of the Turkish crew were rescued by the *Bulbul* the following morning. The *Morina* arrived in the Bosphorous on the morning of 5 August and the *Bulbul* put into Igneada.[2] The Jews feared the Soviets more than anyone else, and wanted to flee from Rumania before their arrival, and the Germans gave them authorisation to escape before the Red Army arrived!

On 11 August, 10 miles north-west of Poti, *U-18* torpedoed and sank a Soviet cargo ship estimated at 1500 tons. On 13 August, 20 miles south of Poti, *U-18* torpedoed and sank a Soviet motor gunboat. On 20 August, 62 bombers, 80 fighters and ground attack planes of the Soviet Black Sea Fleet, after laying preliminary smoke emissions to eliminate the anti-aircraft fire, attacked the harbour of Constanza; *U-9* was sunk, and *U-18* and *U-24* were damaged. Other warships and many similar craft were sunk or damaged. Soviet forces were invading Rumania and, on 23 August, an armistice was signed between the Rumanians and the Soviets. In evacuating the harbour of Constanza, on 24 August, the non-operational warships were scuttled; among them, *U-18* and *U-24*. The last three German U-Boats in the Black Sea,

The U-20 (type IIB) in the Black Sea, at Constanza, in 1943 or 1944. Armed with two 20mm AA guns. The conning tower has been lengthened to allow an emplacement for an additional gun. (Drüppel).

U-19, *U-20* and *U-23*, despite those catastrophic circumstances, operated courageously from 25 August in the area off Constanza, fighting as a point of honour to the last ditch. On 1 September, at 02:30, *U-23* (*Oberleutnant zur See* Arendt) fired a salvo of torpedoes into the harbour of Constanza and hit the Rumanian cargo ship *Oituz* (1905, 2686 tons) which was damaged beyond repair. On 2 September, at 05:22, almost for the fifth anniversary of the beginning of the Second World War, *U-19* (*Oberleutnant zur See* Ohlenburg) torpedoed and sank the Soviet minesweeper *Vzryv* (1939, 441 tons) off Constanza. The Soviet shipping being reduced to a minimum, and targets became scarce. When their fuel was used up, and after an offer to sell them to Turkey was rejected, *U-19*, *U-20* and *U-23* were scuttled by their own crews near Erekli on the Turkish coast: *U-20* and *U-23* on 10 September and *U-19* on 11 September, the crews being interned.

Right to the end the 'canoes' had the upper hand against the Red Fleet. None of the six U-boats was sunk at sea by Soviet warships, mines or aircraft between November 1942 and September 1944, the *Kriegsmarine* remaining undefeated in the Black Sea. It must be recalled that type II submarines were particularly successful against their enemy counterparts, having sunk five of them: the British *Thistle* and the French *Doris* in April and May 1940, the Soviet *M-78* and *M-99* in June 1941 and the Soviet *M-94* in July 1941, only losing *U-144* in July 1941.

Addenda

In their obscure but useful job of training, three 'canoes' were lost accidentally in the Baltic:

- on 19 March 1943, *U-5* (*Leutnant zur See* Rahn) lost in a diving accident, west of Pillau, at 54°25N/19°50E.
- on 18 February 1944, *U-7* (*Kapitän* Loeschke) was lost in a diving accident, west of Pillau, at 54°25N/19°50E.
- on 8 April 1944, *U-2* (*Kapitän* Schwarzkopf) was lost, west of Pillau, by collision with the German fishing vessel *Heinrich Fröse*.

In addition, *U-21* (*Kapitän* Schwarzkopf) was paid-off in Neustadt on 5 August 1944 and scrapped in February 1945, and *U-56* (*Leutnant zur See* Miede) was bombed and sunk on 28 April 1945, in Kiel, by an air raid.

For more specifications of type II submarines, see *Conway's All the Worlds Fighting Ships 1922-1946* (London: Conway Maritime Press, 1980).

Notes:
1   Ed: Remains of this torpedo gave Royal Navy experts detailed information on German torpedoes.
2   J Rohwer and G Hummelchen, *Chronology of the War at Sea 1939-45*, (London: Greenhill Books, 1992), page 295.

ARMOURED CRUISER VERSUS ARMOURED CRUISER:

Ulsan 14 August 1904

During the Russo-Japanese war, 1904-5, Admiral Iessen's armoured cruiser squadron, after failing to aid the breakout of the main Russian fleet at Port Arthur, headed for his base at Vladivostok. However, 36 miles north of Tsushima he discovered four armoured cruisers of Vice Admiral Kamimura's squadron barring his line of retreat. Here **Peter Brook** examines one of only two actions that were fought between armoured cruisers, the Battle of Ulsan.

During the brief heyday of the armoured cruiser, from 1895 to 1916, only two actions were fought between armoured cruisers, Coronel and Ulsan. Much has been written about the former while the second remains largely forgotten. At the beginning of the Russo-Japanese war the Russian Far Eastern Fleet was divided between Port Arthur, where all the battleships were located, and Vladivostok, base to three armoured cruisers, *Rurik*, *Rossia* and *Gromoboi* and a large modern protected cruiser, *Bogatyr*. This squadron's task was to raid the Japanese coast and to disrupt sea communications between Japan and the seat of the war.

By August 1904, in the seventh month of the war, the squadron had made six sorties, only one of which, made in June, had been fully successful, when the squadron sank the *Hitachi Maru* carrying eighteen 11in howitzers, the Port Arthur siege train. In August the Port Arthur fleet had come under shellfire from the Japanese besiegers and in consequence the fleet attempted to make for Vladivostok on 10 August but were engaged by the Japanese; the main part of the fleet returned to Port Arthur, the remainder, with the exception of a small cruiser the *Novik*, which made an unsuccessful attempt to reach Vladivostok, seeking internment in neutral ports. As part of the breakout plan, Admiral Iessen, commanding the Vladivostok squadron less *Bogatyr*, unseaworthy following a grounding, was notified of the sortie of the Port Arthur fleet, but as the message was delayed and boiler fires were out, he did not sail until 13 August, by which time the attempted breakout had been thwarted. Iessen planned to meet the main fleet in the Straits of Korea; at first light on 14 August he was some 36 miles north of the island of Tsushima when he saw

Admiral Iessen, right, on board Rossia. (Klado).

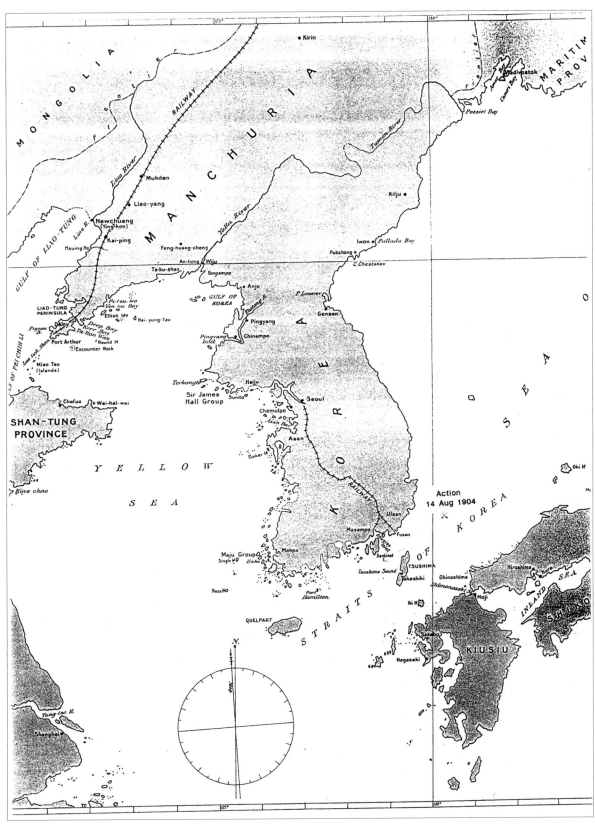

Theatre of Operations. (Custance).

Gromoboi. (Author's collection).

Rurik *before her rigging was reduced*. (Author's collection).

Rossia *pre-war*. (Navy & Army Illustrated).

four warships to the north barring his line of retreat. These were the four armoured cruisers of Vice Admiral Kamimura's squadron, charged with guarding the Straits of Tsushima against any Russian ships that had eluded the main Japanese fleet. Guessing that the Vladivostok squadron would come south he had gone northwards leaving two old protected cruisers, *Naniwa* and *Takachiho*, to guard the straits.

The Two Squadrons Compared.
(Also see table 1)

Russian

The three cruisers were not sister ships but showed a steady improvement from *Rurik* (1892) to *Gromoboi* (1899) via *Rossia* (1896). All were of an out-dated design with their main armament mounted on the broadside. *Rurik*, which caused a great stir in naval circles when launched, was originally barque-rigged with 4-8in guns protected by small shields only, mounted in sponsons on the upper deck, 16-6in QF unprotected on the main deck and 6-4.7in shield-protected on the upper deck between the 8in guns. There was an armour belt 6ft 9in wide of Creusot steel, 10-8in thick terminating in bulkheads which were taken up to the upper deck to provide the 6in battery with protection from raking fire. *Rossia* was a distinct improvement with an 8ft 6in wide, 8in thick belt of Harvey Nickel steel and a patch of 5in armour protecting

Admiral Kamimura. (Author's collection).

the engines and boiler rooms above the belt. Her 20kts speed was about 2kts better than *Rurik's*. Armament was 4-8in and 16-6in, all shield protected; one of the 6in was mounted right in the bow and one in the stern, neither having broadside fire. Twelve 3in replaced the 4.7in guns. *Gromoboi* was a further improvement and could be

Table 1. WARSHIPS TAKING PART IN THE BATTLE OF ULSAN

Russian

	Rurik	Rossia	Gromoboi
Year of Launch	1892	1896	1899
Displacement(tons)	11,690.	13,675	13,220
Dimensions(feet)	435(oa)x67x27ft3in	480ft6in(oa)x68ft6inx26	481(oa)x68ft6inx27
Armament	4-8in/35	4-8in/45	4-8in/45
	6-6inQF 6-4.7inQF	16-6in.QF 12-3in	16-6inQF24-3in
Armour:			
Belt	10-5in	8-4in	6in
Side above		5in	Side above1.5in
Deck	3.5-2.5in	3.75in	3-2in
Bulkheads	10in		
Battery bulkheads	4in		
Casemates			(14)5in.2in rear
Machinery	2 sets VTE	3 sets VTE	3 sets VTE
	8 cylindrical boilers	32 Belleville boilers	32 Belleville boilers
	IHP 13,250=18.7kts	IHP 15,500=20.2kts	IHP 15,500=20kts
Coal	2000 tons	2500 tons	1720 tons

Japanese

	Idzumo/Iwate	Tokiwa	Azuma	Naniwa/Takachiho
Date of Launch	1899,1900.	1898.	1899.	1885
Displacement(tons)	9600	9778	9307	3727
Dimensions(feet)	434(oa)x68ft6in	442(oa)x67	452ft(oa)6inx68ft9in	320(oa)x46
	x23ft9in.	x24ft5in.	x23ft9in.	x 23ft3in
Armament	4-8in/45.14-6inQF	4-8in/45.14-6in QF	4-8in/45.12-6inQF	8-6inQF
	12-12pdr	12-12pdr	12-12pdr	
Armour:				
Belt	7-5-3.5in	7-5-3.5in	7-3.5in	
Side above	5in	5in	5in	
Gunhouses				
& casemates	6in	6in	6in	
Deck	2.5in	2in	2in	3inslopes, 2inflat
Machinery	2 sets VTE	2 sets VTE	2 sets VTE	2sets, horizontal Cpd
	24 Belleville boilers	12 cylindrical boilers	12 Belleville boilers	6 cylindrical boilers
	IHP16,080=21.7	IHP19,400=23kts	IHP17,000=20kts	IHP7000=17kts
Coal	1551tons	1410tons	1275tons	800tons

described as the only true armoured cruiser in that two 8in and 12-6in were mounted in 5in casemates with the remaining 2-8in and 4-6in shield-protected. Armour protection was similar to *Rossia's* but was Krupp cemented. All three had large coal capacities with great endurance.

Japanese

The four armoured cruisers had similar armament dispositions with twin turrets mounted fore and aft with 12-14 6in on the broadside, a more effective disposition than the Russians, doubling the number of 8in guns able to fire on each side. *Idzumo* and *Iwate* were sisters and, like the similar *Tokiwa*, were built by Armstrongs at their Elswick yard from Phillip Watts' designs. All three of the

Armstrong ships mounted their 8in in 6in gunhouses with ten of the 6in mounted in casemates with 6in fronts and 2in rears, the remainder behind shields. *Idzumo* and *Iwate* had Krupp armour and Belleville boilers. *Tokiwa's* armour was the slightly less effective Harvey nickel and her boilers were cylindrical. On trials she made 23kts but only with considerable forcing, so that her continuous sea speed was about 19kts whereas her near-sisters could make 21kts. The fourth armoured cruiser was the French-built *Azuma*, longer and less beamy but otherwise similar, with Elswick guns and mountings but with only 12-6in, 8 of which were in casemates; her speed was ½-1kt less than *Idzumo's*. Two elderly protected cruisers, *Naniwa* and *Takachiho*, were involved in the final stage of battle. Both were built by Armstrongs at their Low Walker yard, launched in 1885; their original Krupp breechloaders had

Idzumo *upon completion*. (Vickers).

been replaced by 8-6in Armstrong QF shortly before the war with five able to fire on each side. Their speed was about 16kts. Because of the Russians poor armament layout they were outgunned nearly twice broadside to broadside:

	8in.	6in	4.7in
Japanese (ACs only)	16	27	
Russian	6	22	3

The one advantage the Russians had was their much greater steaming radius but this counted for nothing in the ensuing battle.

The Action

At 05:00 as soon as the Japanese were sighted, the Russians changed course to the NE; the Japanese followed suit but on a slightly converging course (fig 1) with firing commencing at 05:23 at a range of 8500 metres. Within half an hour *Rurik* was damaged and began to drop astern of her two consorts; Admiral Iessen, flying his flag in *Rossia* headed to starboard in order to open the range but this put the Japanese in an enfilading position, and to make matters worse the rising sun dazzled the Russian gunners. At about 06:00 Iessen made a 180° turn, perhaps hoping to evade the Japanese by going up the Korean coast and at the same time enabling *Rurik* to catch up. After a few minutes Kamimura (flagship

Iwate *in pre-war livery*. (Ogawa).

Naniwa *in 1907*. (WSS).

Tokiwa. (Ogawa).

Azuma. (Jane's FS *1903*).

Takachiho *re-armed and with funnel raised as she appeared at Ulsan*. (WSS).

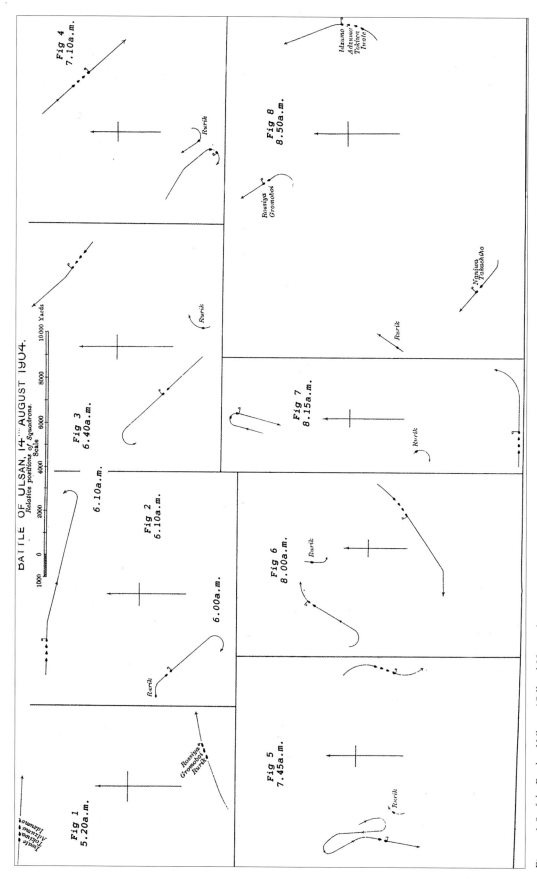

Figures 1-8 of the Battle of Ulsan. (Official History).

The last of the Rurik, *14 August 1904.* (Official History).

Idzumo) responded by making a 180° turn himself but, because he turned to port, this opened the range (fig 2) and he was forced to slow down because *Azuma* had developed engineroom problems, so that firing only recommenced at 06:24 with *Rurik* again suffering, receiving three hits in the stern. The tiller flat flooded and made her unresponsive to the wheel; she then had to be steered by her engines. Her speed steadily dropped, increasingly exposing her to Japanese fire; at about 06:40 her tiller jammed hard-a-port and thereafter *Rurik* was out of control, constantly circling to starboard.

At this point Iessen made a 180° turn to port (fig 3) in order to place his two ships between *Rurik* and the Japanese, but *Rurik* suddenly increased speed and swung to starboard, passing between Iessen and the Japanese with all three Russian ships suffering severely from Japanese gunfire. Kamimura had made a 180° turn so that both squadrons were heading SE, Iessen again altered course by 180° heading about NW so that at one point the two fleets were steaming on opposite courses (fig 4); it was at this juncture that Kamimura's rear ship, *Iwate*, was hit by an 8in shell which struck the 2in roof of the starboard forward casemate, setting off ready-use ammunition and causing enormous casualties (32 killed, 9 mortally wounded and 34 wounded). That 6in gun was put out of action as well as the 12pdr above, the 6in gun below and another 6in further aft. Kamimura again turned 180° to conform with the Russians, but by turning in succession to port the range again opened. Shortly after, Iessen turned back for the third time in an attempt to support *Rurik* (fig 5); his flagship was ablaze forward but the fires were put out in about 20 minutes.

Rossia and *Gromoboi* were now headed northwards but at this point Kamimura made a mistake which resulted in these two making their escape. Kamimura circled the *Rurik*, initially by heading SE and then W (fig 6), allowing the Russians to get to the north of him. At about 08:00 Iessen turned towards the *Rurik* for the fourth time (fig 7) and, believing that she was again able to steer, ordered her to make her own way back to Vladivostok, the two remaining Russian ships heading north at their maximum speed, about 18kts. At about the same *Naniwa* (flag) and *Takachiho*, part of Rear Admiral Uriu's fourth division, came up from the SE, which left Kamimura free to pursue Iessen, leaving the two protected cruisers to finish off *Rurik* (fig 8). A running fight went on for about an hour and a half, with the Japanese scoring hits on the Russians, whose speed gradually fell to about 15kts. *Azuma* again broke down, *Tokiwa* taking her place in the line; for some reason the range closed only slowly to 5000 metres but Kamimura then allowed it to open again to 6500 metres.

By 10:00 Kamimura was becoming anxious about leaving the Straits of Tsushima unguarded and at this point his gunnery officer informed him that *Idzumo* had expended three quarters of her ammunition. This was, in fact, incorrect as about half remained; after five minutes of rapid firing Kamimura reversed course and abandoned the chase, having decided to use his remaining ammunition to sink *Rurik*. Ironically it was just after this time that the Russians had to stop in order to repair damage and at the same time *Rurik* had sunk. An attempt to inform the Admiral of this fact by wireless was unsuccessful. *Rurik* had been in action with Admiral Uriu's cruisers since 08:42 with the range closing to less than 3000 metres at one point. By 10:05 it was clear that *Rurik* was beaten, with all her guns out of action, and Uriu ceased fire. His last shot had burst in the conning tower killing her Captain, who had been rendered *hors de combat* early in the action, and wounding the senior surviving officer, Lt Ivanov, the junior gunnery officer. He was determined that *Rurik* should not fall into Japanese hands

Rossia, *two views of damage after the battle*. (Klado).

and ordered the only unwounded executive officer, Sub Lt Baron Schilling, to bring the wounded up on deck and then explode the torpedo magazine but no fuze was available so the ship was scuttled by opening the Kingston valves, with the wounded being tied to lifejackets or pieces of wood. Her crew abandoned ship with *Rurik* going down by the stern with her bow high in the air. The Japanese were quick to rescue survivors and aided by a calm sea picked up 625 of the crew, of whom 230 were wounded; 170 went down with the ship. Only 4 of the 22 officers were unwounded.

Casualties and Damage

Casualties were particularly heavy on the Russian side partly because of poorer protection to the guns and partly because *Gromoboi*'s 3in guns were kept fully manned, while in contrast *Rossia*'s engaged side QF gunners lay prone on the opposite side and the guncrews on the disengaged side were sent below; casualties among crew in *Gromoboi*'s casemates were negligible.

Japanese Ships

	Idzumo	Azuma	Tokiwa
Killed	3	0	0
Wounded	16	8	3

	Iwate	Naniwa	Takachiho
Killed	40	2	0
Wounded	37	4	13

Rossia, damage to 8in casemate after Ulsan. (Klado).

Russian Ships

	Rossia	Gromoboi	Rurik
Killed	44	87	192
Wounded	156	170	239
Interned			625

Gromoboi's after 8in was damaged but none of the casemate guns was put out of action. Both she and *Rossia* were ablaze at one point because of spare charges being set on fire; *Gromoboi*'s was quickly extinguished but *Rossia*'s forecastle was badly damaged before the fires were put out. *Rossia* received nineteen hits on her hull on the starboard side and nine to port as well as hits on boats, funnels and decks, with half her guns put out of action. *Gromoboi* sustained fifteen hull hits on her starboard side

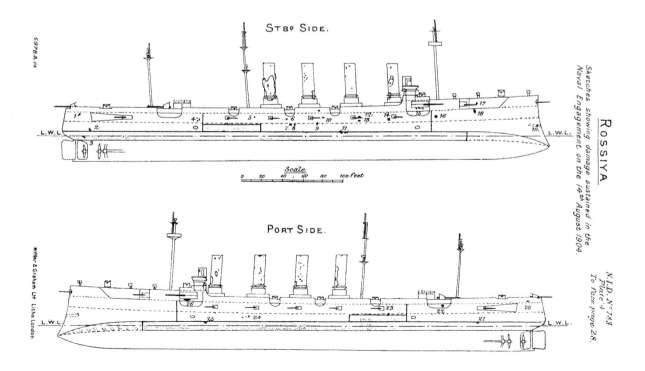

Diagram showing damage to Rossia. (Naval Attaches).

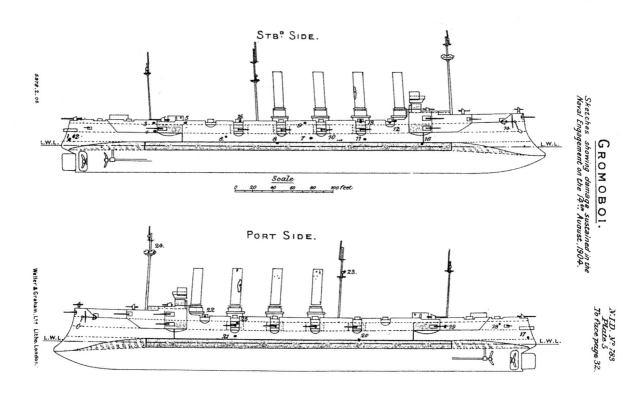

Diagram showing damage to Gromoboi. *(Naval Attaches).*

and seven to port as well as others on boats, light guns etc. A hit on a top killed 16. None of the hits on the belt of either ship penetrated. The Japanese mostly used HE shell but these tended to burst prematurely. Neither ship was badly damaged and both were repaired within two months despite poor dockyard facilities.

Conclusions

Ulsan presaged the Dogger Bank action of 24 Jan 1915, when five British battlecruisers failed to destroy an inferior German force of three battlecruisers and an armoured cruiser by concentrating on the stricken cruiser and not pursuing the fleeing enemy after Beatty's flagship was put

Rossia, *damage after the engagement. (Klado).*

Gromoboi's *damaged conning tower. (Klado).*

Two views of Gromoboi *showing damage sustained at Ulsan.* (Klado).

out of action. At Ulsan the Russians should have been annihilated but throughout the action Kamimura failed to close to a decisive range, made his turns away from the enemy and in succession. This last manoeuvre meant losing ground and was potentially more dangerous as each ship turned at the same point but did have the advantage of the Admiral remaining in the lead. In Kamimura's case this was unnecessary as his second in command, Rear Admiral Misu was flying his flag in the rear ship, *Iwate*, and could have temporarily assumed command. By concentrating on *Rurik* Kamimura allowed the Russians to escape to the north and then compounded his mistake by not pursuing at full speed, finally breaking off the action too early. The Russians, faced with a superior force blocking their path to their base, fought splendidly but their gunnery was inferior, with 2.5 per cent hits compared with the Japanese 6 per cent. Iessen could be criticised for not abandoning *Rurik* to her fate earlier; his reluctance to do so must have been good for morale. In the long run Kamimura's flawed victory made no real difference as two months later *Gromoboi* was put permanently out of action by running onto rocks and *Rossia* made no further attempts to interfere with Japanese sea communications.

Epilogue

And what became of Ivanov? In 1907 he was awarded the distinction of being known as Ivanov the 13th for the rest of his service because at the time of Ulsan he was the 13th Ivanov on the Navy List.

Sources
Corbett J, *Maritime Operations in the Russo-Japanese War*, (Reprint, Annapolis MD, 1994).
Custance Admiral Sir R, *The Ship of the Line in Battle*, (London & Edinburgh: William Blackwood & Sons,1912).
Klado N, *Battle of the Sea of Japan*, (London: Hodder & Stroughton, 1906).
Official History of the Russo-Japanese War (Naval & Military) vol 1, (London: HMSO, 1910).
Russo-Japanese War, Reports of Naval Attaches etc., vol 3, Admiralty Intelligence Department, Jan 1906.
Wilson HW, *Battleships in Action*, (London: Sampson Low & Co., 1926).

THE *RETVIZAN*: AN AMERICAN BATTLESHIP FOR THE TSAR

The American-built battleship *Retvizan* has often been described as the best Russian battleship of her era.[1] Built by Charles Cramp the successful design of the *Retvizan* influenced the next generation of US Battleships. Using Russian and American sources, **Stephen McLaughlin** describes her origins, characteristics, and career under two flags.

An American Armstrong's?

The story of the *Retvizan* properly begins with Charles Cramp of Philadelphia, for it was his determination and persistence that ultimately won the contract for the Imperial Russian Navy's first foreign-built battleship in more than thirty years.

Charles Henry Cramp was born in 1828, the eldest son of the Philadelphia shipbuilder William Cramp.[2] After learning the fundamentals of naval architecture, Charles began working in his father's yard in 1846, and was made a partner in the business in 1859. Charles apparently took over much of the business management of the yard over the next few years, showing sound business sense and a strong interest in the emerging technology of steamships.[3] During the American Civil War Charles designed the hull of the ironclad USS *New Ironsides*[4] and also suggested building a pair of similar but improved broadside ironclads, but the US Navy was caught up in what Cramp called the 'monitor craze' and so showed no interest in his proposal. The Cramp shipyard won a few other contracts during the war, but the two decades after the war were lean ones for all American shipyards; there was no naval construction to speak of, and little merchant ship building beyond coastal vessels. The Cramp yard managed to stay in business, but only by the narrowest of margins. The only warship built at the yard in this period was the monitor *Terror*, theoretically a 'repair' of a Civil War vessel of the same name, but in fact a completely new ship. She was laid down in 1874 but construction was suspended in 1877.

The following year saw Cramp's first encounter with the Imperial Russian Navy when his shipyard was visited by a group of Russian officers, headed by Captain 1st Rank L P Semechkin, aide-de-camp to the Grand Duke Konstantin Nikolaevich, general-admiral of the Imperial Navy.[5] Semechkin was looking for merchant ships that could be converted into commerce raiders, in case the tense relations with Britain caused by the Russo-Turkish War erupted into open hostilities. Three ships building at the Cramp shipyard were selected: *State of California*, *Saratoga* and *Columbus*. These ships were purchased by the Russians, converted by Cramp and taken into the Imperial Navy as *Afrika*, *Aziia* and *Evropa*. A fourth commerce raider, *Zabiiaka*, was ordered as new construction from Cramp. The next year Cramp met Konstantin Nikolaevich in Paris, and the general-admiral expressed his satisfaction with the American-built ships.

William Cramp died in 1879, and Charles became president of the company. Not long afterwards America's naval lethargy began to change with the advent of the 'New Navy' in the 1880s. Although John Roach's yard won the contracts for the first of the new navy's steel ships, Cramp gained a prominent place in the second round of construction, receiving contracts for three ships in 1887. More contracts followed, and soon Cramp was not merely building ships for the navy, but often contributing to their design as well. In addition to proposing modifications to the designs as put out for bid, Cramp on one occasion sat in on a preliminary design meeting of the Secretary of the Navy and his bureau chiefs and helped determine the characteristics of the US Navy's first armoured cruiser, USS *New York*. Having won the bid to build the ship, he suggested a rearrangement of the machinery arrangements that increased her underwater protection.[6]

At the height of the New Navy's building boom Cramp had a chance to get re-acquainted with the Imperial Russian Navy. In 1893 the cruisers *General Admiral*, *Admiral Nakhimov* and *Rynda* visited the United States for the naval review honouring Columbus' discovery of America. Cramp's firm did some repair work on the ships, and many officers of the squadron visited his yard, including the squadron's commander, Vice-Admiral N I Kaznakov.[7] The Russian admiral was apparently impressed with the yard's efficiency and capacity, Cramp had no fewer than five warships in various stages of construction at the time. Cramp nurtured this contact through corre-

Retvizan *at the New York Navy Yard in October 1901; the ship is riding very high, and it is likely that she has just been, or is about to be, dry-docked to have her bottom painted and cleaned before her trials. In the foreground is USS* Holland *(SS-1)*. (Naval Historical Center).

spondence with Kaznakov after his squadron left the United States, and this led in turn to correspondence with other high-ranking Russian naval officers.

Cramp's experience with warship construction continued to grow throughout the 1890s. By 1898 his shipyard had become the largest single contributor to the construction of the New Navy's big ships, building four of eleven battleships and seven of eighteen cruisers, in both types more than any other single shipyard. In addition to ships for the US Navy, Cramp also built the Japanese protected cruiser *Kasagi*. But even though his shipyard was far and away the most successful American shipbuilding firm of the era, Cramp had an even bigger dream: to turn his company into an American version of Sir William Armstrong's fabulously successful shipyards. He once said enviously that Armstrong's yards were not mere shipbuilders, but had become 'navy-builders.' Cramp harboured similar ambitions.

These ambitions were fuelled by more than simple commercial interest; woven throughout much of Cramp's career was a peculiar combination of admiration and loathing for Britain. He believed that British commercial interests had formed a powerful lobby against government subsidies to America's anaemic merchant marine, an opinion he voiced in Congressional testimony, magazine articles and interviews. He bitterly resented the Royal Navy's mastery of the seas, but spoke glowingly of British shipyards and their efficiency. Driven by a mixture of patriotism and mercantile self-interest, Cramp dreamed of shattering the British near-monopoly of the international warship-building market.

This was no idle ambition, Charles Henry Cramp was a very determined man. One gets the impression, in fact, that he was a demanding, opinionated and rather prickly character. Even his admiring biographer noted that Cramp was 'not always charitable in his criticisms and not always liberal in the standards of competency' and also that he 'has at times shown a spirit approaching intolerance when dealing with invasions of his profession by inexperienced, untrained, or incapable men'.[8] It is probably no coincidence that two descriptions of him use the term 'Napoleonic'.[9] In his long campaign for Russian contracts, he showed the determination, and the patience, of a master strategist.

But why single out Russia? At the time Russia was building all her own big ships. The most likely explanation is that Cramp realised that British firms dominated most other available markets. The contract for *Kasagi* was considered more a gesture of goodwill than a harbinger of things to come; Cramp recognised that the Japanese would continue to rely on British yards for their major warships. Russia, on the other hand, was unlikely to order ships from Britain, given the long-standing enmity between the two nations.

So Cramp continued his courting of the Russians. His biographer notes that throughout 1894-1896 he corresponded with:

> high officials in the Russian Ministry of Marine; though little progress was made during those years except to call the attention of the Russians in a vivid and forceful manner to the capacities and facilities which he controlled, and to strengthen the *entente cordiale* which had so long existed between the Russian naval authorities and himself.[10]

His contacts by now included an increasing number of influential Russian officers, among them F K Avelan, Chief of the Main Naval Staff, E I Alekseev, commander of the Black Sea Fleet and soon to be appointed commander of the Far East, and N E Kuteinikov, the chief inspector of shipbuilding. These men had visited Cramp's yard as younger officers and could attest to its capabilities.

In 1897 Cramp published an article entitled 'The Coming Sea-Power' in the journal *The North American Review*.[11] He wrote it quite consciously with an eye toward Russian readers, pointing out the effects of Japan's growing navy on the balance of power in the Far East. The article was reprinted in various European newspapers and journals.

Thus, by the end of 1897 Cramp was on friendly terms with high officials in the Imperial Navy. He could point to extensive experience in the design and construction of warships. He was aware of the growth of Japanese naval power and had written of its effects on Russian ambitions. The ground was thoroughly prepared, and it is hardly surprising that 'Early in the following spring [1898] Mr Cramp received advices from St Petersburg that the Ministry of Marine would be glad to entertain plans and proposals from him'.[12]

'For the Needs of the Far East'

All Cramp's importuning would have been in vain, of course, if Russia did not need foreign-built warships. But Cramp was correct when he wrote in his article:

> The Russian dockyards are efficient, as far as they go, and turn out good work, judging from such specimens as I have seen. But their capacity is not adequate to the task that is presented by the situation.[13]

The 'situation' arose from the changing naval balance of power in the Far East, specifically to the spectacular rise of Japanese seapower. This was particularly disturbing for Russia, as she had by 1898 managed to make of Japan a bitter enemy.

China was forced to cede the Liaotung Peninsula (which included Port Arthur) to Japan after the Sino-Japanese War of 1894-1895, a concession that set off a furore of activity in the foreign chancelleries of Europe, most notably in St. Petersburg, Paris and Berlin. Russia, France and Germany combined in the 'Triple Intervention,' warning Japan that its possession of the Liaotung Peninsula would constitute a permanent threat to China and would render Korean independence fictitious. Japan was forced to back down; unable to stand against the three European powers.

Japan's bitterness was quickly translated into action. In place of Port Arthur she added 30 million taels to the indemnity China had to pay, and a great portion of that money was funnelled into warship construction. The construction programme called for six new battleships by 1905, in addition to the two already building in Britain. This force of eight homogeneous battleships would give Japan overwhelming naval supremacy in Far Eastern waters.

Russia's seizure of Port Arthur in March 1898 was also deeply resented by the Japanese, who wondered why Russian occupation would be less of a threat to the independence of China and Korea than Japanese possession had seemed in 1895. Tsar Nikolai II was too much blinded by the prospects of taking the port to care about Japanese sensibilities; on 27 March 1898[14] the normally restrained sovereign wrote exultantly in his diary, 'At last! An ice-free port!'

But that ice-free port meant little without a naval force based there, and unfortunately Russia's Pacific squadron was not particularly impressive. The largest and most modern ships were the armoured cruisers *Admiral Nakhimov*, *Riurik* and *Rossiia*; the remainder of the squadron consisted of the obsolescent ironclad cruisers *Vladimir Monomakh*, *Dmitrii Donskoi* and *Pamiat' Azova*. In time of war the armoured cruisers were intended for raiding Britain's Far Eastern commerce, a strategy Russia took a step further in 1895-1896 with the laying down of the battleships *Peresvet* and *Osliabia*, essentially hybrid cruiser-battleships designed for long-range operations in the Pacific theatre.[15]

The Russians quickly realised that the anti-British *guerre de course* strategy would serve them poorly in a war with Japan. The new 12in-gunned battleships of the Japanese building programme would easily out-match the 10in-gunned *Peresvet* class ships. Even before Port Arthur was obtained, the 1897 programme, designated 'For the Needs of the Far East', called for the construction of four new battleships, and on 10/22 March 1898 the Tsar authorised the construction of two more. But authorising the new ships was one thing, building them another; Russia's Baltic shipyards were already at capacity with battleship and cruiser construction. The situation was exacerbated by the long building times common in Russian yards, whereas Japan's British-built ships would be available in relatively short order. There was only one way out of this building bottleneck: ordering ships from foreign yards.

Negotiations[16]

Even before the decision was made to order ships from foreign shipbuilders, some basic design work had been done by the Naval Technical Committee (*Morskoi Tekhnicheskii Komitet*, or MTK). In its meetings during the winter of 1897-1898 the MTK proposed raising the displacement of new battleships to 15,000 tons, to match the latest British and Japanese battleships, which displaced 14,650-14,850 tons. In the end, however, the displacement was limited to 12,000 tons for reasons of economy. Since the *Peresvet* class was seen as too lightly armed, the MTK took the *Poltava* class as a model for the armament: four 12in and twelve 6in guns. The increased displacement compared to the 11,000 ton *Poltavas* was to be used to increase the speed to 18kts, using a two-shaft power plant instead of the three-shaft machinery lay-out of the *Peresvet*. The wood and copper sheathing of the *Peresvet* class was to be eliminated.

In early 1898 the MTK worked out a 'Programme for the designing of an armourclad'. They took the improved *Poltava* as a starting point, but added a requirement for a 5000nm steaming range at 10kts (compared with 2800nm for the *Poltava*).[17] Having these basic characteristics in hand and having decided to build ships in foreign yards, the Naval Ministry intended to sponsor an international design competition. They reckoned without Charles Cramp.

Cramp was informed of the Russian plans for foreign construction through his European contacts. As early as February 1897 the Russian Naval Ministry had made inquiries in France and Belgium for the construction of an entire Far Eastern shipyard, probably to be built at Vladivostok. A deal worth 30,000,000 francs was mentioned to the Cockerill firm, with whom the Russians had dealt before on several occasions.[18] The subsequent occupation of Port Arthur seems to have siphoned funds away from this plan, but word of the Russian inquiries very probably reached Cramp through his contacts in the financial markets. One of the company's board members was Theodore Seligman, whose brother Henry was a New York-based lawyer and financier. Henry Seligman was in turn in contact with Max Hellman, head of the Paris firm of Seligman Frères et Cie, who was related to the Seligmans by marriage.[19] Hellman was in contact with unnamed 'parties,' presumably in St. Petersburg. There is no indication of who these 'parties' were, but according to Henry Seligman, they 'were absolutely instrumental in bringing about negotiations'.

The first concrete mention of a Russian project in the Cramp records is a letter to Henry Seligman dated 4 February 1898. In this communication Cramp promised to pay Hellman:

> 10% upon the amount received from such contracts as shall be obtained directly through him and shall be accepted in writing by this Company for the construction of the vessels now under consideration.

At this point Cramp apparently only foresaw the construction of cruisers and destroyers, but Seligman's reply of 18 February must have set the shipbuilder's ambitions afire:

> I would add that I received a letter from Paris, in which they state that the Russians are not only desirous of building 30 torpedo destroyers [sic], 5 or 6 cruisers of 2500 to 3000 tons, and one big cruiser of 5000 to 6000 tons, but also the establishment of a navy yard at Vladivostok, which would get all of the Russian ship-building and repair work in Asia.

But an enormous order like this would not come cheap. On 23 February Seligman asked for 15 per cent if the deal to build a Far Eastern navy yard went through (cash if the contract went directly to Cramp, shares if a new company was formed to do the work). Cramp agreed to this the next day. Meanwhile Seligman was giving Cramp advice on gaining a contract. On 18 February he wrote that:

> General [George] Williams[20] is by this time in Paris, and I have no doubt that in a day or two he will cable you as to the prospects of obtaining a contract for building the war-vessels; and if the outlook is satisfactory, I still deem it of the utmost importance that you should go over there at once.

The prospects revealed by General Williams in Paris were apparently quite favourable, no doubt due in part due to the lobbying of the American Ambassador in St Petersburg, Ethan A Hitchcock, who 'used his influence with the Russian Naval and Finance Ministries in order to promote the solicitation of the shipbuilding company, Cramp & Sons, for orders for cruiser and torpedo boats'.[21]

Cramp departed for St Petersburg in early March 1898, sailing aboard the liner *St Paul*, a ship coincidentally built in his own yard. The board of directors had authorised him 'to take with him such working staff and other persons as he may think advisable,' presumably meaning a small design group. Upon his arrival Cramp was soon able to reinforce his personal contacts with senior Russian officers. He was invited, on 29 March, to attend an annual banquet of officers who had been in the contingent destined for the Cramp-built cruisers of 1878.[22] Among these officers was the influential Admiral F K Avelan. The banquet took place on 9 April, just when Cramp and the Naval Ministry were getting down to serious negotiations.

Cramp opened the discussions with a proposal to build a battleship based on the 11,340 ton USS *Iowa*, recently completed at his shipyard. This was an interesting choice for a prototype; although she had the merit of being familiar to Cramp, she was two classes behind the latest American battleship design, one of which, USS *Alabama*, was at that time under construction at Cramp's yard. Cramp may have picked *Iowa* because of its general similarity to the *Poltava* class, like the Russian battleships, she mounted a powerful secondary battery in turrets on the side-decks, and it had a good steaming range (4,500nm at 10kts).

The MTK, on the other hand, insisted on using the *Peresvet* as a general model, and Cramp was shown the drawings of both this class and *Kniaz' Potëmkin Tavricheskii* to guide him in his proposals.[23] Based on these requirements and drawings, Cramp and his staff had to prepare in very short order new sketch designs or face losing the contract. There followed an intense round of negotiations between Cramp and the Russians, what his biographer described the 'tender mercies' of the MTK:

> For several weeks they subjected Mr Cramp to a species of inquisition which might well have appalled a man of less resources, less determination, or less confidence in his own ultimate mastery of the situation.[24]

Actually, Cramp's 'inquisition' seems to have been no more rigorous than what Russian designers were usually subjected to when putting forward a design. That much being said, it must be admitted that these negotiations could not have been easy. There was a sizeable faction in the MTK that wanted the contract to be awarded to a French shipyard, while both Krupp and Ansaldo had been mentioned as possible builders. But Cramp had allies of his own on the committee, and he had the advantage of being on the spot, while his competitors had yet to arrive in St Petersburg.

The end result of these negotiations was a set of 'preliminary specifications,' to which both Cramp and the MTK agreed:

Displacement:	Not to exceed 12,700 tons
Draught:	Not to exceed 26ft (7.9m)
Armament:	Four 12/40 (2 x 2)
	Twelve 6in (152mm)/45 (12 x 1)
	Twenty 75mm
	Twenty 47mm
	Six 37mm
	Two 2.5in (64mm) landing guns
Armour:	Krupp plate
	Main belt: 9in (229mm) belt over ⅔ of the waterline
	upper belt: 6in (152mm)
Speed:	18kts[25]

It can be seen from these that Cramp had managed to obtain a 700 ton increase in the originally specified 12,000 ton displacement, a change sanctioned by the general-admiral, Grand Duke Aleksei Aleksandrovich. But otherwise the specifications were strict, especially regarding the 18kt speed, which had to be maintained on a continuous 12 hour trial. In order to achieve this performance, Cramp argued that Niclausse boilers would have to be used. The Imperial Navy had used Niclausse boilers in only one vessel, the gunboat *Khrabri*; the Belleville water-tube boiler was preferred. Cramp argued in favour of the Niclausse boilers on technical grounds, but he also pointed out that:

> for any naval power to surrender itself to a single type of proprietary boiler, thereby creating a monopoly against itself, could not be else than unwise; that the era of

water-tube boilers was still in the experimental stage, that perfection was yet to be developed, and was doubtless a long way off...sound marine engineering policy would forbid the exclusion of the Niclausse system.[26]

In reality, however, Cramp's advocacy for these boilers surely owed a good deal to the fact that he was the American agent for Niclausse[27] a fact his biographer failed to mention in outlining the merits of these boilers. Despite all Cramp's arguments, the MTK came down firmly against using the Niclausse boilers only to be overruled by the personal intervention of the general-admiral.

The sketch design based on the specifications was a synthesis of Cramp's ideas and those of the Russians. Although the MTK had pushed for a ship based on the *Peresvet*, the design actually showed strong similarities to the Black Sea Fleet battleship *Kniaz' Potëmkin Tavricheskii*, which was laid down at Nikolaev just before Cramp arrived in Russia. In fact it seems reasonable to assume that *Retvizan* was basically a faster, high-seas version of *Potëmkin*. Most of the differences between the two ships are explained by *Retvizan*'s need for greater range; she sacrificed four 6in guns for the greater internal space required by her much greater coal supply (1,100 tons vs. 2,000 tons), while the forecastle deck was extended right to the stern, also gaining internal space. *Retvizan* also had a longer and slightly narrower hull, the result of the need for higher speed.

Retvizan's general design was thus a product of the Imperial Navy's experience and requirements rather than of Cramp's knowledge of the US Navy's ships. She shows virtually no connection to contemporary American battleship design. For example, the sloped armour deck behind the main belt was a feature not adopted in US battleships until the *Virginia* class of 1901. However, Cramp's role in the design process should not be underestimated. It was up to him to take *Potëmkin*'s 16kt, short-ranged design and convert it into an 18kt, long-ranged ship; her structural arrangements and hull form were apparently entirely his work. Working under enormous time pressure, without the facilities and resources of his shipyard to draw upon, Cramp and his staff had done a virtuoso job in putting their sketch design together.

Once the 'preliminary specifications' and the basic sketches had been approved, things moved quickly. On 23 April 1898, a contract was signed by Cramp and Vice-Admiral V P Verkhovskii, chief of the Main Administration of Shipbuilding and Supply, for the construction of one battleship and one protected cruiser according to 'the most modern practice'. The cruiser was to be completed in twenty months, the battleship in thirty months.[28] The contract received the emperor's approval on 2 May, a remarkable performance for the usually ponderous governmental bureaucracy. One Russian writer hints that both Verkhovskii and General-admiral Aleksei Aleksandrovich had a 'personal interest' in the deal although exactly what that means is left open to interpretation.[29]

Cramp's achievement in St Petersburg was little short of spectacular. Thanks to his 'Phenomenal persistence and business skill' he had short-circuited the Naval Ministry's

THE RETVIZAN: AN AMERICAN BATTLESHIP FOR THE TSAR

One of the starting points for Retvizan's *design, The Black Sea Fleet's battleship* Kniaz' Potëmkin Tavricheskii, *whose construction was begun shortly before Cramp arrived in Russia.* (Naval Historical Center).

intention to hold an international design competition.[30] Moreover he had also stolen a march on his competitors and sailed home with the largest foreign contract yet received by an American shipyard; the battleship had a contract price of $4,360,000, and the cruiser $2,138,000.[31] Nevertheless, he must have left St. Petersburg with some feelings of disappointment. He had hoped to build *two* battleships, four cruisers and perhaps thirty torpedo boats for the Russians, not to mention supplying a complete shipyard at Vladivostok, a sale that would have turned his company overnight into the American version of Armstrong's that had been his guiding vision.

Construction

Two days after Cramp and Verkhovskii signed the contract the United States declared war on Spain. Commodore George Dewey destroyed the Spanish squadron at Manila on 1 May while Cramp was sailing for home. When he arrived in America on 12 May 1898, Cramp's first act was to assure the press that his Russian contract would not 'in any way interfere with our work on the vessels now building for the United States'.[32]

To meet these dual commitments, the shipyard had to be expanded. On 26 May 1898, the board of directors approved a number of improvements to the yard, to increase its capacity: a new slipway, boiler shop and cranes, for a total cost of $135,000.[33]

Cramp had contracted to build the ship in thirty months so he could not afford to waste time. Even before he had left St Petersburg he 'had made a contract with the Carnegie Company, through its representative in

Russia, for the materials entering into the construction of the vessels'.[34] Other contracts followed;[35] on 18 October 1898, a contract with the Sterling Company of Chicago granting license to build Niclausse water tube boilers; on 3 January 1899, a contract with Carnegie Steel Co. Ltd. for armour; on 5 January 1899, a contract with the Bethlehem Iron Co. for armour; and, curiously enough, on 6 January 1899, a contract with the Imperial Russian Marine Ministry for deck armour to be produced at Russian state factories. General Electric was the contractor for the ship's electric plant.[36]

The contract between Cramp's yard and the Naval Ministry left many points open. These were to be settled on the spot by a commission of officers headed by Captain 1st Rank M A Danilevskii, which arrived in the United States on 25 July 1898. The commission was empowered 'to decide all questions during construction...subject to the confirmation of the director of the Naval Ministry',[37] and was equipped with a great deal of documentation, including the specifications for the *Peresvet* class and ledgers with the correspondence relating to that class, to be used as guidance in the detail designing of the new battleship.

There followed 'an enormous volume of correspondence' between Philadelphia and St. Petersburg as Cramp's staff began turning the sketch design into the complete set of plans needed to build a battleship.[38] During this period Cramp tried to extract every possible concession from the Russians, and Naval Minister Vice-Admiral P P Tyrtov noted that 'I fear now that he has concluded the contract, he will demand reductions in the weight first of one thing, then another, pleading that it is impossible to satisfy the requirements'.[39]

Indeed, Cramp was willing to exploit every loophole in the contract to win more favourable terms. It helped him that the definitive version of the contract was the English, not the Russian, copy. There were significant differences between the two, perhaps as a result of its hurried composing; the fact that the Russians were unfamiliar with some US Navy practices also worked against them. For example, the Russian version of the contract for the cruiser *Variag* called for deck protection equivalent to 'the best vessels of corresponding type', which for the Naval Ministry meant the cruiser *Diana*, then under construction in Russia, which had a protective deck of 'extra-mild nickel steel' provided by a French firm. However, the English version of the contract specified deck protection as in 'the best vessels in the fleet of the USA' and the US Navy didn't use extra-mild nickel steel. The Russians were thus forced to pay extra for this steel.

The Russians also were not above trying to gain an edge. The contract specified that moderate forced draught could be used on the trials, another of the general-admiral's concessions to Cramp, since the Imperial Navy's engineers did not like forced draught, believing that it damaged the boilers.[40] The supervisory commission therefore insisted that the trials be run at natural draught. Cramp, however, stuck to the contract, and gained his point.

The first working drawings were forwarded to St. Petersburg at the end of 1898, and at the same time work finally began on the slipway on hull no. 300, soon to be named *Retvizan*. The ship was officially laid down on 29 July 1899, by which time 1000 tons of steel had been assembled on the slipway. Construction did not go smoothly; the Cramp yard, according to one recent history, 'ranked among the nation's most adamant opponents of organized labor [sic] and a shorter workday'[41] and in August 1899 a strike broke out at the yard, involving machinists, boiler makers, blacksmiths, riveters and fitters. Prominent labour leaders such as Samual Gompers were drawn to the cause, and the strike continued until the spring of 1900, when it finally collapsed. But Cramp was forced to invoke a strike clause in the contract, giving him a little more time to finish the ship.

All was not well with the Russian commission, either. Danilevskii took it upon himself to make all decisions and used the other members of the commission merely as clerks, keeping them at their desks, treating them 'as if they were schoolboys'.[42] The members of the commission protested, and a personal order from Admiral Tyrtov, untied them from their desks. Danilevskii's relations with Cramp were also were strained, he refused to sanction the first 10 per cent payment to Cramp because of contractual disagreements. The situation was not finally resolved until 22 November 1899 when Danilevskii was replaced by Captain 1st Rank E N Shchensnovich, who seems to have got on better both with the commission and with Cramp, a relationship no doubt assisted by the fact that he soon released payments to the shipyard.[43]

Work was also slowed by the bureaucratic methods of the Naval Ministry, which required daily reports on the progress of construction and insisted on approving any changes in the plans. There were numerous points where American construction practice differed from Russian, and these proved a source of endless troubles as construction progressed. In at least one case, however, the Naval Ministry's interference was definitely beneficial: Cramp, worried about the ship's ability to reach her contract speed, decided to reduce the beam by 1ft (0.3m). This provoked a sharp telegram from N E Kuteinikov, the chief inspector of shipbuilding, that under no circumstances could the metacentric height be reduced below 4ft (1.22m). Another alteration in the design came as a result of a miscalculation of the weights; detailed accounting showed that the ship would be 272 tons overweight, and so Cramp was forced to increase the length by 8ft (2.44m) in order to maintain the desired draught.

The ship was finally launched on 23 October 1900, complete with Russian Orthodox ceremonies presided over by the Reverend Alexander Hotovitsky.[44] One local newspaper described the ship's condition at launch:

> Nearly if not quite all of her water tube boilers and much of her other machinery are already in her, and her engines are ready to be dropped aboard as soon as she strikes the water....Her guns have already arrived from Russia and will be installed and ready for service before the preliminary trials.[45]

After the launch work was slowed for a while as efforts were shifted to the completion of *Variag*; nevertheless, despite some difficulties with the Russian-made turrets (see armament notes, below), *Retvizan* ran her acceptance trials in October 1901. On 17 January 1902 the ship was inclined, the results of which indicated a normal displacement of 12,409.93 tons, as opposed to the designed figure of 12,745.56 tons. Metacentric height was about 38in (93.3cm), well short of the required figure, but since the ship was underweight, it was decided that 227 tons of ballast would restore her stability without compromising the design. Trials revealed a fair amount of incomplete work, which Cramp was obliged to fix before receiving his final payment. She was accepted into the Russian Imperial Navy on 23 March 1902. Even after *Retvizan*'s arrival in Russia her guns and turrets required further work due to the somewhat incomplete state of the equipment that had been shipped to America by the Russian manufacturers.

General Features

Retvizan's characteristics are given in table 2.

Retvizan had a complete double bottom, 3ft (0.9m) deep under the machinery spaces and 5ft (1.5m) deep under the 12in magazines. The double bottom continued around the turn of the bilges and up to the armoured deck over the extent of the machinery spaces. Additional anti-torpedo protection was provided in this region by deep coal bunkers; the inner bulkhead of the coal bunkers was about 15ft from the ship's outer side.[46] There were fourteen transverse watertight bulkheads, and a

Retvizan, *probably during the review by emperors Nikolai II of Russia and Wilhelm II of Germany held at Reval in August 1902.* (Courtesy of Sergei Vinogradov).

Table 2: RETVIZAN – GENERAL CHARACTERISTICS

Ordered:	14/26 April 1898
Construction begun:	circa December 1898
Laid down:	17/29 July 1899
Launched:	10/23 October 1900
Entered Service:	10/23 March 1902
Displacement:	12,780tons normal
Dimensions:	376ft pp, 382ft 3in wl, 386ft 8in oa x 72ft 2in x 25ft
	114.6m pp, 116.5m wl, 117.85 oa x 22.0m x 7.6m
Armament:	Four 12in (305mm)/40 (2 x 2)
	twelve 6in (152mm)/45 (12 x 1)
	twenty 75mm/50
	twenty-four 47mm/43
	six 37mm/23
	six 15in (381mm) torpedo tubes, four above water (bow, stern, after broadside tubes),
	two below water (forward broadside tubes)
Protection:	Krupp armour; main belt 9in (229mm) tapering to 5in (127mm) at the lower edge;
	upper belt 6in (152mm); forward and aft waterline 2in (51mm); casemates 5in (127mm);
	fore and aft bulkheads 7in (178mm); armour deck 2in (51mm), 2.5in (63mm) slopes;
	forward and aft protective decks 3in (76mm); turret sides and faces 9in (229mm), roofs 2in (51mm);
	barbettes 8in (203mm); conning tower sides 10in (254mm).
Machinery:	Two sets vertical triple expansion engines, 24 Niclausse watertube boilers; 17,112ihp
Speed:	17.99kts
Endurance:	1016tons coal normal, 2000tons maximum; 4900/8000nm at 10kts
Complement:	28 officers, 722 men.

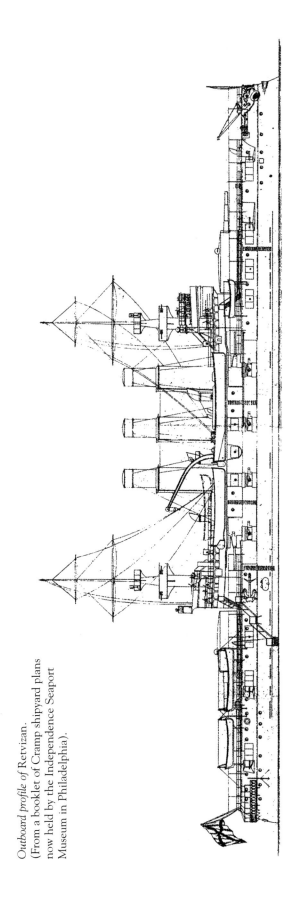

Outboard profile of Retvizan.
(From a booklet of Cramp shipyard plans now held by the Independence Seaport Museum in Philadelphia).

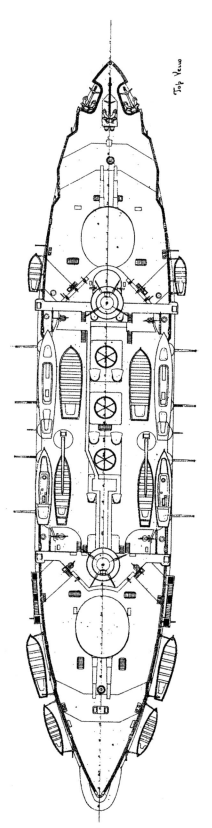

Plan of Retvizan. (Independence Seaport Museum).

centreline bulkhead in the engine room; the bulkheads rose to the berth (armour) deck. Pumping arrangements featured autonomous systems in each main compartment, as opposed to the older 'main drain' system with its numerous bulkhead penetrations.

Retvizan was outfitted to act as a flagship, with admiral's quarters aft (including a sternwalk) and cabins for the staff.

Armament[47]

Retvizan's main battery consisted of four 12in/40 guns in two twin turrets. These guns were made by the Obukhovskii Works and had the following characteristics:

Bore:	12in (304.8mm)
Bore length:	38.4 calibers
Weight incl BM:	43.08 tons
Weight of AP shell:	730lbs (331.7kg)
Propellant charge:	234.3lbs (106.5kg)
Muzzle velocity:	2592fps (790mps)
Rate of fire:	one round every 80-90 sec

Penetration (Krupp armour)

At muzzle	15.0in	381mm
2000yds	12.25in	311mm
4000yds	9.88in	251mm
6000yds	7.91in	201mm
8000yds	6.26in	159mm
10,000yds	5.08in	129mm
12,000yds	3.66in	93mm

Ammunition stowage was 77 rounds per gun. Compared with the guns of contemporary Japanese and British battleships, the Russian guns fired a lighter shell at a higher muzzle velocity; this gave better penetration at ranges out to about 3000yds. After that the greater residual velocity of the heavier Japanese and British shells allowed greater penetration, although unreliable fuzes generally meant that neither Russian nor Japanese shell were likely to penetrate heavy armour before exploding.

The turrets were a separate contract from the ship itself. Cramp initially hoped to win this bid as well, and some early reports said that the ship would receive American-style turrets. Danilevskii, the head of the Russian supervisory commission, also wanted American turrets. He reported that 'The Yankees have available large electrical firms and a wide range of electrical techniques, surpassing in this regard not only what we have in Russia, but also the whole of western Europe, which serves as a guarantee of the quality of those installations

which could be made by Cramp'.[48] But at a meeting in June 1898 the Artillery Department of the MTK insisted that the contract be awarded to the Metallicheskii Works, where they would be better able to supervise the quality of the work. The resulting turrets were typical of Russian practice of the time, based upon the French centre-pivot type. They were electrically powered, but the Metallicheskii Works sent the disassembled turrets to Philadelphia with cables missing and incomplete documentation, forcing the electricians at the Cramp yard to piece things together for themselves. This they did (Cramp charged an additional $50,000 for the work), and the gunnery trials, held in October 1901 under the supervision of Major-General A F Brink of the Artillery Department, were satisfactory.

The intermediate battery was made up of twelve Canet-pattern 6in/45 QF guns with the following characteristics:

Bore:	6in (152.4mm)
Weight incl BM:	5.82 tons
Weight of AP shell:	91.3lbs (41.5kg)
Propellant charge:	28.4lbs (12.9kg)
Muzzle velocity:	2600fps (793mps)
Rate of fire:	3-5rpm

Penetration (Krupp armour)

At muzzle	6.14in	156mm
2000yds	3.90in	99mm
4000yds	2.60in	66mm
6000yds	1.69in	43mm
8000yds	1.26in	32mm
10,000yds	1.14in	29mm
12,000yds	1.06in	27mm

Eight guns were mounted in casemates on the battery (main) deck, and another four on the upper deck. Ammunition supply amounted to 2400 rounds (200 per gun). An American observer noted that:

> The breech mechanism…is considerably more complicated than the modified Welin breech mechanism which was recently adopted by our navy.[49]

Some of the complexity noted by this writer was due to extra safety features of Russian guns. Fred T Jane noted that 'before the gun can be discharged, at least two, and occasionally three, safety devices have to be loosed'.[50] These extra safety devices were regarded as necessary because Russian sailors were not accustomed to complex machinery. The inevitable consequence of this was a somewhat slower rate of fire than equivalent guns in other navies.

The heavy anti-torpedo boat battery was made up of twenty 75mm (12pdr) Canet-pattern guns; fourteen of

Retvizan, *probably on her way to or from trials, the ensign aft appears to be the Cramp house flag, and her paint scheme is not yet the 'standard' Russian scheme, with black gun barrels.* (National Archives).

these were mounted in embrasures on the main deck, four forward and three aft on either side, and six on the upper deck, three on either side between the upper 6in casemates. Ammunition stowage was 325 rounds per gun. There were twenty-four 47mm (3pdr) guns: four in each fighting top, another eight at the forward end of the superstructure (one on either side on the first superstructure deck and three on the platform above flanking the conning tower) and eight at the after end (three on either side of the lower platform at the base of the mainmast, with another pair on the upper platform). There were six 37mm (1pdrs) in the bridge wings, as well as two Maxim machine guns. The ship also carried two 2.5in (63.5mm) landing guns of the Baranovskii pattern. The torpedo armament comprised six 15in (381mm) tubes, with four above water (bow, stern, and the after broadside mounts) and two submerged tubes (broadside forward). Seventeen torpedoes were carried. The ship could also carry 45 mines, and there were six 75cm searchlights.

Fire control consisted of the Geisler 1894 system, which was installed after the ship's arrival in Russia. This used a series of electrical indicator dials (not unlike engine-room telegraphs) to transmit range and target data from the gunnery post in the conning tower to the individual guns. Ranges were determined by the Liuzhol'-Miakishev 'micrometer', a sextant-like device that could measure the angle subtended by a prominent feature on the enemy ship, such as the waterline-to-masthead distance; this could then be converted to a range if the actual height were known. Ships of the Imperial Navy carried reference books giving the known heights of various features on foreign warships.[51]

Like several of her contemporaries, *Retvizan* was designed to carry two 'second-class torpedo boats', launches equipped with torpedo tubes. Five such craft were built for *Retvizan* by the Crescent yard of Lewis Nixon at Elizabethport, New Jersey (presumably three were intended as spares). Each launch was equipped with a single torpedo tube in the bow and a small-caliber QF gun forward.

Protection[52]

The total weight of *Retvizan*'s armour was 3,300 tons, or 25.8 per cent of the normal displacement; all vertical armour was made by the Krupp process. The main belt was 9in (229mm) thick, tapering to 5in (127mm) at the lower edge; it ran for 256ft (78m) along the waterline and was 7ft (2.13m) high, of which about 3ft (0.91m) was above the design waterline. Above this was the upper belt of 6in (152mm) armour, 7ft 6in (2.29m) high. The upper belt was as long as the main belt; it was closed off fore and aft by 7in (178mm) armoured bulkheads. The main deck casemate guns were protected on all sides by 5in (127mm) armour, with 1.5in (37mm) screens between the guns; the upper deck guns had 5in armour on their outer sides, and inboard were enclosed by 1.5in semicircular bulkheads. The extremities of the ship were protected by 2in (51mm) armour that had a vertical extent equal to the combined heights of the main and upper belts.

The armour deck was level with the top of the main belt; it was 2in (51mm) thick on the flat and 2.5in (63mm) on the slopes, which angled down to meet the lower edge of the main belt. Forward and aft of the citadel there were 3in (76mm) protective decks extending to the bow and stern. The forward protective deck also served to reinforce the ram. The 12in turrets had 9in (229mm) faces and sides and 2in (51mm) roofs, with 8in (203mm) barbettes above the level of the upper belt; from this level down to the armour deck the barbettes were 4in (102mm) thick. The walls of the conning tower and its communicating tube were 10in (254mm) thick.

Machinery and Trials

Retvizan's machinery plant consisted of two vertical triple expansion engines with a total designed output of 16,000ihp. The engine cylinder diameters were 38.5in (97.8cm), 42in (106.7cm) and 92in (233.7cm) for the high, medium and low pressure cylinders, respectively. Steam was supplied by twenty-four Niclausse boilers operating at a pressure of 18 atmospheres.

The MTK had been forced to accept the Niclausse boilers, and its misgivings were proved to be well-founded. The Niclausse boilers on *Variag* gave a great deal of trouble, in practice reducing the ship's speed and range. At the Battle of Chemulpo she could make no more than 16kts because only 22 of 30 boilers were operational.[53] US Navy experience was similar: the Niclausse boilers originally installed in the USS *Maine* were subject to 'continual breakdowns'[54] and had a very high coal consumption; they were replaced in 1910. *Retvizan* herself suffered a boiler accident on her voyage to Russia; however, she otherwise seems to have suffered no particular boiler problems during her brief career in the Russian Imperial Navy.

The trials of *Variag*, with a similar plant to that of *Retvizan*, had been very successful, so great things were expected from the battleship. Preliminary trials of both the machinery and guns were held in September 1901 off the Delaware Capes.[55] The ship developed a speed of 17kts, and the gunnery tests were satisfactory. *Retvizan*

then returned to the Cramp yard for final preparations for the official trials.

After docking at the Brooklyn Navy Yard, *Retvizan* headed for Boston on 17 October; the official trials were to take place on the US Navy course off Cape Ann. Edwin Cramp, brother of Charles and the company's chief representative on the voyage, proposed that the trip up to Boston be made at full power, and the somewhat surprised Russian officials agreed. The run was made during a stormy night, and the initial results seemed successful beyond anyone's hopes: 'During one hour the speed reached 19 knots, and at no time did it fall below 18'.[56]

But things did not go so well during the more controlled conditions of the progressive trials, held on 21-24 October. Although the use of forced draught and picked stokers permitted the engines to develop a maximum output of 17,111.7ihp, well above the contracted power of 16,000ihp, the speed, according to calculations by the Russian officials, never exceeded 17.99kts. The company, however, disputed this result reckoning that the ship had made 18.01kts.[57]

It seems certain that the remarkably high speeds recorded during the trip to Boston owed a great deal to

Retvizan in Russian service. The inset shows Captain 1st Rank Eduard Nikolaevich Shchensnovich, the ships first, and only, Russian commander. (Author's collection).

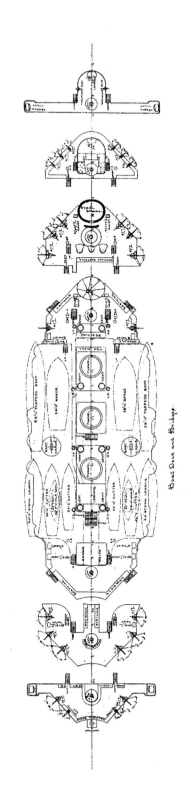

Inboard profile of Retvizan.
(Independence Seaport Museum).

Boat deck and bridge platforms of Retvizan. (Independence Seaport Museum).

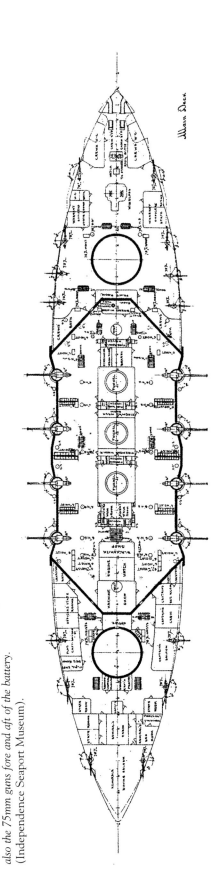

Main deck plan of Retvizan, showing the 6in gun battery. Note also the 75mm guns fore and aft of the battery. (Independence Seaport Museum).

the stormy conditions. The argument between Cramp and the Naval Ministry over what speed *Retvizan* had actually achieved on trials continued for some time. The Naval Ministry eventually agreed that another trial should take place after the ship arrived in the Baltic. This second trial seems never to have taken place, and the 17.99kt speed is often given as *Retvizan*'s maximum. However, it should be noted that at the time of the trials the MTK had expressed doubts that this speed could be duplicated under service conditions, and it is likely that her actual speed was somewhat less.

Career

Retvizan was named after a 62-gun Swedish ship, *Rättvisa*, captured in 1790 by the Russians at Sveaborg.[58] The Swedish name means 'Justice'. *Retvizan* was accepted into the Imperial Russian Navy on 23 March 1902 under the command of Captain 1st Rank E N Shchensnovich. The crew had arrived only shortly before, in order to reduce the number of desertions, this having earlier been a considerable problem in *Variag*'s case. She left the US on 13 May of that year, stopping at Cherbourg to coal. On 14 June, during the voyage from Cherbourg to Kronshtadt a tube burst in one of the boilers, and six stokers were scalded, three of them fatally.[59]

After her arrival in Russia the ship was fitted with wireless equipment. She took part in a naval review at Reval (Tallinn) on 6-8 August staged for the meeting of Nikolai II with Kaiser Wilhelm II.

While under construction *Retvizan* had been fitted with an experimental system for coaling at sea, using a system of winches and cables running from her mainmast to the foremast of a collier steaming in her wake.[60] On 30 August 1902 she tested this system, with the old Cramp-built auxiliary cruiser *Aziia* playing the part of a collier. On another occasion coal was transferred from the battleship to a torpedo boat. These trials were deemed successful, and similar gear was later installed on ten ships of the Second Pacific Squadron. Before she left for the Far East, *Retvizan*'s equipment was transferred to the battleship *Sisoi Velikii*.

On 13 November *Retvizan* set sail for the Far East from Libava in company with the battleship *Pobeda* and the cruisers *Pallada*, *Diana* and *Bogatyr*. Other ships joined en route, but the detachment did not arrive in the Far East together, *Retvizan* and *Pallada* arrived alone at Port Arthur on 4 May 1903.

Retvizan had searchlight duty on the night of 8-9 February 1904. The watch officer noticed two unknown torpedo craft headed toward his ship and sounded the alarm, but it was already too late. At 22:35 (Russian time) a Japanese torpedo struck *Retvizan* on the port side forward, which blasted open a 220ft^2 hole. Five men in the torpedo flat were killed and the electric power went out. The ship took on a list of 11° to port; this was soon reduced to 5° by counter-flooding the starboard magazines. A sail was worked over the hole (the collision mat proved too small for the job). Steam was raised after 45 minutes and the ship got

Retvizan under repair at Port Arthur in 1904, the sheer legs are positioning the caisson used to repair her torpedo damage. Note the ship's dark wartime paint scheme, probably dark grey hull and cinnamon-coloured upper-works. (Courtesy of Sergei Vinogradov).

The end of Retvizan's Russian career, wrecked by Japanese howitzer shells and Russian attempts to destroy her fighting value before Port Arthur surrendered. Her bow lies on the bottom but her stern is still afloat. Other photographs show the ship resting entirely on the bottom. (National Archives).

under way for the harbour entrance, but grounded in the narrow channel with 2200 tons of water aboard. One of the culprits in spreading the water was the ventilation system, which used American-style automatic ball-cocks to seal shafts. As the water level rose, the hollow steel ball would rise into a constriction in the shaft and close it off. However, in some cases the shafts were distorted by shock damage, so the seals proved to be imperfect.

Retvizan proved to be thoroughly stuck in the harbour entrance. While there, her guns and searchlights played an important role in defeating a Japanese attempt to seal up the entrance to the port with blockships on the night of 23-24 February. She was finally towed into the harbour on 8 March 1904, and repairs began on the ship immediately. She was ready for service on 3 June 1904, and she sailed with the squadron on 23 June 1904 in an abortive sortie; the Russians returned to harbour after encountering the Japanese fleet.

On 9 August Retvizan was struck by seven 4.7in shells from a Japanese battery that had a narrow view of the harbour through the surrounding hills. Captain Shchensnovich was slightly wounded, a barge alongside was sunk and the ship was holed below the waterline. She took on 400 tons of water and a 1° list, which was corrected by counterflooding. The water was still in the ship the next day when the squadron sortied with the intention of reaching Vladivostok. Prior to departing the squadron's commander, Vice-Admiral V K Vitgeft, give permission for Retvizan to return to Port Arthur if the temporary plating over the hole began to give way.

The sortie of 10 August resulted in the Battle of the Yellow Sea. During the battle Retvizan was short of her designed armament by two 6in, two 75mm, two 47mm and six 37mm guns, which had been landed for use in the port's landward defences. In addition the left 12in gun in her forward turret gave trouble throughout the battle. Retvizan's moment of glory came when two 12in shells struck the bridge of Tsesarevich, killing Admiral Vitgeft and throwing the flagship out of control; she circled toward the Japanese line. Retvizan was the second ship in the Russian line and at first followed, but Captain Shchensnovich soon realised that something was wrong with the flagship. Seeing Tsesarevich come under the combined fire of the entire Japanese battleline, Retvizan's captain steered straight toward the Japanese, with the intention of distracting their fire and perhaps trying a ramming attack, an action that probably saved the flagship. As the range dropped down to less than 4000yds a hit jammed the forward turret and Shchensnovich himself was seriously wounded. She was forced to sheer off.

Most of the squadron, including Retvizan, returned to Port Arthur. Retvizan had suffered eighteen hits in the battle from guns of 8in to 12in calibre, two of which were below the waterline. Six men were killed and 43 wounded; the forward turret was out of action for a while, as were two 6in guns.

The squadron made no more sorties. Many of its light guns were dismounted for use as artillery ashore. On 1 October Retvizan was hit by an 11in howitzer shell, fired as part of a random bombardment of the harbour. However, on 5 December the Japanese captured 203

Hizen, ex-Retvizan, in Japanese service. Note that while the fighting tops have been removed and the funnels replaced, the ship is otherwise little changed from her original configuration. (Naval Historical Center).

Retvizan's American cousin, USS Maine, *designed by Cramp and based on his experience with the Russian design. The external resemblance between the Russian and American ships is striking, and in fact* Maine *bears an even stronger resemblance to* Retvizan's *prototype,* Kniaz' Potëmkin Tavricheskii, *thanks to the lower quarterdeck. (Naval Historical Center).*

Metre Hill, which afforded them a panoramic view of the harbour. The 11in howitzers already in place could now be accurately directed, and they soon sank the remnants of the squadron. *Retvizan* was hit by numerous 11in howitzer shells (sources disagree on the exact number) at least one of which penetrated to the boiler rooms.[61] She sank in the shallow waters of western basin on 6 December 1904.

On 2 January 1905 *Retvizan's* Captain Shchensnovich signed the instrument of capitulation on behalf of the navy. *Retvizan* was raised by the Japanese on 22 September 1905 and taken to Sasebo. She was under repair in Japan from January 1906 to November 1908. *Retvizan*, now renamed *Hizen*, had her fighting tops removed, her light guns replaced with Japanese-pattern weapons and her Niclausse boilers replaced with Miyabara boilers.[62]

Hizen was at Sasebo when the First World War broke out. In early October 1914 she was ordered to Esquimalt to reinforce the relatively weak British squadron operating off the North American coast, in case Vice-Admiral Graf von Spee's Asiatic Squadron headed that way. Towards the end of the month, while still on her way, she was diverted to Honolulu to keep an eye on the German gunboat *Geier*, which had turned up there on 15 October. She watched the port with the armoured cruiser *Asama* until *Geier* was interned on 8 November. She and *Asama* then went south in pursuit of Spee's squadron, but never sighted the enemy.

Her career during the war seems otherwise to have been a quiet one. Starting in 1918 *Hizen* was often to be found at Vladivostok and other points off Russia's Pacific coast, supporting the Japanese intervention in the Russian civil war. She was re-rated to a first class coast defence ship on 1 September 1921, and was disarmed at Sasebo in April 1922 under the terms of the Washington Treaty. She was finally stricken on 20 September 1923, and was sunk as a gunnery target ship in the Bungo Straits on 12 July 1924.

Conclusion

Retvizan compared well with her contemporaries, and in fact she became the model for the next generation of American battleships, the *Maine* class. The U.S. Navy's original intention had been:

> practically to duplicate that class [the *Illinois*] as regards size, speed, armament, etc. It was decided, however, to invite bidders to submit their own designs, offering preference — other things being equal — to bids guaranteeing the highest rate of speed and greatest coal endurance.[63]

The impetus for this increase in speed came from reports of the Russian battleship's 18kt speed.[64] The winning design was submitted by none other than Charles Cramp, and featured Niclausse boilers and an 18kt speed. In fact *Maine* was very close in size and characteristics to *Retvizan*, with a strong outward resemblance to the Russian ship. In fact the superficial resemblance to *Kniaz' Potemkin Tavricheskii* was even stronger, thanks to the lower quarterdeck, which *Maine* also had. The most significant difference between the Russian and the American ship was in the arrangement of the protection. *Maine* had a thicker belt but no inclined armour deck to back it up, and there was no waterline belt aft. She also had two more 6in guns.

Thus some of the features selected by the Naval Technical Committee in St Petersburg eventually came to be embodied in a class of American battleships.

Sources

1 See, for example, *Conway's All the World's Fighting Ships 1860-1905* (London: Conway Maritime Press, 1979), p. 183; R Gardiner (ed.) *Steam, Steel and Shellfire: The Steam Warship 1815-1905* (London: Conway Maritime Press, 1992), p. 120; A Preston, *Battleships of World War 1: An Illustrated Encyclopedia of the Battleships of All Nations 1914-1918* (New York: Galahad Books, 1972), p. 192; S Vasil'evich Suliga, *Korabli Russko-Iaponskoi voiny 1904-1905gg* (Moscow: Izdatel'stvo 'Askol'd,' 1993), p. 6. The latter source goes so far as to call Retvizan 'One of the better armourclads of its time'.

2 For biographical information on Cramp, see A C Buell, *Memoirs of Charles H. Cramp* (Philadelphia: J B Lippincott, 1906), *National Cyclopaedia of American Biography*, vol. 5, pp. 254-255; *Dictionary of American Biography*, vol. 2, pp. 499-500; *New York Times*, 7 June 1913, p. 11.

3 This period in Charles Cramp's life is covered best in G E Farr and B F Bostwick with the assistance of M Willis, *Shipbuilding at Cramp & Sons: A History and Guide to Collections of the William Cramp & Sons Ship and Engine Building Company (1830-1927) and the Cramp Shipbuilding Company (1941-46) of Philadelphia*, (Philadelphia: Philadelphia Maritime Museum, 1991), pp. 9-12.

4 While the proposal for the ship was put forward by Merrick & Sons, this engine-building firm had no shipyard, so it subcontracted to Cramp's for much of the design and construction work. See W H Roberts, *USS New Ironsides in the Civil War* (Annapolis: Naval Institute Press, 1999); Buell, *Memoirs*, pp. 62-71.

5 L I Strakhovsky, 'Russia's Privateering Projects of 1878: A Page in the History of Russian-American Relations', *Journal of Modern History*, vol. VII, no. 1 [March 1935], pp. 22-40; Buell, *Memoirs*, pp. 209-224.

6 Ivan Musicant, *U.S. Armored Cruisers: A Design and Operational History* (Annapolis: Naval Institute, 1985), pp. 17-18; Norman Friedman, *U.S. Cruisers: An Illustrated Design History* (Annapolis: Naval Institute Press, 1984), p. 35.

7 *Cramp's Shipyard founded by William Cramp 1830* (Philadelphia: The William Cramp & Sons Ship & Engine Building Company, 1902), p. 147.

8 Buell, *Memoirs*, p. 205.

9 *National Cyclopaedia*, vol. 5, p. 255; N N Afonin, 'Eskadrennyi bronenosets "Retvizan"', *Sudostroenie*, no. 4, 1993, pp. 43-47, p. 43.

10 Buell, *Memoirs*, p. 227.

11 C H Cramp, 'The Coming Sea-Power' *North American Review*, vol. 165, no. 4 [October 1897], pp. 444-451; Buell, *Memoirs*, pp. 251-252.

12 Buell, *Memoirs*, p. 253.

13 Cramp, 'The Coming Sea-Power,' p. 449.

14 All dates are according to the western calendar; in using Russian sources it must be remembered that the Russian calendar was 12 days behind in the 19th, and 13 days behind in the 20th century. Transliteration of Russian words and names is according to the Library of Congress system.

15 S McLaughlin, 'From *Riurik* to *Riurik*: Russia's Armoured Cruisers', *Warship 1999-2000*, pp. 44-79, p. 54.

16 Unless otherwise noted, the description of the early technical discussions is taken from Afonin, 'Eskadrennyi bronenosets "Retvizan"'.

17 V I Gribovskii, 'Eskadrennye bronenosety tipa "Borodino"', part 1, *Sudostroenie*, nos. 5-6, 1993, pp. 46-51, pp. 46-47.

18 J P McKay, *Pioneers for Profit: Foreign Entrepreneurship and Russian Industrialization 1885-1913*, (Chicago: University of Chicago Press, 1970), p. 273.

19 Information on Cramp's relationship with Henry Seligman and Max Hellman is taken from the Minute Book (1895-1902) of the Board of Directors, Manuscript 86a, Accession Number 82.140.8, held at the Independence Seaport Museum in Philadelphia, which includes handwritten copies of the correspondence between Cramp and Henry Seligman regarding Max Hellman. It is interesting to note in passing that in September 1898 Henry Seligman replaced his brother Theodore on Cramp's board of directors. Information on Max Hellman is taken from a brief obituary that appeared in the *New York Times*, 6 January 1911, p. 9.

20 I have been unable to identify General George Williams of Washington; he is not in the contemporary Register of US Army officers. The *New York Times* described him as having 'accompanied Mr. Cramp as an advisor', *New York Times*, 13 May 1898, p. 5.

21 Alfred Vagts, quoted in E H Zabriskie, *American-Russian Rivalry in the Far East: A Study in Diplomacy and Power Politics, 1895-1914* (Philadelphia: University of Pennsylvania Press, 1946), p. 42, note 112.

22 Buell, *Memoirs*, pp. 225-226. Such banquets seem to have been fairly common in the Imperial Navy.

23 Afonin's articles on Retvizan mention only the *Peresvet* as a model, but R M Mel'nikov, *Bronenostsy tipa 'Borodino'*, (St. Petersburg: Nauchno-populiarnoe izdanie, 1996), p. 14, specifically mentions that Cramp was shown the *Potëmkin's* drawings.

24 Buell, *Memoirs*, pp. 253-254.

25 Mel'nikov, *Bronenostsy tipa 'Borodino'*, p. 15.

26 Buell, *Memoirs*, pp. 260-261.

27 F T Jane, *The Imperial Russian Navy* (London: Conway Maritime Press, Reprint ed., 1983), p. 543.

28 *New York Times*, 13 May 1898, p. 5.

29 Mel'nikov, *Bronenostsy tipa 'Borodino'*, p. 15.

30 Afonin, 'Eskadrennyi bronenosets "Retvizan"', p. 43.

31 Cramp Minute Book (1895-1902), 26 May 1898.

32 *New York Times*, 13 May 1898, p. 5.

33 Cramp Minute Book (1895-1902), 26 May 1898.

34 Cramp Minute Book (1895-1902), 26 May 1898.

35 Cramp Minute Book (1895-1902), 7 November 1898 and 26 January 1899.

[36] Cramp Minute Book (1895-1902), 23 February 1899.

[37] Afonin, 'Eskadrennyi bronenosets "Retvizan"', p. 43.

[38] S A Balakin, *Bronenosets 'Retvizan'*, (Moscow: Modelist-konstruktor, 1999), p. 3.

[39] R M Mel'nikov, 'Istoriia sozdaniia bronenostsa "Retvizan" i kreisera "Variag"', *Sudostroenie*, part 1: no. 2, 1973, pp. 57-59 and part 2: no. 3, 1973, pp. 56-60, part 1, p. 57.

[40] The contract specified a forced draught of no more than 1 to 1.5 inches of water pressure in the boiler rooms; see E N Shchensnovich, *Plavanie eskadrennogo bronenostsa Retvizan s 1902 po 1904 g.g. (Vospominaniia komandira)* (St. Petersburg: Tsitadel', 1999), pp. 67; the Royal Navy generally allowed forcing to higher pressures, up to 2in; see R Sennett, *The Marine Steam Engine: A Treatise for the Use of Engineering Students and Officers of the Royal Navy*, (London: Longmans Green, and Co., 1885), p. 68.

[41] T R Heinrich, 'Ships for the Seven Seas: Philadelphia Shipbuilding in the Age of Industrial Capitalism, 1860-1900', (Ph.D. dissertation, University of Pennsylvania, 1993), pp. 349-351.

[42] Afonin, 'Eskadrennyi bronenosets "Retvizan"', p. 44.

[43] Mel'nikov, 'Istoriia sozdaniia bronenostsa "Retvizan" i kreisera "Variag"', part 1, p. 58.

[44] 'Launch of the Retvizan', *Philadelphia Record*, 24 October 1900. Father Alexander Horovitsky returned to Russia in 1914 and served there until 1937, when he was arrested and disappeared, presumably dying in one of Stalin's gulags. He was canonised as a martyr-saint in 1994. 'The Life of Saint Alexander Hotovitsky, New Hieromartyr of Russia, Missionary to America', *Your Diocese Alive in Christ*, vol. XI, No. 2 (Summer 1995), pp. 11-15. My thanks to Archpriest Mark Shinn of St. Andrew's Church in Philadelphia for information about both *Retvizan* and Saint Alexander Hotovitsky.

[45] 'Retvizan Will be Launched To-day', *Public Ledger-Philadelphia*, 23 October 1900.

[46] The dimensions of the double bottom and the depth of the coal-bunkers are based on measurements of Cramp's booklet of blueprints (Independence Seaport Museum, accession number 85.57.2).

[47] Information on the ship's armament comes chiefly from Suliga, *Korabli Russko-Iaponskoi voiny 1904-1905gg*; S I Titushkin, 'Korabel'naia artilleriia v ryssko-iaponskoi voine' *Gangut*, no. 7, January 1991, pp. 64-79; 'Carries a Miniature Fleet: New Russian Ship *Retvizan* Will Have Five Small Vessels of War Aboard'. *New York Times*, 4 August 1901, p. 1.

[48] Afonin, '"Retvizan"', p. 39.

[49] 'The Russian Battleship "Retvizan"', *Scientific American*, vol. LXXXV, no. 17, 26 October 1901, p. 263.

[50] F T Jane, 'Russian Naval Guns' *Scientific American*, vol. XC, no. 22, 28 May 1904, pp. 418-419, p. 418.

[51] A V Platonov, 'Otechestvennye pribory upravleniia artilleri-iskoi strel'boi', *Tsitadel*, no. 1, 1998, pp. 92-115, pp. 96-97.

[52] The description of the armour protection is based on Suliga, *Korabli Russko-Iaponskoi voiny 1904-1905gg*, pp. 6-7 and Afonin, 'Eskadrennyi bronenosets "Retvizan"', p. 46.

[53] A Smigielski, 'Imperial Russian Navy Cruiser *Variag*', *Warship*, vol. III, no. 11, pp. 155-167, p. 165.

[54] J J Fee, 'The Rise of American Naval Power', *Naval Engineering and American Sea Power*, ed. by R W King (Baltimore: Nautical & Aviation Publishing, 1989), p. 75.

[55] 'Cruiser *Retvizan* a Success: Trial of American-Built Russian Vessel Highly Satisfactory', *New York Times*, 17 September 1901, p. 14.

[56] 'The New Russian Battleship: *Retvizan* Breaks All Records, Making 18.8 Knots for Twelve Hours', *New York Times*, 19 October 1901, p. 1.

[57] Afonin, 'Eskadrennyi bronenosets "Retvizan"', p. 46; 'Russia's New Battleship: The *Retvizan*, in Another Trial, Proves Satisfactory to Officers', *New York Times*, 22 October 1901, p. 6.

[58] R C Anderson, *Naval Wars in the Baltic During the Sailing-Ship Epoch 1522-1850*, (London: G. Gilbert-Wood, 1910), pp. 367. Tomitch, *Warships of the Imperial Russian Navy*, p. 44, says the name means 'pathfinder' in Swedish; Afonin, '"Retvizan"', p. 38, says it means a 'war cry.' However, a quick check in a Swedish-English dictionary reveals the meaning given here.

[59] Afonin, 'Eskadrennyi bronenosets "Retvizan"', p. 46; Jane, *The Imperial Russian Navy*, p. 543.

[60] S Miller, 'Coaling Warships at Sea — Recent Developments', *Transactions of the American Society of Naval Architects and Marine Engineers*, 1904, pp. 177-200, pp. 184-191.

[61] D K Brown, in 'The Russo-Japanese War: Technical Lessons as Perceived by the Royal Navy', *Warship 1996*, pp. 66-77, p. 73.

[62] Information on the career of *Hizen* (ex-*Retvizan*) in the Japanese navy is taken from: Hangeorg Jentschura, D Jung and P Mickel, *Warships of the Imperial Japanese Navy, 1869-1945*, (Annapolis: Naval Institute Press, 1977), pp. 20-21; Preston, *Battleships of World War I*, p. 192; and A J Watts and B G Gordon, *The Imperial Japanese Navy*, (Garden City, NY: Doubleday & Company, Inc., 1971), pp. 23-24.

[63] P Hichborn, 'Designs of the New Vessels for the U.S. Navy' *Transactions of the American Society of Naval Architects and Marine Engineers*, 1898, pp. 115-138, pp. 115-116.

[64] N Friedman, *U.S. Battleships: An Illustrated Design History*, (Annapolis: Naval Institute, 1985), pp. 38. Friedman expresses some surprise over the fact that reports about *Retvizan's* speed came from the American naval attaché in Paris, but the attaché in question, William S. Sims, was also accredited to St. Petersburg and Madrid see E E Morison, *Admiral Sims and the Modern American Navy*, (New York: Houghton Mifflin, 1942), p. 48.

NILE AND TRAFALGAR; THE LAST BRITISH IRONCLADS

The revival of French naval development in the aftermath of the Franco-Prussian war, 1870-71, coupled with technological developments such as the mine and torpedo rather clouded British Naval policy in the period 1870-1890. The need to combine armament, armour and speed within a reasonable displacement led to many different warship concepts. Here **Keith McBride** examines the development of the *Nile* class as a response to French policy and these conflicting technological demands.

During the 1880s, the Royal Navy was slowly climbing out of the trough into which it had fallen in 1870s: a whole series of technical developments were becoming practical naval propositions, and the revival of French naval development after the Franco-Prussian War caused much concern in Whitehall. The modern torpedo and torpedo-boat had been invented in the late 1870s and were thought by many to have made the battleship, or ironclad as she was usually called, obsolete. The Northbrook Naval Programme of 1884-85 included two ironclads, the *Renown* (later *Victoria*) and *Sans Pareil*, but it was felt that more were needed in the short term, though the torpedo seemed to rule them out in the more distant future.

Design work on what became the Nile class began in July 1885, when 'The Way Ahead' was far from clear. The 'Admiral' group, built round a main armament in open barbettes, were well in hand, but were already much criticised for a combination of low freeboard and poor protection. The *Renown* had heavier protection, though less than was desirable, a low freeboard and a single turret containing two mighty 16.25in (412 mm) guns; the preferred 13.5in (343 mm) gun was having extended teething troubles. The Italians were building two huge ships with 17.7in (450mm) guns in open barbettes, many shielded 6in, the fantastic speed of 18kts and no side armour whatsoever.

However, the only opponent taken seriously was France, whose latest ships featured a very thick but low *ceinture complete*, protecting the whole waterline, an unprotected secondary battery in the upper part of the hull, and a main armament carried at a high level at the top of heavily armoured barbettes, with the guns themselves unprotected. Apart from the threats of rival ironclads and of torpedo boats, the newly-developed Elswick cruisers were intended partly as 'Killers of Ironclads',

Nile at anchor, probably in the Mediterranean, with Inflexible *in the background. (CPL).*

using their heavy guns, speed and manoeuvrability, while their lighter, quick-firing guns would be effective against a variety of 'soft' targets, including the unarmoured areas of ironclads.

One school of thought looked back to the *Devastation* of 1869, which when designed possessed impenetrable armour all over, a small number of very powerful guns and what was intended to be reasonable seaworthiness, habitability, speed and radius of action. Progress in guns (though not in their use) had rendered her armour and armament obsolete, and the basic concept had had to be modified, first into the *Dreadnought* of 1873 and then into the series of 'Citadel' ships with turrets *en echelon*. Mingled with these were the belated broadside ships *Alexandra* and *Temeraire* of 1873.

The impossibility of covering a ship with effective armour had led to what Edward Reed called 'Ships armoured in parts', and the French secondary battery was a means of attacking unarmoured areas, though it was itself vulnerable to medium and light calibre fire. The 1884 designs for the *Renown/Victoria* included a substantial secondary battery, as yet of slow-firing BL guns, and one of these designs, 'C' of October, 1884, was still very much in contention. It was in effect a turreted 'Admiral' with a powerful 6in battery.

The 111-ton 16.25in gun had apparently been adopted solely because of delays in the production of 13.5s (they suffered from 'slippage' even then). The 1885 ships were designed throughout for 13.5in guns. The men of the 1880s tended to look back to the *Devastation*, authorised in 1869, and her half-sister the *Dreadnought,* as the ideal ships of a golden age, and in July 1885, the Controller Sir Arthur Hood, rejected previous plans and instructed the senior Constructor to start work on a 'New *Dreadnought*'. This was a continuation of sailing-ship tradition, where no-one quite knew why some ships were good and some bad, though they knew that there were good and bad ships, and worked forward empirically from past 'good' designs.

The new design was conceived at an awkward moment. Sir Nathaniel Barnaby, the serving Director of Naval Construction (DNC), was in the process of being eased out and replaced by William White, who was brought back to the Admiralty after a four-year stint at

Elswick, under a package deal arranged between the Admiralty and the firm. Design proceeded under the direction of W H Morgan, aided by Messrs Crossland, Allington and Cardwell.

As described in Oscar Parkes' *British Battleships*, on 22 August 1885, the old and the new DNCs submitted a joint memorandum on design. In the *Nile* Ship Cover is an anonymous and undated document on design policy, which is apparently the latter part of this memorandum. It makes many points, one being that only the 22,000-ton design put forward some years before could meet all requirements, and even it would be vulnerable to 'ground mines' (presumably moored mines, which had not quite reached their final form). The 22,000-tonner had, as expected, been rejected as far too expensive, but any smaller ship was a compromise. With England being the richest and most technically advanced country in the world it was to her advantage to go for the biggest and most powerful ships she could afford, so as to beggar her neighbours. The *Alexandra* and *Temeraire* of 1873 were obsolete when laid down, and had only been built to match the *Kaiser* and *Deutchland* (sic) laid down on the Thames, still England's leading shipbuilding centre, for the up-and-coming Imperial German Navy.

The Italian giants, *Italia* and *Lepanto*, were regarded with some awe on account of their prodigious speed of

Nile *at anchor, showing her low freeboard and old style cat-head and billboard anchor gear.* (CPL).

Trafalgar showing her forward turret, secondary armament, top gun and boat arrangements. Her short funnels distinguished her from her sister. (CPL).

18kts, and high freeboard, while the powerful guns of the French ships won respect, but it was felt that England should develop her own ships on her own lines (Russia had virtually abandoned battleship construction after the *Petr Veliky*, which was much like the *Devastation*). Calibre of gun and thickness of armour were not the only criteria: the lighter guns and the loading mechanisms of the big ones in foreign ships were vulnerable to the new small quick-firing guns and even to machine guns, while the torpedo boat threat was potentially very serious.

The memorandum mentioned that during the year's 'Russian Scare', the need for protection against torpedoes (which probably included the mine at that period) outweighed the need for more ironclads. Smaller ironclads would have been welcome, except for the other danger of being outclassed by bigger ones.

In one passage, the memorandum envisaged attack on enemy ironclads by RN ironclads, aided by lightly protected ships armed with heavy guns. These would probably have been the new Elswick protected cruisers or the same firm's Rendel gunboats. Such tactics would have required skilful teamwork and a very efficient signalling

system. Design 'C' would be big, expensive and in part vulnerable, but her many 6in BL would have been effective against a similar attack by the enemy or against the unarmoured parts of his ironclads.

The choice seemed to come out as between, on the one hand, a true revival of the *Devsatation/Dreadnought* family, with heavy guns, a few small, light quick-firers and very heavy protection, and on the other hand, 'C', or something similar. The decision was for the former. In this connection, David K Brown, an experienced warship designer, has argued that secondary batteries were a dangerous source of weakness; they could never be effectively protected against heavy calibre fire (though the Italians tried in the *Littorios*), and offered a path for flash into the magazines. The Admiralty seems from the first to have chosen enclosed heavily-armoured turrets for the main armament, rather than the high open-topped barbettes used by the *Admirals*, the French ships and the latest Italian designs.

Work began in early July 1885 when Admiral Hood, the First Sea Lord, instructed Sir Thomas Brandreth the Controller 'to cause a sketch design and report on first-Class armour-clad battleship described in enclosed papers to be prepared for the consideration of the Board'. What the Americans would call the 'Characteristics' were:

The basic design was to be an 'Improved Dreadnought', with four heavy guns in two turrets, low freeboard, heavy armour and a very light 'auxiliary armament'. The 'C' concept was clearly rejected.

Armament four 68-ton guns in two turrets.

Auxiliary armament twelve rapid-firing 6pdr BL guns, ten Gardner and Nordenfeldt machines guns.

'Coal carrying power' was to be 1000 tons, with arrangements for 1200 tons in war.

Speed was to be 16kts with forced draft, which was much favoured at the time.

There were to be 80 rounds for each gun of the main armament (firing all these might well have worn the gun liners out!); the papers were to go via the Director of Naval Ordnance (DNO) for advice on the outfit for lighter guns.

The displacement was, if possible, not to exceed 11,400 tons with this load.

Nathaniel Barnaby (DNC) sent lithographs of a design of November 1880 and Design 'D' of 1881 to give an idea of what was involved. Four days later, the DNO replied that the outfit for a 6pdr (57mm) QF was 500 rounds and that for a 1in (25.4mm) Nordenfeldt for ten guns (presumably a 10-barrelled gun) 4800 rounds per gun. Ten Nordenfelts would weigh 22.5 tons, one 6pdr four tons and four Gardners 3.75 tons. The Gardner was a two-barrelled machine gun. Though almost forgotten today, it was much used by the Victorian Royal Navy afloat and ashore, being more portable and reliable than the better-known Gatling. The projected ships' *raison d'etre*, their main armament, seems to have been the 13.5in BL, usually referred to as the 60-ton gun, throughout. Its weight varied considerably during a protracted research and development process.

A few days later, apparently, a drift towards a substantial secondary battery appeared. The battery was to be lengthened to the same as the *Dreadnought*, while the armour in the central part of the citadel amidships was to be cut down to a maximum of six feet above the water line. Turrets and gun mountings were to be like those of 'C', while the auxiliary battery was to be like that of 'C', but on one level only. The problem was that the 13.5in gun would probably not pierce the thickest (19in/483mm) armour of the latest foreign ships, while spreading the limited armour weight possible in the *Nile* would make it thinner and hence vulnerable. Any significant auxiliary armament would also require a substantial increase in weight. By 15 July the new design had crept up to 11,420 tons, and the '60-ton' guns to 68 apiece. Even this meant skimping on some of the armour. As compared with the *Benbow*, the last of the

'Admirals', there was less deck armour and much more on the sides.

Cost would be £725,000 for hull and engines against £750,000 for design 'C'. The proposed beam of 70ft would permit building at Chatham, Portsmouth or Pembroke, and also allow the magazines to be placed on the centre-line, where the armoured deck would be 11ft above the waterline, against 2.5ft in 'C'. The much weaker auxiliary battery at least permitted the turrets wider arcs of fire.

In forwarding the 'New Dreadnought' design to the Controller Barnaby stated that it was the best that could be done on the dimensions; protection was good, but not perfect. The latter would have required the 22,000-tonner; he would have preferred 'C', though he felt a 6in auxiliary battery unnecessarily heavy; 4in or 5in would be adequate.

His views made an impression. On 20 July he discussed the matter with the Naval Lords, and they called for a fresh design, with less citadel armour and a gun deck carried out to the side for an increased auxiliary armament, boat stowage and living space. This was ready by 24 July and was approved. Even the DNO was fairly happy, though he wanted a shorter mast with a stump military mast and fighting top forward and four 5in guns on each side instead of five. Although the *Niles* are usually thought of as ships with extremely heavy armour, they were much less so than originally proposed. Metacentric height came down to 5ft, which was thought adequate. Displacement had crept up to 11,800 tons, though the 13.5in guns were now listed as of 66 tons not 68. Orders were given for the lead-ship *Trafalgar* to be laid down at Portsmouth and this was done on 18 January 1886, *Nile* following at Pembroke on 18 April, which was in the next financial year.

The design team of Messrs Morgan, Crossland, Alington and J H Cardwell had as usual to deal with many problems; the 5in guns increased from six to eight and in September 1887 were replaced by the new 36pdr (4.7in or 120mm) QFs. On the advice of the Ordnance Committee the shells of the latter were later increased to 45lbs and the outfit to 300 rounds per gun, a net increase of 1000lbs per gun. These guns were protected by a 5in steel screen (more topweight to plague the designers!) The torpedo 'discharges', one on each beam, one forward and one aft, increased in weight and two more 0.45in Nordenfeldts were added. Altogether, 169 tons of extra ordnance were added. Not surprisingly, either 'J C' or 'J H C' had to take leave to drink the waters, at Llandidrod Wells naturally. The *Nile* was definitely a Welsh battleship.

In May 1886 when William White became DNC, he insisted on careful records of all designs changes being kept: the lack of these caused much trouble in other ships. On 10 September 1887, M Todd wrote to Williams for detail of all *Trafalgars* prior to the one launched in 1841 (by 1887 named *Boscawen*). The reply two days later was that there had been only one, which was ordered to be built in 1807 as a 2nd rate of 98 guns. She was laid down at Chatham in May 1813, but in 1814 was ordered to be registered as a 1st rate of 104 guns. She was launched on 26 July 1820, first cost being £89,367.

Table 1: COMPLEMENT OF BOTH SHIPS 25 OCT 1886:

1 Capt
1 Comdr
6 Lts (1 Torp)
1 Nav Lt./Staff Comd/Nav Lt.
2 Sub Lts.
2 Gnr (1 torp)
1 Boatswain
1 Carpenter
2 WO for QD Duties
12 Midshipmen/Cadets
1 Fit or Staff Surg.
1 Fit/Staff/Paymaster
1 Surg.
1 asst. Pay or Chaplain

1 Master-At-Arms
1 Ch Gnrs Mate
1 Ch Qm
1 Ch Y of Sigs
1 Skilled Carpenter's Mate
1 Naval Schoolmaster
1 Writer
1 Ship's Steward
1 Ship's cook
1 Ch Bandmaster

1 CI.P.O.
3 Ship's Corporals ("Crushers")
4 Gunners Mates
4 Boatswain's Mates
1 Captain's Coxswain.
2 Capts of Forecastle
3 Quartermasters
1 Yeoman of Signas
1 Coxswain 1st Cl.
2 Captains of Maintop
2 Captains of Foretop
2 Captains of Quarterdeck Men
1 Captain of Hold
1 Sailmaker
2 Skilled Carpenter's Mates
1 Caulker
1 Blacksmith
2 Armourers
1 Plumber
1 Painter 1st Class

1 Sick Bay Steward (Old) or 1 Sick
   Bay Steward 1st class (new)
1 Torpedo Artificer

2nd Class Petty Officers

5 Coxswains 2nd Class
2 Captains of Mast
2 2nd Captains of Forecastle
2 2nd Captains of Maindrop
2 2nd Captains of Foredrop
2 Signalmen
2 2nd Captains of Quarterdeck Men
1 Sailmaker's Mate
1 Cooper
1 Caulker's Mate
1 Painter 2nd Class
1 Musician

Seamen

18 leading Seamen
1 Yeoman of Store Rooms
1 2nd Captain of Hold
1 Sailmaker's Crew
1 Signalman 2nd or 3rd Class
146 AB/OS or OS 2nd Class

4 Skilled Shipwright
2 Shipwright
1 Blacksmith's crew
3 Armourer's Crew
4 Carpenter's crew
1 Cooper's crew 1 Plumber's crew
15 Bandsmen
1 Tailor 1 Shoemaker
1 Butcher (or Royal Marine in lieu)
3 Lamptrimmers (or Marines in Lieu)
1 Ship's Steward's Assistant
1 Assistant Sick Berth Attendant
   (Old) or S.B.A. (New)
1 Cook's Mate

Domestics

1 Capt's Steward
1 Capt's Cook

1 Capt's Servant
1 Capt's Cook's Asst.
1 Cmdr's Servant
1 Wardroom Steward
1 Wardroom Cook
1 Wardroom servant
1 Wardroom Cook's asst.
1 Gunroom Steward
1 Gunroom Cook
2 WO's Servants
1 WO's Cook

Boys

1 Ship's Steward's Boy
25 Boys 1st Class (inc 3 Signal & 2
   Bugler Boys)

Steam Department

1 Fleet/Staff/Chief Engineer
4 Engineers/Asst. Engineers
2 Chief Engine Room Artificers
11 Engine Room Artificers
2 Chief Stokers
14 Leading Stokers
90 Stokers/Coal Trimmers/ Stokers 2nd
   Class

Royal Marines

1 Major/Captain
2 Sgts/Royal Marine Artillery
3 Cpl/Bombardier RMA
1 Drummer/Bugler RMA
50 Pte (inc 20 Gnrs RMA, 7 Ptes as
   W.O./Offrs' Servants)

All to include 2 Gunnery Instructors
2 Gnry Instrs with rate of Capt of
   Turret,
1 Torpedo instructor,
1 Torpedo Artificer,
8 Ldg Torpedomen
105 Seamen Gunners/Torpedomen

Renamed *Camperdown* in February 1825, she was fitted as a coal depot 1861. Her name changed again to *Pitt* in 1882, and she was still in existence in 1887. There were apparently no name problems over *Nile*.

There was a doubt whether the wing passages were adequately sub-divided, and an extra bulkhead was worked in during construction. Portsmouth's estimate of turret, glacis and conning tower armour weight was much heavier than either Pembroke's or that by the DNC; Pembroke's proved to be correct. *Trafalgar* was launched on 20 September 1887 and *Nile* on 27 March

1888. Completion was long delayed for lack of the 13.5in guns and *Nile*, like some earlier ships, ran her trials without them. The two ships were not ready for service until 1890/91. Total cost came out at £885,718 for *Nile* and £859,070 for *Trafalgar*.

In service, they steamed well, but their speed was greatly reduced in rough seas. *Nile* once rolled 22°. Fortunately, they served mainly in the Mediterranean, for which they were very suitable. Like the American *Oregon* they were really 'seagoing coast defence battleships', not confined to coastal waters, but unsuitable for oceanic

Nile starboard quarter. (CPL).

warfare. Neither ship fired a shot in anger, though *Nile* was next astern to *Victoria* on the eventful 22 of June 1893 when the flagship was rammed and sunk by HMS *Camperdown*. Minor troubles occurred as they often do; the lagging on the boilers had to be increased, the bacon in the Captain's store was pre-cooked by the heat of the ships, and there were worries about the heat in the magazines, especially after cordite charges were adopted. From 1898/9 onwards, both were in reserve (quite modern ships were often paid off to make their crews available for newer ones). During 1904 Admiral Fisher described them as hopelessly obsolete, to which the First Lord, Lord Selborne, replied that 'The Japs would give us a million apiece for them'. Then came another *Dreadnought*; the 1905 one. In 1909-10, orders were given for high-powered Type II radio to be fitted, to suit the ships for their planned wartime role, but on 28 November 1910 further expenditure on them was forbidden. *Trafalgar* was sold on 9 March 1911 for £29,500 and *Nile* for £34,900 on 9 July 1912.

Though neither was ever in action, the fate of a foreign ship may provide a clue to their performance; the Russian *Navarin* was similar in many ways. She was laid down in 1889 and completed seven years later. She carried four 12in and ten 6in and, like the British sisters, served for a time in the Mediterranean. In 1904, like other obsolescent or obsolete Russian ships, she was assigned to the ill-fated Second Pacific Squadron. At Tsushima, she was badly damaged aft by gunfire during the day action and after dark was torpedoed in the same area. Despite her many injuries, she was still struggling along at 02:00 on 28 May 1905 when three of the Japanese 4th Destroyer Division sighted her. They challenged, and receiving no reply, steamed ahead and laid eight mines apiece across her path. If she saw them, she was probably unable to turn and avoid the trap. One mine exploded aft and one on the starboard side amidships. As foreseen in the 1880s she was quite unable to withstand this damage, and capsized rapidly, with all but three of her crew of 674.

THE NAVY OF VICTORIA, AUSTRALIA

The Colonial Naval Defence Act of 1865, allowed British colonies to support their own warships within their territorial waters. Here **Colin Jones** examines the naval procurement of the Australian state of Victoria, which had long been anxious over naval security since the development of Melbourne as a major colonial city.

In the year 1890 Melbourne stood as the seventh largest city of the British Empire, after London, Bombay, Calcutta, Manchester, Glasgow and Liverpool. It was, however, as one English visitor put it, a fine place, but a long way from town. Although they might not have quite thought of it that way, the distance from town was what made the citizens of Melbourne nervous, and encouraged them to provide for their own naval defence. The following overview, therefore, follows the history of one of the least known British naval forces, the Victorian Navy.

During the nineteenth century the city of Melbourne grew as a phenomenon, due to the influence of the great Victorian gold rushes and the confidence which they engendered. Melbourne is located at the head of Port Phillip, a large area of landlocked water, some 750 square miles, with access to the sea via a narrow opening onto Bass Strait, a dangerous channel known as The Rip. It is 37 miles direct from there to Melbourne, though sandbanks near the heads require most shipping to take an indirect path. Forts were built to protect the seaward approaches to the city, but the nature of the environment meant that floating defences were an absolute necessity. They had to fulfil two roles:

1. Support of forts in defence of Melbourne and Port Phillip. The forts, especially in the earlier period, were unable to command sufficient of the area to deny it to an enemy. Warships were therefore required to project the defence forward and to fill gaps between the command of the gun batteries.
2. Denial of Bass Strait to an enemy. This was a very important focal point for shipping, where an enemy cruiser might expect to find many rich pickings. In particular, for sailing ships it was the end of the Great Circle route from the southern Atlantic to Australia. Sailing ships had to make their landfall so as to pass between Cape Otway on the Victorian coast and Cape Wickham on King Island. Steamships also would be making the same landfall, even if they had first called at a port in South Australia or Western Australia.

Of the two, probably the defence of Bass Strait was the more important, as there were severe difficulties in the navigation of The Rip. In specifying the type of cruiser which would be appropriate for Australia in 1885, Admiral Tryon noted 'the seas that run at the entrance to these harbours are often heavy, and the "Rip" inconvenient'.

The Royal Navy kept a force of cruisers on the Australia station, but they were usually absent from Melbourne; based at Sydney and oriented to the South Pacific. In 1885 the Governor of Victoria noted, 'The area included within Your Excellency's command is very extensive, and the numerical strength of your squadron is not large for the duties which, under such an eventuality as war, they would be called upon to perform, while the requirements of the more distant parts of your command might further reduce the strength of the squadron in the immediate vicinity of Australia, and, moreover, the first line of defence may lead to the concentration of your squadron at some distance from the shores of these Colonies'.

In the circumstances, it is not surprising that Victoria should have raised its own naval force and that, as early as 1860, it should have been given legal status as the legitimate arm of the state.

William Laird Clowes in his history of the British Navy called England the Mother of Navies, because of the many other forces that it had nurtured. The Victorian Navy was not the least of these. This then was the progression of its ships of war and their associates.

As early as July 1853, the Governor of Victoria had decided to buy a 'war steamer' to protect the substantial gold shipments which went through the port of Melbourne. It was to be a vessel of 250 tons measurement and 80nhp, armed with either 2-32pdr 56cwt guns and 4-24pdr howitzers, or 1-32pdr and two carronades. In view of rising costs, however, work was suspended within a few months. By April 1854, the threat of war in Europe ensured that a much larger vessel was specified. It was also appropriate that a warship should be owned locally instead of being a vessel of the Royal Navy supported by a subsidy. The sloop *Electra* was on station on this basis from April 1853 to December 1856. The result was the steam sloop *Victoria*, the first real Australian warship.

During 1860 the ship was at war along with Royal Navy vessels in New Zealand, and to ensure the discipline of her men and protect her from possible charges of piracy, the colonial parliament enacted the Armed Vessels Regulation Act 1860. The Imperial government saw this as a dangerous action for a colony which was not itself a sovereign state and disallowed the Act. Nevertheless, the need to accommodate the vessel within a legal framework led to the passing at Westminster of the Colonial Naval Defence Act 1865, which allowed colonies to support their own warships within their territorial waters. These vessels might if appropriate be placed 'at Her Majesty's disposal, when any such vessel would become to all intents a vessel of Her Majesty's regular navy'. The colonial government had matched this legislation with the Paid Naval and Military Forces Act of 1864.

Victoria

Sloop designed by Oliver Lang, laid down 1/1855, launched 30/6/1855, completed 22/11/1855, by Young Son Magnay & Co, at London.
880 tons displacement (580 tons measurement)
167ftbp x 27ft 5in x 12ft
1-32pdr 56cwt
6-32pdr 25cwt
150nhp, single screw, 9.5kts (12kts under sail)
manned by 53 permanent and 42 naval brigade (establishment of 32 in 1878)

The full armament was never carried, as a second pivot gun, intended to be mounted aft, would have interfered with the working of the ship. It was carried on board in case of emergency, however, until 1859 she mounted only the forward pivot gun and two broadside guns. She was rearmed in 1878 with 1-64pdr 45cwt gun and 4-12pdr howitzers. The ship was put at the disposal of the hydrographer to replace the schooner *Loelia* for the Victorian coastal survey in 1865-69 and 1873-78. She passed to the Customs Department in 1880, though still available as a gunboat. She was sold in 1882 as an excursion steamer, sold again in 1888 and scrapped in 1895.

The continued need for greater naval defence led to a variety of expedients, including further subsidies for British warships on the station. The building of gunboats had been recommended in 1859. A subsidy was paid to maintain the sloop *Pelorus* on station for six months of each year from 1860 to 1862, and in 1863 the colonial parliament voted a large sum for the purchase of a floating battery. One design for such a craft featured an internal paddle wheel. Another suggestion was the building of a group of gun rafts, each mounting a single heavy gun. One, named *Elder*, was constructed in the Government Marine Yard at Williamstown in 1864, partly to emphasise the need for proposed ironclads. It used the hulls of two lighters and although fitted for sails and sweeps, it would mostly be towed into position and fight from anchor. The whole exercise was overly optimistic, and the vessel was not used after its initial few months. It was offered for sale, ashore, in 1878. The need for a gunboat was met by the *Pharos*.

The first Australian warship, the steam sloop Victoria, *as depicted on her completion in November 1855. (Illustrated London News).*

74

The battleship Nelson *in the new Alfred Graving Dock at Williamstown in March 1875.* (RAN).

Pharos

Gunboat, tender called 12/4/1864, designed by J.
Wilson, launched 14/3/1865 at
Government Marine Yard, Williamstown.
156 tons gross or 110 tons net
120ft oa x 19ft 6in x 10ft 7in
one pivot gun
47hp, single screw 9kts

Although built to the specification of a gunboat, following the recommendation of the Commodore commanding the station, and regarded as part of the Victorian fleet, she was never used for a naval role and never armed. Her main role was in the servicing of lights, as a replacement for the schooner *Empire*. In time of war she would probably have taken 2-12pdr howitzers which were held on the *Nelson* as boat guns. She was used by the hydrographer on the Victorian coastal survey in 1865 and 1869-72. A proposed sale to Fiji in 1872 did not eventuate. She was sold in 1881 as a tug. She became a coal hulk in 1895.

The inadequate reach of the guns of the Hobsons Bay forts was a serious worry and Hugh Childers proposed in 1863 to build a pair of small ironclads for the defence of Port Phillip. Designs were submitted by Lairds of Birkenhead. This proposal was vetoed by the Admiralty and an agreement was reached in November 1866 whereby the Imperial government subsidised the cost of the *Cerberus*, an ironclad specially designed for Victoria, and provided the obsolete battleship *Nelson* as a gift. The value of the service of the *Victoria* in New Zealand was taken into account. The *Nelson* would replace the hulk *Sir Harry Smith*, which had been used as an armed blockship since 1859 and was obtained as a naval training ship in 1864. Victoria for its part built a graving dock of a size 'so as to receive the largest vessels of war now built'. Ships of the Royal Navy were to have absolute precedence over any other vessels for the use of the dock. The acquisition of the two ships was the first major expansion of the Victorian navy. The Alfred Graving Dock at Williamstown took its first ship in March 1875.

The sloop *Victoria* was the only ship of the Victorian navy to be fully manned by a professional crew. By 1863, all ships had a core of professional experts and their complement was completed as required by reservists. The *Nelson*, which would have been worked by a full complement of 850 men in the Royal Navy, could muster some

131, plus boys, in Victoria. The naval brigades also had shore training depots. While the *Nelson* was rebuilding in December 1878 the Sandridge drill hall boasted 8-32pdr and 1-7in guns.

Nelson

Line of battle ship, trials as a steamer 21/6/60, to Victoria 7/1/1867,
commissioned 22/7/1867.
4096 tons displacement (2736 tons measurement)
224ft bp x 56ft x 24ft 9in
2-7in 116pdr MLR 96cwt converted Palliser
20-64pdr MLR 58cwt shunt
20-32pdr ML SB 43cwt
6-12pdr ML SB 6cwt howitzer (boat guns)
2002hp, single screw, 10.89kts
manned by 37 permanent and 94 naval brigade (establishment of 61 in 1878)

The *Nelson* had been laid down in 1809 and launched in 1814 as a three-decked battleship of 120 guns, but she had never been commissioned. In 1859-60 she was converted to steam, lengthened and cut down as an 87-gun two-decker, but once again, never commissioned. Her fitting out for Victoria was the nearest she came to being a fully-fledged man of war. For the voyage she carried 6-9in

fortress guns and 6-12pdr field guns as cargo, and so 1-7in and 4-64pdr of her own guns had to be sent separately. These arrived in 1870. For mounting 40 guns on decks designed to carry 66, the guns were arranged in batteries, fore and aft, with the area amidships available for other purposes. The ship saw no service outside Port Phillip, and was usually moored as a boys training ship. In view of the continued need for a cruiser in the Victorian fleet she was cut down and re-rated as a frigate during 1878. There were proposals for rearming her with heavier guns and light QF's, which came to nothing. As first converted to a frigate she mounted 2-7in, 19-64pdr and 10-32pdr guns. Her armament in 1884 comprised 2-7in, 18-64pdr, 12-32pdr and a gatling gun. The 32pdrs were removed by 1888 for use ashore by the Naval Brigade. As it was impossible to raise and train enough men to handle the vessel under sail, her rig was removed in 1887. Her boilers were condemned in 1888, after which she was towed in manoeuvres for four more years. By 1896 her structure was deteriorating and her armament was 14-64pdr for training, 2-12pdr BL saluting and 2-9pdr BL saluting guns. She was sold on 28 April 1898 and cut down for use as a coal lighter. Her guns were widely distributed to towns throughout Victoria. She sank at her berth in 1911 but was raised in 1914 and sold in 1920. Her remaining timbers were scrapped by 1928.

The ironclad monitor Cerberus *as built. This photo was taken before her departure for Australia, about June 1870.* (RAN).

The Cerberus, *late in her career, steaming manoeuvres on Port Phillip.* (From a dusty lantern slide, A. Woodley collection).

Cerberus

Monitor designed by Edward Reed, laid down 1/9/1867, launched 2/12/1868, completed 5/5/1870, by Palmer Shipbuilding & Iron Co, Jarrow.

3344 tons displacement (2107 tons measurement)

225ft oa x 45ft 1in x 15ft 6in

4-10in 18 ton 400pdr MLR

Armour: sides, 6-8in, breastwork 8-9in, turrets 9-10in iron, on backing of 9-11in teak

1369ihp, twin screw 9.75kts

bunkers for 10 days' steaming at economical speed

manned by 82 permanent and 73 naval brigade (establishment of 123 in 1878)

The *Cerberus* was obtained by Victoria under a special dispensation from the Admiralty, and could have been, in wartime, withdrawn from Victorian waters at the discretion of the commander of the Australia Station. As she was not to be accompanied by another steamer, she was built up and given a sailing rig for her voyage to Australia, and did not emerge in her proper form until 25 August 1871. She had a four foot double bottom which would 'admit of flooding and semi-sinking during active service, so as to present a smaller mark for the enemy's fire'. There is no record of this ever having been done in the frequently choppy waters of Port Phillip. The big guns had a range of 4800yds, a penetration of 11.7in of wrought iron at 1000yds and a rate of fire of one round every four minutes. Her steam

launch was fitted as a spar torpedo boat and 2-12pdr howitzers were shipped temporarily in 1878. She was refitted in 1879 with steam steering gear, a military mast and 4-1in Nordenfelt guns. On 26 August 1884 she suffered the cracking of a gun in the after turret after a misfire. It was replaced from the armoured cruiser *Nelson*, then on station, on 12 February 1885. Two more Nordenfelt guns were added in 1885. She was refitted in 1888 with a shortened flying deck and net defences. Her armament in 1896 comprised 4-10in MLR and 2-6pdr QF. She suffered the cracking of a trunnion of the left gun in the after turret in 1898 and the gun was replaced by the Imperial authorities in November. The damaged gun is now on display at HMAS *Cerberus*. By 1900 her armament had been augmented by 4-14pdr and 4 four-barrelled Nordenfelt guns. Two of the 14pdrs were taken for use by the Naval Brigade in China on field carriages in 1900. Although there had been suggestions that she should be rearmed with modern breech-loading guns several times after 1893, this was not done and she was reduced to harbour service after her boilers were condemned in 1906. She was partly dismantled in 1909 and renamed *Platypus II* as a submarine depot ship in 1921. She was sold on 23 April 1924 and scuttled at Sandringham on 2 September 1926, where she still lies. Moves towards permanent preservation started in the 1970s, but were unsuccessful. She suffered a partial collapse of her structure in a storm in December 1993 and has deteriorated since.

When a serving captain of the Royal Navy was appointed in 1883 to head the Victorian navy, some sleight of hand was required, as the *Cerberus* was only a Commander's command and service in Victoria was not counted towards seniority, as it was not 'service commanding Ships-of-War at sea'. He was therefore posted as 'Captain of the *Cerberus* and in command of the Naval Force'.

Expansion of the Victorian Navy was based on the 1877 recommendations of the military engineer Sir William Jervois, whose plans for coastal defences embraced most of the Australian colonies. In the case of Victoria, floating defences and minefields were important adjuncts to the new forts which were built to guard the entrance to Port Phillip. Jervois specified the need for gunboats and torpedo boats in particular. As some capacity for blue water operation was needed, he had urged the replacement of the *Nelson* and *Victoria* by 'one good, swift, unarmoured vessel'. The final impetus came with the visit of a Russian squadron in early 1882 and suggestions that it could have been scouting possible bases for operations in time of war. Two gunboats and three torpedo boats were ordered in Britain in June 1882, and the locally built mine-laying steamer was recalled to service. The gunboats were modified versions of Rendel designs, specially fitted for service in Australia.

Miner
Coastal minelayer 1882, ex *Octopus*, built in 1878-9 by
  Robison Bros, South Melbourne.
36.4 tons
55ft oa x 12ft2in x 5ft 6in
35hp, twin screw 8kts
4 men

This vessel had been built as a minelayer but the easing of international tensions had seen her assigned to duty as a tug. After tending a dredge in Gippsland, she reverted to the defence forces in 1882. She was refitted in 1890 to have a fresh water tank to supply the forts. She was returned to the Victorian government by the Commonwealth in 1904 and scrapped in 1924.

Albert (ex *Melbourne*)
Gunboat laid down 30/9/1882, launched 6/6/1883,
  completed 26/1/1884, by Armstrong Mitchell, Elswick
  (y.n. 454).
370 tons
120ft oa x 25ft x 9ft 6in
1-8in 12.5 ton BLR 27cal
1-6in 4 ton BLR 29cal
2-9pdr BLR
2-3pdr Nordenfelt
376ihp, twin screw 10.18kts
55 men

Used as guardship at Port Phillip heads during war scares and for occasional coastal training. Laid up in 1895 and fruitlessly offered for sale, she passed to the Department of Works in 1897 and was used as a buoy tender. A pro-

The Miner *laying mines off the incomplete South Channel Fort during the war scare of 1885.* Nelson *is in the background.* (Illustrated Australian News).

posal to reacquire her to send with the expedition to China in 1900 was not proceeded with. She was reacquired by the navy during the Great War for conversion to a tug, but this was abandoned in 1917 and she was sold as a lighter.

Victoria
Gunboat laid down 30/9/1882, launched 25/6/1883,
  completed 26/1/1884, by Armstrong Mitchell, Elswick
  (y.n. 455).
530 tons
145ft oa x 27ft x 11ft 3in
1-10in 25 ton BLR
2-13pdr BLR
2-3pdr Nordenfelt
807ihp, twin screw 12.58kts
53 men

As her single 10in gun was regarded as unduly heavy for coastal patrol work the ship was intended to do, she was rearmed in February 1888 with 1-8in and 1-6in instead. The gun was then placed in one of the forts. Laid up in 1895, she was sold to Western Australia as a survey vessel in 1896 and disarmed. She was sold for use as a mercantile tug in 1902, hulked in 1920 and scrapped in 1935. Victoria had been seeking a torpedo boat, against resistance by the Colonial Office, which cancelled an order placed with Thornycroft in 1878. On 15 August 1879 Thornycroft offered Victoria a first class torpedo boat, but

The gunboat Victoria *prepares to leave Portsmouth in February 1884.* (West & Son, Gosport).

this was not accepted. An improved design was offered on 2 March 1880, for a 20kt vessel of 100ft. Subsequently, as a result of these approaches, Thornycroft was able to supply torpedo boats to four colonies. These were the three Victorian boats:

Childers
First class torpedo boat launched 18/8/1883, completed
  16/11/1883, by Thornycroft, Chiswick (y.n. 172).
60.5 tons
113ft oa x 12ft 6in x 5ft 6in
2-15in TT
2-1pdr 1.5in Hotchkiss
679ihp, single screw, 19.11kts
18 men

Four sets of 14in side dropping torpedo gear were fitted in 1888. As a result of damage after a cruise in Bass Strait in 1905, she had her twin bow torpedo tubes replaced by a single tube. She was sold as a hulk ashore on 5 August 1918.

Nepean
Second class torpedo boat launched 22/2/1884,
  completed 20/3/1884, by Thornycroft, Chiswick (y.n. 189).

Lonsdale
Second class torpedo boat launched 12/3/1884,
  completed 20/3/1884, by Thornycroft, Chiswick (y.n. 190).

10 tons
67ft oa x 7ft 6in x 3ft 2in
2-14in TT
168hp, single screw, 17.16kts (*Lonsdale* 17.59kts)
7 men

The original design called for steam impulse-ejection gear for the torpedoes, but this was replaced by air-ejection, to match the *Childers*. Both were fitted with side dropping torpedo gear in 1886. These vessels proved very wet and the forward torpedo launching gear was removed and the bows plated up in 1888. All the steel torpedo boats were kept out of the water on slipways at Williamstown when not in use. These two were stricken in 1912 and subsequently scrapped.

In addition to the purpose-built naval vessels, some other government steamers were used as naval auxiliaries. Those employed on a regular basis were the steam hopper barges *Batman* and *Fawkner* and the 531-ton paddle tug *Gannet*, all fitted as gunboats with a 64pdr gun (in 1886 replaced by a 6in), and the steam launches *Commissioner*, fitted as a torpedo boat, and *Spray*, fitted as a picket boat. The tug *Eagle* (later *Osprey*) was used to tow the *Nelson* after her boilers were condemned. The *Fawkner* was given compressing gear to allow her to act as tender to the torpedo flotilla. The 17kt Huddart Parker packet steamer *Courier* was built in 1887 to carry 4-14pdr QF guns as a lookout steamer for Bass Strait, but she was never used as such. It was envisaged that a second vessel would also be taken up in time of war as a scout. The relevant guns were not obtained until 1891. The customs

The torpedo boat Childers *lies on one side of a pier at Williamstown while the* Nelson, *reduced to a frigate and stripped of her rig, lies on the other, about 1893.* (RAN).

The torpedo launch Gordon *lies outboard of the torpedo boats* Nepean *and* Lonsdale *in the boat harbour at Swan Island.* (Author's collection).

cruiser *Lady Loch* of 1886 was also fitted to mount a gun, but was never used as a warship.

The force remained on its usual mixed basis, with vessels fully commissioned only for occasional manoeuvres. The torpedo force was seen as important, and received continued investment, the next boat being a 'turnabout' torpedo launch.

Gordon

Torpedo pinnace, 1885, by J. S. White & Co, Cowes
  (y.n. 606)
12 tons
56ft x 9ft 6in x 4ft 10in
2 sets of torpedo dropping gear
3-1in Nordenfelt
150ihp, single screw 15kts
11 men

The tender for this vessel was awarded on 5 February 1885, with the torpedo gear under an additional order dated 2 July 1885. She ran trials in April 1886 and was able to complete a circle in 40 seconds in twice her own length. In 1888 she was listed with just one gun. She was rammed and sunk by the *Picket* on 14 November 1914 and was not considered worthy of repair.

In operational terms, the gunboats were a disappointment and the *Nelson* should have been replaced by a cruiser. The Victorian fleet needed upgrading. As the commander of the force wrote in 1888, 'they resemble a weak body of troops that may be able to hold the mountain passes against a powerful foe, but dare not venture into the open for fear of annihilation'. In the event, all development plans were overtaken by the negotiations which led to the creation of the Australian Auxiliary Squadron. This would provide a fleet of modern Royal Navy vessels to be based in Australia for local defence, supported by a subsidy from all of the colonies. In March 1885 Admiral Tryon recommended a cruiser based on the *Scout* and the deliberations of the Colonial Conference in 1887 resulted in the Australasian Naval Defence Act of 20 December 1887. Victoria asked Armstrong for an alternative and their design arrived in October 1888. The accompanying table (Fig. 1) indicates the relative merits of Tryon's first suggestion, the Armstrong design for Victoria, and the type of vessel which actually served in the Australian Auxiliary squadron.

The crew of the Childers *prepare to bring a torpedo up from its storage under the deck during manoeuvres, Easter 1885.* (Illustrated Australian News).

Victoria paid a subsidy in proportion to its share of the Australian population, initially 29 per cent of the total, for the maintenance of the four cruisers and two torpedo gunboats of the squadron, which were all based in Sydney and arrived in 1891. Ten years later, economic recession and population change had seen Victoria's share of the subsidy drop significantly. With the development of the fixed defences, the Victorian Army obtained two vessels for use around the forts and another was built for the navy. A fortified depot for minelayers and torpedo craft was established at Swan Island, close to Port Phillip heads.

Vulcan

Coastal minelayer, launched 25/5/1889, by Melbourne
  Coal Shipping & Engineering Co, Williamstown; trials 31/8/1889
125 tons
103ft x 17ft 3in x 8ft
295hp, single screw 12.5kts
6 men

She was built with two rudders on the 'turnabout' principle. She was sold for mercantile use in 1918 and renamed *Clamin*. She was scrapped in 1935.

Figure 1

	Archer	Armstrong design	Mildura
Displacement	1770 tons	1040 tons	2575 tons
Speed	16.5kts	16.0kts	19kts
Range	7000 miles at 10kts	2500 miles at 10kts	6000 miles at 10kts
Armament	6-6in BL (3 for broadside)	3-6in BL (3 for broadside)	8-4.7in QF (4 for broadside)
	8-3pdr QF	4-40pdr QF & 8-3pdr QF	8-3pdr QF
	2 electric lights	1 electric light	1 electric light
	3 torpedo tubes	2 torpedo tubes	2 torpedo tubes

The torpedo boat Countess of Hopetoun *was named for the wife of the Governor. Here she presides over a yacht race in Corio Bay, off Geelong.* (A. Woodley).

Picket
Picket boat, completed 1/1891, by D & R Buchanan, South Melbourne

Mars
Picket boat, completed 6/1891, by Melbourne Coal Shipping & Engineering Co, Williamstown
65ft oa x 13ft 4in
65ihp, single screw 10.5kts
5 men

The *Picket* had fresh water tanks to supply the fleet as well as fire fighting gear. She was run down and sunk by the *Courier* in 1908, but raised. She was subsequently in several other accidents, chartered by the Customs Department during 1917, and was towed to Geelong in 1921. The *Mars* filled an urgent need for water transport around the forts, as well as communications and target towing, and was not sold until 1947. During World War II she was known as *ST 140*. She was lost as a fishing boat in 1957. Another vessel used by the defence forces was the 100ft water lighter *Macedon* of 1891.

Despite the coming of the new Australian squadron, Victoria still had need of torpedo craft. A 323-ton turn-about torpedo gunboat, *Sea Serpent*, was built by White in 1887 as a speculation, probably in the hope that it would be purchased by Victoria. This vessel eventually went to China as the *Fei Ting*. In the event, the Victorian choice went to a Yarrow torpedo boat, ordered in January 1890.

Countess of Hopetoun
First class torpedo boat completed 25/8/1891, by Yarrow & Co, Poplar (yard no. 905)
80 tons
130ft oa x 13ft 6in x 5ft 7in
3-14in TT
4 sets torpedo dropping gear
3-1in Nordenfelt 1pdr
1186hp, single screw 24kts
19 men

She suffered an accident on trials when she ran down a sailing barge at 18kts. She was subsequently delivered to Melbourne under sail, and commissioned on 25 July 1892 with the breaking of a bottle of champagne by the firing of the bow torpedo. The gun on the conning position was replaced by a searchlight. She led the yacht *Franklin* at the royal fleet review of 28 May 1920 at Melbourne and was sold in April 1924.

The Victorian Navy was the first in the colonies to have its own flag. A special ensign was raised for the first time aboard the *Nelson* on 9 February 1870. Victoria was the first Australian colony to form a Defence Department, in 1883. Unfortunately, the navy was always too small to absorb the number of boys trained. In 1890 the Victorian Navy had 235 permanent and 382 reserves, figures which had applied for a number of years. The reserves were required to take part in the Easter cruise and monthly afloat drills. In 1900 a contingent was sent to participate in the fighting in China. It comprised 86 officers and men of the permanent naval forces and 121 of the reserves. To a large extent, it was the existence of the Victorian Navy, and the influence of its officers in the political decisions of the federation created in 1901, that ensured that Australia would have its own fleet before the Great War. Unfortunately, the decades during which Australia became a federation and decided on its future defence priorities saw no investment in new naval vessels until the ordering of three destroyers in February 1909. These were vessels of 700 tons, built to a special design for Australia. The subsidy scheme was extended to the maintenance of Royal Navy vessels for the drilling of local forces from 1902. In the case of Victoria, this was the cruiser *Psyche*.

When the first destroyers, *Parramatta* and *Yarra*, arrived in Melbourne on 10 December 1910 their officers were men who had come up through the Victorian Navy. They were the first new Australian warships which had been built for almost 20 years. Yet until 1911 they flew the Australian blue ensign, indicating their restricted status under the Act of 1865. They were the last colonial warships.

Sources:
The information is drawn from a large number of mostly Australian sources.

Colin Jones is the author of a number of works covering the Victorian Navy, published as follows:
Australian Colonial Navies, (Canberra: Australian War Memorial, 1986).
'The Voyage of the Colonial Ship *Victoria*', *Mariner's Mirror*, May 1986.
'The Colour of the Flag', in T Frame, J Goldrick and P Jones (eds.), *Reflections on the RAN*, (Sydney: Kangaroo,1991).
'The Purchase of the Australian Colonial Gunboats', *Mariner's Mirror*, May 1995
'Ruling the Waves', *Warship 1997-1998*.
'The View from Port Phillip Heads', in D Stevens (ed.) *Southern Trident*, (Sydney: Allen & Unwin, 2001).

WAR AGAINST THE WOUNDED

During the First World War Germany's unrestricted submarine campaign specifically targeted non-military vessels including Hospital Ships, a direct contravention of the 1907 Hague Peace Conference. Here **Peter Kelly** examines Germany's controversial 'War Against the Wounded'.

Spawned in the early days of the Great War as a by-product of haphazard mine warfare operations against Allied merchant shipping, Germany's 'War Against the Wounded' evolved into a concerted offensive against the helpless at sea. Initially mines were the main underwater danger for shipping, with several Allied hospital ships falling victim to this terrible weapon, but rapid development of the German U-boat arm saw the submarine eclipse the mine as the dominant threat. In its infancy the submarine acquired a reputation as an invisible weapon, against which there was no known strategic defence. Contempory naval men feared the submarine for its ability to strike unseen, then melt into the depths from whence it came. British naval opinion condemned it as an underhanded and cowardly weapon of stealth.

With a view to limiting the submarine's propensity for 'operations by stealth' a Peace Conference, held at The Hague in 1907, revised international maritime laws governing the capture or sinking of merchant vessels in war. The Second Hague Convention, as it became known, codified the right of a belligerent to visit and search all ships suspected of carrying contraband. The new code meant merchant vessels could no longer be sunk without warning, and adequate arrangements were to be made for the safety of the crew before a merchantman could be sunk. The revised laws also guaranteed immunity from attack for hospital ships bearing the prescribed distin-

Kyarra *as a Hospital Ship. Originally a freighter she was taken up as a hospital ship in 1914, but converted to a transport in March 1915, finally being refitted as an Invalid transport in 1918.* (Ship Lover's Society of Victoria-Australia (SLSV)).

guishing marks, though they remained subject to visitation and search by a belligerent, but under no circumstances could a hospital ship be sunk. For daylight identification, hospital ships flew a prescribed Red Cross Society flag and carried a broad green band around a white hull, interrupted at strategic points by huge Red Cross symbols. Military hospital ships differed only in that they carried a red band around a white hull in place of the green. At night all hospital ships steamed with navigation lights and internal lights at full brilliance, while Red Cross markings on the hull were brightly illuminated and lights were rigged to delineate the coloured band around the hull. In addition, names and details of hospital ships were notified to all belligerents. Germany and Britain were bound by the same code for the treatment of hospital and merchant ships at sea, but the commencement of hostilities in 1914 set the two nations upon diverging paths.

As the conflict broadened, hospital ship traffic increased proportionately. The sheer volume of hospital ship traffic passing back and forth through volatile theatres of war created a situation ripe for disaster. Fluctuations in the level of immunity enjoyed by Allied hospital ships appear almost relative to Germany's military fortunes. Sadly the great white hulls with their red crosses and green or red bands, gradually came to represent plump targets for German U-boats, until eventually the temptation became too great. Early successes indicated to the Germans that an officially sanctioned offensive against Allied hospital ships could become a desirable adjunct to German U-boat operations, resulting in the destruction of significant numbers of Allied soldiers.

Sick and Wounded

Wounded Allied troops received initial medical treatment at forward aid posts, located within easy distance of the front line. Critical cases were transported to Casualty Clearing Stations for further treatment and evacuation to England by hospital ship. The antiquated military tactics of the Great War resulted in high casualty figures, though often volume did not equate with combat intensity. Poor food and hygiene conditions at the front produced a steady stream of disease victims to augment the number of wounded. The aggregate flow of sick and wounded kept a fleet of hospital ships employed in European and Mediterranean waters. In the Middle-East, sick and wounded arrived at British hospitals in Mudros, Malta and Gibraltar, for on-forwarding by hospital ship to Britain.

The Ophelia Incident

The 'official' German campaign against Allied hospital ships began on 1 February 1917, when Germany announced a zone from which it debarred all Allied shipping. The Germans threatened to sink all Allied and neutral ships, including hospital ships, found in the 'barred zone.' While history correctly denounces the deliberate sinking of hospital ships, the 'Ophelia Incident' is often identified as the flash point which ignited the German campaign. In reality it was the first of a series of incidents which fuelled German allegations of British breaches of the Hague Convention. The Ophelia Incident began on Saturday 17 October 1914, when four destroyers of Germany's 'Emden Patrol' were sunk off the Dutch coast in a spirited encounter with a division of the Third Rear Destroyer Flotilla. The following day Admiral Hood[1] began a naval bombardment of enemy positions along the Belgian coast, using a motley collection of obsolete warships rushed into service for the purpose. When British Naval Intelligence advised a strong German naval force was massing for a counter-offensive against the bombardment vessels, Commodore Tyrwhitt[2] put to sea on Sunday 18 October with the 'Harwich Force' of light cruisers and destroyers to meet the impending threat. The Harwich Force was joined at sea by the British submarine E8, under Lieutenant-Commander Francis H H Goodhart.

About midday the German hospital ship Ophelia[3] was sighted, ostensibly searching for German survivors of the previous day's destroyer action. On sighting the British submarine, Ophelia reportedly took evasive action and attempted to flee the scene, but surface forces overhauled her near the Goodwin Sands off Kent. A search revealed Ophelia was a floating hospital of 100 beds, complete with medical equipment and prescribed markings under the Geneva and Hague Conventions. Searchers also found wireless equipment on board. Wireless was still a new innovation in the Royal Navy, and apart from flagships, very few vessels carried it. In contrast, most German vessels had wireless equipment. This discovery led to claims Ophelia was a radio signalling ship, relaying positions of the British coastal bombardment fleet to German forces. Her wireless equipment was dismantled and she was dispatched to Yarmouth Roads under escort of the cruiser Undaunted. While claiming her as a prize of war, the Secretary of the Admiralty announced on 5 November:

> The German vessel Ophelia was detained because her name had not been notified to the British Government as a hospital ship in accordance with the requirements of the Convention, and at the time she was behaving in a manner inconsistent with the duties of a hospital ship.

A report in The Times next day suggested she was arrested on suspicion of being a minelayer, and that 'a large number of explosives' had been found on board.

The German Press immediately denounced the British seizure as a violation of the Hague Convention. Subsequent German claims that documents found on dead German sailors proved that British warships had prevented Ophelia from effecting their rescue, lacked credibility. A British Prize Court condemned Ophelia, stating she was 'not constructed or adapted or used for the special and sole purpose of affording aid and relief to the wounded, sick, and shipwrecked'. It also found she was 'adapted and used as a radio signalling ship for military purposes of the enemy'.

The Varela, *essentially a transport, was hurriedly converted to carry wounded while serving in the Persian Gulf. She was not marked or notified as a hospital ship and continued to carry munitions.* (SLSV).

Wreck of the Rohilla

Sea mines are usually laid as barrier minefields to protect a harbour or some other feature from invasion. Since mines cannot distinguish between friend and foe, civilian or military, they are a potential danger to the unwary of either side. This was amply illustrated when the 7000-ton British hospital ship *Rohilla*[4] came to grief in a British minefield off Whitby. She mistook her position in a severe storm enroute from Leith to Dunkirk to collect wounded. Her captain believed himself some seven miles to seaward, but violent east-south-easterly gales and lashing rain reduced visibility to almost zero, and prevented confirmation of his position. Shortly after 03:00 on Friday 30 October 1914, the ship entered the minefield. While manoeuvring to extricate herself from this predicament she struck a mine. Less than a minute later *Rohilla* was smashed upon the rocks half a mile south of Whitby. Constant rescue attempts with rocket apparatus failed, and local lifeboats managed to bring only 13 ashore before rising seas forced them to retire. The storm did not abate until Sunday morning, but by then more than 70 lives were lost and heavy seas had smashed *Rohilla* to pieces.

British Closure of the North Sea

Britain announced a closure of the North Sea, east of a line from the Hebrides through the Faroe Islands to Iceland, from 5 November 1914. The Admiralty asserted the closure was in response to indiscriminate German minelaying on the main Atlantic trade route. They believed the mines had been laid during the previous week by a disguised German merchantman flying a neutral flag. Further statements accused Germany of conducting reconnaissance with trawlers, neutral vessels and hospital ships. Neutral Governments were directed to re-

route shipping via the English Channel, where they would receive sailing directions to carry them safely to Scandinavia. They were also warned of the 'fatal consequences' of straying 'even a few miles' from the courses given. In reality the closure allowed the Admiralty to begin the great barrier minefield across the North Sea as a measure for controlling U-boat ingress and egress via the north of Scotland. It also simplified contraband control by channelling merchant shipping into one route, especially those bound for German ports or to countries suspected of German sympathies. The closure effectively tightened the British blockade of Germany eventually strangling enemy military operations in Europe and reducing the German civil population to starvation point.

The Varela Incident

British and Allied hospital ships paid a heavy price for the *Varela* incident. It evolved from the landing at Fao in the mouth of the Shatt-el-Arab River at the head of the Persian Gulf, and the subsequent Battle of Sahil, when Turkey entered the war against the Allies. Troop transports in these operations were not accompanied by a hospital ship. Two transports, *Varela*[5] and *Erinpura*, were hurriedly converted to carry wounded, though they remained essentially troop transports with a section for the wounded from these operations. As transports, their munitions and other materials of war remained on board, and the vessels were not marked or notified as hospital ships. Later, following an accident while munitions were unloading from *Varela*, a British newspaper published the almost prophetic but sadly misleading statement, 'the unloading of munitions from the hospital ship *Varela* might lead to the justification later on for sinkings of hospital ships'. Much of Germany's early rhetoric to justify the sinking of Allied hospital ships was based on this report.

First Tentative Step Towards Treachery

The first reported U-boat attack on a hospital ship came when *U-21*[6] fired a torpedo at the British hospital ship *Asturias*[7] on 1 February 1915, just 15 miles from Le Havre Roads. The daylight attack was delivered in clear weather conditions with good visibility, despite *Asturias* being clearly marked as a hospital ship under the Hague and Geneva Conventions. Pursuing Admiralty instructions for countering torpedo attack, *Asturias* turned her stern towards the U-boat to avoid the torpedo, then clapped on all speed to out-run her attacker. The submarine surfaced and chased the hospital ship, fortunately without success.

A Taste of 'Unrestricted Naval Warfare'

With the British blockade exacting a terrible toll on the German population, Admiral Behncke of the German Marine Department, announced his country could no longer feed its population 'and therefore must resort to a

RMS Asturias, A-class liner of the Royal Mail Steam Packet Co. Despite being clearly marked as a hospital ship she suffered the first reported U-boat attack on a hospital ship on 1 February 1915. The attack, in daylight and with clear weather conditions was unsuccessful as Asturias turned her stern to avoid the torpedo, then out-ran her attacker. (SLSV).

blockade of Britain by submarine'. The German Admiralty declared an area surrounding the British Isles to be a 'war zone,' effective from 18 February 1915, pledging intensified submarine and minelaying operations in those waters. Germany announced that Allied merchant ships entering this zone would be sunk without warning, while neutral shipping also risked attack 'owing to the use of neutral flags by British merchantmen'. This last proviso was aimed at ship-owners who followed the British Government's suggestion to re-register their ships under neutral colours to avoid U-boat attack. Germany also used this trick to import liquid fuels in German tankers flying the American flag. Britain believed the German announcement amounted to little more than 'political grandstanding,' since German mines had been regularly sown around the British Isles and U-boats had already sunk Allied and neutral shipping in British waters without warning. The first Hopsital ship attacked after the Greman announcement of the 'warzone', was the converted Channel steamer *St Andrew*, employed in the cross-Channel 'Hospital Ferry Service' avoided a torpedo off Boulogne. Suspicion for this attack centred on *U-8*, sunk a few days later in the English Channel by HMS *Ghurka*.[8]

Allied and neutral merchant shipping suffered an appalling toll in the months of unrestricted warfare at sea, which culminated in the sinking of the Cunard liner *Lusitania* in May 1915. This act ignited a storm of international outrage and condemnation, and eventually became the catalyst which ended the first period of 'unrestricted' naval warfare. America's President Wilson

warned 'torpedoing without warning would produce a rupture in diplomatic relations'. Fearing American alienation, the Kaiser ordered the suspension of unrestricted operations, and temporarily diverted U-boats to disrupt England's arterial trade routes in the Mediterranean.

Anglia Mined

For a short period there remained more mines than U-boats in British waters, and it became only a matter of time before a hospital ship fell victim. *Anglia*[9] became the first Allied hospital ship sunk in the First World War whilst carrying wounded. At 12:30 on Wednesday 17 November 1915 she struck a mine in the Dover approaches, about three miles from shore, with some 366 wounded on board. The mine exploded under the port bow, smashing the bridge and throwing the captain to the lower deck, where he landed relatively unharmed. Within minutes the ship was listing heavily to port and sinking rapidly by the head, preventing the starboard boats from launching. Passing between *Anglia* and the shoreline *en route* from London to Lisbon, the collier *Lusitania* responded to *Anglia*'s cry for help, without heeding her own danger in entering a mined area. As *Lusitania* approached she stopped engines and lowered two boats, which began dragging survivors from the water. *Anglia* filled so quickly that her bows were soon submerged to the forward funnel. When the first of *Anglia*'s boats reached *Lusitania*, survivors began climbing aboard, but *Lusitania* struck a mine as the first two reached her deck. She sank quickly, leaving rescued and rescuers to be gathered by other vessels now arriving on the scene. *Anglia* stood on end until her bows struck the sea-bed, then slewed round to sink on an even keel. Her mast heads, still flying the Red Cross flag, remained visible above the surface. One hundred and thirty-four died in the disaster, most in the two forward hospital wards.

U-boats Target Hospital Ships Again

Despite the risk of international outrage, an emerging breed of younger U-boat commanders began to see Allied hospital ships as tempting targets. The next spate of hospital ship outrages began in March 1916, when public indignation focused on the Franco-Russian hospital ship *Portugal*, torpedoed in the Black Sea at 08:00 on Thursday 30 March 1916. *Portugal*, a French steamer manned by a Russo-French crew, was on loan to the Russian Government as a properly marked hospital ship. The Turkish Government had been the first to officially recognise her hospital ship status. *En route* to the port of Ofau[10] to load wounded, she stopped near Cape Fathia to facilitate repairs to a small craft in company. As she lay motionless a submarine appeared and circled her, then fired two torpedoes from less than 100yds. One missed, but the other struck her engine-room. *Portugal* filled and sank in less than a minute, taking 115 men and women with her.

The *Portugal* incident evoked howls of international outrage. Russia denounced the attack as a 'flagrant infraction of the rights of man,' and an 'act of common maritime piracy', lodging protests with each of the Central Powers. In the absence of protests from enemy Red Cross organisations, the Russian Red Cross withdrew from the forthcoming International Red Cross Commission meeting in Stockholm. The *New York Times* denounced the Germans as 'Blood Maniacs' and launched a tirade of invective against Teutonic savagery, while Spain called for a conference of neutrals to define measures against German piracy.

Public condemnation had little effect on German submarine warfare. Three months later the Russian hospital ship *Vperiode*, which replaced *Portugal*, was torpedoed in almost the same place and in the same manner as her predecessor. *Vperiode* was also torpedoed in a daylight attack, despite being clearly marked as a hospital ship. She was *en route* from Batum to Rizeh, near Trebizond, to load wounded. Fortunately only seven lives were lost in this incident.

Enemy Surface Vessels Respect Hospital Ship Immunity

It appears that disregard for the immunity of hospital ships was, in 1916, restricted to a few rogue commanders in the Central Powers' submarine arm. German surface ships still respected the conventions, as illustrated by the destroyer raid of 26 October. The hospital ship *Jan Breydel*, bound from Boulogne to Dover with wounded, sighted German destroyers some seven miles north-west

HMHS Britannic, at 48,158 tons, remained the world's largest liner until overtaken by the Queen Mary. *Just after 08:00 on Tuesday morning 21 November 1916, while sailing through the Kea Channel, the ship was rocked by a huge explosion and she sank with a death toll of 29, while a further 21 were injured.* (SLSV).

of Cape Griz Nez, at about 23:00. After an action near Calais, the enemy destroyers approached *Jan Breydel*, steering to cross ahead of her. Bound by the Geneva and Hague conventions to take no part in any conflict, the hospital ship could not signal their presence. The German destroyers recognised her immunity, and allowed her to pass astern of them unchallenged. A short time later the hospital ship *St Denis*[11] passed the empty transport *Queen* on an opposite course between Dover and Boulogne. The *Queen*, with navigation lights at full brilliance, was followed by five enemy destroyers. The captain of *St Denis* did not suspect the destroyers were German, so sent no message. They allowed her to pass before sinking the *Queen* in accordance with correct procedure under the conventions.

Return to Mine Warfare: The Galeka Sinking

The *Galeka*[12] sinking delivered a painful reminder of the twofold nature of the underwater menace. The former Union Company liner *Galeka* was converted to a hospital ship in June 1915, and served with the cross-Channel 'Hospital Ferry Service'. She struck a mine off La Hogue on 28 October 1916. When damage reports indicated the vessel was slowly sinking her complement abandoned her and took to the boats, but before she could sink, the derelict drifted ashore onto rocks where in a short time she became a total loss.

The Britannic Controversy

Although mines are a potential menace in all theatres of war, hospital ships in the Mediterranean remained 'incident free' until November 1916. Mudros, the advanced base for Allied operations at the Dardanelles, became the fulcrum of Mediterranean hospital ship operations. Red Cross vessels brought sick and wounded soldiers to Mudros from Allied operations in the Middle East, Africa, and India, where they transferred to larger hospital ships fbound for England.

The recently completed four-funnelled White Star liner *Britannic*, larger half-sister of *Olympic* and *Titanic*, had entered service as a hospital ship on the Mediterranean run in December 1915. Like her ill-fated sister, controversy still haunts her memory. On her trip to the Mediterranean in late October 1916, *Britannic* carried almost 500 medical personnel and some 15 tons of medical supplies for British hospitals in Egypt, Malta and Mesopotamia. Following her arrival at Mudros on Saturday morning 28 October 1916, medical personnel and supplies were off loaded into smaller hospital ships bringing wounded for transfer to England. The interned enemy national Adalbert Franz Messany, a 24-year-old opera singer suffering with tuberculosis, waited on board the Australian hospital ship *Wandilla*[13] for transfer to England and eventual repatriation to Austria. He saw medical staff and stores transferred from *Britannic*, and

during his trip to England, noted the presence on board of many apparently uninjured soldiers (the sick and walking wounded).

Britannic's final trip became her most controversial. She sailed from Southampton on 12 November, with a full complement of crew and medical staff of both sexes on board, arriving at Naples on Friday 17 November for coal and water. After two days' delay, occasioned by stormy weather, she finally sailed on Sunday afternoon for Mudros. In the Kea Channel, just after 08:00 on Tuesday 21 November, the ship was rocked by a huge explosion near her starboard bow. *Britannic*'s distress call brought French harbour vessels hurrying to her rescue from Port St Nikolo on Kea Island, along with the converted auxiliary cruiser *Heroic* and other nearby British warships. *Britannic* sank with a death toll of 29, and a further 21 were injured. A single explosion had destroyed the world's largest contemporary liner.[14]

Just two days after the *Britannic* sinking, on Thursday 23 November 1916, another hospital ship suffered a similar incident in the Mediterranean. The four-masted 'intermediate' liner *Braemar Castle*,[15] converted to a hospital ship in October 1915, was struck in the Mykoni Channel in similar circumstances to *Britannic*, but she remained afloat and was beached. The death toll was mercifully low, with only four killed in the explosion. After temporary patching *Braemar Castle* was refloated and towed to Malta for repairs, where she found the naval dockyards working to capacity on naval vessels. *Braemar Castle* was redirected to Italy's La Spezia dockyards for repairs, before resuming her service as a hospital ship.

Conflicting evidence raised doubts about the weapons used in both incidents. Official reports suggested they were probably mines, but remained inconclusive. Subsequent snippets of fragmented evidence added to the controversy.

The Australian hospital ship *Warilda*,[16] carrying the prescribed markings of a hospital ship, passed through the Kea Channel with wounded from Malta on the night of 20/21 November 1916. She was one of six vessels ferrying wounded to Mudros for transfer to *Britannic*.

Whilst returning to Malta following the loss of *Britannic*, *Warilda* passed through the Mykoni Channel just hours ahead of *Braemar Castle*. (Following the sinkings of *Britannic* and *Braemar Castle*, six hospital ships returned to Malta where they were ordered to deliver their wounded to England).

Shortly after daybreak on 21 November, the White Star liner *Heroic*, then an Armed Merchant Cruiser (AMC), passed through the Kea Channel steering an opposite course to *Britannic*. The two ships exchanged greetings as they passed.

In contrast with denials published in the German newspaper *Lokalanzeiger*, the *Kieler Zeitung* stated on Monday 27 November 1916, that *Britannic* had been torpedoed. The editor wrote:

> The *Britannic* was transporting fresh troops for our enemies. If she had not been doing so our submarines would never, of course, have torpedoed her.

Karapara, *depicted in her wartime role as a Hospital Ship. The green band, interspersed with huge red crosses, can clearly be seen around her hull.* (SLSV).

The Admiralty refuted the allegations, stating:

> British hospital ships are employed solely in the conditions set forth in the Geneva and Hague Conventions, and they carry neither personnel nor materiel other than that authorized by those conventions.

A German prisoner-of-war, captured after the sinking of *U-109* off Dover in August 1918, claimed to have been in the crew of *U-73* when she laid mines in the Kea Channel, less than an hour before *Britannic* was lost. (This appears to be somewhere around the time *Heroic* passed through the same channel). Captain Gustav Seiss, former captain of *U-73* confirmed this story after the war.[17]

A French intelligence report of 2 January 1917 also confirms the sea-mine theory, but suggests *U-72* was responsible for the sinkings:

> 10 [mines] have been exploded or have been swept in Zea Channel[18] ~ 1 struck by *Burdigala*,[19] 1 struck by *Britannic*, 8 raised and destroyed. 4 have been discovered in the Mykoni Channel ~ 1 struck by *Braemar Castle* and 3 swept. . . .We attribute these various mine-layings to *U-72* which was reported to us as having left Pola on the 7th November.

Germany Closes the Channel to Allied Hospital Ships

Upon his repatriation, the opera singer Adalbert Messany told German interrogators all he had seen since his internment in Egypt at the outbreak of war. His testimony provided the Germans with further 'proof' that Allied hospital ships had abused their Red Cross immunity. On 29 January 1917 Germany published 22 such allegations, followed by a declaration delineating a 'barred zone' which effectively closed the Channel and the Mediterranean to Allied hospital ships from 1 February. Abandoning all pretence of legality under international law, Germany publicly announced its intention to sink Allied hospital ships:

> the German Government can no longer suffer that the British Government forwards troops and munitions to the main theatre of war under cover of the Red Cross, and it therefore declares that from now on no enemy hospital ship will be allowed in the sea zone comprised between a line drawn from Flamborough Head and Terschelling on the one hand, and from Ushant to Land's End on the other. If in this sea zone after the expiry of the stated time any enemy hospital ship is encountered, it will be considered as a vessel of war and it will be attacked without further ceremony.

Germany further stipulated sick and wounded should be disembarked at Avonmouth near Bristol, to keep hospital ships outside the 'barred zone'. Britain refuted the claims of misuse, and quoted Germany's right to visit and search hospital ships at sea, to ascertain the veracity of such claims. In the 'verbose posturing' which typifies the era, the Foreign Office issued this threat in reply:

> His Majesty's Government have requested the United States Government to inform the German Government that His Majesty's Government have decided that, if the threat is carried out, reprisals will immediately be taken by the British Authorities concerned.

Britain was slow to heed the German warning, preferring instead to cling to a tenet of hospital ship immunity under the relevant conventions.

Hospital Ships Attacked as 'Vessels of War'

Disregarding British threats of reprisal, Germany implemented her programme of aggression. The *Glenart Castle*,[20] *en route* from Le Havre to Southampton with wounded, was damaged by explosion on 1 March 1917 off the Owers lightship. As in previous cases, the hospital ship was clearly marked, and the incident happened in clear weather and good visibility. Although crammed with wounded, no lives were lost in this case. When the ship stopped, every soul on board transferred safely to the boats. The ship remained afloat and, manned by a volunteer crew, was towed to Portsmouth for repairs. Again an enquiry could not determine the cause of the explosion as either a mine or a torpedo, but popular naval opinion believed it was a torpedo.

Definite Proof

In a second attack, *Asturias* fell victim to a German submarine off Start Point about midnight on 20/21 March 1917. *Asturias* was steaming with all navigation lights and hospital ship markings brilliantly illuminated. She had unloaded some 900 sick and wounded at Plymouth for transfer to British hospitals, leaving only crew and medical staff on board. As *Asturias* rounded Start Point *en route* to Le Havre for more casualties a torpedo struck her stern, damaging the rudder and detonating in the engine-room. The resultant explosion damaged machinery and knocked out the lighting system.[21] Destroyers and patrol boats answered her distress calls, retrieving survivors from the water and taking lifeboats in tow. Some 380 persons were rescued, while 43 died and a further 39 were injured.

A German wireless message of Tuesday 26 March 1917 included the attack in a 'List of Achievements' by the U-boats. A German communiqué issued on Friday 30 March announced Germany would begin sinking hospital ships in the Mediterranean, again alleging Allied violations of the conventions. The communiqué also reinforced the earlier wireless message, stating:

> the *Asturias* was sunk in accordance with the declaration issued by the German Government on January 31.

The Admiralty responded by suspending all Mediterranean hospital ship sailings until adequate protection for them could be arranged.

Admiralty Fears for Safety of Hospital Ships

Shortly after the *Asturias* incident the Admiralty expressed anxiety for the safety of commercial traffic in British waters, especially for hospital ships. Although the underwater menace was now largely attributable to intensified U-boat activity, the problem remained twofold, with an increasing list of hospital ship losses from enemy mines. The Admiralty considered mines as much a part of the underwater problem as submarines. Minelaying U-boats could follow a minesweeper without detection, resowing mines almost in its wake. The only measure for dealing with minefields was to increase minesweeping patrols, but the preferred method was to destroy greater numbers of U-boats, especially the minelayers. It was also the preferred method for countering torpedo attacks, though the task was difficult. Clearly the hospital ships displaying the Red Cross were no longer guaranteed immunity from direct attack. In an alternative strategy the Admiralty removed a number of hospital ships from the list, preferring instead to designate them 'Ambulance Transports'. They could now be armed, provided with naval escorts, and given camouflage schemes similar to those used by troop transports.

Gloucester Castle

As if to emphasise Admiralty fears, the hospital ship *Gloucester Castle*[22] was torpedoed in mid-Channel on the night of 30/31 March 1917. The attack took place in clear weather conditions and with good visibility. The victim was clearly marked as an Allied hospital ship. British destroyers rushed to the rescue, some searching for the U-boat in a bid to prevent further attack, while others went alongside to remove some of the 450 wounded on board. *Gloucester Castle*'s wounded, along with medical staff and crew, were removed without loss of life. Many of the wounded were lifted over the rail to the destroyers' decks, complete with their stretchers. When all deck space had been filled, the destroyer alongside would move off to allow the next in her place. Military authorities ashore received the wounded, transporting them to hospital in a fleet of hastily assembled ambulances. German wireless later confirmed that a U-boat had torpedoed *Gloucester Castle*.

Private Samuel Arnold Bodsworth, RAMC

In heavy weather on 10 April 1917, the hospital ship *Salta* struck a mine and sank in Le Havre Roads. Fortunately she carried no wounded, but 52 of her medical staff lost their lives, including nine nursing sisters. A tenth nursing sister owed her life to the bravery and tenacity of a medical orderly from *Salta*. The destroyer HMS *Druid*[23] rushed to the scene to begin rescue operations. She went alongside a swamped boat and dragged the occupants aboard, except for one nursing sister too exhausted to hold the lines thrown to her, and Private Samuel Arnold Bodsworth, RAMC, who refused to leave her. When the sister lost consciousness and was washed overboard, Private Bodsworth dragged her back again. He finally succeeded in securing a line round her, allowing her to be hauled on board *Druid*. Private Bodsworth received the Albert Medal for this rescue.

Reprisals Short-lived

Although no wounded troops had died in recent sinkings, the attacks were labelled an 'illegal and inhuman mode of warfare', waged 'in direct and flagrant contravention of [the] Hague Convention'. It fell to the Royal Naval Air Service to fulfil Foreign Office promises of reprisals. A combined Franco-British aerial force attacked Freiburg, a university town of nearly 80,000 people located in Baden, some thirty miles from the French front in Alsace. At noon on Saturday 14 April 1917 a squadron of 12 aircraft dropped bombs and leaflets on the town. The primary bombing targets were municipal buildings and medical facilities, while the leaflets explained the raid was a reprisal for sinking Allied hospital ships. A second raid followed at 17:00 hours, conducted in a similar manner by 23 aeroplanes, but local defenses were not caught napping a second time. German aeroplanes rose to meet their attackers, shooting down three British aircraft in the ensuing dogfight. German reports claimed civilian casualties numbered seven women, three men and one soldier killed, with 17 women, eight men and two children injured. The attack provoked public outcry on both sides, which effectively ended Allied 'reprisals'.

WAR AGAINST THE WOUNDED

The Australian hospital ship Warilda. *Refitted as an ambulance transport, she was camouflaged and armed with a single 4.5-in gun and employed on the cross-Channel 'Hospital Ferry Service'. En route* from Le Havre to Southampton, on 2 August 1918, *she was torpedoed. 102 wounded and several engine-room personnel were lost in the tragedy as* Warilda *capsized and sank. (SLSV).*

British and German Wounded Drown

The Freiburg raid sparked a further intensification of U-boat operations. On Tuesday evening, 17 April, the ambulance transport *Lanfranc*[24] and the hospital ship *Donegal*[25] were torpedoed within 30 minutes of each other. Both were under naval escort, *en route* to British ports with wounded. As an Ambulance Transport *Lanfranc* carried no markings. She had on board 234 British wounded, most of whom were cot cases, 167 German wounded prisoners-of-war, 52 medical personnel, and 123 crew. Nineteen British lives were lost in *Lanfranc*, along with 15 Germans. The torpedo struck on the port side abaft the engine-room, smashing two boats and tearing a huge hole in her side. Cot cases, including Germans, were transferred to the remaining boats, with everyone clearing the sinking vessel within 45 minutes of the attack. The captain and those unable to board the overcrowded boats, were taken off by the first rescue vessel. *Lanfranc* sank by the stern some thirty minutes later.

Because the exigencies of war had prevented *Donegal's* conversion to 'Ambulance Transport', she retained her hospital ship markings. She carried British walking wounded, of whom 29 were drowned along with 12 of her crew. *Donegal* was torpedoed abaft her engine-room on the port side, smashing lifeboats and tearing a great hole in the ship. She sank by the stern within thirty minutes.

Plan to Keep Wounded Abroad

The loss of *Lanfranc* highlighted flaws in the 'Ambulance Transport' stratagem. An alternative was required to counter the alarming increase in attacks against hospital ships. Increased hospitals and expanded medical facilities in Europe and the Middle-East, provided an answer which allowed casualties to receive treatment at safe distances from the fighting, and reduced the need for hospital ships. The plan created a series of 'Field Hospitals', which required the immediate influx of vast numbers of doctors and medical staff. A poor response from Britain's already over-taxed medical profession almost resulted in the complete mobilisation of all British physicians.

German Protest and Talk of Reprisal

On 22 April 1917 the International Red Cross Committee addressed a rather belated note of protest to the German Government over the torpedoing of the hospital ships, *Asturias*, *Britannic*[26] and *Gloucester Castle*. The note emphasised that sinking hospital ships was 'in contradiction to the humanitarian conventions which [Germany] pledged itself solemnly to respect'. The Committee drew attention to a belligerent's right to search hospital ships, but stressed that nothing could 'excuse the torpedoing of a hospital ship'. Next day the French Government issued an official statement in Paris, informing the Germans they would begin embarking German prisoners in French hospital ships to protect them from U-boat attack. Britain also considered embarking German prisoners in hospital ships as a measure of protection. Germany retaliated by placing French prisoners-of-war in front line battle areas.

On 26 April a Centre Deputy in the Reichstag demanded German reprisals be exacted in cases where Britain or France transported German prisoners through the 'forbidden zone' in Allied hospital ships. The German Government adopted the proposal, and General Friedrich sent a communiqué to both Britain and France stating that the Germans would order the 'sharpest measures of reprisal' if prisoners were exposed to the danger of being torpedoed while on board Allied hospital ships.

Revised Sailing Tactics for Hospital Ships

Allied hospital ship sailings recommenced in the Mediterranean on 15 April 1917, under a new strategy. Following the same precautions as troopships, they now steered a 'zig-zag' course at sea, and 'darkened ship' at night. At least two destroyers would escort them, with the supply of hospital ship escorts taking a higher priority than troopships. The new tactics automatically negated hospital ships' immunity, but the precautions were necessary since Germany did not respect that immunity.

In British waters, all hospital ship movements were redirected to Avonmouth or Newport in the Bristol Channel, in compliance with the German directive of 1 February. This measure temporarily eliminated the danger for hospital ships arriving in home waters with their cargoes of sick and wounded, and attendant medical staff.

Loss of the Dover Castle

Anxious to show the threat to Mediterranean hospital ships was not idle bluff, a German U-boat attacked the two hospital ships *Karapara* and *Dover Castle* in the early evening of 26 May 1917. Bound for Malta in clear weather and good visibility, the two hospital ships steered east along the Algerian coast, escorted by the destroyers *Cameleon* and *Nemesis*.[27] Both ships were clearly marked, though by now such markings mattered little. A torpedo struck *Dover Castle* at 19:00. She stopped engines and immediately transferred her wounded to the boats, and by 20:00 all were clear of the ship. *Nemesis* laid a smoke screen to hide her charges, then shepherded *Karapara* to safety at Bona (now Annaba), which was the nearest port. *Cameleon* collected patients from *Dover Castle*'s boats then put her self alongside the crippled ship. She took off crew and medical staff, leaving only the captain and a volunteer crew to prepare for towing, while *Cameleon* departed for Bona with a total of 950 persons on board. Before *Cameleon* had passed from view, another torpedo struck *Dover Castle*, sending her to the bottom in three minutes. The towing party manned the remaining boat, to be rescued by a French vessel some six hours later. Six stokers died in this incident. The attack was attributed to *UC-73*.

German Position Reiterated

In a semi-official telegram on 26 May, Germany reiterated its position on Allied hospital ships:

> the German Government will in future prevent all traffic by hospital ships in the entire barred zone and in the Mediterranean, including the route left open for Greece, and will regard enemy hospital ships appearing there as vessels of war, and attack them immediately.

A contradictory statement followed, listing conditions to ensure safe passage for hospital ships on the route left open for Greek shipping. In effect, Germany required six weeks' advance notification of the hospital ship's name and speed, with expected arrival and departure times. The vessel could collect her wounded only from Salonika for direct transfer to Gibraltar. Prior to departure a neutral government representative should declare the vessel to be carrying 'only sick and wounded, and nurses, with no cargo other than material for the use and treatment of the sick and wounded'.

Spanish Commissioners Appointed

Whilst a majority of British sick and wounded were now treated in Field Hospitals near the battlefields, a steady flow of critical patients still required transportation to British hospitals. To prevent further German outrages, the British and French Governments agreed to a Spanish proposal to carry a Spanish naval officer as a neutral Commissioner in each hospital ship, to guarantee against alleged abuses of Red Cross immunity. When Germany accepted the Spanish proposal, France disembarked German prisoners from her hospital ships and Germany removed French prisoners from forward danger areas. Italian hospital ships were granted the same conditions a few weeks later. To streamline the operation, King Alfonso of Spain negotiated free passage for Allied hospital ships in the Mediterranean and the Atlantic as far north as the English Channel. The revised plan reduced time and distance commitments for Spanish Commissioners. Immunity was restored to hospital ships in the Mediterranean from 10 September 1917, but that immunity could not extend to the double-edged weapon of mine warfare. When the hospital ship *Goorka*[28] struck a mine off Malta in October 1917, crew and medical staff worked quickly and efficiently to evacuate the ship. Fortunately there were no lives lost in this incident.

Further crisis loomed in British waters as improved Allied anti-submarine measures began to reduce the effect of Germany's 'submarine blockade' of the British Isles. In November 1917 the German Government introduced a desperate countermeasure to restore the naval bias to her favour by announcing a massive extension of its 'barred zone', and closing previous 'safe' navigation zones. From a German viewpoint, the redirection of British hospital ships to the Bristol Channel meant U-boats need now only wait near Lundy Island for an assured 'kill'.

Kyarra, *Although not a true hospital ship, she was refitted as an Invalid Transport for the repatriation of 1000 Australian invalids from Plymouth. At 09:00 hours on 26 May 1918, en route from London to Devonport, a torpedo was seen approaching the ship. It tore a huge hole in the forward stokehold on the port side,* Kyarra *rapidly foundered with the loss of five lives.* (SLSV).

Renewal of Hospital Ship Outrages

Leutnant Wilhelm Werner of *U-55* torpedoed the hospital ship *Rewa*[29] in the Bristol Channel at 23:15 on 4 January 1918, signalling the renewal of 'unrestricted submarine warfare' against hospital ships. *Rewa* had collected casualties from Salonika, Malta and Gibraltar and was bound to Avonmouth with 279 invalids, some 80 medical staff and 207 crew. A Spanish Commissioner boarded the ship at Salonika and disembarked at Gibraltar, which was her last port of call before home waters. *Rewa* carried the correct identification lights of a hospital ship, and her navigation lights burned at full brilliance. She was steaming at 9kts when at 23:00 the captain and third officer noticed two small white lights four points on the port bow, distant one mile. Unsure of the lights the captain determined they could be an improperly lit local sailing vessel, and ported his helm about two and a half points to pass clear of her. Although the hospital ship altered course, her position relative to the lights appeared not to alter. Again the helm was put over, but within seconds a torpedo crashed through her port side. It struck almost amidships, passing through the red cross and holing the starboard side. Distress calls were immediately sent. While the ship settled quickly on an even keel, her 30 cot cases were lifted into the boats. The four female nurses and medical staff followed, then the crew. By 23:50 the ship was clear, the captain being the last to leave. *Rewa* took her final plunge at midnight, her casualties being three Lascar crew killed

in the initial explosion. All fourteen boats kept together as much as possible, burning flares to attract attention, but it was some three hours before two trawlers and a small oiler arrived to begin rescue operations.

Germany responded to this outrage by wireless, stating four Spanish Commissioners had returned to Madrid in protest at the misuse of Allied hospital ships. In a statement issued on 13 January, Germany denied responsibility for the sinking, suggesting *Rewa* had probably encountered a recently-laid German minefield in the Bristol Channel. British minesweepers quickly proved the Bristol Channel 'minefield' as a hoax. The Spanish Commissioner who disembarked at Gibraltar released a statement on 16 January in which he said: 'I can guarantee that all conditions agreed on were scrupulously observed'. Later it was established *U-55* had sunk *Rewa*.

German propaganda could not disguise the renewed offensive against hospital ships. As German military power deteriorated in Europe, U-boat attacks increased in volume and viciousness. Like *Asturias*, the hospital ship *Glenart Castle* was lost in a second attack by U-boat. She sank when a torpedo from *U-56* struck her at 04:00 on 26 February 1918 off Lundy Island near the mouth of the Bristol Channel. She was bound from Newport (opposite Avonmouth) to Brest to embark wounded when the attack occurred. *Glenart Castle* sank in five minutes, dragging some of her boats down with her. The submarine surfaced after the attack, and cruised among

The Australian hospital Wandilla, *built in 1912 for the Adelaide Steamship Co and loaned to the Admiralty in August 1916 for use as a hospital ship. In May 1918, she was stopped by a U-boat in the Mediterranean. The U-boat captain exercised his right to thoroughly search her for contraband, uninjured troops, or munitions of war, and when she proved to be a hospital ship under the conventions, he allowed her to pass unmolested. (SLSV).*

the survivors and wreckage before submerging and leaving them to their fate. Of the 182 people on board only 38 survived. They had been immersed for more than twelve hours before French and American vessels arrived to rescue them. Later evidence suggested the submarine had machine-gunned survivors in the water, but the allegation remained unproven.

Although not a true hospital ship, the Australian steamer *Kyarra*[30] was refitted as an Invalid Transport for the repatriation of 1000 Australian invalids from Plymouth. A former troop transport and freighter, she was camouflaged and refitted at Tilbury Docks early in 1918. When about two miles off Anvil Point at 09:00 on 26 May 1918, en route from London to Devonport, a torpedo was seen approaching the ship. It tore a huge hole in the forward stokehold on the port side, and in sixteen minutes *Kyarra* had foundered with the loss of five lives. A sixth was so seriously injured when the torpedo struck that he died shortly after.

Lucky Escapes

Several hospital ships and ambulance transports had lucky escapes during the war. By 1918 Ship Masters were acutely aware of the U-boat problem, and employed tactics to counter torpedo attack. Intelligence reports indicated the

quality of German torpedoes had declined since 1914, due to the blockade which had prevented raw materials reaching Germany. Most lucky escapes of 1918 can be attributed to these two factors.

In February 1918 the Australian hospital ship *Warilda* was struck by a torpedo. *Warilda* had been employed on the cross-Channel 'Hospital Ferry Service' since returning to England with wounded after the sinking of *Britannic*. Refitted as an ambulance transport, she was camouflaged and armed with a single 4.5-in gun. *En route* from Le Havre to Southampton with a full cargo of wounded, she was attacked at 02:00. The torpedo struck abaft the bridge on the starboard side, but failed to explode.

The hospital ship *Western Australia*[31] chartered from the Western Australian Government for the duration of the war, escaped unhurt when she avoided a torpedo on 20 March 1918. Following the German declaration of 'unrestricted submarine warfare' she was refitted as an ambulance transport and resumed her regular 'Hospital Ferry Service' run between Southampton and Le Havre.

Just twelve days after the loss of *Glenart Castle*, the clearly marked hospital ship *Guildford Castle* escaped destruction in the same area. She was inbound to Avonmouth with 438 wounded on board. A torpedo was seen approaching the ship at 17:35 hours on 10 March, but it passed harmlessly astern. A minute later another torpedo struck the ship on the port side abreast the mainmast, but failed to explode. The torpedo rebounded from the ship and returned to bump along her side. As it passed astern it was struck by a propeller but again failed to explode! It is believed that two submarines delivered this attack.

Searched and released

Not all U-boat commanders were prepared to sink hospital ships on sight. In February 1917, the hospital ship *Dunluce Castle* was stopped by a U-boat in the Mediterranean and searched. After ascertaining the ship was solely employed as a hospital ship, she was released. In May 1918, as if to demonstrate the reinstatement of hospital ship immunity in the Mediterranean, the Australian hospital ship *Wandilla* was stopped by a U-boat. The U-boat captain exercised his right to search her thoroughly for contraband, uninjured troops, or munitions of war, and when she proved to be a hospital ship under the conventions, he allowed her to pass unmolested.

A Most Callous Atrocity

The hospital ship *Llandovery Castle*,[32] Captain R A Sylvester, was chartered early in 1918 by the Canadian Government to transport Canadian wounded to their homeland. After successfully completing her westward crossing, the clearly marked *Llandovery Castle* sailed from Halifax with seven Canadian doctors as supernumeraries. Torpedoed by *U-86* on the night of 27 June 1918, some 114 miles west of Fastnet Rock off Southern Ireland, *Llandovery Castle* sank in ten minutes, leaving crew and medical staff barely time to launch the boats. The U-boat surfaced and her commander, *Leutnant* Helmut Patzig, ordered Captain Sylvester to approach the submarine. Patzig demanded the captain hand over eight American airmen travelling as passengers on board. When the captain insisted there were no Americans on board, only seven Canadian doctors, Patzig smashed every boat with his submarine then shot the survivors in the water, leaving only the captain's boat unscathed. The U-boat then submerged, leaving behind 234 dead. A later report suggested enemy nationals acting as spies in Halifax were responsible for Patzig's misinformation.

Second Time Unlucky

Although not technically a hospital ship, the Australian steamer *Barunga*[33] was refitted to repatriate Australian casualties. *En route* from London to Plymouth on 7 July 1918 to embark the invalids, a torpedo was sighted approaching about 200yds off the port side at about 11:45. By putting her helm hard-a-starboard *Barunga* avoided the torpedo by mere inches. It failed to explode, surfacing some distance away. *Barunga* loaded 855 Australian invalids the next day, but was delayed until 14 July, when she sailed with the cruiser HMS *Kent* and the destroyers *Midge*, *Lance* and *Victor* as her escort. Some 150 miles south of the Scilly Isles the escort turned for home. A few minutes later, at 16:20 on 15 July, a torpedo smashed into *Barunga's* starboard bow. The submarine surfaced, but two shots from *Barunga's* gun forced her to submerge again. The destroyers laid patterns of depth charges over the area then stood by the sinking ship. Casualties from the 'tween-decks hospital were ferried in boats to the waiting destroyers, while others dived overboard and swam to floating wreckage from where they were soon rescued. *Barunga* settled slowly, allowing every person on board to be saved. Several attempts to tow her failed, and she sank just before midnight.

Ambulance Transport tries to Ram

With approximately 800 persons on board, including seven female passengers, the ambulance transport *Warilda* departed Le Havre for Southampton at 22:15 on 2 August 1918. When a submarine was sighted off the starboard bow shortly after 01:30, the Officer of the Watch tried unsuccessfully to ram it. The submarine retaliated with a torpedo which smashed through the starboard quarter into 'I' ward, where 102 walking wounded were accommodated. The ship was travelling at 14.5kts at the time of impact, and although the blast disabled her starboard engine, she retained much of her speed on the port engine. Her steering gear was damaged in the explosion, and the valves could not be reached to shut off her port engine, which left the ship charging round in circles too fast to launch her boats. While the destroyer escort dropped depth charges round her, some 400 cot cases were brought on deck to wait until she slowed enough for rescue operations to begin. In an hour the ship had slowed to 1.5kts, although her stern was now submerged. When sixteen people died in two mishaps while launching the boats, destroyers took large numbers off in a direct transfer from the deck of the sinking ship. The 102 cases from 'I' ward, and several engine-room personnel were lost in the tragedy. *Warilda* capsized and sank at about 04:00 on 3 August.

Cessation of Hostilities

The Armistice in November 1918 did not end the role of the hospital ship, it merely altered the focus. Hospital ships continued in service for some time, repatriating prisoners-of-war from both sides. They could now sail 'upon their lawful occasion' without fear of an unseen menace beneath the surface.

The cessation of hostilities sent shock waves through the German U-boat Service. Many of its officers and men believed the service should not surrender, since it had never been beaten in war. Fortunately their sentiment did not prevail. While a number of U-boat commanders deserved trial as war criminals for atrocities against the Red Cross at sea, responsibility for the deliberate operation against sick and wounded, must rest squarely with the German Government of the day. Only a few U-boat commanders sank hospital ships, despite Germany's declaration of 1 February 1917, but the inaction of the German Government indicated the ruthlessness of its rogue U-boat commanders was not accidental. It failed to punish any officer, or disclaim his action, for attacking Allied hospital ships in the Great War. Patzig and two of his officers were charged with war crimes after the war, but Patzig could not be found. His officers were found guilty, but 'escaped' shortly after the trial. Unfortunately the 'War Against the Wounded' in the Great War sowed the seeds of another campaign, which bore its bitter fruit a generation later.

Sources

The Times, London.

The New York Times.

Sir J S Corbett, *Official History of the War*, (London: Longmans Green & Co., 1921)

A W Jose, *The Official History of Australia in the War of 1914~1918*, vol 9, (Sydney: Angus & Robertson, 1943)

S Mills, *HMHS Britannic, The Last Titan*, (Dorset: Waterfront publications, 1992)

L Thomas, *Raiders of the Deep*, (London: Wm. Heinemann Ltd., 1929)

J P Eaton and Charles A Haas, *Falling Star*, (Wellingborough: Patrick Stephens Ltd., 1989)

W H Miller Jr, *The First Great Liners in Photographs*, (New York: Dover Publications Inc., 1984)

J H Isherwood, *Steamers of the Past*, (Liverpool: Sea Breezes, 1966)

P J Fricker, *Beken of Cowes, Ocean Liners*, (London: Thos. Reed Publications Ltd., 1992)

Capt T D Manning, *The British Destroyer*, (London: Putnam, 1961)

Time-Life International, 'The Seafarers' series, *The U-boats*, (Amsterdam: Time-Life Books, 1984)

Notes

1 Rear-Admiral the Hon, Sir Horace L A Hood, Rear Adm. Dover Patrol.

2 Became Admiral of the Fleet Sir Reginald Tyrwhitt in 1934.

3 *Ophelia*, freighter of 1153 tons, one of 22 steamers owned by Adolf Kirsten of Hamburg.

4 *Rohilla*, 7409 tons, built 1906 by Harland & Wolff. Owned by BISN Co.

5 *Varela*, British troop transport of 4645 tons, built 1914 for BISN Co's Bombay/Karachi/Persian Gulf service.

6 Lieutenant-Commander Otto Hersing.

7 SS *Asturias*, 12,029 tons, twin screw, A-class liner of the Royal Mail Steam Packet Co. Built 1908 by Harland & Wolff.

8 *U-8* was sunk and her crew captured on 4 March 1915.

9 *Anglia*, twin screw steamer of 1862 tons, built 1900 by W Denny.

10 Near the town named Of on the south-eastern shores of the Black Sea, now in the Republic of Turkey.

11 RMS *St. Denis*, cross-Channel steamer of 2435 tons. Built 1908 for the Harwich to Holland service.

12 *Galeka*, twin screw G-class liner of Union Castle line. Built 1899 for the South African service.

13 *Wandilla*, Captain C C Mackenzie. Australian coastal liner of 7785 tons, built 1912 for the Adelaide Steamship Co. Loaned to the Admiralty in August 1916 for use as a hospital ship.

14 At 48,158 tons, *Britannic* remained the world's largest liner until overtaken by the *Queen Mary*.

15 *Braemar Castle*, single screw Intermediate liner of the Union Castle line. Built 1898 by Barclay Curle & Co, Glasgow, for the East Africa service.

16 *Warilda*, Australian coastal liner of 7785 tons, built 1912 for the Adelaide Steamship Co. Loaned to the Admiralty in July 1916 for use as a hospital ship.

17 See also L Thomas, *Raiders of the Deep* (London: Wm Heinemann Ltd., 1929), pp. 64.

18 Former name of the Kea Channel before the First World War.

19 *Burdigala*, French twin screw troopship of 12,480 tons, built 1898 by Schichau at Danzig, as *Kaiser Friedrich* for Nord-Deutscher Lloyd. Sunk near the Mykoni Channel a week earlier.

20 *Glenart Castle*, twin screw G-class liner of Union Castle line. 6757 tons, built 1901 as *Galician* by Harland & Wolff.

21 The Admiralty bought the wreck and refitted it as a store ship at Plymouth until after the war. The Royal Mail line then re-purchased the ship and refitted her as the cruise liner *Arcadian*.

22 *Gloucester Castle*, twin screw G-class liner of Union Castle line. 6575 tons, built 1900 by Harland & Wolff.

23 HMS *Druid* 'I' class destroyer, built 1911 by Denny. Armament 2 x 4-in, 2 x 12-pdr guns, and 2 torp tubes.

24 *Lanfranc*, twin screw steamer of Booth Steamship Co. 6287 tons, built 1907 at Dundee.

25 *Donegal*, twin screw steamer of Midland Railway Co. 1885 tons, built 1904 by Caird & Co.

26 The International Red Cross believed *Britannic* was torpedoed.

27 *Cameleon* and *Nemesis*, 'H' class destroyers of approx. 740 tons. Armament as for 'I' class.

28 *Goorka*, 6300 ton twin screw G-class liner of Union Castle Line, built 1897 by Harland & Wolff

29 *Rewa*, Captain J E Drake of BISN Co. Turbine steamer of 7308 tons, built 1906 by Denny for British India Company's mail and passenger service. Refitted as a hospital ship in August 1914.

30 *Kyarra*, Captain A J G Donovan, AUSN Co. Ltd. steamer of 6953 tons, built 1903. Originally taken up as a hospital ship in 1914, but converted to a transport in March 1915.

31 *Western Australia*, Western Australian Government coastal steamer of 2937 tons. Built at Trieste for the Russian Government as the *Mongolia*, she was used as a hospital ship in the Russo-Japanese war of 1904/5.

32 *Llandovery Castle*, 11,423 tons, twin screw Union Castle Line steamer, built 1914 by Barclay Curle & Co for the East Africa service. Converted to a hospital ship in 1917.

33 *Barunga*, former German-Australian line steamer *Sumatra*, of 7484 tons, captured in Sydney on the outbreak of war in 1914.

SWEDISH STEAM TORPEDO BOATS

The Royal Swedish Navy was one of the first to take an interest in the development of fixed and moveable mines and torpedoes, not least because the Archipelago favours ambush tactics. **Daniel Harris** describes the transition from spar torpedo boats to the 'torpedo boat destroyer'.

In February 1868, the Swedish Cabinet approved the Navy Administration Board's request for funds to carry out research into 'underwater mines', and to acquire a special mining vessel. The 'underwater mine' named in the funding application was the spar torpedo. No doubt, both the Swedish and Norwegian navies knew of the spar torpedo's development from the connections established with the United States Navy by the naval constructor J C A d'Ailly. The latter visited America in the years 1861-64 to examine monitor construction and the other naval developments.

An Order in Council dated 23 April 1869 instructed the Navy Minister to arrange the construction of an iron vessel to carry a spar torpedo. Its dimensions were: length 28ft, beam 8ft, draft 5ft. Four men operating levers turned the boat's single propeller. It was soon realised that this iron boat was, owing to its slow speed, unable to meet the navy's requirements. Nevertheless, it was not struck off the strength until 1880.

Articles by serving naval officers, published in the 1870 and 1871 journals of the Royal Society for Naval Sciences, suggested the increasing number of boats with single-cylinder steam engines used for commercial transportation in the skerries should be requisitioned in wartime and adapted to carry spar torpedoes.

In 1871, the Lindholm yard, Goteborg, completed a 9 ton steam launch for the Navy to carry one spar torpedo. This vessel's dimensions were: 40ft long, 14ft beam and 3ft draft. A 28hp steam engine gave a maximum speed of 7kts. The complement for this launch, named *Nordstiernam*, was five men. The navy believed that the steam launches belonging to the fleet's major units could be adapted to carry spar torpedoes, operate the Harvey Otter system[1], or the spar torpedo to attack vessels anchored in confined waters during the dark hours.

The Floating Target

Early in 1872, the Navy Board sent Lieutenant C F Ekermann to London to arrange for the construction of a floating target, built to represent the midships section of a double-bottom iron ship for exercises with the Spar Torpedo or the Harvey Otter System. He resided at 57 Gracechurch Street in the City of London. The board had authorised Ekeman to sign a contract dated 14 January 1871 with Earle's Shipbuilding Company of Kingston-upon-Hull to build the floating target for £2400. It was probably delivered to Karlskrona, but unfortunately, neither draughts of its construction, nor any information about its use have survived. Presumably it was anchored in the Blekinge Skerries.

The First Torpedo Launches

The *Naval Sciences Journal* for 1873 suggested that the speed of ships' launches, and of the *Nordstiernan's* were too slow for effective attacks with spar torpedoes. The article stated that torpedo craft based on Thornycroft's high-speed steam launches would be ideal for torpedo attacks. The article included particulars of Thornycroft's launch *Miranda*, which was 59ft long and had a beam 6ft 8in. *Miranda* had two saloons aft. On trials, it had made 20.45kts with the tide and 14.75kts against the tide. Its engine developed 176ihp.

The reports of the *Miranda's* speed, no doubt, provoked the interest of both the Norwegian and Swedish navies in the possible uses for high-speed launches in defence. In 1873, the Norwegian Navy ordered a high-speed steam launch from Thornycroft which was named *Rap*. The dimensions were length 58ft, beam 7ft, and a draft of 3ft 11in. *Rap* was propelled by a 100hp compound engine designed to give a speed of 15kts. The Norwegians had initially intended for *Rap* to operate the Harvey Otter System. That proved to be unsuccessful. It was replaced by two spar torpedoes. The Norwegian Navy paid £1517 for the *Rap*. Her hull is now preserved at the Horten Naval Museum.

On 28 November 1873 the Swedish Navy Board signed a letter of intent, and on 23 February 1874 a contract with Thornycroft & Co Ltd, Church Wharf, Chiswick, London to build a high-speed launch similar to the Norwegian *Rap*, to be named *Spring* (fig 1 and 1a)

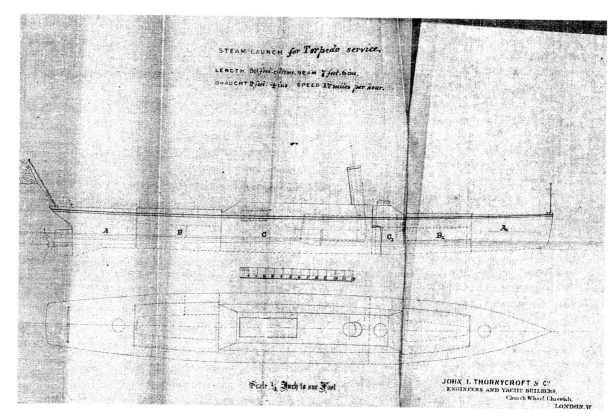

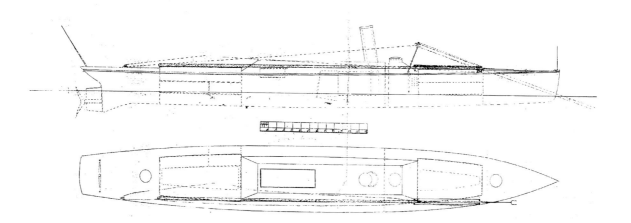

Figures 1 and 1a. Plans of the torpedo launch Spring. (Courtesy of Krigseerkevit).

for £1800. For some reason, the builder's price was £287 higher than that charged for the Norwegian craft. Spring's dimensions were length 58ft, beam 7½ft, draft 3ft 11in. The launch's displacement, including 1½ ton of coal and a crew of 5, was 15.8 tons. The contract stipulated that the hull plating was to be of Bessemer steel and of the same thickness as the Norwegian vessels. The frames of 3/8 x 3/4 x 1/8in angle iron were to be 17in apart. There were also to be six watertight compartments. The flush steel deck was to be covered with canvas. A 90hp inverted compound engine drove the single propeller. Its cylinders were seven and eleven inches in diameter and had an 8in stroke.

The contracts stipulated the engine to be as noiseless as possible. In addition, it was to have a surface condenser. Thornycroft was to make the locomotive boiler of either Lowmoor or bowling iron, or Bessemer steel, and the firebox of copper. The boiler's working pressure was to be a 120lbs per sqin. The fuel consumption was about 26lbs per hour. The navy required Spring to maintain 17mph or 15kts with full load for three hours. However, on the acceptance trials, the maximum speed reached was 14.7kts. The launch's normal operating speed was 12kts, the propeller making 505rpm.

The merchant ship Atlanta delivered Spring to the navy at Stockholm in the summer of 1875. Her Norwegian sister had already been handed over earlier at Goteborg, whence a Norwegian crew had steamed her to Oslo. King Oscar II was later to be on board for one of the speed trials in Oslo fjord.

Spring was intended to operate the Harvey Otter system but it proved to be a failure. She was then fitted to carry four spar torpedoes. The 1877 issue of the Royal Society's Journal reporting the 1875 and 1876 exercises stated that Spring was found unsuitable for Spar Torpedo operations owing to its limited turning circle.

In 1879 the navy returned Spring to the builders for two major changes. The first to move the rudder aft of the propeller, and to install forced draft to the locomotive-type boiler. In 1884, Spring was fitted to carry two 11in torpedoes, one on each side, and a 25mm machine gun. Before being stricken in 1893, Spring was renamed Mining Boat No 1, later Glimt, and finally Mining Boat No 10.

In 1874, the Stockholm Navy yard built a 12-ton vessel to carry four spar torpedoes, two forward and two aft, named Shrick. It was 47ft (14½m) long, had a beam of 8ft, and a draft of 3ft. A sister named Ulven was built at the same time for the Norwegian navy. The 124hp engine gave Shrick a maximum speed of 7kts, considered too slow for any attacking craft. A correspondent to the Society's Journal of 1878 wrote that the minimum speed of an attacking spar-armed torpedo boat should be at least 10kts. Shrick became a dockyard tender, and in 1902 sank after collision with a merchant vessel.

In 1878, the Stockholm Naval Yard laid down a series of five iron 21 ton torpedo boats numbered 3, 4, 5 and 7 (Fig 2); their dimensions were length 56ft, beam 11ft, draft 4ft. Two 80hp compound engines driving two four-bladed propellers gave maximum speed of 10kts. Coal-fired locomotive-type boilers provided the steam. The complement was seven men. No 7 was originally fitted

with an experimental waterjet propulsion system. The maximum speed reached was 6kts. Consequently, 80hp steam engines and propellers replaced the experimental equipment. The five's armament was one 12mm machine gun and four spar torpedoes. The spars' length was about 35ft. The charges weight was 28lbs. The spar's length from the bow was 22ft, the distance at which an attack was possible. Such an operation could be as dangerous for the vessel's crew as for the target.

In the 1877 issue of the Naval Sciences Journal, O Norrbom suggested that 'mining boats' be fitted with some light armour to protect the crew. The journal published a reply in the 1879 issue in which the author stated that the best defence was speed, not armour, moreover spar torpedo vessels ought to be able to attain at least 16kts. The author held that a weaker power's defence was speed. The author discussed the probable manning difficulties of the spar torpedo boats. He dismissed the call for volunteers, practice common in the larger navies, as impractical. In support of his opinion, he stated that when the commander of an American corvette called for volunteers 'to furl the mainsail, nobody volunteered so the mainsail was lost'. 'Calls for volunteers was an unknown practice in the Swedish Navy and should so remain'. The writer stated that when Lieutenant Cushing, USN, had destroyed the Confederate Albemarle, and the Russian Schestakov had attacked Turkish vessels with spar torpedoes, in spite of 'murderous fire', no crew member had been lost. The author suggests, however, that the officer in command of a spar torpedo boat should carry a revolver.

The Naval Defence Policy

The self-propelled torpedo, invented by Luppis of the Austrian Navy and the British engineer Whitehead in 1868, made the French towed system, the Harvey Otter and the Spar Torpedo obsolete. It brought about the need for small, fast vessels able to carry the launching equipment. Naval staff planners in Sweden and Norway believed these torpedo-carrying craft would be ideal for local defence. The Norwegian and Swedish coasts with the many islands and the skerries were ideal for torpedo boat operations. French naval experts, quoted in the Royal Socieity's Journal, suggested the small fast torpedo boats be stationed in every port for harbour defence. In addition, larger torpedo craft should be based on the channel ports to attack large British vessels operating in those waters.

The French naval defence proposals probably influenced the Swedish decision to begin in the late 1870s construction of a series of torpedo boats not exceeding 60 tons. These boats with the monitors would provide naval defence in the confined waters of the skerries. The initial construction program for 'First-Class Mine Boats' was authorised in 1878. That designation was changed in 1883 to second-class torpedo boats when the building of vessels over 60 tons began. All torpedo craft built between 1879 and 1905 had to be able to pass through the Göta canal system which joins the Baltic to the Skagrrak, sometime called the Western Sea. The canal provided a quicker means of transferring small torpedo boats from Stockholm to the west coast, avoiding long voyages south and passage through the sound and Kattegat.

The Second-Class or First-Class Coastal Defence Torpedo Boats

In July 1879, the King-in-Council authorised the navy to buy or build a vessel that could launch 'a torpedo through a tube'. The Naval Administration Board had already ordered ten 14in torpedoes from Whitehead's Fiume factory. The board had intended to place an order with a British yard for the first torpedo boat with a fixed launching tube. Unfortunately, at that time, the Crown lacked funds to pay the British yard's quoted price. Consequently, in December 1879 the Stockholm naval yard was ordered to build Sweden's first steam torpedo boat with tubular torpedo launching gear, in accordance with draughts approved by King Oscar II. This first torpedo boat, named *Rolf* (fig 3) had the following dimensions: length 90ft, beam 12ft, draft 5ft. A locomotive-type coal-fired boiler and a 350ihp compound engine gave *Rolf* a maximum speed of 16kts. The vessel's armament was a twin-barrel 25mm machine gun and one fixed torpedo tube. The complement was 13 men. The total displacement with 9 tons of coal was 40 tons. The yard was able to complete *Rolf* within the available financial resources. *Rolf*'s completion and trials, attended by King Oscar, took place in the autumn of 1882. In 1887, *Rolf* was renamed *Mining Boat No 61* and in 1895, to 2nd class torpedo boat *Blink*. In 1903, after removal of the torpedo tube and armed with a 36mm gun, *Blink* became Tender *B6* and was scrapped in 1909.

The Seid Class (fig 4)

In March 1882, the parliament released sufficient funds for the navy to purchase a torpedo boat from either France or Britain. The plan was to purchase a vessel that could be used as a model to be copied or used as basis for Swedish-designed small vessels. These were to be classified as second-class torpedo boats. The naval board's choice was a 45 ton torpedo boat similar to that designed for Italy by J Thornycroft & Co of Chiswick on Thames, London.

On 4 March 1882 the Swedish Government signed a contract with John Thornycroft & Co, steam yacht and launch builders, for a steam torpedo boat to be named *Seid*, dimensions: length 100ft, maximum beam 12ft, draft forward 1ft 9in, aft 5ft, 49 tons at full load, complement 11 men. The price was £8000. The builder was to supply, fit and mount a double ejecting apparatus for discharging 14in Whitehead torpedoes. The hull was to be built of the best-quality steel plate and angle bars. The contract required heavier deck plating above the torpedo, boiler and engine rooms. Corticene was to cover all decks. The bulkheads of the boiler and coal bunker were

to be double and lined with rock wool 'to intercept heat'. The plates for the conning tower were to be 1in thick. Its windows with wiping gear were to be so placed to enable 'the man at the wheel to command the whole horizon'. In addition, the wheel was to work both bow and stern rudders. The conning tower was 'to be so arranged to meet the torpedo gear designed by Mr Whitehead'.

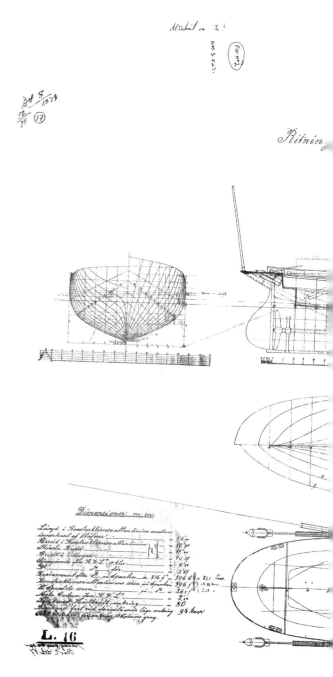

Compartments abaft the engine room were to be 'fitted out comfortably for the officers and engineer'. The petty officers' accommodation included three 'comfortable berths' in the torpedo room in which hooks were fixed for the hands' hammocks. All woodwork was to be finely varnished; cabin tops were to be painted white. A 'Downton patent water closet' was to be fitted in the after cabin.

Seid's machinery consisted of a vertical surface condensing compound engine capable of developing 500ihp. The cylinders were 13½ and 22in in diameter and stroke 12in. The builder was to make the locomotive-type boiler of open hearth steel with firebox and tubes of lowmoor iron, able to stand a working pressure of 180lbs per sqin and a hydraulic pressure of 260lbs. It was to be fitted

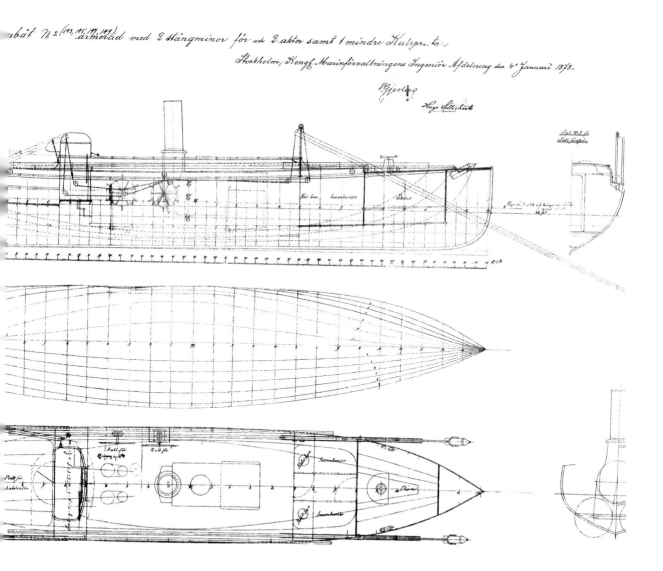

Figure 2. Plan of torpedo boats Nos. 3, 5, & 7. (Sjöhistoriska Museét, Stockholm).

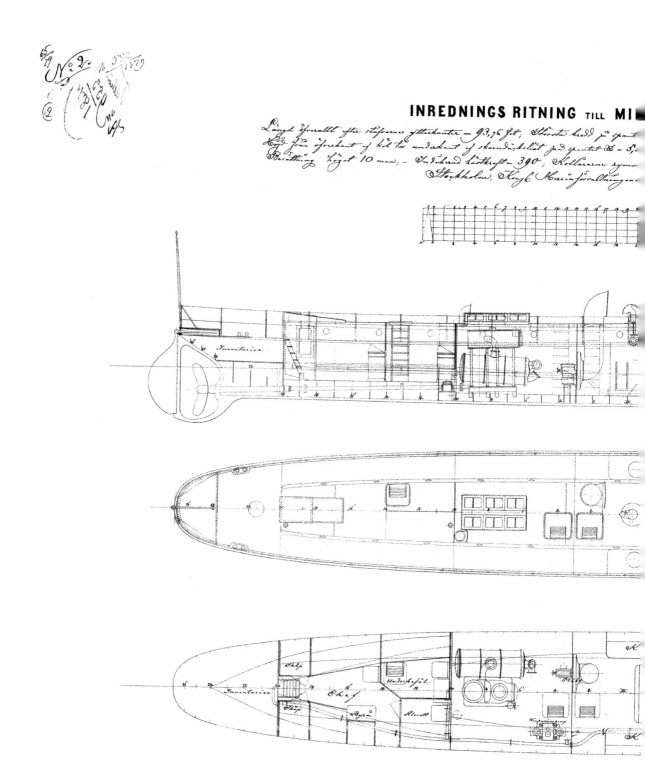

Figure 3. Plan of torpedo boat Rolf. (Sjöhistoriska Museét, Stockholm).

ROLF.
Fastställes
Minrum

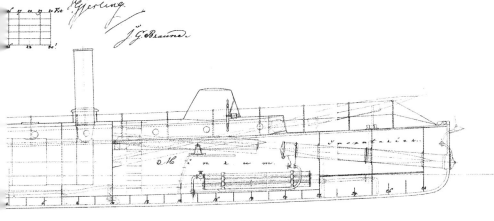

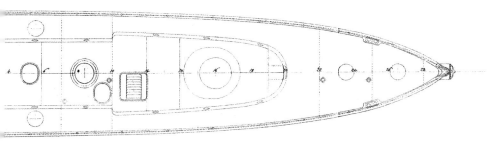

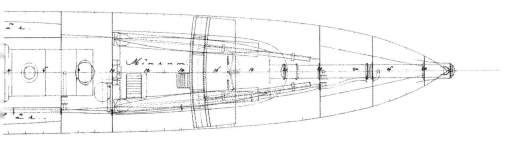

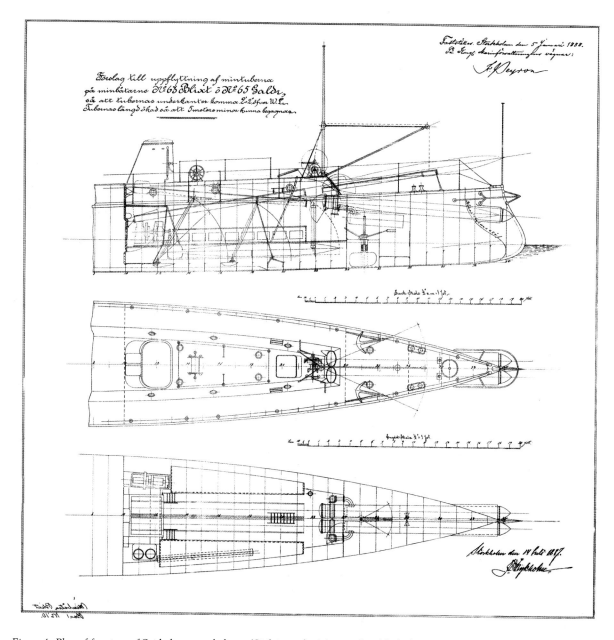

Figure 4. Plan of fore part of Seid class torpedo boat. (Sjöhistoriska Museét, Stockholm).

with 'Thornycroft's patent arrangements for protecting the men tending the boiler against accidents'. The contract contains no particulars of 'the patent arrangement'. Steam heating was to be fitted for below decks. In winter, when the vessel was laid up ashore, steam from dockyard boilers would then be connected. The contract stipulates that 'the machinery be of the same quality as that in the boats built for the English government'.

The torpedo gear of Whitehead & Co comprised two launching tubes with inside and outside doors, two accumulators, each able to make one shot when charged to 30 atmospheres, two half tubes to receive the torpedo from deck and an air-compressing pump installed in the engine room.

The contract required the builder to supply a complete set of construction drawings on delivery. Thornycroft, under the agreement's terms, supplied spare parts, tools, twenty-five coal bags and two campstools.

Thornycroft had guaranteed that Sied at full load would attain a speed of 18kts. At the three-hour speed trials on the measured mile, *Seid* attained a speed of 19kts. *Seid*'s armament was two above-water, fixed bow tubes for 14in torpedoes and one 25mm twin-barrel machine gun.

In 1883, the Stockholm navy yard laid down *Galor*, in all essentials a copy of *Seid. Galor* joined the fleet in 1885 and twelve years later, was an exhibit in that year's Stockholm art and industry exhibition. Downgraded to Patrol boat *B8* in 1907 she went to the breakers in 1928.

Six vessels were built on *Seid*'s lines. The first two were *Narf* and *Norve*, launched by the Stockholm naval yard in 1886. Their dimensions were: length 100ft, beam 11ft, draft 6ft, tonnage full load 46 tons, complement 14. Both had the same armament as *Seid*. Their compound engine gave 430ihp, and a maximum speed under trials at full load, including 12 tons of coal, of 20kts. Locomotive-type boilers provided the steam. Both became patrol boats B9 and B10, armed with 37mm gun, and were broken up in 1928.

In 1888, the Stockholm yard completed *Bygve* and *Bylgia* (fig 5): length 102ft, beam 12ft, draft 6ft, 48 tons displacement with full load including 12 tons of coal. Both had locomotive-type boilers and vertical triple-expansion engines, to provide 460ihp. The designed speed was 18kts, which was exceeded by 1kt during acceptance trials. The triple-expansion engines were the first installed in Swedish naval vessels. The armament was similar to *Seid*'s. In 1915, both were downgraded to patrol craft, and re-armed with a 37mm gun. In 1916, both vessels, on neutrality patrol in the Åland sea, prevented the German submarine *UB20* from seizing a Swedish steamer *en route* to Finland, then still under Russian occupation.

The last two of the *Seid* class were *Agne* and *Agda*. In 1891, the former was laid down in the Stockholm naval yard and the latter in the Karlskrona dockyard. The hulls had about the same dimensions of *Seid*, but the positions of torpedo tubes changed. A single trainable torpedo tube was mounted amidships, and a single above-water tube in the bow for 14in torpedoes. The 25mm twin-based machine gun was fixed to the forecastle. The compound engine and the Yarrow water-tube boiler supplied by that British firm enabled *Agda* to make a maximum speed of 19kts. *Agne*, having a similar compound engine but only a locomotive-type boiler, made only 18kts in the high-speed trials. Yarrow water-tube boilers and triple-expansion engines were to become the standard for class 2 torpedo boats. The water tube boiler's advantages were shorter time needed to raise steam, and higher working pressures. In 1915, both vessels had the torpedo tubes removed and a 37mm gun replaced the 25mm machine gun. Both were downgraded to patrol vessels and renamed *Vb 13* and *14*. On August 8 1916 the Russian submarine *Kaiman* attacked the German SS *Schbawen* in Swedish waters without result. *Vb13* and *Vb14*, enforcing Swedish neutrality, found the Russian sub in Swedish territorial waters and forced it to leave.

In 1899 the Stockholm navy yard laid down two torpedo boats, *No 79* and *81*, dimensions: length 108ft, beam 12ft, and draft 7ft, displacement at full load 56 tons. Yarrow boilers supplied the steam for the triple-expansion 670ihp engines. The designed speed was 20kts and 21 was reached on trials. The armament was one 15in bow torpedo tube, a second trainable tube on the after deck, and one 37mm quick-firing gun, 14 men made up the complement. Neither joined the active fleet before 1903 for unknown reasons. In 1915, *No 79* was on patrol off Gotland's east coast when the German minelaying cruiser *Albatross* was run ashore to avoid destruction by superior Russian forces. In spite of the presence of the Swedish torpedo boat, which stationed herself between the wreck and the Russian force, the latter fired several rounds, most of which landed on Gotland, before steaming north, *Albatross* and her surviving crew were interned for the duration of the war. Nos 79 and 81 became tenders in 1918 and were sunk as targets in the late 1920s.

In 1901, the Crown authorised the building of two second-class torpedo boats to be *No 83* and *85*. It requested bids from commercial yards and awarded the contract to Motala's Norrköping yard. The hulls, still based on Thornycroft's original design, had improved sterns and balanced rudders. Their dimensions were: length 107ft, beam 12½ft, draft 7ft, displacement (full load) 54½ tons. Both had Yarrow watertube boilers and Motala's triple-expansion 700ihp engines, and on trials made an average speed of 21½kts. The armament was the same as in *79* and *81*; 83 and 85 joined the fleet in 1903. In May 1916, *No 83*, on patrol alone in the Åland Sea, suffered an engine breakdown. As there were no other craft nearby, the skipper made sails out of the vessel's collision mats, and reached a nearby harbour. Both 83 and 85 were sunk as targets in 1929.

Between 1904 and 1909, the navy had a series of ten second-class torpedo boats built by the royal and private dockyards. The ten were the last of the small type built for the navy. They were numbered 5 to 15 but 13 was omitted to allay the superstitions of Admiral W Dyrssen, the deputy minister for the navy. The dimensions of all were length 104ft, beam 12ft, draft 6ft. The displacement of these varied between 58 and 61 tons. A 700ihp triple-expansion engine and coal-fired Yarrow boiler gave these vessels to make a maximum speed at full load, including 11 tons of coal, of 21kts. The complement was 14 men. All ten vessels carried the same armament, two 18in torpedo tubes, one fixed in the bow, a second trainable on the after deck, and a 37mm gun. In contrast to the earlier built second-class torpedo boats, this last series carried 18in torpedoes.

The vessel's construction took five years, because parliament was parsimonious with the necessary funds. The Karlskrona Naval Yard laid down and completed *No 5* and *No 6* in 1905 and 1907 respectively. The Stockholm Naval yard laid down and launched *No 7*, *8* and *9* in 1905 and 1907. That yard completed *No 10* and *11* in 1909. The Motala yard at Norrköping built *No 12*, *14*, and *15* in the years 1907 and 1908. These were the last built on *Seid*'s lines. Most had become tenders to coastal fortresses by 1928, all were stricken by 1953. The Customs Department purchased *No 7* and *8* in 1947 for use in chasing liquor smugglers. No information about the success in those operations is available. In 1953, both went to the scrap yard.

The First-Class Torpedo Boat Programme

In June 1880 the Naval Defence Committee released its proposals for naval construction that included armoured coastal defence ships designed to operate against an aggressor in open waters. The committee held that new armoured ships would need torpedo boats both for scouting and protection. To meet these responsibilities, the fleet needed vessels able to operate under all weather conditions. The existing torpedo boats, intended to operate with the monitors in the confined waters of the Skerries, failed to meet these requirements.

In 1883, the Swedish government authorised the purchase of a torpedo boat from J Thornycroft & Company of Chiswick, London. That vessel was to be the prototype for the future domestic construction of torpedo boats. The contract written in fine copperplate handwriting, and signed by John Thornycroft, is dated 11 December 1883. The company agreed to build the torpedo boat for £10,200 in seven months.

The Thornycroft torpedo boat, named *Hugin* (fig 6), had the following dimensions: length overall 113ft, breadth moulded 12ft 6in, draught forward about 2ft,

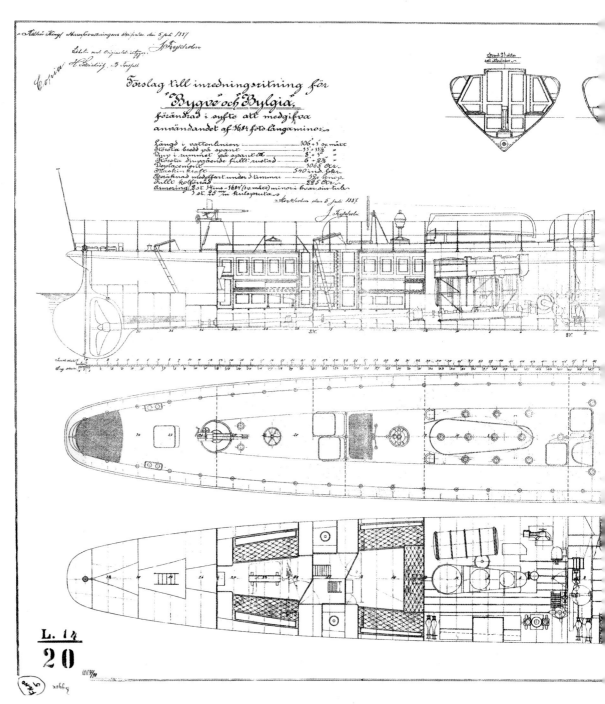

Figure 5. Plan of torpedo boat Bygue. (Sjöhistoriska Museét, Stockholm).

draught aft about 6ft 6in. Displacement at full load was 65 tons. The hull's plating was to be of the best quality steel to be ¼ inch in thickness amidships, and to BWG standards elsewhere. The frames were to be 1¼ x 7/8 x 5/32in angle bars but 1¼ x 1 x 3/16in amidships.

The contract specified that the hull was to be divided into 13 watertight bulkheads. The bulkheads forward of the boiler and coal bunker were to be double and 'lined with slag wool to intercept heat'. Two special clauses inserted in the contract state, 'The vessel to be so built, and the bulkheads forward of the boiler room and aft of the engine room so strengthened and fitted that the vessel can either be lifted in slings, or rested on two keel blocks placed under the above-mentioned keel without sustaining any damage'. 'The bulkhead forward of the boiler room and after of the engine to be strengthened and fitted with lifting gear'. It was the practice to lay up the torpedo boats on shore for the winter in the old galley section of the

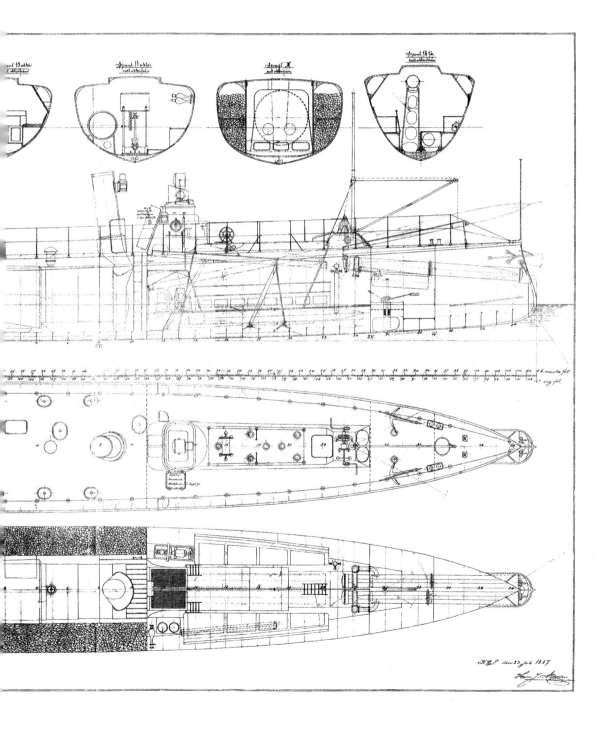

Hugin, *probably at Chiswick.* (Sjöhistoriska Museét, Stockholm).

Stockholm naval dockyard. (The author recalls seeing these old steam torpedo boats resting on blocks in the old galley yards from Strandvagen in the 1940s).

The conning tower was to be of ¼in steel plate with windows to enable 'the man at the wheel to command the horizon and arranged for Mr Whitehead's Torpedo gear'. The rudder was to be '[ab]aft the propellers and an auxiliary bow rudder forward', both to be worked by a wheel in the conning tower; 'the bow rudder to lower from deck'. The navy board agreed in a supplementary agreement 'to pay £100 for the installation of Mr John Donaldson's patent steam steering engine and gear arranged to work both rudders and capable of being changed simultaneously from steam to hand steering'.

Hugin's machinery comprised a vertical compound condensing engine having cylinders 24¼in x 14½in x 15in stroke capable of developing 800ihp, steam donkey and circulating pumps. The two locomotive-type boilers were to be made of open hearth steel, and the firebox and tubes of 'low moor iron – all rivet holes to be drilled'. The working pressure was 130lbs, and there were to be two safety valves. In addition, the builder was to install 'the special arrangements for getting up steam quickly' similar to those used in English boats, 'and their patent arrangements for protecting men from accidents while tending fires'. The bunker was to hold 10 tons of coal.

The compartments aft of the engine room were to be fitted out 'comfortably for the officers, engineer and petty officers'. The torpedo room would serve as the seamen's mess. The after cabin had Downton's patent WC with cock fitted to ship's side to prevent water running in the vessel when heeled over. The builder was to supply a portable WC on deck for the hands' use. Thornycroft was to supply a 'steam cooking apparatus to be placed in the engine room'. The complement was ten men.

Hugin's armament was two fixed 15in torpedo tubes in the bow, with two reloads, and one twin barrel 25mm Palmkrantz gun. On the acceptance trials, Hugin at 650ihp reached a speed of 18.5kts. For the voyage from Chiswick to Sweden, she had three masts rigged for sails, also for some reason, the twin funnels were painted white. Refitted in 1899, Hugin was classified as second-class torpedo boat in 1906 and as a tender in 1915. She was scrapped in 1923.

After Hugin's arrival in Sweden, parliament granted funds for the construction of three similar torpedo boats named *Munin*, *Freke* and *Gere* by the Bergsund Company, Stockholm. The three with Hugin would form a squadron to operate with the coastal fleet. The only difference between these three and the prototype Hugin were improved wheelhouses, higher freeboard in the bow and the installation of French Sautter Harlé searchlights. All four joined the offshore, or coastal fleet late in 1887. In 1888, as an experiment, sixteen 15in bronze torpedoes were ordered from Schwartzkopf of Berlin for trials with these new vessels. These were unsuccessful and the navy returned to its normal supplier, Whitehead. In 1906, all were downgraded to second-class torpedo boats for local defence and to tenders in

1915. *Munin* was sunk as a target in 1926, the other three went to the breakers in 1923.

An anonymous writer of an article published in the Society's 1885 *Journal* expressed satisfaction with the new 113ft torpedo boats. He had found the new 113ft boats were more mobile than the older boats. He noted that the British 113ft craft had a third torpedo tube mounted aft. The author held that more and larger torpedo boats ought to be acquired. He stated that the British Navy had just placed orders with Thornycroft and Yarrow for 40 125ft vessels to be armed with five torpedo tubes, and two Nordenfeldt guns; moreover, the German navy had ordered 127ft torpedo boats from Thornycroft, the Austrian navy 135ft vessels from the same yard, and the Imperial Japanese Navy had ordered 160ft two-screw boats from Yarrow. He noted that since the German navy had 75 torpedo boats, the French 50 and the Russian over 100, Sweden ought to add more torpedo craft to its fleet.

Gondul *and* Gudur

In 1891 parliament released sufficient funds for the construction of two 83 ton (at full load) torpedo boats to be named *Gondul* and *Gudur*. The royal dockyard at Karlskrona was to build both vessels, were the first built entirely to a Swedish design. The dimensions were length 125ft, beam 13ft, and draft 6ft. The machinery to drive a single propeller, and designed to drive the vessels

at over 20kts, comprised a 840ihp triple-expansion engine. A locomotive-type boiler provided the steam. Neither vessel reached her designated speed on trials at full load. The pair were armed with two twin-barelled 25mm machine guns mounted on special platforms on each side of the funnels that slightly exceeded the hull's camber, and two torpedo tubes, the one above the waterline in the bow, the other mounted on the stern. The original plans were for *Gondul* and *Gudur* to carry 18in torpedo tubes but the trials with that calibre of tube were unsuccessful. The Navy Board's engineer held the chief constructor, G Svenson, was responsible for the failure. He, in defence, held that torpedo calibre ought to be suitable for the torpedo boat and not the contrary. The result was that 15in tubes and torpedoes replaced the larger calibre. In 1918 minesweeping equipment replaced the torpedo tubes; in 1922 both were reclassified as tenders and laid up on a minimum maintenance basis. Scrap yards purchased both in 1926.

The Komet *Class*

In July 1895, the Women's League for Sweden's Defence presented the Minister for the Navy with the funds that it had collected for purchase of a new torpedo boat. In that year, the Norwegian Navy had ordered three 130ft torpedo boats, *Hval*, *Delfin* and *Hal* from the German Schichau yard in Elbing. Austria, Japan, China and

Komet underway. (Sjöhistoriska Museét, Stockholm).

Russia had also placed orders with Schichau for the same type. Concern for the increased numbers of German and Russian torpedo boats caused additions to the Swedish defence budgets. In the autumn of 1895, the navy board, perhaps influenced by the Norwegian decision, and having the funds raised by the Women's League, placed an order with the Schichau yard for one torpedo boat of its latest and successful design, to be named *Komet* (fig 7). At that time, Norway and Sweden were united and the relations between the two navies were close. Both had agreed that to ease identity Swedish torpedo boats should have even identification numbers, the Norwegian odd.

Komet was to be the model for a series of eleven torpedo boats to be built in Swedish yards. The dimensions of *Komet* were length 126ft, beam 14ft, draft 7ft. Total displacement at full load was 104 tons. *Komet*'s machinery was to consist of two Schichau locomotive-type boiler, 14 atmospheres and an 850ihp triple-expansion condensing engine, driving a three-bladed bronze propeller. The engine's reversing gear was to be Stephenson's link motion. The coal bunker was to hold 17 tons. Auxiliary machinery included electric generator, fans, pumps and distilling equipment to provide 100 litres of fresh water in one hour. The *Komet*, during four hours sea trials off Elbing, averaged 23kts. The design required *Komet* to have 100 hours radius of action at 10kts.

The original armament was a single, 15in above-water tube in the bow, a single fixed tube aft, one 47mm QF gun on the roof of the conning tower and a second on the stern. In 1901, more modern 37mm guns replaced the two 47mm. The contract with the Elbing yard dated 27 September has 20 hand-written pages. It contains more details of the hull's construction than earlier contracts made with Thornycroft. The hull is to be built of 'good German steel' of the same quality as used for German naval vessels. The hull plating varied in thickness from 2.5 to 4.5mm. The conning tower's plating was to be 3mm thick. The roof was to carry the 47mm gun but its gauge of plate was not specified in the contract.

Komet's complement was 18 men. The space for 12 ratings was behind the bow torpedo tube, for two officers behind the engine room, and for four petty officers in the stern. The wardroom was to have two sofas that would serve as bunks, and 'polished walnut siding with cypress mirrors'. Schichau was also to provide a tea service, a coffee pot, a coffee grinder, three soup plates, twelve other plates and two spittoons. The petty officer's mess had four bunks. Schichau supplied all the equipment for the galley including frying pans. The officers and seamen were to have separate heads.

Trials in Swedish waters began in August 1896 and continued until October. King Oscar II, having been trained as a naval officer, was on board for one of the October runs. *Komet* was adapted for minesweeping during the First World War, became a tender in 1922, and was sold for scrap in 1926.

Between 1896 and 1901, parliament authorised the construction of eleven torpedo boats, based on the Schichau draughts. The first three, *Blixt*, *Meteor* and *Stjerna* had the same dimensions and armament as the prototype. Yarrow supplied two water-tube 14-atmosphere

boilers, in place of Schichau's locomotive type. The triple-expansion engine placed between the two boiler rooms developed 1200ihp. The maximum speed reached by these three was 23.91kts. All became minesweepers after 1918 and were downgraded to patrol craft in 1918. *Stjerna* was broken up in 1937, the other two in 1947.

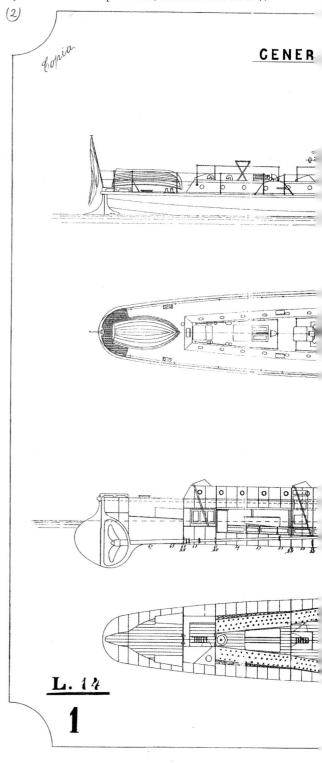

The Karlskrona yard built the second batch named *Orkan*, *Bris* and *Vind* in the years 1898-1900. All were identical to the *Blixt* series and made over 24kts on speed trials. All were gone by 1937. *Virgo* and *Mira*, product of the Karlskrona dockyard in 1901 and 1902, had balanced rudders and a modified stern. *Mira* had no bow torpedo tube, but one mounted on the forecastle, the other on the stern. Neither made more than 23kts. *Virgo* had the above-water bow tube and the single tube on the stern. In 1921, both became minesweepers. In 1935, the department of Customs and Revenue acquired *Mira* to use in the suppression of the illegal import of spirits from the

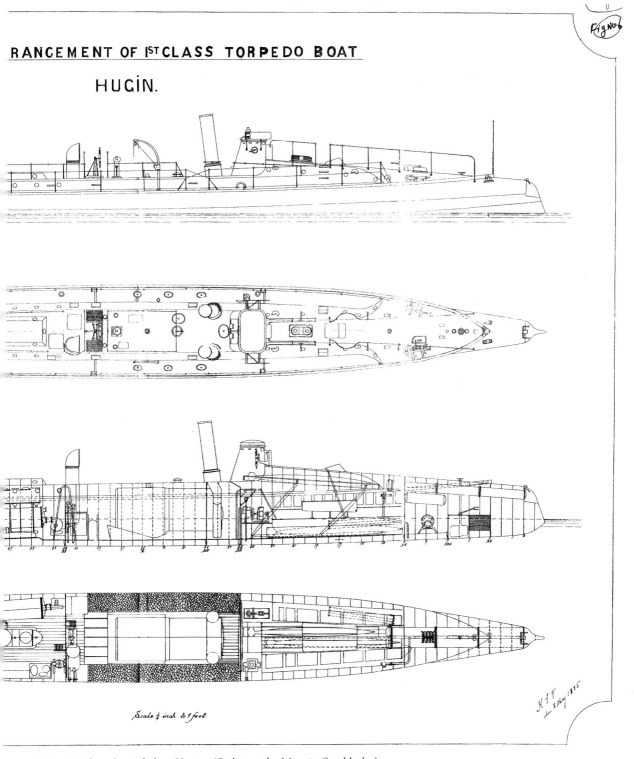

RANCEMENT OF ISTCLASS TORPEDO BOAT

HUGIN.

Scale ⅛ inch to 1 foot

Figure 6. Plan of torpedo boat Hugin. (Sjöhistoriska Museét, Stockholm).

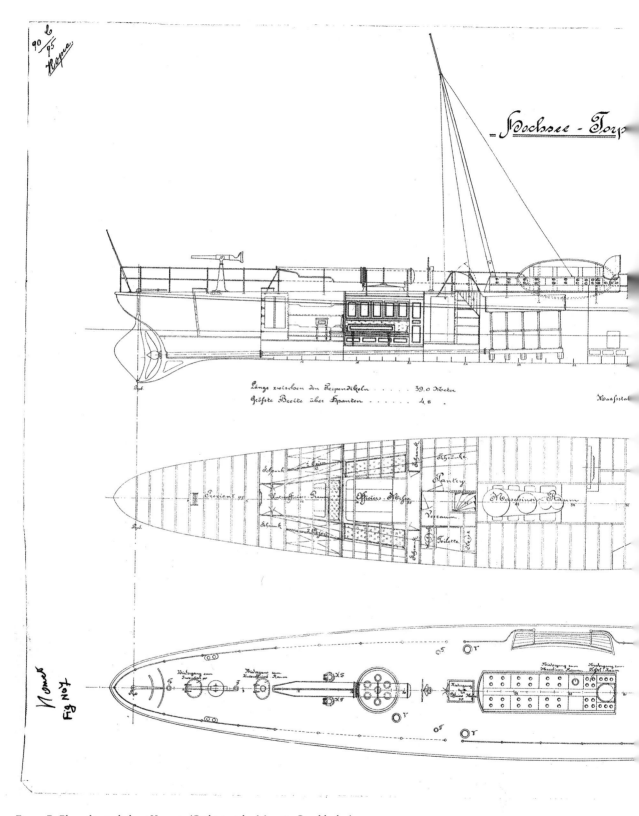

Figure 7. Plan of torpedo boat Komet. (Sjöhistoriska Museét, Stockholm).

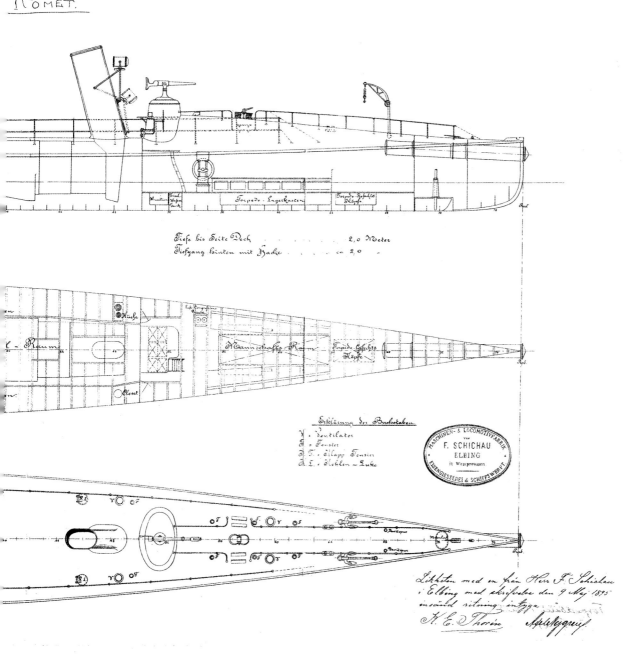

Baltic countries and Finland. The department had no objections to the removal of the torpedo tubes, but insisted that the two 37mm guns would be retained. The customs believed that the sight of guns would encourage smugglers to surrender. *Mira* returned to the navy in 1940 and was sold for scrap in 1943.

In 1901, parliament authorised the construction of three more *Komet* class torpedo boats. The navy board accepted the Bergsund yard's bid to build *Orion* and *Sirius* and the Goteborg Lindholm Works offered to lay down *Kapella*. All had slightly fuller bows than their predecessors, and at full load displaced 96 tons. Minesweeping gear replaced the deck torpedo tube at the end of the war. *Kapella* was stricken in 1936, *Sirius* went for scrap in 1942 and *Orion* lasted until 1947.

The Plejad Class

The Navy Board's 1899 report stated that the fleet's torpedo boat arm consisted of fifteen first-class, and eleven second-class vessels. To bring the strength to the 1892 recommended numbers, the fleet needed fourteen more. In its 1901 report the board's construction committee recommended that the navy's torpedo boats ought to be larger vessels than the *Komet* or *Blixt* class, and able to operate the 18in torpedo developed by Whitehead. The board accepted he committee's recommendation, proposing to cabinet that the navy acquire an example of the latest type of torpedo boat developed for one of the major navies. The vessel purchased would again be a prototype for torpedo boats to be built in Sweden, adapted to meet Swedish service conditions.

Following investigations, the board concluded that the 106 ton torpedo boat, built for the French navy by Normand of Le Havre was the most suitable available (fig 8). Normand had built several for the French navy. In 1902, the cabinet agreed to the purchase of one torpedo boat and in November, a year later, parliament released funds to buy a torpedo boat from the French yard. The contract, dated November 1903, was signed by Augustin Normand in January 1904. The name of the vessel was to be *Plejad*, and the others of this class were also to bear stars' names. The Karlskrona Royal Dockyard, the Bergsund and Gotaverken yards were to build sixteen *Plejad*-type boats between 1904 and 1910.

The dimensions of the prototype *Plejad* were as follows: length overall 132ft, beam 14ft, draft 8½ ft. The displacement at full load was 106 tons. The contract with Normand, in contrast to the Schichau agreement, included a schedule to show the weights in kilograms of those items to be supplied by builder and those to be furnished by the Swedish Navy Board. For example: Normand to supply propelling machinery, spare parts and tools equal to 37,331kg, the Board torpedo tubes, guns, boats, and the furnishings for officers, petty officers and men's accommodation, including the heads. Presumably the French type was unacceptable to

Launch of Plejad *at Normand's yard Le Havre* (Sjöhistoriska Museét, Stockholm).

Plejad *class torpedo boat*. (Sjöhistoriska Museét, Stockholm).

Swedish seamen. The contract specified that steel used for the frames and plating was to be the same quality as that used in the French navy. All plating was to be lap-riveted. The conning tower's plating was to be 4mm thick. *Plejad*'s machinery comprised a 2000ihp condensing triple-expansion engine and two Normand water-tube boilers these covered 17kg pressure with fireproof insulation and provided the steam for the main engines, auxiliaries and the steam steering gear. The water tubes could be galvanised. The boilers water capacity was 1480 litres. Exhaust steam from auxiliaries was to be condensed. The engine room contained an evaporator to supply emergency fresh water. The coal bunker could hold 17 tons of coal, or 20 tons of briquettes used by the French navy.

The single rudder's plating was to be galvanised. Normand was to provide two four-bladed propellers, the one of steel, the other of bronze. Presumably, the steel would be used during the northern winters when ice was prevalent. Merchant vessels trading in the Baltic, at winter's onset, made a practice of exchanging bronze propellers for steel.

During the three hours trials off Le Havre, *Plejad*, at full load, attained a maximum speed of 26kts. Her radius of action at 14kts was about 1500nm. *Plejad* had one 18in above-water torpedo tube in the bow and a trainable second tube on the stern. When fully armed, the bow torpedo compartment carried two extra 18in torpedoes. Single 37mm guns were mounted on the forecastle and abaft the trainable torpedo

tube. The complement was two officers, four petty officers and 19 men.

Plejad arrived in Swedish waters in August 1905. A year later, parliament authorised the construction of *Castor* and *Pollux* by the Karlskrona dockyard, both exact copies of the prototype. In 1908, Gotaverken and Bergsund laid down *Iris*, *Thetis*, *Spica* and *Astrea*. In 1909, Gotaverken completed *Antares*, *Arcturus*, *Altair* and *Argo*; Bergsund *Polaris*, *Perseus*, *Regulus* and *Rigel*. In 1910, as a make-work project, the Karlskrona yard built the last two, *Vega* and *Vesta*, in which 57mm guns replaced the 37mm.

During the First World War, from 1914 until the end of 1917, the *Plejad* class vessels were continuously engaged in neutrality patrols or escort duties in Swedish waters. They were not the best seaboats because they tended to plough through the short waves of the Baltic rather than riding them. In heavy weather, the watchkeeping officer and the helmsman had to lash themselves to the open bridge to stay on board.

Neutrality patrols caused incidents with the Imperial German Navy. In November 1915, when British steamer *Thelma* was under escort of *Pollux* in the sound, a German destroyer attempted to force *Thelma* into international waters. *Pollux* took action by placing herself between the German ship and *Thelma* to end interference. In January 1916, *Castor*, commanded by Prince Wilhelm, the younger son of King Gustav V, prevented two German naval vessels from forcing the British *F. D. Lambert* from the buoyed channel off Falsterbo. In July

1916, *Polaris* prevented the seizure by German destroyers of the *George Allen* and *Ambassador* at the Sound's southern entrance. At the end of the war the whole *Plejad* class were converted to minesweepers and laid up. At the beginning of 1939, surveys of *Argo*, *Antares*, *Castor*, *Pollux*, *Regulus*, *Rigel*, *Vega*, and *Vesta*, revealed that all were only fit for scrap.

During the Second World War, *Astrea*, *Iris*, *Spica*, and *Thetis*, from 1942 to 1944 were stationed on Vanern, Sweden's largest lake, as an anti-invasion force under military command. In 1944, *Astrea* and the *Komet* class *Orion*, assisted a Danish Great Belt ice-breaking train ferry in its escape from a German M class minesweeper to Swedish waters at the Sound's

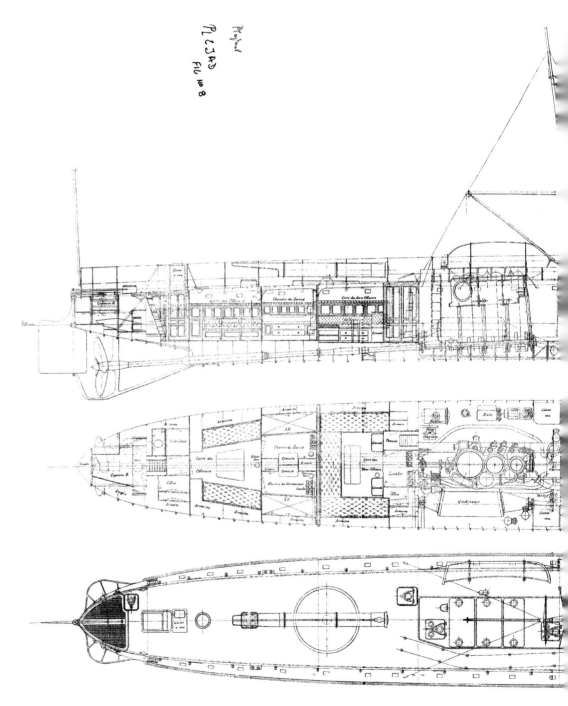

Figure 8. Plan of torpedo boat Plejad. (Sjöhistoriska Museét, Stockholm).

northern end, by placing themselves between the escaping Dane and the German vessel. They then escorted the Dane to Helsingborg. At the end of 1945, all the remaining *Plejad* class torpedo boats, except *Iris*, went for scrap. This latter vessel was used until 1947 to recover practice torpedoes fired by the motor torpedo boat squadrons.

The Torpedo Boat Destroyers – Mode *and* Magne

The development of the torpedo from the late 1860's had enabled small fast vessels to make attacks on large vessels such as battleships and large cruisers. Steel nets

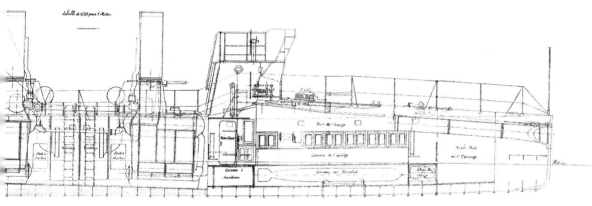

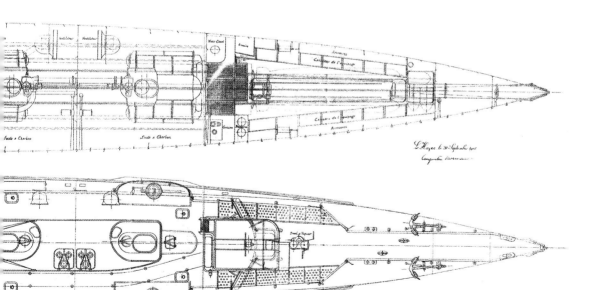

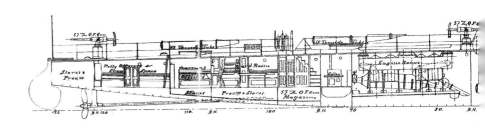

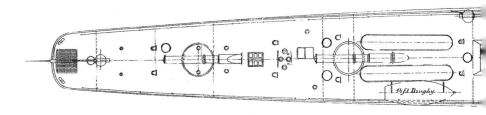

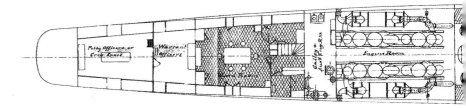

Figure 9. *Plan of torpedo boat destroyer* Mode. (Sjöhistoriska Museét, Stockholm).

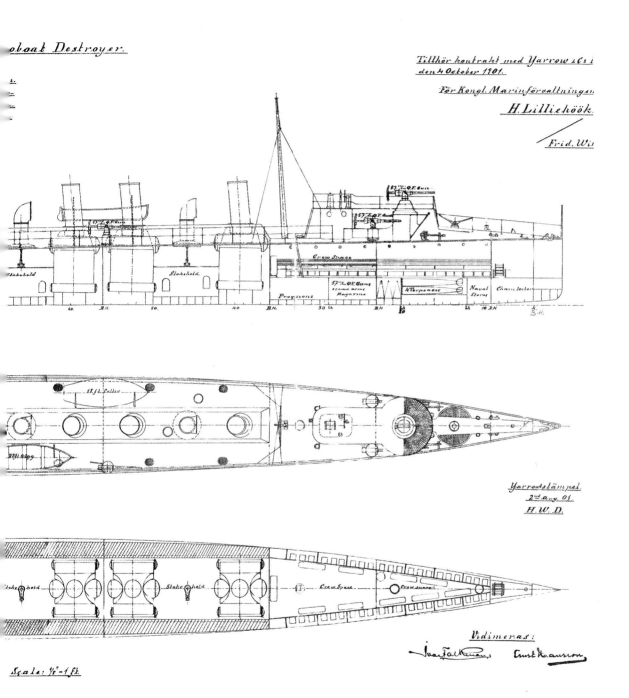

hung over both sides of an anchored vessel gave some protection, but made any rapid movements difficult. Small calibre guns were the best defence for major units against small torpedo boats. Nonetheless, major navies in the nineteenth century's closing years began to construct fast, better-armed vessels to combat the torpedo boat. In 1886 the British navy had begun to build such larger, fast craft armed with a 4in gun that came to be known as torpedo gunboats, and these evolved into 'torpedo boat destroyers' (TBDs) in the American and British navies. Destroyers were also to take over the role of the torpedo boat.

The Swedish Navy Board, aware of the British development, began studies about the size of TBD or 'hunter' (the name given to this type in Sweden) suitable for scouting for the fleet. They were to have a speed of 30-31kts with 15 tons of coal on board, bunkers for a further 80, good sea keeping qualities and not to exceed 350 tons. The plan was to follow earlier precedents, buy the most suitable vessel abroad, and have copies built in Swedish yards with improvements on the original design.

According to the Thornycroft records, in 1899 the Navy Board had begun negotiations with the yard as well as Beardmore's and Yarrow's. In September 1899, Thornycroft's representative, S W Barnaby, had submitted an offer to the Navy Board for a 30kt destroyer. In January 1900, Thornycroft requested leave to amend its offer, stating that as a result of 'recent experience gained on trials of six 30-knots destroyers we have just completed for the Japanese – show improvements can be made in machinery – to guarantee a speed of 31 knots'. Apparently, as the Navy Board was unfamiliar with the Thornycroft boiler, the makers desired an opportunity of proving its worth. The price for the Thornycroft vessel was '£54,500 ex armament'. The Board placed no order owing to fund shortages.

In July 1901, the Navy Board asked Thornycroft to tender again for alternatively 30, 31 and 32kt vessels. In August, the firm offered three alternative designs, 'a 30-knot vessel similar to those built for the British and Japanese navies, or a copy of HMS *Albatross* but with larger boilers, or a 31-knot vessel'. The prices were £50,000, £52,000 and £60,000, delivery in 15 to 18 months. Barnaby wrote on 23 August 1901 from Stockholm that the 'matter looks hopeful' noting he had special relations with the Board. Thornycroft asked him to obtain the prices quoted by competing yards. Five days later, Barnaby called John Thornycroft and his fellow directors that 'in spite of some adjustments in the price, the offer of a £48,000 vessel from Poplar (the Yarrow yard) had been accepted'. The Chiswick yard's price was £52,250.

The *Naval Sciences Journal* for 1901's autumn reported that parliament had approved the expenditure of 1,212,000 kronor for the acquisition of a torpedo-boat destroyer to be named *Mode* (fig. 9). In addition, that the best offer came from that 'world-famous builder of torpedo boats and destroyers, Yarrow & Co of England – delivery will be made at the latest by 14 November next year'. Yarrow had built two experimental vessels for the British Navy in 1893, and the *Sokol*, the first to exceed 30kts, for the Imperial Russian Navy in 1905. Another

reason, besides the lower price, for the Navy Board's decision to place the order with Yarrow may have been familiarity with the Yarrow straight watertube boiler, whereas it had no experience of the Thornycroft-Schulz boiler with its curved tubes.

The contract between the Royal Swedish Naval Board and 'Messrs. Yarrow & Co. Ltd., Engineers & Shipbuilders of Poplar, London' was signed on 4 October 1901. The agreement's terms specified that Yarrow was to build 'one twin-screw torpedo-boat destroyer as described in the specification annexed and accompanying drawing (fig. 6) for $48,300'. The dimensions were:

Length Overall	220ft 3in
Beam	20ft 6in
Depth Amidships	13ft 2in

Speed during a continuous run of 3 hours carrying a load of 35 tons – 31kts
Total displacement at full load 453 tons

The speed trials were to be carried out in the Thames Estuary's deep waters. The contract specified 'Penalty & Premium' as follows:

> On trial the average air pressure in ash pan is not allowed to exceed 3 inches. If to obtain a speed of 30 knots, a higher air pressure is required, the vessel shall be subject to rejection. Should speed exceed 31 knots, a premium shall be added to the contract price at the rate of £500 for every entire quarter of knot greater than 31. Should the speed fall below 30 knots, a penalty shall be deducted from the contract price of £500 for every quarter of a not less than 31 knots. Should the speed fall below 30 knots, the vessel shall be subject to rejection.

The Navy Board, after accepting the proposal and examination of the draughts and specifications, required Yarrow to make changes to the stern and strengthen the hull. Yarrow's, in its letter dated 29 November 1901 agreed that 'alterations to the stern and strengthening of the hull desirable'. The board was surely aware of the British Navy's problems with destroyers' lightly constructed hulls. In 1898 the new HMS *Cobra* had broken up in moderate seas.

The specification required the hull 'to be designed for the greatest strength, speed, and manoeuvring power, and of strong steel'. In addition, it was to have 'uniformity of elasticity'. Every plate was to be 'hammered into shape cold'. The stem and stern posts were to be of forged steel, not cast. The hull was to be divided into seven watertight compartments, each to have a steam ejector with a capacity of 80 tons per hour. In addition, Yarrow was to install seven hand pumps to be worked from the deck. The whole deck was strengthened to carry two single 18in torpedo tubes aft and six 57mm QF guns. The turtleback form of the forecastle was held to improve the vessels' seakeeping qualities. Coconut matting was to cover the steel decks aft.

Mode's main engines were two 6000ihp four-cylinder triple-expansion condensing engines driving two 3-bladed bronze screws. The diameter of the high-pressure

Mode, *built by Yarrow & Co., served as a convoy escort until laid up in 1918.* (Sjöhistoriska Museét, Stockholm).

cylinder was to 20½in, the intermediate 31½in and the two low-press cylinders 34in. The engines were to have reversing gears and an arrangement for hand turning. Four Yarrow watertube boilers, coal fired and having a working pressure 'not to exceed 250 lbs', provided the steam for the main engines and auxiliaries. Two boilers had equipment for oil firing 'such as supplied to the Dutch first-class torpedo boats recently delivered'. The coal-bunker could hold 87 tons. The auxiliaries included electric light machinery, air compressor, capstan, evaporator and steering gear.

The complement of 62 comprised four officers, 13 warrant and petty officers and 45 ratings. The commander's quarters were between the wardroom and the petty officer's mess. Four officers were to be accommodated in separate cabins if space was available, or 'in a ward room fitted with berths enclosed by draperies'. The five warrant officers' mess was situated forward of the wardroom and next to the dynamo room. The petty officer's mess was aft of the captain's cabin. The ratings' space was below the conning tower and the turtleback forecastle. The inner hull was to be insulated with cork to make winter conditions bearable.

Mode's sea trials took place in August 1902 close to the Maplin Sands.[2] No armament had been mounted but she carried the equivalent weight. A special crew provided by Yarrow and first-grade coal, and some oil firing enabled *Mode* to reach 6500ihp, 420rpm giving a speed of 32.4kts. However, after arrival in Karlskrona and the installation of the two torpedo tubes, guns and ammunition, on high-

speed trial, *Mode* hardly made 29kts. *Mode* was in commission from arrival in Swedish waters until 1919. Most of her service was escorting merchant vessels in convoy from the northern east coast ports to the entrance to the Sound and Kattegat. These convoys only sailed in daylight hours anchoring well inside territorial waters during night time. In April 1918, *Mode* was laid up and in 1920, placed in minimum care and maintenance. In 1928, she was sunk as a target.

Early in 1904, Parliament agreed to the Navy Board's purchase of a second destroyer similar to *Mode*. It was prudent to consider the type of vessel built by Yarrow's rival, J Thornycroft & Co. of Chiswick, London. In July 1904, the Board accepted Thornycroft's offer to build a destroyer for £50,000. The price was for the completed vessel but without any armament, the name to be *Magne* (fig. 10). The Thornycroft records classify *Magne* as a 'Shirakumo type and as proposed to the Argentine government'. The Thornycroft contract's terms and specifications differ from those of the Yarrow contract for the *Mode*.

Magne's dimensions were: length 216¼ft, beam 20¾ft, draft 8¼ft. The contracted speed was 30.5kts, 7200ihp, displacement at full load 460 tons. The hull plating was to have a tensile strength of 37 to 43 tons per sqin. The contract states that the hull was to be divided into nine compartments by watertight bulkheads and half bulkheads as approved. Bilge ejectors were to be in each 'principal compartment'. The agreement requires a 'conning tower and turtleback of 3/8in mild steel befitted forward'. *Magne's* hull differed from *Mode's* with its longer turtleback, which was more effective in the Baltic's short seas to aid the flow of water over the bow to the scuppers. The hull had a flat stern and a balanced rudder. The two-cylinder steam-steering engine placed in the engine room could be worked from the conning tower, bridge and from the deck aft. The deck plating and lower plates of bulkheads were to be galvinised. The deck and conning tower were to be strengthened to six 57mm guns, one on the conning tower's roof, two alongside the conning tower, two in the waist and one on the stern; in addition, two 18in torpedo tubes aft.

The starboard side was fitted with rails for moving torpedoes stored under the forecastle aft to the torpedo tubes. The Karlskrona dockyard would install all armaments on *Magne*'s arrival. As regards the division and fitting out of the space for the 67-man complement, the particulars contained in the contract are few. It only stipulates that 'suitable accommodation for officers, warrant officers, petty officers are to be arranged'. Adding that 'officers' cabins are to have mahogany fittings and other space fittings are to be of painted white pine', also a seamen's head and urinal and WC for officers use are to be fitted. Steam heating and electric light are to be installed in the crew space, which was to be lined with rock wool.

Magne's machinery comprised two 7200ihp four-cylinder triple-expansion condensing engines driving two three-bladed bronze propellers. (The contract stipulated these must be cast in one piece). The high-pressure cylinder had a diameter of 2in. The diameter of the intermediate lower pressured cylinders were 29½ and 31in respectively. The reversing gear was to be of the continuous motion type. Four Thornycroft Schultz water-tube coal-fired boilers provided the steam. Two boilers had oil-spraying jets. The working pressure was 240lbs per square inch. The bunkers were to hold 80 tons of coal and 16 tons of fuel oil. In addition, there were two extra bunkers in the stoke hold to hold 16 tons of coal. These were not be fitted for the speed trials. *Magne*'s speed at full load was to be 30.5kts and her range 2800 nautical miles at 15kts. On acceptance trials, *Magne* averaged 30.713kts for three hours. The contract contained no penalty or premium clauses for failing to reach, or exceed 30.5kts. Thornycroft was to supply

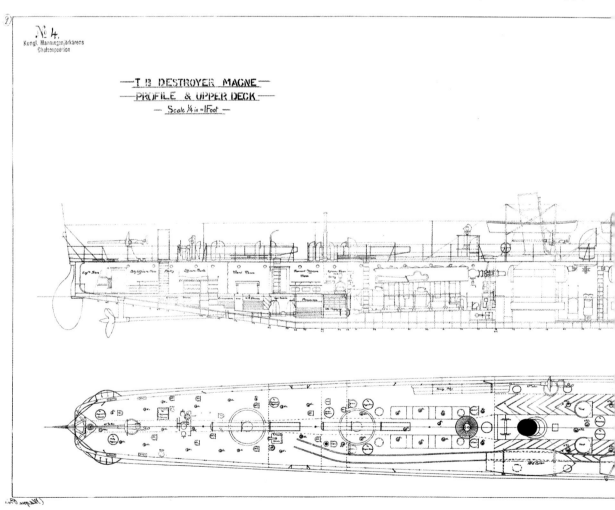

Figure 10. Plan of torpedo boat destroyer Magne. (Sjöhistoriska Museét, Stockholm).

amongst the list of miscellaneous items 'a brass watch bell engraved with the ship's name, thirty life belts, two mops, two camp stools, crockery, cutlery suitable for five officers'. The board was to supply the vessel's boats.

Magne was the last vessel launched at Chiswick Works. After final acceptance, the tug *Little Briton* towed her to Karlskrona for installation of armament. In the summer of 1905 she joined *Mode* on the west coast force during the period of the dissolution of the union with Norway crisis. *Magne* was active in the neutrality patrols and escort duties during the First World War. In 1916, she forced the Russian submarine *Alligator* to leave territorial waters off Gotland. Laid up at the end of 1918 *Magne* was never again commissioned. Struck off the strength in 1936, she was used as a gunnery target and was broken up in 1943.

The Navy Board chose the superior *Magne* as the prototype for the construction of six destroyers between 1907 and 1911. All were to have Yarrow watertube boilers instead of the Thornycroft-Schulz type. In 1908, Kockums of Malmo built *Wale*, *Ragnar* and *Vidar*; and Lindholm of Goteborg, *Sigurd*. All had the same four-cylinder, triple-expansion engines as *Magne*. In the last two of the class,

Hugin, built by Gotaverken and *Munin*, built by Kockums in 1911, Curtis AEG 10,000ihp turbines, replaced the triple expansion engines, but as these were direct drive with 800rpm, the speed increase obtained was only of the order of 1-2kts more than their older sisters. However, the astern turbines on trials gave *Hugin* and *Munin* a maximum speed of 20kts. All were engaged on neutrality patrols and escort service during 1914-18.

In 1916, *Sigurd* prevented German destroyers from seizing a British merchant off Landsort. *Hugin*, in June 1918, fired shots at the German submarine *UB20* that had refused to leave the outer Stockholm Skerries. All were recommissioned during 1939, in October, *Munin* prevented the German auxiliary *Hansestadt Danzig* from interfering with four Finnish merchantmen in Swedish east coast waters. *Wale* and *Hugin* were stricken in 1940 and the rest in 1946.

After the completion of the *Magne* class, the Swedish navy no longer turned to foreign sources for destroyer prototypes. Nonetheless, the navy purchased prototypes for submarines in 1912 and motor torpedo boats in 1940 from Italy. In 1941 the navy had construction drawings for cruisers prepared by an Italian shipyard.

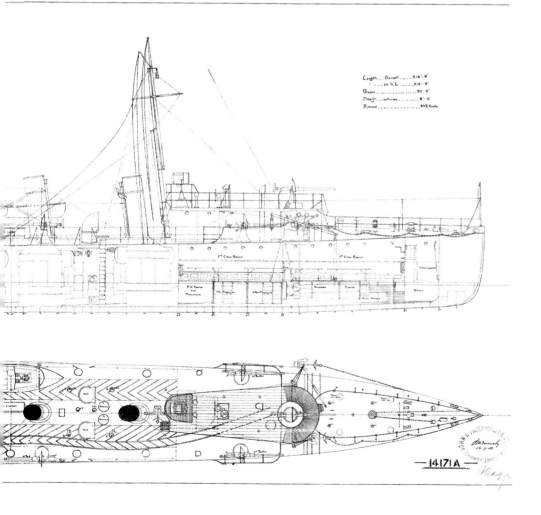

Magne *was the last vessel launched at Thornycroft's Chiswick Works.* (Sjöhistoriska Museét, Stockholm).

Sources

Policies

J Hegland, *Norske, Torpedbatar gjonnom 100ar*, (Oslo: 1973)

R Llindsjo, *Marin Historia*, (Stockholm: 1993)

O Lybeck, *Svenska Flottans Historia*, vol. III, (Malmo: 1945)

P Wedin, *Amiralites Kollegiets Historia*, vol. III, (Malmo: 1977)

Tidskrift – I – Sjovasendet 1870, 1871, 1872, 1874, 1877, 1881, 1885, 1889, 1901, 1902, 1904

A Zettersten, *Svenska Flottans Historia*, vol. 7, (Stockholm: 1886)

Construction Machinery and Armament

Navy Board Contracts- held at Royal Military Records Office, Stockholm

Earle's Shipbuilding	14 January 1872
Thornycroft contract	23 February 1874
" "	4 March 1882
" "	11 December 1883
Schichau Contract	27 September 1895
Normand Contract	2 January 1904
Yarrow Contract	4 October 1901 (& as amended)
Thornycroft Contract	8 July 1904

Thornycroft Archives re: *Magne, Rap* and *Spring* (National Maritime Museum, Greenwich)

Note: Yarrow Poplar records were destroyed during 1939-45.

Other

Borgenstam C. et al, *Jagare*, (Karlsrona: 1989)

Westerlund et al, *Svenska Orlogsfartyg 1855/1905*, (Karlsrona: 1993)

General Bibliography

C Borgenstam, et al, *Attack till sjoss*, (Karlskrona: 1985)

P Ekman, *Havs vargar*, (Jacobstad: 1983)

G Halldin, et al, *Svenskt Skeppsbyggen* (Malmo: 1963)

G Halldin, et al, *Skepps byggmastare*, (Malmo: 1948)

O Lybeck, et al, *Svenska Flottans Historia*, vol. III, (Malmo: 1943)

In addition to the above, correspondence with the late Cmdr J E Olow, RSwN

Notes

[1] The Harvey Otter System comprised canister containing gun cotton towed at speed then swung out at an angle of 45 degrees from the towing vessel to strike the anchored opponent. An illustration in Amiralitets Kollegiets Historia, vol. 4 page 27 shows a French-made towed torpedo, but no information is available about its method of operation.

[2] Ed: Much later the Admiralty refused to accept trials run on the Maplin Mole; the shallow water led to an artificial increase in speed.

SIR WILLIAM WHITE

KCB, FRS, LLD, DSc[1]

As Director of Naval Construction, 1885-1901, Sir William White was responsible for 43 battleships, 26 armoured cruisers, 21 first class protected cruisers, 48 second class, 33 third class and 74 other warships. Here **David K Brown** argues these ships were the best of the period and that White may have been the greatest warship designer of all time.

Introduction

It is 100 years since Sir William White retired from the post of Director of Naval Construction, arguably the greatest warship designer of all time.[2] He was born at Devonport on 2 February 1845, becoming an apprentice in that Dockyard in March 1859 with indentures which bound him for seven years, starting at 3/- per week. He was described as of slight build, very fair and only just reached the minimum height. His first task was helping to convert the sailing three-decker *St George* into a steam-ship with guns on two decks.

In 1864 White won a scholarship to the new Royal School of Naval Architecture and Marine Engineering in South Kensington, passing top of the eight Dockyard entries. White, Elgar and W G John led the academic race for the next three years and there were many other well known names amongst both staff and students. Work at the School lasted from November to April with very long hours. Practical work in the Yards filled the rest of the year, during which students were required to write a 'Diary' which was a factual record of the equipment and procedures in each department of the Yard which would form the basis for tutorials.[3]

Early Achievements

White passed out in 1867, top by a wide margin, and was appointed to the Admiralty as a Third Class Draughtsman, soon becoming professional assistant to Edward Reed, the Chief Constructor. Reed was to acknowledge White's help in writing his Royal Society paper on strength[4] and his book *Shipbuilding in Iron and Steel*.[5]

The capsize of the transport *Perseverance* in 1855 led the Admiralty under Isaac Watts to initiate studies into various aspects of stability. By the time White joined these studies were flourishing and he joined Barnes, Barnaby and John in further work leading to papers to the Institution of Naval Architects (INA).[6] In 1870 White was appointed as Instructor in Naval Architecture at the Royal School, moving with the School to Greenwich in 1873. He was also professional

Sir William White, KCB, FRS, LLD, D Sc. Founder of the Royal College of Naval Constructors and, possibly, the greatest warship designer of all time. (Authors collection).

assistant to Reed's successor, Nathaniel Barnaby, paid as a Second Class Draughtsman plus £2-2-0 for each of two afternoons a week at Greenwich. During 1875 White began to write a book based on his lectures, *The Manual of Naval Architecture*, published in 1877. It is a most readable book with a fine blend of theory and practice; it was translated into four other languages and was revised several times.

Design Work

The report of the 1871 Committee on Designs, set up to review current and future policy in the light of the loss of the *Captain*, was generally favourable, but it was decided to redesign the breastwork battleship *Fury*.[7] The concept of the redesign, now called *Dreadnought*, was Barnaby's but White carried out all the detailed work. This required frequent spells working at Pembroke, where in 1873 he became engaged to Alice Martin, daughter of the Chief Constructor of the Yard.

White was then much involved with the *Inflexible*, first on the initial design, then to Portsmouth for the building and back to the Admiralty where he carried out a vast number of novel calculations for the *Inflexible* Committee. This committee was set up to consider criticisms of the design by Sir Edward Reed and its report justified the design.

Steel Hulls

The potential advantages of steel rather than iron for ship construction had been apparent for some time and increasing amounts had been used in the hulls of warships. The only steel available in quantity was that made by the Bessemer process which in the mid-1870s was too unreliable for use in highly stressed areas.[8] In 1863 the Frenchmen Martin, father and son, adapted Siemens' reverbatory furnace for the manufacture of high-quality steel. The chief constructor at Lorient, de Bussy, decided to build the *Redoutable* almost entirely of this new steel and in 1874 Barnaby and White visited Lorient to see the work in progress. White and de Bussy struck up a lasting friendship.

On their return, Barnaby read a paper to the INA in which he challenged British industry to match the quality of French steel. Riley, the managing director of the Landore works (founded by Siemens), claimed and later demonstrated that their material met all requirements. Steel thus produced had a theoretical strength some 30 per cent greater than iron, but White decided that in the first all-steel ship (*Iris*, designed by White under Barnaby's direction) no thickness should be reduced by more than 15 per cent. Even so, the weight saving was considerable, a major factor in making *Iris* the fastest ship in the world.[9] In 1877 the cost of steel was about double that of iron but prices soon fell and by 1888 iron shipbuilding had died out.

In March 1875 White was given the new title of Assistant Constructor while working on the 'Admiral' class battleships. In 1879 the Argentine Government asked for a new cruiser, the *Almirante Brown*, to be designed by a constructor, and White was allowed to accept the task for a commission of one per cent of the building cost. It was his first independent design and seems to have been very satisfactory; the ship was modernised in 1897 and not scrapped until 1930.

The Royal Corps of Naval Constructors (RCNC)[10]

In the 1870s all Admiralty constructors began as shipwright apprentices in one of the Royal Dockyards.

Formal education was good but extremely competitive with 50 per cent dropping out at the end of each year. At the beginning of the sixth year a few of the very brightest were selected to take the naval architecture course at Greenwich. The success rate was poor; between 1873 and 1890 only nine out of twenty-one students reached an acceptable standard. Even when they passed out promotion was very slow; the work of a junior assistant was boring and many resigned.

Early in 1880 White submitted a memo which suggested improvements in entry standards, education and, above all, career development. This memo was amplified in August 1880. White's scheme was largely based on the French *Genie Maritime* but with a shift of emphasis from a purely theoretical base.

White distinguished between the graduate from Greenwich and the technician in the Dockyards, who, though well educated by the standards of the day, was below the Greenwich level. Both categories were to have separate lines of promotion instead of fighting directly for jobs on a basis which was almost bound to be unfair to one or the other. White envisaged an interchange between constructors and similar men in industry to mutual benefit. He was particularly keen on frequent moves between the Admiralty design office and the Dockyards. The Controller gave enthusiastic support and the Royal Corps officially came into being under an Order in Council signed by Queen Victoria on 23 August 1883.[11]

Armstrongs

By the time the Royal Corps was set up, White had left the Admiralty to work at Armstrong, Mitchell & Co. His Admiralty salary was £600 pa plus a lecturing fee of £51. Armstrongs paid him £2,000 pa plus 2/- per ton for all warships built at Elswick and 1/- per ton for merchant ships. During the next two years at Armstrongs, White designed the protected cruisers *Naniwa* and *Takachiho* for Japan, the torpedo cruisers *Panther* and *Leopard* for Austria, two small cruisers for Spain, the *Dogali* for Italy and two Chinese cruisers. They were all highly regarded and did much to

Inflexible. White was much involved with her design and with demonstrating her safety to a Committee. (Authors collection).

Repulse of the Royal Sovereign *class, the first class of battleship for which White was responsible.*(Authors collection).

enhance White's reputation, particularly for the design of fast, heavily armed cruisers.[12]

White was the author of three influential articles to *The Times* in 1884 on 'The State of the Navy', dealing mainly with cruiser policy.

Director of Naval Construction

Nathaniel Barnaby resigned in 1885, fed up of quarrels with Reed.[13] The First Lord, Lord George Hamilton, asked White to return and, following protracted negotiations, White became DNC on 1 August 1885. White accepted a very considerable drop in pay to £1500 pa without bonuses. Philip Watts was released by the Admiralty to take White's place at Armstrongs and White was to be available for consultation for the remainder of his original five-year contract. (This was to give rise to accusations of conflict of interest, but there is no evidence to justify such charges). Before leaving, Barnaby and White wrote a joint memo expressing concern over the building programme and the *Nile* in particular.

It had been agreed that White should also have the title of Assistant Controller and that the Director of Dockyards should be responsible to him. White planned an extensive review of the management of the Dockyards with the aim of separating their function of a naval base from the civilian management of shipbuilding and repair. He proposed that the Chief Constructor should become the general manager of the civilian side. A Dockyard could not be run in quite the same way as a commercial yard since it was subject to the scrutiny of Parliament. He brought in a new accounting system with an independent audit office. All this was approved and came into force on 1 February 1886 but, that very same day, a new government under Gladstone took office with the Marquis of Ripon as First Lord. Ripon did not like White's plan and removed the Dockyards from his authority, putting them under Elgar.

Though Elgar was a classmate of White, they disliked each other intensely; Elgar had been a strong supporter of Reed in his battles with Barnaby and White saw the change as a breach of the agreement for which he had sacrificed so much. With hindsight, one may well think that White was over-loaded and hence that the separation of the Dockyards was correct.

The year 1886 was a tragic one, with the death of his first wife in November. Only a month later White himself nearly died when he went for a trial dive in the French submarine *Nautilus*. They got stuck on the bottom off Tilbury and White took charge, rocking the boat till it broke free. White was encouraging the development of all-steel armour and increasing the capacity for its manufacture.

The Naval Defence Act

These preparatory moves were vital to the new building programme which White saw as essential. In June 1887 White, aged 42, sent a memo to the Board, drawing attention to the increasing number of obsolete ships and recommending a scrap-and-build programme costing £9 million. The First Naval Lord and the Controller proposed an alternative programme and there was angry debate in the Admiralty, Parliament and the press. The report on the manoeuvres of 1888 given to Parliament in February 1889 was the last straw, showing that the Navy was well below the traditional 'Two Power Standard'. Eventually, in March 1889, the Naval

Defence Act was put to Parliament, authorising the building of seventy ships up to 1894 at a total cost of £21.5 million; an enormous sum in those days.

Naval Defence Act Ships:

8 First class, 2 second class battleships
9 First class cruisers, 33 smaller cruisers
18 Torpedo Gun Boats

There were special and very novel financing arrangements by which money unspent in one year could be carried forward to the next, contrary to normal Parliamentary accounting.[14] The bulk of the ships were to be built in the Royal Dockyards but White's detail planning showed that slips would not be available for all of them, his sense of detail extended to the need for more lifting gear at Pembroke.

Royal Sovereign

In August 1888 there was a meeting of the Board to consider the requirements for the new first class battleships. The First Sea Lord, Hood, wanted an improved *Nile*, a low-freeboard turret ship.[15] He was surprised to find that these improvements brought the displacement to 16,000 tons with a 25 per cent increase in cost over *Nile*. White developed further studies, including barbette ships for another meeting in November. The main topics for debate were:

Turret ship versus barbette
Guns, main and secondary, and their disposition.
Freeboard (Top weight virtually precluded a high free-
    board turret ship)
Armour arrangement (Single or two citadels)
Speed.

Both professional and naval opinion was divided on all these issues, but eventually there was general agreement that seven ships should be high freeboard barbette ships with a twin 13.5in mounting at each end.[16] The secondary armament was to consist of ten 6in guns, widely distributed. The armour belt was to be 18in compound with an upper belt of 4in steel backed by coal bunkers which would stop any high capacity (HE) shell and make it unlikely that the 3in deck would be hit by an intact projectile. Most people saw these ships as a great success, though the advocates of turret ships and those wanting thicker armour were critical. Reed was particularly strong in his criticism. Eventually, the Board took the unusual step of permitting, even encouraging, White to read a very detailed paper on their design to the INA (Reed was given a copy in advance). It was one of the longest and most savage debates held by the Institution. Every point made by Reed was demolished by the result of full-scale trials, by model tests or by exact and well proven calculation[17]. White's design office was highly professional and world leaders in every aspect. Reed never again saw fit to criticise White and his team and, indeed was sometimes to support him.

The cost of the powerful secondary battery was not always understood. The ten 6in and their equipment weighed 500 tons compared with 140 in *Nile* and needed about 140 men in action. The four main deck guns were in casements weighing 20 tons each (the six upper deck guns were in light shields until 1902-05, when casemates were added).

This class was never tried in action but the very similar Japanese *Fuji* and *Yashima* did well in the Russo-Japanese war. There were two weak points which were not recognised at the time and hence were perpetuated in later classes. There was an ammunition passage running from the forward to the after barbette which could transmit an explosion. Partly to accommodate this passage, there were centreline bulkheads in the machinery spaces, which could cause large heel angles in the event of underwater damage.[18]

The last first class battleship was *Hood*, a low freeboard turret ship, which was a failure. The two second class ships were diminutives of the *Royal Sovereign* with 10in guns and, within their limits were quite successful. A third second class battleship, *Renown*, was part of the 1892 programme and marked a great advance. Her armour belt was 8in of the new Harvey cemented armour, equivalent to 12¾in of compound. The middle deck, level with the top of the belt was 2in thick but the protective deck was sloped down at the sides, 3in thick, to support the bottom of the belt. (Fig) The great advantage of this arrangement was that any shell penetrating the belt would meet the deck at 45° and almost certainly fail. This arrangement became standard in most navies until the end of the Second World War; one of the last ships with this style of protection was the *Bismarck*, where it was fairly successful at close range. Much of White's ideas

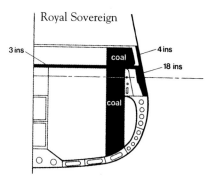

Diagram showing the disposition of armour. White's arrangement for Renown was used up to the end of the First World War in the RN, and in the Second World War by Bismarck. (Authors collection).

Bacchante. *One of White's armoured cruisers.* (Authors collection).

on protection were derived from trials on protective structures, both above and below water, built into the old battleship *Resistance*, which was fired on in trials from 1885 to 1889.

In March 1890 White married Annie Marshall, daughter of an old Newcastle friend.

Renown may be seen as the definitive White battleship though there were many improvements in later classes.[19] One improvement rarely noted is the reduction in hull weight from class to class. This is best represented by (Hull weight/Product of dimensions LBD).

Hull Weight Reduction

Class	Hull weight (W_H)	WH/L.B.D x 10⁻³
Renown	5040	4.25
Majestic	5650	4.7
Canopus	5310	4.2
Formidable	5650	4.21
Bulwark	5625	4.3
Duncan	5400	4.13
K E VII	5900	4.11
L Nelson	5720	4.01

Just over half the hull weight was main structure, the remainder including supports and seats, pumping and ventilation, paint etc. It is tempting but incorrect to think that savings in hull weight can be used to increase armament. Both cost considerations and upper deck layout will usually preclude such a trade-off. Some increase in armour would be possible, and a lighter ship is easier to power.

There followed eight *Majestics* with an 8in Harvey belt and the new 12in gun. Then came the *Canopus* class with a shallow draught and a thinner belt of 6in Krupp, equivalent to 8in Harvey. Three *Formidables* and five *Londons* were generally similar to *Canopus* but with a 9in belt. The six *Duncans* were a knot faster and 1000 tons lighter with a 7in belt. The eight *King Edward VII* ships were designed while White was sick and his place was taken by H E Deadman but they may be seen as the last of the White style.

Twenty-five of the battleships from *Majestic* to *Lord Nelson* were built in Royal Dockyards, with an average building time of 36.6 months, Portsmouth managing an average of 32.6 months. The 14 built in commercial averaged 42.9 months. The difference was largely due to the lack of strikes in the Dockyards but this, in turn, was associated with better management at both professional and foreman level; a tribute to White's reforms.

Cruisers

The development of the cruiser from White's *Iris* is fairly straightforward. The earlier ships were designed on the protective deck *system*. Emphasis is needed on 'system' since protection depended not only on the deck itself but on a complex arrangement of coal bunkers to preserve both buoyancy and stability in the event of damage causing flooding.[20] A few bigger ships were given a belt but with compound armour there was no weight available to protect any large area of the ship. Once cemented armour, Harvey then Krupp, became available, the armoured cruiser was reborn with a 6in belt capable of resisting all high capacity shells and any shell up to 6 inch.

White's reputation at Armstrongs for fast, heavily armed cruisers led some to criticise his Admiralty designs. White justified his designs pointing out their endurance, the extent of the armour and the final clincher that he gave the Board what they asked for![21]

Torpedo Craft

White's first attempt at an anti torpedo boat vessel was the Torpedo Gun Boat, a scaled-down cruiser. The first was *Rattlesnake* laid down 1885 of 550 tons and 19kts. These ships were derided as too slow to catch a torpedo boat even when *Speedy* reached 21kts, 6kts slower than the early destroyers. However, in 'a moderate sea' *Speedy* beat the destroyer *Havock*.

The torpedo boat destroyer depended on light weight for its success and White realised that this style of construction needed specialist firms with and integrated team of designer and builder. With experience, standard designs from the Admiralty were preferred.

The Royal Yacht Victoria and Albert

The design of the yacht started in 1897 and she was completed in dry dock at Pembroke. When she was floated out she lolled, heeled due to negative metacentric height. An investigation showed that she was 700 tons overweight, 20ins deeper in the water with a metacentric height of 3in in the load condition and less at lighter draught.[22] Drastic changes were made; the forecastle and one layer of superstructure were removed, the masts and funnels were lowered, the beam was increased by wooden girdling and ballast was placed in the double bottoms.

She now had a metacentric height of 2ft 6in and was safe to go anywhere.[23] White accepted responsibility and was gently reprimanded by the Board. In Parliament he was defended by his old enemy Reed. As a result White had a nervous breakdown and when he returned to office in September 1900 he was unable to delegate the most trivial tasks, infuriating his staff until he retired in 1901.[24]

Dreadnought

White had always believed in the smallest ship for the job and, rightly, saw that *Dreadnought*, though not much bigger than previous ships, would start a building race leading to much bigger ships making existing ships obsolete. He also believed in a powerful secondary armament, incorrectly reading the lessons of the Russo-Japanese War.[25]

Achievement

As DNC White was responsible for 43 battleships, 26 armoured cruisers, 21 first class protected cruisers, 48 second class, 33 third class and 74 other warships. They were the best ships of the day, a statement which is justified by the frequency with which they were copied, particularly by UK commercial yards building for export. One may see the Russo-Japanese war as fought between a Japanese fleet whose major vessels were largely copies of White's fleet and a Russian fleet of French style.[26]

White's ships were worn out and obsolescent by the time the First World War broke out and only used in subsidiary roles. However, of the ten White battleships mined or torpedoed, all but one capsized. The one that did not, *Irresistible*, shows why. The centreline bulkhead between the engine rooms was destroyed in the explosion

A fine builder's model of Latona, *a second class Naval Defence Act cruiser.* (Authors collection).

whereas in the other ships the asymmetric flooding led to rapid capsize. His other design error, the fore and aft ammunition passage, has already been mentioned.

His gifts as a designer have obscured his management skills. His re-organisation of the Dockyards, conception of the Royal Corps and the meticulous planning of the building of the Naval Defence Act ships show him at his best. Even the greatest men have their faults but White had very few. His biggest failing was in bringing on a successor.[27] He is even alleged to have told Controllers that there was no one good enough. If this is true, and I doubt it, it was White's fault. This can be linked with his inability to delegate and obsession with detail, both symptoms of depression. Finally, Phillip Watts came back from Armstrongs. White had a difficult relationship with successive Controllers; they were bright young admirals on the way to the top, but however brilliant, White could advance no further.

As a young man White complained that Reed had not given him enough credit for his work on structure. As DNC White hardly ever gave any credit to his staff even though he could not possibly have written the numerous papers published in his name as well as all his official work. There are virtually no accounts describing White as a person other than Manning, and that was severely criticised in a review by Abel, supported by Berry. Let the last word lie with a younger constructor, Lloyd Woolard:[28]

'Sir William White, like all of us, had certain foibles, but he has always appeared to me to be one of the great of the profession and one could not be in his company without respecting his powerful personality. He had a phenomenal memory and his assistants, after specialising in some branch of the work, were often disconcerted by finding that Sir William knew more about it than they did. He had a perfect command of the King's English in both the spoken and written word; his style was heavy, perhaps a little reminiscent of Gibbon. But no one could ever misunderstand him. A great man.'

He died suddenly on 27 February 1913.

Notes

1 F Manning, *The Life of Sir William White*, (London: John Murray, 1923). This book was commissioned by Lady White after her husband's death. It is reasonably impartial but Manning was not familiar with technology and failed in some aspects to give White enough credit. It would seem that many of the private papers were destroyed when the book was complete.

2 My other heroes were Sir Stanley Goodall (*Warship 1997-8*) and Sir Rowland Baker (*Warship 1995*)

3 This was still a major item in my training ca 1950.

4 E J Reed, 'On the Unequal Distribution of Weight and Support in Ships', *Phil Trans*, London, 1871.

5 It was most unusual in those days for senior men to acknowledge help from anyone. Later, White rarely mentioned the help he had received.

6 D K Brown, 'British Warship Design Methods 1860-1905', *Warship International*, Toledo, I/1995.

7 The bulk of the calculations for this committee were carried out by White and John.

8 D K Brown, *Warrior to Dreadnought*, (London: Chatham, 1997), p74-5; Sir N Barnaby. 'Iron and Steel for Shipbuilding', *Trans INA*, 1875.

9 It is surprising that Manning hardly mentions White's great involvement in the introduction of steel, see Manning, *op cit*, p. 56.

10 See D K Brown, *A Century of Naval Construction*, (London: Conway Maritime Press, 1983) for fuller account of the formation of the RCNC.

11 This writer was in charge of the Centenary celebrations in 1983.

12 P Brook, *Warships for Export*, (Gravesend: World Ship Society, 1999).

13 Reed was married to Barnaby's sister and professional disagreement carried over into the domestic scene.

14 For a fuller account of the Naval Defence Act see Brown, *Warrior to Dreadnought*.

15 The old Coles meaning of turret, not the modern shielded barbette.

16 There was a preference for a new 12in gun but it would not be ready in time.

17 White was formidable in debate and very rarely beaten. I would give Beresford the sole victory in discussion of watertight doors in 1896.

18 A very crude calculation suggests one wing space flooded would lead to a heel of about 8°. A second space flooded would reduce the stability and more than double the heel, often causing capsize.

19 *Renown* was Fisher's favourite flagship. (He then said the lightest practicable big gun and the heaviest secondary gun).

20 Brown, *Warrior to Dreadnought*, p. 113 explains the protective deck system.

21 There is some evidence that this was not entirely true and that he frequently presented the Board with a fait accompli, completing the design before the Board had agreed the requirements.

22 Much of the extra weight was over thick cement insulation in the Royal Apartments.

23 The author had to certify her safe to be towed to the scrap yard.

24 It has been suggested by Dr P Brook that several of White's early periods of sick leave were due to depression. He instances 1869, 1888, 1894 and 1902 as well as that following the debacle on the Royal Yacht.

25 D K Brown, 'Technical Lessons of the Russo-Japanese War', *Warship 1996*.

26 It was our editor, Anthony Preston, who first described this war as White against the French.

27 Modern management schools would probably suggest that he should have developed at least three possible successors to allow for accidents and leave a choice.

28 Graduated 1904.

THE CONTRE-TORPILLEURS OF THE LE FANTASQUE CLASS

The six ships of the *Le Fantasque* class are generally considered to represent the high point of *contre-torpilleur* construction between the world wars. **John Jordan** examines their origins in the context of the tactical concepts which dominated the *Marine Nationale* of the 1920s and 1930s, and the way in which their design evolved from their four-funnelled predecessors.

As naval historians we are in the happy position of being able to apply hindsight to our analysis of the merits and defects of particular concepts and designs. It is therefore easy to forget that not only were these insights unavailable to those who were responsible for them but that, in the absence of experience, concepts have a tendency to acquire an irresistible momentum of their own. So it was with the *contre-torpilleur* of the inter-war *Marine Nationale*, a concept which grew from a projection of a particular wartime scenario which, failed to materialise.

Subsequent analysis of these revolutionary vessels has tended to concentrate on their shortcomings when put to the test in wartime in tactical contexts for which they were not originally designed. Should we really be surprised that ships optimised for high-speed artillery engagements in Mediterranean waters lacked the hull strength, endurance, manoeuvrability and anti-submarine warfare (ASW) weaponry required for arduous low-speed convoy escort duties in the North Atlantic theatre?

L'Audacieux dressed overall at Royan on 10 May 1936, shortly after she entered service with the 2ᵉ Escadre (Brest). Note the black face of the range clock on the forward face of the upper bridge. (Marius Bar).

L'Indomptable departs Royan on 11 May 1936. Note the prominent brass 'guttering' around no.3 and no.4 mountings, which was used to stow ready-use rounds prior to action. It was not fitted to no.5 mounting so as not to obstruct access to the quarterdeck. (Marius Bar).

Unfortunately this line of analysis has tended to obscure more valid criticism of the extent to which these ships lived up to their designers' expectations. The *contre-torpilleur* was a high-technology answer to an age-old maritime problem: how to secure high-quality intelligence about the composition, disposition and intentions of the enemy's battlefleet whilst at the same time shielding one's own heavy ships from the prying eyes of the enemy's scouting forces. Whether it was the right answer remains open to debate, but evaluation of the *contre-torpilleur* must also focus on the proposed technical solutions to the perceived tactical problems. For, compared to a run-of-the-mill fleet destroyer of the period, the *contre-torpilleur* was a high-value ship at the cutting edge of naval technology, incorporating the very latest developments in construction, armament and propulsion.

To what extent was the *Marine Nationale* successful in matching the advanced technology increasingly available during the 1920s to the original tactical concept? Were the relatively small and lightly-built *contre-torpilleurs* able to accommodate all this new technology satisfactorily, without serious imbalances in design and without the sort of hull growth that would push them into the cruiser category? Finally, was the increasingly high level of specialisation inherent in the later designs a potential weakness? These are the questions this article aims to address.

On learning lessons

The six ships of the *Le Fantasque* class were the last in a series of 30 *contre-torpilleurs*, beginning with the *Jaguar* class of the 1922 programme, continuing with the four-funnelled *Bison/Valmy* classes of the 1925-26 programmes, then progressing to the *Aigle* class ('*les rapaces*') of the 1927 programme and their successors of the *Vauquelin* class of the 1928 programme. Each new type had seen incremental improvements in power and performance, and with the *Le Fantasque* class the *Marine Nationale* aimed to make further improvements and to correct the all-too-apparent defects of the early ships.

However, when the initial studies were begun in the summer of 1928 (the *Le Fantasques* were originally to have been funded in the 1929 programme) only the *Jaguar* class had yet been completed and had run trials. Three ships of the *Bison/Valmy* class had just been launched, but the first unit was not due for sea trials until the following year. The first unit of the *Aigle* class would not be laid down until October, and the inability of the French shipyards, both public and private, to keep pace with the naval programmes already sanctioned would result in the construction of the six *Vauquelins* being delayed until 1930-31.

In the absence of any fundamental change in the *modus operandi* of the *contre-torpilleur*, the basis for the new design would therefore be the *Vauquelin* class, which was currently still on the drawing-board, while incorporating lessons learned from the *Jaguar*. The preliminary drawing dated 3 June 1929 (and subsequently approved by the *Comité Technique* on 28 June) is therefore of a ship virtually identical to the *Vauquelin*, with the distinctive four funnels and the fifth gun mounting immediately abaft the fourth funnel. The only significant change in layout was the position of the searchlight projectors, relocated on the centre-line fore and aft (in the *Vauquelin* class they were side by side forward of the third funnel).

However, this preliminary sketch tells us little about the more fundamental changes envisaged as a consequence of the lessons learned during trials of the *Jaguar* class. There were two fundamental problems which needed to be addressed: the inability of the main guns to score hits on a target in anything but a calm sea and the high fuel consumption, which was responsible for an operational radius far smaller than had been anticipated.

The lightness of the ships' construction with the excessive topweight combined to make the *Jaguars* lively gunnery platforms. Despite the 40-metre bilge keels fitted, they rolled badly: 25° with a beam sea, with a roll period of only 8-10 seconds. They also heeled badly in high winds or when turning: 20° at 35kts with only 5-6° of rudder.

The topweight problem proved so severe that it precluded a number of much-needed modifications to the guns, and ultimately resulted in the removal of several items of equipment. When thirty 138.6mm Mod.1923 (the model installed in the *Bison/Valmy* class) were purchased in 1925 to replace the 130mm Mod.1919, fitting was precluded by the additional 10 tonnes of topweight this would have entailed. A sophisticated director fire control system (FC) still under development when the *Jaguars* were completed was abandoned when it was realised how overweight these ships were. It proved impossible to provide FC directors for the single 75mm anti-aircraft (AA) guns for the same reasons, and the latter ultimately had to be removed and replaced by lightweight machine guns. Reserve depth charges were no longer carried from 1928, torpedoes were embarked only for exercises until the outbreak of war, and in 1932 the

two Thornycroft 240mm antisubmarine mortars were removed for a saving of 5.5 tonnes. In 1929 there was even a proposal to shorten the anchor chains!

Fire control problems

The practical solution to the fire control problem, adopted as a result of trials with the *Jaguar* class, was to fire the main guns only when the ship was at the midpoint of her roll, which seriously slowed the rate of fire when the latter was not in harmony with the period of roll. Since the maximum rate of fire for the 130mm Mod.1919 was only 4-5rpm in conditions of flat calm, this would inevitably be reduced to around 3rpm in any sort of seaway. This figure was totally unacceptable to the *Marine Nationale*, which expected a three-ship division of *contre-torpilleurs* to greet any opponent that presented itself with a deluge of fire, using its high speed to extricate itself from combat before the enemy could acquire the range.

The latest 138.6mm Mod.1927, which had a German-pattern semi-automatic sliding breech and spring-loaded rammers, had a theoretical rate of fire of 14-15rpm. However, if the 'rapaces' and the *Vauquelins* had a similar roll-period to the *Jaguars*, which seemed likely, this would inevitably be reduced to around 6rpm, double the rate of fire of the early ships but still well below the potential of the gun. So the General Staff demanded that the gun mountings to be fitted in the *Le Fantasque* class, which would mount an even higher performance 50-calibre gun with a theoretical range of 20,000 metres, should have

Le Malin *at speed on 30 May 1938. The fineness of the hull-form forward meant that there was virtually no bow wave below 15kts. No.2 gun housing is painted in 'neutrality' colours.* (Marius Bar).

Le Terrible departing Toulon on 11 February 1941 for Oran. From there she would proceed to Dakar as a replacement for L'Audacieux, crippled in the action against British and Free French naval forces on 23 September of the previous year. Again note the neutrality markings on no.2 gun. (Marius Bar).

full remote power control (RPC), a system in which electric motors would compensate for the movement of the platform and keep the gun trained on the target.

The first French RPC system, devised by Paquier-Laurent and derived from the British Vickers system, underwent trials in the *Lorraine* during 1923. It failed to deliver the promised accuracy and was temporarily abandoned, but a further experimental installation was tested in the elderly gunnery training cruiser *Gueydon* in 1928, and subsequently in her successor *Pluton* from 1933. These were all large ships with the weight reserves and electrical generating capacity to accommodate such a system. It would be quite a different matter to install full RPC in a small, lightly-built ship where space, weight and generating capacity were at a premium.

Superheated Steam

The other major innovation in the *Le Fantasque* design was the adoption of high-pressure superheated boilers, which held out the promise of even higher performance. The Royal Navy and the Italian Navy had already embarked on the construction of destroyers powered by superheated machinery. Following successful trials with the competitive *Amazon* and *Ambuscade*, the British Admiralty adopted a Thornycroft boiler rated at 21kg/cm², and the eighth ship of the 'A' class, *Acheron*, had experimental boilers rated at 35kg/cm². The Italian *Nullo* class destroyers of the 1924 programme also had Thornycroft superheated boilers. All these ships achieved 37kts comfortably.

The *Marine Nationale* was a little way behind, but in the same year the seaplane carrier *Commandant Teste* was authorised with small Yarrow superheated boilers rated at 20kg/cm². Indret was already engaged in the development of superheated boilers rated at 40kg/cm² for 10,000t cruisers, and from September 1927 A.C. Loire and St Nazaire-Penhoët were invited to submit designs for advanced propulsion systems capable of delivering 72,000shp. Two competitive designs were to be evaluated in two *contre-torpilleurs* of the 1927 programme, *Milan* and *Epervier*, with a view to developing a tried and tested propulsion system for the *Le Fantasques*. Two types of superheater, Yarrow and Penhoët, were to be evaluated in conjunction with two types of turbine, Parsons and Rateau. However, the backlog of construction in the shipyards delayed the construction of these ships. They were laid down at Lorient Naval Dockyard only in late 1930, and ran sea trials from late 1932, by which time the design for the *Le Fantasque* class had been finalised and all six ships had been laid down.

Because of these delays, decisions regarding the propulsion system for the *Le Fantasque* class had to be taken on a purely theoretical basis. It is therefore unsurprising that the *Marine Nationale*, frustrated in its aim of adopting a tried and tested system, continued its earlier policy of hedging its bets and distributing orders among the maximum number of contractors. The Yarrow superheated boilers for the *Le Fantasques* were built by a wide variety of manufacturers, and three ships had Rateau direct-action turbines while the remaining ships were fitted with Parsons reaction turbines. This lack of uniformity was a recipe for the regular machinery failures

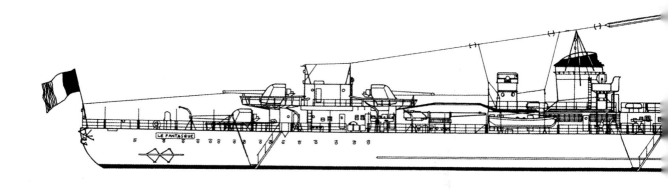

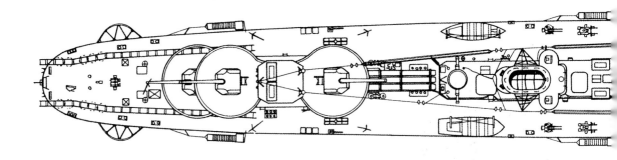

Profile and Plan Views:
The profile and plan views are based on official plans for Le Fantasque *and* L'Audacieux *(Arsenal de Lorient) dated 5 November 1936. Note that they show the projected twin 37mm Model 1933 abeam the midships deckhouse rather than the single 37mm Model 1925 fitted as a temporary measure on completion. The twin Hotchkiss 13.2mm MG, originally to have been installed on the forecastle, are mounted on the after 37mm pivot; these would subsequently be relocated to specially-built platforms projecting from either side of the bridge. (Drawn by the author).*

and maintenance problems that had plagued the earlier ships, both on trials and in service.

Fundamental Flaws

There were other defects that quickly became apparent during trials with the *Jaguar* class which were more difficult to address. The lightly-constructed hull did not stand up well to operations in heavy weather conditions, especially in the rougher waters of the Atlantic. Manoeuvrability was poor; the fineness of the hull-form (length-to-beam ratio was 10.6:1) contributed, but the single centre-line rudder, which had a surface area of only 14.4m² and was powered by an inadequate servo-motor, was primarily responsible. At 30kts it took 25-30 seconds to turn the rudder to its maximum 35°angle, and

trials with *Tigre* in 1925 gave a turning circle of 1050m at 20kts and 1140m at 25kts. Ten years later the *contre-torpilleurs* of the *Le Fantasque* class turned in similar figures. At the slightly higher speed of 33kts *L'Indomptable* had a turning circle of 1,425m to starboard and 1205m to port (the disparity was a function of the asymmetric arrangement of the propeller shafts). These figures were higher than the corresponding ones for contemporary French cruisers and capital ships (the cruisers of the *La Galissonnière* class had a turning circle of 900m at 30kts), which sometimes made it difficult to keep station when in company with them. Moreover the rudder only had any effect at all from 10kts, making the *contre-torpilleurs* difficult to manoeuvre in harbour.

These problems could not be effectively addressed because they were a direct result of the *Marine Nationale's* obsession with high-speed straight-line performance. The

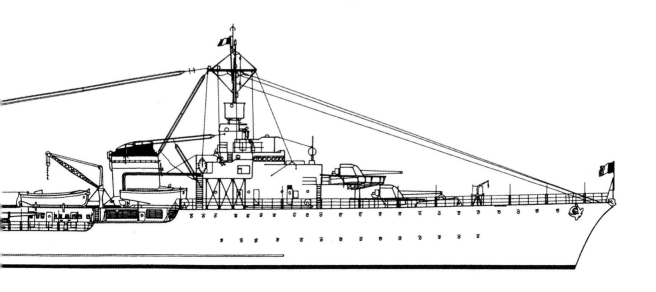

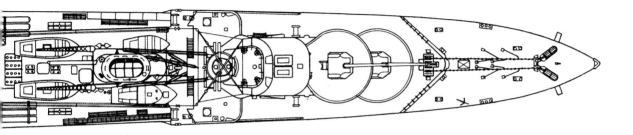

light construction and fine lines of the ships were essential in order to minimise resistance, and the single counter-balanced rudder was designed to minimise disturbance to water from the propellers.

However, the poor manoeuvrability of these ships would surely have impacted on their performance in their intended missions, even if we discount the disastrous effect it was to have on their performance in the anti-submarine role, for which they were not designed. Scouting operations in the presence of more powerful enemy cruisers would undoubtedly have required rapid manoeuvres. The night encounters which so exercised French designers in their consideration of torpedo-tube disposition and centralised FC arrangements, would also have made demands on the ships' ability to manoeuvre effectively in order to extricate themselves from a potentially fatal close-range artillery engagement.

The other major flaw which was perhaps less apparent at the time was the total inadequacy of the anti-aircraft armament. The *Marine Nationale*, in line with other navies of the period, was unconvinced by the potential aerial threat to these fast, agile ships. It was thought that the major threat would be air attack while the ships were stationary, in harbour, a not-unlikely scenario given the proximity of the major French base, Toulon, to airfields in Italy. Apart from the 76mm gun, which proved too large and unwieldy for installation in the *contre-torpilleurs*, the only AA weapons available during the late 1920s were the single 37mm Mod.1925 and smaller-calibre machine guns such as the elderly 8mm Mod.1914 and a new Hotchkiss 13.2mm MG under development, the Mod.1929. The former had a poor rate of fire, while the machine guns were designed to counter strafing by slow biplanes constructed of traditional wood and canvas, and

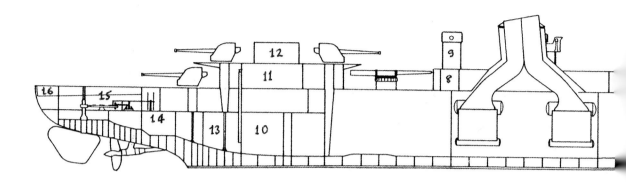

Inboard Profile:

Inboard profile of Le Fantasque. *Note the proportion of the ship's length taken up by the machinery.* (Drawn by the author).

Key to Inboard Profile:

1. *fwd 138.6mm magazine*
2. *intermediate handing room*
3. *upper handing room*
4. *navigation bridge*
5. *main gunnery DCT*
6. *torpedo r/f platform*
7. *W/T office (reception)*
8. *W/T office (transmission)*
9. *secondary FC director*
10. *aft 138.6mm magazine*
11. *intermediate handing room*
12. *upper handing room*
13. *37mm magazine*
14. *depth charge magazine*
15. *steering gear compartment*
16. *depth charge tunnels*

would prove virtually ineffectual against the fast metal-skinned monoplanes developed during the 1930s.

During the construction of the *Le Fantasque* class development began on a variety of new 37mm twin mountings, of which only the Mod.1933 (a twin variant of the Mod.1925) saw light of day. But AA guns were a very low priority for these ships, and they began to receive the Mod.1933 only in 1940, when the Second World War was already some months old. Even when these weapons were fitted there was nowhere to put them. All the best positions were taken up by the main guns, and they were simply located on the existing Mod.1925 pivots at upper-deck level abeam the midships deckhouse, where they had poor arcs and consequently could engage targets only on the port or starboard beam. No effective system of fire control was provided, policy being to direct a hail of fire ahead of an incoming aircraft following target designation by a simple rangefinder with a 1-metre base.

New lessons, new plans

Although plans for the new class, designated 'contre-torpilleur de 2610t type 1929', were approved by the *Comité technique de la marine* on 28 June 1929, the delays experienced with the preceding classes due to shipyard overload resulted in the project being effectively suspended for two years. This enabled experience with the first of the four-funnelled *contre-torpilleurs*, the *Bison/Valmy* class, to be taken into account.

Many of the lessons learned from this second group of *contre-torpilleurs* served to reinforce experience with the *Jaguar* class. Stability was still inadequate, and the *Bison/Valmy* group rolled badly in a seaway and heeled badly when turning at speed. The ships could easily sustain 31kts in formation, but fuel consumption at lower speeds was unexpectedly high, so that they never attained their designed operational radius. Considerable attention would therefore be paid to reducing topweight

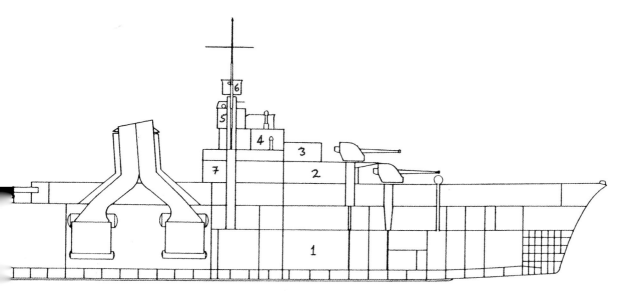

and improving stability in the new design, and in late 1929 the General Staff requested an increase in fuel bunkerage from 360t to 580t, with the aim of improving endurance to 4,000nm at the cruise speed of 15kts.

During trials with the *Bison/Valmy* class it became apparent that at speed exhaust gases from the fore-funnel were drawn into the bridge spaces. In late 1930 it was therefore proposed that the funnel should be moved farther away from the bridge structure. However, this would have placed it so close to the second funnel that it made sense to combine both uptakes into a single, broader funnel, and to extend this modification to the after pair of funnels.

At the same time it was decided that the third 138.6mm mounting, which in all previous *contre-torpilleur* types had been mounted immediately abaft the after funnel, and could therefore be fired only on the broadside, be relocated at the forward end of the after deckhouse, which would enable it to fire on forward bearings. The other advantage of this modification was that the mounting could now be served directly from the after shell hoists. Previously this mounting had to be replenished via an overhead cable system, its relative isolation from the after hoists being compensated by a larger ready-use ammunition park (30 rounds as compared to 24 in the *Jaguar* class, 48 compared to 24 in the later ships).

Revised plans drawn up by the Service Technique des Constructions Navales (STCN) were duly approved in early 1931, and the class was now designated 'contre-torpilleur type 1930'. The suppression of the mainmast, implicit in the repositioning of the third 138.6mm mounting, did not meet with universal approval. There was concern that shorter radio aerials would make Medium Wave reception less reliable; a simple pole mainmast was therefore reinstated. However, these reservations were overtaken by moves to reduce still further the distinctive top-hamper of the early *contre-torpilleurs*. Further modifications to the design in July 1933, when all ships of the class had been laid down, resulted in the revolutionary new silhouette which set the *Le Fantasques* apart from their predecessors: two broad low funnels, the forward tripod replaced by the distinctive *mât de flèche* with the gun and torpedo fire control directors seated around its base, and outriggers for the radio aerials on the second funnel to replace the former mainmast.

Construction

The six ships of the *Le Fantasque* class were laid down in 1931-32. Two were ordered from Lorient Naval Dockyard, the remaining four from private shipbuilders. Construction proceeded smoothly; the hulls were launched 1933-34 and all entered service from late 1935 to mid-1936.

Hull construction was essentially unchanged from the *Vauquelin* class, the clipper bow with marked sheer and flare being complemented by the *cul de poule* stern, adopted to facilitate minelaying, and which had the additional benefit of preserving trim at high speeds. The hull and main deck were of 6-14mm steel plate with a resistance of 50kg/cm², and were of riveted construction.

Concerns had been expressed regarding the extensive use of the light alloy duralumin for the superstructures of the *Aigle* and *Vauquelin* classes. The external panels of the bridge structure and deckhouses of the *Le Fantasque* class were therefore of steel, and were reinforced where exposed to blast from the main guns. Duralumin was used only for partitioning within the superstructures.

L'Indomptable departing Toulon on 25 August 1941 for machinery trials following repairs at the naval dockyard. Although she still carries her pennant number as lead-ship of the 8ᵉ division de contre-torpilleurs, the latter had effectively been dissolved on 1 August. L'Indomptable was reallocated to the 6th Division, together with Volta and the damaged Mogador. In this photo the main DCT is trained on the beam; note the white-paint applied to the rangefinders, intended to reflect the heat of the sun and thereby minimize distortion of the optics. (Marius Bar).

These improvements were possible because of the considerable weight saved by reducing the height of the superstructures, masts and funnels.

There was light plating over the magazines (1.31t!), but the ships were otherwise unprotected. According to operational doctrine they were not intended to stay around long enough to get hit. However, subsequent experience in the Second World War was to suggest that the lightness of their construction was in some ways an advantage when faced with 'heavy' ships, whose shells tended to pass straight through their light plating without exploding. Damage from even the heaviest shells was therefore often limited to broken pipework and severed cabling.

A more serious problem was their vulnerability to damage in heavy seas, particularly as the *Le Fantasques* were deployed on completion with the Atlantic Squadron based on Brest (due to a sea-change in the political situation, in which Germany was now viewed as the potential enemy). The 8ᵉ *division de contre-torpilleurs* took severe structural damage in the Bay of Biscay in November 1939, and this experience was repeated with *Le Fantasque* in 1943. French steel was also of poor quality, and an inspection of the hull of *L'Indomptable* in January 1940 (when the ship had been in service less than four years) revealed pitting to a depth of 8mm.

Sea keeping was otherwise much improved as compared with the earlier *contre-torpilleurs*. The *Le Fantasques* proved to be excellent sea-boats, with insignificant roll and only 6-7.5° heel with 25° of rudder. They therefore proved to be relatively steady gunnery platforms, and their lower silhouette also made them less sensitive to wind. However, funnel gases were still drawn into the bridge spaces at high speed, presumably because of the reduction in the height of the funnels, and prominent cowlings were fitted from 1942 onwards.

Machinery

As in *Milan* and *Epervier* there were four Du Temple vertical small-tube boilers with superheaters, rated at 27kg/cm² and operating at a nominal temperature of 225° (+100° with superheaters); higher temperatures of 360-370° were regularly obtained. The superheaters were of the Thornycroft type, except in *Le Terrible*, which had a Yarrow-Loire model, characterised by a greater number of tubes. As in earlier types the boilers were paired, and although the uptakes were paired in the funnel sleeves they were kept separate to minimise the effects of action damage.

Three ships had the classic Rateau direct-action turbines, the remaining three being fitted with Parsons reaction turbines; the latter were more complex but allowed a slower rotation of turbines, resulting in reduced wear and lower fuel consumption. The Rateau turbine sets comprised three main turbines (HP, MP, LP) with single reduction gearing, and with the reversing turbine inte-

A fine builders model of L'Indomptable *showing the sleek hull form of the* Le Fantasque *class.* (CPL).

grated into the LP turbine. Two cruise turbines worked in series via the MP turbine, and could power the ships up to 21kts; they were declutched only above 25kts. The layout of the Parsons turbines was similar, but there was only a single cruise turbine acting via the LP turbine.

Speed performance on trials was remarkable, and sent shock waves through other European navies. *Le Terrible* attained just over 45kts, thereby breaking the world speed record. All six ships exceeded 43kts on trials, and comfortably exceeded 40kts in service. Maximum speed in formation was 40kts for the Rateau ships, and 38/39kts for the Parsons ships.

However, there was a downside to these impressive figures. Because of the economic recession a conscious effort was made to distribute work on the propulsion systems to the largest possible number of sub-contractors. It was hoped this would ensure prompt delivery of components, but it also resulted in a marked lack of uniformity and quality of manufacture which was to have a number of adverse consequences.

There were frequent turbine problems on trials. In September 1934 *Le Triomphant* stripped blades on the starboard HP turbine, and had to undergo repairs at ACF Dunkerque for three months; subsequently, in January 1935 the reversing turbine was found to be seriously damaged and had to be removed for repairs which took a further six months. *L'Indomptable* experienced similar problems with her port-side HP turbine in February 1934, leading to repairs at La Seyne; and *Le Malin* was unable to shift to her main turbines in May 1934. *L'Audacieux* experienced problems with her boilers in January 1935 and the brickwork had to be completely rebuilt; there were further problems when trials recommenced, leading to a further two months of repairs. Indeed the succession of machinery incidents with this class was considered so serious that an official enquiry was set up headed by the *Inspecteur général des machines*.

The bronze three-bladed propellers were initially provided by the propulsion machinery contractors, but this led to marked variations in performance, and in 1935 they were replaced by a standard model with a superior profile designed to reduced the number of revolutions at maximum speed. The lack of uniformity in the propulsion systems also led to an interesting tactical measure.

Table 1: LE FANTASQUE CLASS: PROPULSION MACHINERY CONTRACTORS

	Le Fantasque	L'Audacieux	Le Malin	Le Terrible	Le Triomphant	L'Indomptable
Forward Boilers:	Ateliers et Chantiers de la Seine Maritime (Le Trait)	Ateliers et Chantiers de la Seine Maritime (Le Trait)	Chantiers Auguste Normand (Le Havre)	Ateliers et Chantiers de la Loire (St Nazaire)	Babcock & Wilcox (Cherbourg)	Forges et Chantiers de la Gironde (Bordeaux)
After Boilers:	Ateliers et Chantiers de Bretagne (Nantes)	MM Schneider & Cie (Le Creusot)	Forges et Chantiers de la Mèditerranèe (La Seyne)	Ateliers et Chantiers de la Loire (St Nazaire)	Ateliers et Chantiers de France (Dunkerque)	Ateliers et Chantiers de la Seine Maritime (Le Trait)
Turbines:	Ateliers et Chantiers de Bretagne (Nantes)	MM Schneider & Cie (Le Creusot)	Forges et Chantiers de la Mèditerranèe (La Seyne)	Ateliers et Chantiers de Bretagne (Nantes)	Compagnie de Fives-Lille (Lille)	Ateliers et Chantiers de la Loire (St Nazaire)

In order to avoid the vibrations experienced at different speeds by individual vessels combat speed was fixed at 28kts (there was no vibration whatsoever between 26 and 30kts).

Despite the increase in fuel bunkerage to 580t (640t max.) the theoretical endurance was never attained, even by the more economical Parsons ships. At the standard cruise speed of 14/15kts, operational radius was estimated at only 2,700-2,900nm, as compared to the 4,000nm requested by the General Staff.

Gunnery and fire control

The 138.6mm/50 Mod.1929 was derived from the 40-cal. Mod.1927 fitted in the *Aigle* and *Vauquelin* classes. It had a theoretical rate of fire of 14/15rpm (in practice 5/6rpm in Sea State 3-4) and employed separate munitions of the established types. The longer barrel, with its higher muzzle velocity, gave the gun a theoretical range of 20,000m at its maximum elevation of 30°, although accurate observation of the fall of shot was still difficult at this range, despite improvements in range-finding (the inadequate 3-metre base coincidence rangefinder fitted in the early *contre-torpilleurs* had by now been superseded by a stereoscopic model with a 5-metre base). It also served to increase the recoil forces from 43.5 tonnes to 57 tonnes, which placed additional stresses on the gun mounting, and the blast effect was markedly greater (hence the reinforced steel plating on the superstructures). As in earlier types the light 5mm gunshields were barely adequate to protect the crew, who were exposed to the elements particularly when the ships were firing on the beam at speed.

As with their predecessors the *Le Fantasque* class relied on ready-use munitions in combat, the latter being replenished only during lulls in the action. Twenty-four ready-use rounds were provided for each gun, the shells being stowed horizontally in brass 'guttering' which encircled each mounting (the guttering for no.5 gun was not fitted as it obstructed access to the quarterdeck), and the propellant cartridges to the rear of the mounting. In theory this allowed for only 1min 30secs of continuous firing, although in practice five minutes was a more likely figure. In peacetime 100 rounds of AP and HE per gun were provided plus 75 rounds of starshell for no.2 mounting; in wartime this would increase to 200rpg.

No changes were made to the Sautter-Harlé tubular double hoists (one for shells, the other for cartridges) fitted in earlier types. These could handle a maximum of 20rpm, adequate for two guns only. It was therefore decided that no.5 mounting would not be replenished during engagements, and would have a double ready-use munitions park (ie 2 x 24) as compensation. To speed up ammunition supply to the guns, intermediate handing rooms were fitted at the level of no.1 and no.5 mountings. However, this proved unsuccessful; if shells were not instantly realigned at the intermediate level the hoists jammed. Lack of confidence in the reliability of the hoists led the ships' crews to overload the ready-use parks, contrary to safety regulations; remedial action

Table 2: CHARACTERISTICS OF 138.6MM/50 MODEL 1929

Gun Data

muzzle velocity	800m/s
max. range at 30°	20,000m
projectiles	AP: OPFA Mod.1924 (39.9kg)
	HE: OEA Mod.1928 (40.2kg)
	starshell: OE 1925

Mounting Data

weight of mounting	11.6 tonnes
gunshield	5mm
elevation of guns	-10° / +30°
firing cycle	14 / 15rpm (theoretical)
	5 / 6rpm (practical)

therefore became necessary. In a refit at Lorient during the Spring of 1940 *Le Fantasque* had the intermediate handing positions suppressed; she subsequently fired off 250 rounds at Dakar without a single jam.

Fire control was centralised on the (open) upper bridge, where two pairs of target designation binoculars fed the target bearing via Granat transmitter to the main director. The Director Control Tower (DCT), which was fitted with a new-model 5-metre base stereoscopic rangefinder, aligned itself automatically on the target bearing, which was then fed continuously to the transmitting station (*PC artillerie*) below decks. The latter was equipped with an electro-mechanical computer Mod.1929, and transmitted firing data to the guns via Granat transmitters. The gunhouses were trained manually to conform to the pointer on the Granat dial. The guns could be fired locally or by the gunnery officer in the DCT by electro-mechanical transmission. In action firing was automatic when the breach closed. A secondary fire control position equipped with an identical 5-metre stereoscopic rangefinder and a Mod.1919 computer *type aviso* was provided for use in emergency; orders were transmitted to the guns by telephone.

Remote power control (RPC) was intended to sustain the firing solution throughout. Two Janney motors on each mounting and the DCT powered by a 26kW electrical generator provided continuous current: one for lateral movement, the other to maintain elevation. A complex servo-mechanism ensured that the guns and DCT remained fixed on the target despite the movement of the platform; the rangefinder operator simply had to keep the target in his sights. Unfortunately the bearing rheostat was insufficiently sensitive for small movements of the rangefinder, so that any movement threw all the elements out of line. Moreover the lack of commonality in the electrical mechanisms frequently resulted in false readings when corrections of the same value but opposite direction failed to cancel one another out.

RPC for elevation to compensate for the roll of the ship proved to be relatively valueless, because the major problem under these conditions was the manual reloading of the guns. The rheostats were similarly insensitive to small movements. Moreover, sudden movements of

Bow and stern quarter views of Le Terrible, *departing Toulon on 18 May 1942 for magnetic signature measurement following an extensive refit which involved the complete retubing of her boilers. She would leave for Dakar two days later. She has an experimental cowling on the fore funnel, intended to keep funnel exhaust gases clear of the bridge. The after deckhouse has been extensively modified to accommodate a twin 37mm Mod.1933 on the centre-line, a second mounting to port, and a single 37mm Mod.1925 to starboard. The bridge wing positions are now occupied by Browning single 13.2mm MG, the Hotchkiss twin 13.2mm Mod.1929 mountings being relocated in tubs projecting from the forward end of the midships deckhouse. (Marius Bar).*

Le Malin, damaged by gunfire from the USS Massachusetts, photographed in Casablanca harbour after the Allied landings in November 1942. To starboard of her is an older four-funnelled contre-torpilleur, possibly Albatross, while in the background is the battleship Jean Bart. This is one of a number of photographs taken during the operation by an officer on board the USS Wilkes (DD-441); further images from the assualt are included in this year's Warship Gallery. (Robert P Largesse).

the ship often actuated the circuit-breakers, putting the system out of action when theoretically it should have been of most use.

Four of the six ships entered service with a provisional RPC installation; *Le Terrible* and *L'Indomptable* entered service without. Only the bearing element was thought to show genuine promise. Further installations were made in dribs and drabs over the prewar years. However, an operational RPC system was never successfully evolved, and for a time the motors were disembarked altogether in *Le Fantasque*.

Underwater weapons

The early *contre-torpilleurs* up to the 'rapaces' had two centre-line triple banks of torpedo tubes. The principal disadvantage of this arrangement was that torpedoes could be launched through only limited arcs on the beam. This was acceptable in daylight, when the ships could choose the range and angle of approach, but was considered to be a disadvantage in night time operations, when the ships could be surprised at close range. In the *Vauquelin* class the forward bank of tubes was therefore superseded by two twin tubes disposed port and starboard close to the deck edge, with the ability to fire close to the ship's axis on fore and after bearings.

The *Le Fantasques* took this arrangement a stage further, the forward tubes being boosted to triple banks, with two spare reload torpedoes in upper-deck lockers close to the mountings. The forward banks of tubes had training arcs of 20° to 150° on either beam, as compared with only 60° to 120° for the after bank. The torpedoes were fired by compressed air, with explosive charges for back-up. To minimise the risk of accidental explosion the warheads were fixed and the compressed-air bottles filled only just prior to action. The tubes had electrical training with manual back-up, and firing was normally controlled centrally from a special platform equipped with a stereoscopic 5-metre rangefinder located directly above the main DCT. There were optical sights Mod.1935 on the tubes for back-up, but these positions were found to be dangerously exposed to the elements and were provided with protection from 1936.

The anti-submarine and minelaying capabilities were virtually identical to the *Vauquelin*. Two stern depth charge tunnels each with eight 252kg depth charges were fitted, the chain mechanism being operated from the bridge. Reloads (32 in wartime) were carried in a magazine beneath the quarterdeck. It was initially planned to fit two 100/250kg mortars Mod.1928 as in the *Vauquelins*, together with Walser listening apparatus, but both were suppressed in 1931-32, a clear indication of the General Staff's priorities for these ships. There were also two

Décauville 30m tracks for 40 Bréguet B4 mines. Only the after section (five mines per side) was fixed, allowing for the regulation annual minelaying exercise; the other sections were normally landed, and could be reassembled in only a few hours.

Conclusions

The *Le Fantasque* class was in many respects a remarkable design, let down in part by inadequacies in French industrial technology and defects in manufacture. The superheated steam propulsion system gave the ships outstanding high speed performance. The famous sweep of the Skaggerak by the *8ᵉ division* (l'*Indomptable, Le Malin* and *Le Triomphant*) in April 1940 during the Norwegian campaign was conducted at a sustained formation speed of 36kts, and even higher speeds were maintained by individual ships throughout their service lives. The 138.6mm Model 1929, on the few occasions when it was tested in combat, proved to be an effective weapon capable of a high sustained rate of fire once the replenishment hoist arrangements were modified. These were ships that earned the respect of allies and enemy alike.

However, like the earlier French *contre-torpilleurs*, the degree of specialisation inherent in the ships' design created serious imbalances in their capabilities. So much attention was focused on the main hardware that auxiliary systems crucial to their optimal performance were neglected. The regular failure of elements of the propulsion machinery, the frequent breakdowns experienced with the hoists, the inadequacy of the anti-aircraft provision have already been commented on. It was difficult to keep the ships in action for sustained periods; for example it proved impossible to repeat the sweep of the Skaggerak as planned, due to two separate breakdowns in the auxiliary machinery of *Le Malin* during the sweep itself, and damage to the port propeller shaft of *Le Triomphant* from a near-miss.

There were numerous other sub-standard systems which had an adverse effect on the ships' performance. The major increase in demands on electrical power supply was not matched by a comparable upgrading of the electrical generating systems. The power supply from the two 80/106kW turbo-generators proved inadequate during combat, and the low voltage (115/118V) of the system was not compatible with the requirements of RPC. It would have been difficult to install more powerful generators, given that the propulsion machinery already accounted for 39 per cent of the ship's displacement. The internal communications systems were outdated, and were much criticised by the ships' commanding officers during the war. Although the mess decks were considered spacious and well-lit, there was never sufficient accommodation for the designed complement, resulting in a decision to 'double-up' on certain crew functions (the main guns and the anti-aircraft weapons could not be manned simultaneously).

Some of these deficiencies were remedied when the four surviving *Le Fantasques* were rebuilt in the USA during 1943. Others, however, proved difficult to tackle because they were inherent in the imbalances of a design optimised for performance in a role which had been overtaken by events.

Sources

Jean Lassaque, *Les CT de 2 800 tonnes du type Le Fantasque,* (Bourg-en-Bresse: Marines, 1998)

Official plans of *Le Fantasque* & *L'Audacieux*, Centre d'Archives de l'Armement

CF Caroff, *La Campagne de Norvège 1940,* (Service Historique de la Marine, 1955)

John Campbell, *Naval Weapons of World War Two,* (London: Conway Maritime Press, 1988)

SOVIET AND RUSSIAN AIR-INDEPENDENT SUBMARINES

The Imperial Russian Navy investigated air-independent propulsion (AIP) for submarines nearly ninety years ago. The Soviet Navy turned it into reality after 1945 and the Russians today are marketing such systems. **Antony Preston** looks at this obscure area of submarine history.

Although in recent years a number of navies have invested in air-independent propulsion (AIP) systems for submarines, the Russian Navy and its predecessor, the Soviet Navy, have pursued the goal for much longer than is generally realised.

As far back as 1912 *michman* Nikol'sky designed a system featuring a closed-cycle internal combustion engine (the Imperial Russian Navy had been the first to introduce the diesel into a submarine), and it got as far as running on a test-rig in the Baltic Shipyard. But more systematic research and development began in the 1930s, with what Western intelligence agencies claim was a Project 95, probably M-92. She used liquid oxygen as a stored oxidiser, exhausting overboard. The installation was known as YeD-VVD.

On 1 July 1941 another experimental boat, the Project 95 Series XII 'M' class, M-401, was launched and ran a series of trials with a Kreislauf closed-cycle diesel (CCD) engine until the end of the Great Patriotic War in 1945. Her YeD-KhPI plant (also known as REDO) plant rectified the failings of the prototype, which did not consume all the oxygen and had very short endurance. As a result of these trials one of the early Project 615 boats (known to NATO as the 'Quebec' type) was given a Kreislauf CCD plant, and was designated Project A615; over 30 were built. In service, however, the A615 series suffered a number of fires and explosions, and M-256 sank in September 1957 as a result of flooding to put out a bad fire. Although modifications were made to improve safety and fire-resistance, the unreliability of the plant was such that all Project A615 boats were taken out of service in the late 1960s and early 1970s.

Other as-yet unidentified AIP designs, probably also using the Kreislauf CCD, were Projects 618 and 661.

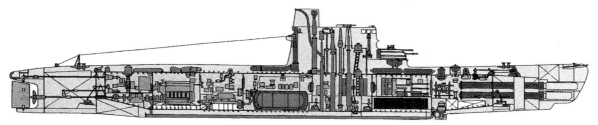

Soviet Project 'Quebec' class submarine, driven by Kreislauf closed-cycle diesel plant. (Rubin Bureau).

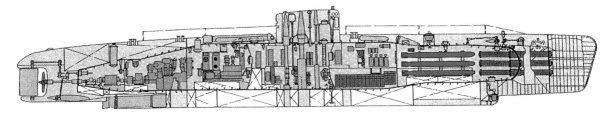

Project 617 'Whale' prototype, driven by Walther HTP turbine plant. (Rubin Bureau).

146

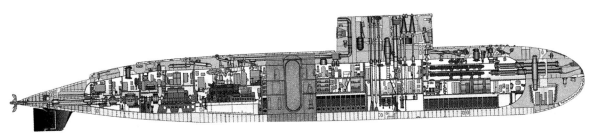

A Project 636 'Improved Kilo' lengthened for fuel-cell AIP plant. (Rubin Bureau).

Informed sources such as Friedman and Pavlov say that 618 was probably a medium-sized boat. From 1947 the TsKB-18 bureau began work on designing a boat using the German Walter turbine, fuelled by perhydrol (enriched hydrogen peroxide) burnt with diesel fuel to provide oxygen for combustion. In effect the bureau recreated the *Kriegsmarine*'s Type XXVI U-boat as Project 616, capable of 22.5 knots and armed with ten torpedoes. This design was rejected, and TsKB-18 then produced Project 617, retaining the Walter plant developed for 616; a new bureau, SKB-143 (now the Malakhit Bureau) was hived off to develop the new design, identified by NATO as the 'Whale' class.

Only one Project 617 boat, S-99, was completed, by Sudomekh in 1952, although trials lasted until 1958. During that period she went to sea nearly 100 times and logged over 315 hours running on the Walter plant. In May 1959, however, she suffered an explosion in a blocked fuel line while starting the Walter plant at a depth of 80 metres. The resulting explosion tore a hole in the pressure hull, and although S-99 survived she was never repaired. Project 683 may have been a long-range

version of 617, but all work on closed-cycle engines for AIP stopped in 1960.

Although the Soviet Navy had no option but to keep pace with the US Navy in developing nuclear power, AIP remained on the agenda, and the Rubin Bureau (formerly TsKB-18) decided to follow the same route as the German Navy, developing fuel cell technology. This is now available for both the *Amur* export variant of the Project 677 *Lada* design and the Project 636 Improved 'Kilo'.

It has been reported by *Jane's Navy International* that some officials in the Rubin Bureau have reservations about their AIP fuel cells and believe that the cells really need several years of testing by the Russian Navy before they can be exported.

The main problem is said to be the inefficiency of metal hydride storage and the buoyancy problem it creates for larger submarines (over 2000 tonnes displacement) after around 14 days' submerged endurance. Given that cryogenic storage is not regarded as a feasible option, the only alternative is to carry hydrogen in the form of a hydrocarbon such as methanol, and then use a catalyst to convert the hydrocarbon to hydrogen and CO_2.

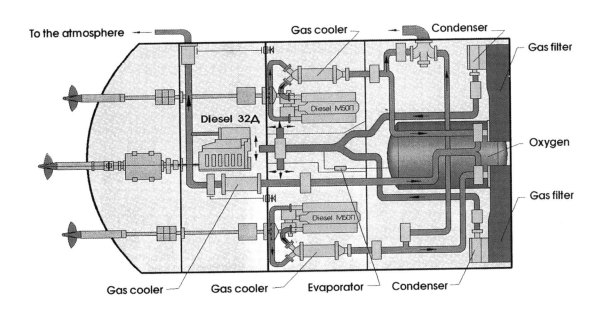

The three-shaft arrangement for the Project A615 boats. (Rubin Bureau).

THE 'WEAPON' AND GALLANT CLASS DESTROYERS

The destroyers designed for the Royal Navy at the end of the Second World War marked a radical departure from previous practice, both in layout and propulsion. **George Moore** examines the 'Weapon' and *Gallant* classes, and their place in RN destroyer development.

Destroyer Production 1939 – 1942

The quest for new destroyers by the Royal Navy (RN) in the years 1939 to 1941 followed broadly to the pattern anticipated at the outbreak of the war, with flotillas of intermediate type vessels being ordered on a regular basis. By late 1941, however, the needs of the fleet were beginning to change as a result of the hard lessons of war experiences and the new fleet destroyers of the 'Battle' class were ordered in 1942, incorporating a gun armament where all weapons could be used effectively against aircraft, a feature lacking in the destroyers being produced up to this point in the war. When the 1942 Programme was drawn up it was originally believed that virtually all new-construction destroyers would be of the new fleet type but they were more expensive to build both in resources and time. The state of the war meant that production had to concentrate on turning out destroyers in numbers as rapidly as possible and as a result of this need 16 'Battle' class were ordered in 1942, the balance and bulk of the programme being made up by 26 units of the 'C' class, a development of the 'Q' class of 1939 which was effectively the standard destroyer-type in production for the Royal Navy up to this point in time. The Programme was duly approved by the War Cabinet on the 27th April 1942.

The problem, however, was that the bulk of the destroyers authorised, on order or under construction were not now going to be fully effective units of the fleet.[1]

Analysing the Problem

The ink was barely dry on the 1942 Programme when a whole series of ideas on how best to improve the armament of the intermediate destroyers initiated a very necessary debate. The Captain of HMS *Excellent*, as it turned out, prophetically proposed first of all that three twin 4in mountings should be carried in a 'Q' class hull.

Other proposals suggested that four or five fully high angle 4.5in (80°) single mountings should be carried, a mounting which did not exist, an alternative main armament suggested was two twin 4in Mark XIX mountings. All were to be fitted with remote power control (RPC). The view of the Director of Naval Construction (DNC) as expressed on 6 May 1942 was that the 'Q' class hull would not be capable of carrying a main armament larger than two twin 4in mountings, and he duly produced a design known as 'Q1'. The result was an 'L' class-sized destroyer with 4–4.5in (55°), two sets of quadruple torpedo tubes, one predictor-controlled twin Bofors, four Oerlikons and a ten pattern depth charge armament. Alternative suggested armaments included 4–4.5in single (80°) or 3–4in twin (80°) mountings. The debate was clearly inconclusive at this stage and no progress was being made.[2]

The next stage of the debate was to involve a more focused forum; by August 1942 the Future Building Committee was formally constituted. One of the first tasks of the committee was defining the destroyer's role, a matter largely instigated by the Prime Minister, Winston Churchill, who expressed his dislike of the 'Battle' class destroyers when the construction of nine light fleet carriers was agreed by the War Cabinet on 1 August 1942. The Assistant Chief of Naval Staff (Weapons), a member of the committee, duly asked in a memorandum dated 29 August 1942:

What are the functions of Fleet Destroyers?
What types of Destroyers do we require?
Are close range Fleet Escort Vessels also required?
Assuming there is a need for a large type Fleet Destroyer, what alterations to the 1942 (Battle) design are desirable?
If we accept that part of our Fleet Destroyers must be on Intermediate Class hulls, what armament should they carry?
What provision should be made for twin speed destroyer sweeps?

HMS Crossbow *photographed in March 1948, as built.* (WSS).

He then went on to stress points which he considered as being particularly important to assist the new committee in their deliberations:

If the intermediate class is larger than 1700 tons it cannot be built at some destroyer building yards.

A fleet destroyer takes 18 months to build compared with 16 months for an intermediate destroyer, costs £250,000 more and requires 44per cent greater complement.

Is the Board Margin of 2 per cent needed?

The ideal anti-aircraft armament should have Radio Direction Finding (Radar), Prediction, RPC and a high rate of fire.

The price of 80° mountings instead of 55° mountings in a destroyer is about 300 tons.

The 80° mounting is only required against steep dive bombers.

Mounting three twin 4.5in mountings cannot be achieved in the *Battle* class without greatly increasing displacement.

In the Intermediate class. 80° mountings, Remote Power Control or an increased close range armament cannot be mounted if displacement limited to 1700 tons.

A fully high-angle destroyer can probably be obtained with 6–4in guns on about 1700 tons displacement.

A predictor controlled Bofors is effective up to about 1,600 yards at which it has a 20 per cent chance of bringing down an aircraft with six seconds fire.

Having asked the questions the Assistant Chief of Naval Staff (Weapons) now set out the array of answers to the questions raised as set out in earlier relevant papers which had been produced over many months:

The Director of Plans described the functions of Fleet Destroyers as:-

To attack enemy ships with torpedoes.

To attack enemy light craft with gunfire.

To screen heavy ships against submarine, aircraft and E boat attack.

To act as supporting forces in combined operations.

He expanded his answer by referring to the increased role which it was anticipated would be the function of aircraft particularly in offensive operations. He did not however see the destroyer being entirely relieved of its offensive function and thus be turned into a close-range escort vessel. No one expressed views which countered this opinion.

The DNC put forward what were described as 'appropriate' designs for both intermediate and fleet destroyers. An intermediate destroyer design designated 'QA' displaced 2000 tons (standard), mounted four single 4.5in (55°) with RPC, two twin Bofors, four Oerlikons and two quadruple torpedo tubes. 70 depth charges 10 patterns were also carried. Machinery produced 47,500 shaft hp to give 36.5kts/32kts. The fleet destroyers foreshadowed the *Daring* class being 2750 tons standard (BA) and 3250 tons standard (BC). Both carried three twin 4.5in guns 'BA' having 55° elevation and 'BC' 80° elevation. There was general agreement that two types of destroyer were needed but no consensus existed amongst members of the Naval Staff on the armament to be mounted in the intermediate class.

No one other than the Director of Gunnery Division supported building close-range fleet escorts. He suggested a ship with maximum close-range anti-aircraft armament, no large-calibre guns, full anti-submarine equipment and one set of torpedo tubes.

The discussions here subsequently evolved into considering the elevation of the main armament. The Director of Gunnery Division stated that the advent of

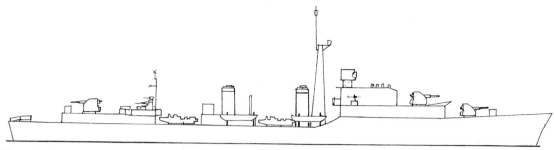

'Weapon' Class - *Two conventional funnels.*
(Drawing by Len Crockford based on original plan provided by David K. Brown RCNC) (RN College notes).

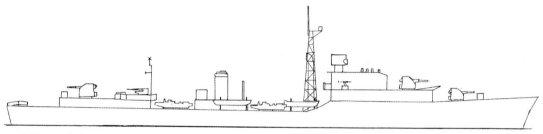

'Weapon' Class - *6–4in main armament.*
(Drawing by Len Crockford based on original plan held by the National Maritime Museum, London).

the Radio Proximity Fuze then being developed with the highest priority made it undesirable to limit elevation to 55°. Mountings with at least 80° elevation were, he considered, an essential requirement.

Perhaps surprisingly in this section no one came up with specific judgements other than the Director of Training and Staff Duties Division who supported Design 'QA'. A main armament of 6–4in was equated for anti-aircraft and anti-ship performance with 4–4.5in given comparable fire control when considering the fleet destroyer armament.

Twin-speed destroyer sweeps were felt to be needed in a well balanced fleet. However the cost of fitting, which meant the removal of one mounting, was not felt to be acceptable. One idea was to build a small special type of intermediate destroyer carrying the sweep, the main armament being twin 4in mountings.

The Director of Naval Ordnance (DNO) emphasised the advantage of producing of one type of destroyer. The DNC saw no advantage in changing the types being produced for Design 'QA' did not differ greatly from the 'Q' type design then in production.[3]

The Intermediate Destroyer question came before the Future Building Committee on 7 September 1942. It was agreed that it appeared impracticable to arm a vessel of intermediate tonnage with more than 4in guns with 80° mountings. In order to give further consideration to the class the committee called for three designs of 1750 tons to 1800 tons armed with either: (i) 6–4in guns, (ii) 4–4in guns and (iii) 4-4.5in (55°) in RPC mountings.[4]

The requested sketch designs were duly presented to the Committee on 21 September 1942. Design 'QC' carried two twin 4in mountings and displaced 1,730 tons, 'QD' carried three twin 4in mountings and displaced 1915 tons whilst 'QE' was armed with two twin 4.5in guns and

displaced 1870 tons. All were designed to achieve 36.5kts (31kts deep) with endurance being 4700 miles. None of the designs could use the existing intermediate hull, however, and there was general agreement that none of them offered a very satisfactory ship. It was decided to ask the DNC to produce two further designs using the existing intermediate class hull which (i) mounted 4-4.5in singles (55°) with one barrage director and (ii) 6–4in (twin 80° mountings) with two barrage directors. It was indicated that a reduction in speed of one knot was acceptable. The destroyer programme was also looked at as a whole and here it was reported that of the 40 slips used to construct destroyers only seven were unable to accept the new 'Battle' class destroyers.[5]

The Committee duly discussed the response of the DNC on 5 October 1942. Three designs were presented: (i) 'QF' 4-4.5in singles (55°), one barrage director: Displacement 1800 tons. (ii) 'QG' 3–4in twins (80°), two barrage directors: Displacement 1760 tons. (iii) 'QH' 3-4.5in singles (80°), one barrage director: Displacement 1800 tons. Each design included two fixed torpedo tubes on each side, one twin Bofors, four twin Oerlikons with endurance being 4700 miles at 20kts.

It was accepted that these vessels would have to be regarded as a good utility escort with a good anti-aircraft defence. They were not seen as anti-submarine vessels for the Committee did not want to see them loaded up with depth charges. Although there was some doubt as to the lethal effects of a 4in shell the preponderance of opinion favoured Design 'QG'. The DNC was asked to proceed with the design but the following departures were suggested:

One additional twin Bofors.
An additional barrage director forward.
Two twin Oerlikons only.

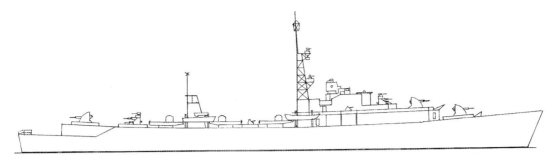

Thornycroft Design.
(Drawing by Len Crockford based on original plan in the Thornycroft Collection held by the National Maritime Museum, London).

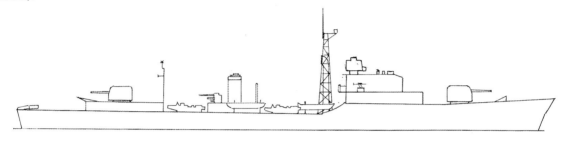

'Weapon' Class with modified armament. Design 'QN'
(Drawing by Len Crockford based on original plan in Ships Cover ADM 138 711 held by the National Maritime Museum, London).

Ten depth charge pattern with 70 depth charges.
Three or four fixed torpedo tubes each side forward.
Type 272 Radar dispensed with and its functions performed by Type 275 set when it is introduced.

The DNC, Sir Stanley Goodall, who was present at the meeting, pointed out that all these requirements could not be met on the present displacement. It was agreed that he would see what could be done on the principle of alternative armaments while retaining a displacement in the neighbourhood of 1800 tons.[6]

After many trials and tribulations the basis of the 1943 Intermediate Destroyer design had at last been agreed but it was not only the armament of the new class which were causing difficulties. The Prime Minister was, as ever, probing into the logic behind the Admiralty new construction programme. On 13 September 1942 he asked how many more 'Hunts' would be obtained if construction of both fleet and intermediate destroyers was stopped. In their reply the Sea Lords skilfully made the point that to design a destroyer like the 'Hunt' but with the necessary endurance would mean a hull very similar to the intermediate class with a correspondingly lengthening in the time to build. The new intermediate design was now on firmer ground with the main armament acceptable politically as well as operationally.[7]

Designing the Ship

The new intermediate class destroyer design was at the time of presentation to the Future Building Committee basically a modification of the type already in series pro-duction. In appearance the ships would have had the single funnel profile of the earlier ships and shared the same hull and machinery designs. What in later years would be defined as the 'concept design' stage was however not yet over for as early as 2 October 1942 it was being suggested that a staggered machinery layout should be adopted. This idea was originally rejected on account of the increased beam that would be necessary. The reason why staggered machinery was wanted was that the action damage report on the experience of the destroyer USS *Kearney* indicated that a ship with this layout would be far less liable to fatal damage or total machinery failure. The unit system could ensure that one boiler and machinery set could remain operational when the second set was out of action. A further development, again involving lessons from United States experience, was the possibility suggested by the Engineer in Chief on 9 October 1942 that new machinery with higher temperatures and pressure could be produced. I hesitate to use the word recommend for the Engineer in Chiefs Department appeared a conservative body and difficulties were outlined. The machinery was expected to take nine months to design, the production period was expected to lengthen and there was expected to be an initial reduction in reliability. Another factor working against any change was that only eight intermediate destroyers were then projected in the 1943 Programme, a factor which did not justify a major re-design. The programme numbers were however far from certain for Thornycroft was seen as able to take either three fleet destroyers or four intermediates.[8]

The subject did not die away, however, for the Controller gave indications that he would like to see a new machinery design used in the new destroyers and even minuted that he was prepared to accept a lower degree of reliability. Needless to say the Engineer in Chief did not feel happy about any loss in reliability. The DNC and the Engineer in Chief discussed the machinery issues on 30 October 1942 when the questions of both a staggered machinery layout and machinery with increased temperature and pressure were discussed the aim being to improve economy by some 15 per cent. To ensure reliability meant that 'economisers' had to be fitted high up. This cost 30 tons of extra weight a figure which increased to 60 tons if staggered machinery arrangements were adopted. Fitting staggered machinery meant that two funnels would have to be fitted which in turn made it more difficult to fit the armament on the upper deck.[9]

Nevertheless, it was decided that higher steam pressures and temperatures should be accepted in the future. The issue was discussed by the Future Building Committee on 10 November 1942 when it was accepted that pressure should not exceed 400 lb/sqin and temperature 750°F. Up to this time for production reasons the 1937 design with steam at 300 lb/sq in and temperature at 650°F had been specified. By adopting the new standard a 20 per cent gain in efficiency was expected at speeds over 20kts which in turn enabled the DNC to meet Staff Requirements. The penalty was a six months delay in production which it was foreseen would mean only nine intermediate destroyers being delivered in 1945. This loss of production however rather flew in the face of the Sea Lords aims which were expressed as recently as 1 July 1942 when letters were dispatched to the shipbuilding firms indicating that they required destroyers to be built in fifteen months, the aim being to 'speed up' production. Another innovation which could now be worked into at least some members of the class was welding where Milne of J S White indicated to

Goodall at the end of October that he was ready to weld destroyers, clearly a useful potential gain in a weight sensitive design. The flow of design studies kept pace with the new thinking. 'QG' was modified to give 'QJ' also 1800 tons. Then came 'QJ' five feet longer and displacing 1825 tons. 'QK' displaced 1865 tons and was given an additional four inches beam and a pattern of ten depth charges. Then new machinery was worked in which took the displacement to 1920 tons.[10]

The Sea Lords were presented with details of the new destroyer after a Board meeting on 6 November 1942 at the instigation of the Deputy First Sea Lord, Admiral Sir Charles Kennedy-Purvis, Chairman of the Future Building Committee. A model was produced showing the general appearance. For comparative purposes details of the existing intermediate design and the 'Hunt' class were also set out. It was not too long before the Sea Lords were describing the new class as 'in effect a 'Hunt' class with increased endurance'; no doubt to assuage any criticism which the size of the new destroyers might provoke in the mind of the Prime Minister.[11] By the end of November 1942 a tentative new construction programme for the following year was becoming more firmly based. A study by the Future Building Committee had indicated that only half the anticipated destroyer requirements needed would be available the result being that the proposed programme was now to build 26 fleet destroyers and 17 intermediate destroyers, a fair change from the numbers expected to be ordered only a few weeks previously. Volumes remained an important factor.[12]

The debate over the design of the new destroyer was, however, far from over. The Controller was described by Goodall in his diary as being 'fussed over the armament' whilst the Deputy Controller considered them to be very

HMS Battleaxe pictured in October 1947, as originally built. (WSS).

large ships, comparable in size to the 'Tribal' and 'L' class destroyers. He said this factor was going to inevitably advance the building time by some three or four months and at first sight he felt that the advantage over the 'S' class destroyer was not apparent. His comments were countered by pointing out that the new design could engage three aircraft with reasonable local control arrangements whilst the 'S' class could only engage one aircraft. The 1943 class with its main armament capable of being fired at 80° could engage the vast majority of steep bombing attacks which was far from the case with the 'S' class design. There was also the factor that the new ship would be capable of engaging twice as many targets with its Bofors anti aircraft guns. The logic behind these facts meant that for an extra 245 tons more than an 'S' class, anti aircraft gunfire was twice as efficient and just as good in low angle gun power particularly at moderate and short ranges. No change was made.[13]

The design of the class was moving rapidly forward by February 1943, with the Admiralty Experiment Works at Haslar preparing preliminary effective horsepower curves. Some features were facing uncertainty; the fixed torpedo tubes were questioned with the Director of Training and Staff Duties Division strongly urging that eight conventional torpedo tubes should be carried at the expense of either a twin Bofors or a five pattern depth charge. The fixed tubes were given up at the expense of a twin Bofors, the alteration being agreed by Goodall on 1 March 1943. Another change was made in April 1943 when the fire control arrangements were reconsidered. The Deputy Controller, CEB Simeon, considered the provision of individual control for each 4in mounting to be generous. It was duly agreed that a set could be removed. Consideration was also being given to mounting the 'Buster' control system for the 40mm Bofors mounting.[14]

The 1943 New Construction Programme

By March planning was underway for the allocation of drawing work to the firms who would build the ships. This task was divided between Scotts, Thornycroft, White and Yarrow. The Controller was also considering the dates when the ships could be laid down. On 29 March 1943 he anticipated that the first ship would be laid down in September 1943 and the final pair laid down in September 1944. In mid-April however, homes had only been found for thirteen members of the class and timings were slipping. Thornycroft was to build three which were to be laid down in March, June and September 1944. Yarrow had four ships to lay down in March, June, August and November 1944. Scotts was to be given five ships which were to lay down in October 1943, January, May, July and August 1944. White was to lay down one ship in November 1944. The balance of the programme was later made up by bringing in Denny, which took two ships, and allocating one more class member to both Thornycroft and Scotts. Denny was not introduced to the Programme until May 1943 when Goodall visited the yard. The firm indicated that they would take the order but would not be in a position to lay down the

destroyers until late in 1944. Scotts accepted an order for a sixth, again as a result of a visit by Goodall. The 1943 Programme was, of course, anticipated to authorise the construction of 17 destroyers of the new class. The number was increased to 19 when in March 1943 it was decided to build the 'C' class destroyers Centaur and Celt of the 1942 Programme as units of the new class.[15]

On 20 March 1943, the First Lord of the Admiralty, AV Alexander duly put his name to the 1943 New Construction Programme. The 17 intermediate destroyers included, as anticipated, were said 'to have been designed for building in those berths which cannot accommodate the larger type'. The policy was to order 'as many destroyers as we can find berths for'. The Programme also included 26 'Battle' class destroyers. The budget for the ships anticipated expenditure of £700.000 in 1943, £5,000,000 in both 1944 and 1945 with £775,000 being spent in 1946, that is £675,000 per ship. The Cabinet discussed the Programme on 1 April 1943. The debate as far as it concerned destroyers was far from straightforward! The Prime Minister, as always, deprecated the growing size of destroyers and the time taken to build them. He wanted more resources devoted to vessels which could be completed more quickly. The First Lord and First Sea Lord, Admiral of the Fleet Sir Dudley Pound, responded by explaining the raison d'etre of the 'Battle' class, indicating that they would have liked all destroyers to have been built to this design. A lack of slips meant that 17 destroyers had to be built to the intermediate design. Rather optimistically, the First Lord said that it was hoped to reduce the building time for both types to between 16 and 18 months, a comment which rather flew against the Deputy Controllers opinion in January, when he was predicting an increase in the time taken to build the new destroyers. The question was then raised whether some reduction could be made in the destroyer numbers, with frigates and corvettes being substituted for them. The Cabinet asked for this matter to be considered but in order to avoid delay they agreed that orders for up to say 20 fleet destroyers ('Battle' class) could be ordered and all except a few of the 1943 Intermediate design could proceed. Orders for the first six members of the new class of intermediate destroyer were placed only one day later; a very rapid response. The Admiralty report titled 'The effect of replacing Fleet Destroyers by additional Frigates' was produced on 12 April 1943. It dismissed the idea stating 'it would not compensate for the proportionately greater loss in fleet destroyer strength and the disadvantageous effects on warship production'. The Cabinet duly accepted the report and approved the programme without amendment.[16]

Detailed Staff Requirements were finally produced in April 1943, no doubt after the first six vessels had been ordered, whilst the 'Weapon' Class legend and drawings together with a description of the design was prepared for consideration by the Board of Admiralty on 29 May 1943, several weeks after the first orders were placed. The Board duly approved the Legend and Drawings on 18 June 1943, the cost now being £651,000 per vessel.[17]

The timetable for building the class was extremely optimistic and it proved impossible to lay down any members of the class until April 1944. Clearly there were pressures on the shipbuilding yards and in August the management at Scotts went so far as to ask Goodall for their 'Weapon' class destroyers to be taken away from them. Nothing was done as there was no where else to place the ships. The next difficulty to arise was the placing of landing craft orders with the naval yards, which occurred in the Autumn of 1943. The programme did not cause too much chaos in yards building 'Weapon' class destroyers but J S White of Cowes and Thornycroft at Woolston were affected by the imposition of one landing craft order at each yard. Worse was to follow in December 1943, when the Transport Ferry (*LST mk3*) programme was being planned. Orders were placed for one ship (*LST 3035*) at Denny and another vessel (*LST 3043*) at Scotts. With the new landing ships and landing craft being given priority over existing programmes delays were inevitable. The only yard seemingly unaffected by the new demands was Yarrow. Another difficulty was labour recruitment, and here both Denny and Scotts lost men to the new frigate fitting-out complex at Dalmuir, further adding to their problems. Meanwhile, on a brighter note, construction of a prototype boiler for the class was underway in August, with trials expected to start in October 1943. If successful it was anticipated that the 1944 Fleet Destroyer design would be fitted with boilers of a similar design to those ordered for the 'Weapon' class.[18]

The 1944 New Construction Programme

Although not realised at the time, an event which would quite dramatically effect future members of the Weapon class occurred in October 1943, when the First Sea Lord, Admiral of the Fleet Sir Dudley Pound resigned and then died from overwork. His successor was Admiral of the Fleet Sir Andrew Cunningham, a fighting Admiral if ever there was one. He was soon to make his mark on the new construction programme.

The Future Building Committee discussed the 1944 New Construction Programme on 20 December 1943. The Director of Plans indicated that slips could be found for four 'Weapon' class destroyers by March 1945, a figure which was expected to increase to nine by September 1945. At this stage no change in design was envisaged other than replacing the existing quadruple torpedo tubes with quintuple 'Pentad' mountings, a suggestion made on 10 December 1943 which was duly approved in March 1944. The Director of Plans subsequently produced an undated memorandum which proposed the construction of the 14 'Battle' class and nine 'Weapon' class destroyers but he did state that this was the maximum number that could be built and that it was a figure that could reduce when the effect of the transport ferry programme (*LST mk3*) had been assessed. Warship production capacity was also in the thoughts of the Prime Minister, for early in 1944 he was wondering 'if we are ordering far more warships than we can ever lay down during the war'.[19]

The proposed programme was now discussed at a meeting held on 13 January 1944 called by the First Sea Lord. The formal minutes stated that 'it was decided to ask for 24 destroyers. The type of destroyer and the proportion between large and medium was left undecided. The First Sea Lord wished attention specially directed to providing the medium type with a heavier gun armament than is at present being considered for the 'Weapon' class'. Goodall made his own note which was a little more illuminating. He added that the Vice Chief of the Naval Staff wanted to build 24 destroyers, the response of the Controller being that this number could be asked for but that it was doubtful if capacity to build could be found. The First Sea Lord then criticised not only the 'Weapon' class as we have seen, but also the 'Battle' class on account of their size. Goodall then went on to say that it was agreed to ask for 23 or 24 destroyers without specifying the type. This meeting incidentally was to result in the demise of the new 5.25in cruiser design which was also strongly opposed by the new First Sea Lord. The Future Building Committee duly discussed developments at meetings held on 17 January and 28 January 1944. The result was that the Director of Gunnery Division was asked to prepare a paper on the merits of the destroyers' armament. His report, which compared the merits of a main armament of (a) the present design (b) four 4.5in guns in single 55° mountings and (c) three 4.5in guns in single 80° mountings, was produced on 5 February. The conclusion was that the 4in armament of the existing 'Weapon' class provided the best low-angle armament and the best defence against air attack. He did not however consider a main armament of 4–4.5in guns in Mark VI mountings. His report was, however, effectively bypassed, when it was produced, for the Sea Lords at a meeting held on 4 February 1944 discussed the main armaments of new designs of battleships, cruisers and destroyers. The subject was referred back to the Future Building Committee but the First Sea Lord did indicate that guns of less than 4.5in were unacceptable in the 1944 Programme destroyers. The results of the Sea Lords' meeting were reported to the Future Building Committee on 7 February 1944; their reaction was ask the DNC to look into a design with 4–4.5in high angle/low angle on a 'Weapon' class hull. What became the *Gallant* class had been conceived.[20]

The memorandum for the War Cabinet setting details of the 1944 New Construction Programme was not produced until 1 May 1944. The policy continued to be production of as many destroyers as possible using existing capacity to the full. It was expected that facilities would become available to produce 14 'Battle' class and eight 'Weapon' class destroyers, with the last ship expected to be laid down in the Autumn of 1945. The Prime Minister, as ever, commented on the increasing size of destroyers, observing that they had become virtually little cruisers. He was referring to the 1944 'Battle' class, which became known as the *Daring* class. The First Sea Lord 'cordially agreed with the importance of reducing the size of destroyers but in the circumstances of the Japanese war he saw no prospect of reducing the size of destroyers included in the 1944 Programme'. No comment was made about the redesign of the 'Weapon' class and it seems likely that most of the Cabinet were unaware that a major design change had occurred. The financial details indicated 22 destroyers were proposed at a cost of £21,520,000; no division between the 'Fleet' and

HMS Battleaxe *pictured in May 1959 after her AD conversion*. (WSS).

'Intermediate' types being indicated. This was a change in presentation compared with 1942 and 1943, when each class was presented separately in the financial table.[21]

The Department of Naval Construction were informed by the Deputy First Sea Lord that the designs of the 1944 Destroyers were 'in the melting pot' the day after the January meeting called by the First Sea Lord. The immediate reaction was to produce sketches of the earlier designs which were used in the presentation produced the Director of Gunnery Division in his paper. By the end of the month however an outline drawing of a destroyer with 4–4.5in guns in mkVI mountings, which has now been lost, was produced by the Department. It may well have been shown to the First Sea Lord, for by early February the new armament was incorporated in Design 'QM' produced at his instigation. By 11 February the new armament was clearly accepted, for the DNC directed that a sketch design be prepared with the main armament of 'QM' but retaining all the functions of a 'Weapon' class destroyer. He permitted an increase of 1ft6in (originally only 6in) in the beam, welding was to be used to the fullest extent and aluminium used wherever practical for superstructure and bridges. The use of this material was a new development, for aluminium could not have been provided earlier in the war and by July, when the design had been refined, it was calculated that some 23.4 tons had been saved by use of the material. The 13-ton Board Margin was sacrificed and the 44in searchlight mounted in the earlier design eliminated. As a first shot displacement was not to exceed 2000 tons. By March the design and been prepared and the details circulated. At this stage the design, in addition to the two twin 4.5in mkVI, carried 2–40mm twin Buster, 2–20mm twin Oerlikon, 2 Pentad quintuple revolving torpedo tubes, two depth charge throwers with one rail and fifty depth charges. One potential problem quickly came into focus. The manufacture of 4.5in Mark VI mountings, as planned, was clearly unable to keep up with the destroyers ordered in the 1944 Programme if

they were to start being laid down at the end of the year. The plan was to produce three mountings a month from September 1945; however something nearer five mountings per month were now going to be needed from mid-1946. This fact may perhaps explain the failure by the Director of Gunnery Division to include the 4.5in Mark VI in his options. There also may well have been some reluctance by shipbuilders to include so much welding in the new destroyers. A year earlier they had indicated their opposition to the technique in discussions with Goodall which are recorded in his diary. The Controller pointed out that the design showed the possibilities of making use of welding but that such a design would initially slow up production due to changes in technique, layout of yards and the training of labour, restrictions which could not have been accepted during the critical years of the war. It was however also pointed out that the result of a lack of welding would be an increase of 100 tons in displacement, which in turn translated into an increased length in order to maintain speed. Logic was slowly overcoming conservative forces.[22]

Plans for building the 1944 destroyers were quickly in train and as early as 5 February it was anticipated that Denny would lay down two ships in September and December 1944, Thornycroft was to lay down its pair in January and May 1945, White was allocated two which were to be laid down in December 1944 and March 1945 whilst Yarrow was given the final pair with keels to be laid in March and June 1945. It does seem likely however that when this plan was drawn up it was expected that the 1944 ships would be identical to the 1943 'Weapon' class. By 22 February 1944 Plans Division reported that the Prime Minister had indicated that vessels should not be ordered from the 1944 Programme which could be laid down by March 1945. The dates now slightly slipped at this stage, with six of the class expected to be laid down in the first quarter of 1945 and the remaining two following in the next quarter, outside the parameter set by the Prime Minister.[23]

Designs and Plans Evolve

The ambitious nature of the 'Weapon' class programme was clearly evident by January 1944. It was becoming abundantly clear that Scotts had little hope of building their six members of the class within any reasonable time and at the end of January Goodall, in a memorandum to the Engineer in Chief indicated, that he was looking for a home for the last two vessels of their order. At that point in time the pair were not due to lay down until the end of 1945, which was later than the dates given for the new 1944 class. The quest for slipways on which to build the two destroyers was to prove unsuccessful and for the time being the orders stayed in place. The transport ferry (*LST mk3*) programme was also having specific effects. In January 1944 the Director of Plans estimated that two 'Weapon' class destroyers due to be delivered in July and August 1946 would be delayed for seven months by the interlopers. The yards effected (although not mentioned) were Scotts and Denny.[24]

Meanwhile the designs of both classes kept evolving. The deck layout of the 'Weapon' class was clearly rather cramped and to improve matters the Constructor in charge of the design, A J Vosper, suggested incorporating the fore-funnel in the mast. Up to this time a conventional two-funnel layout had been adopted. This idea was incorporated into the 1944 class from the start of its life. The plan was accepted but it was to be October 1944 before the new design had been refined and proved at tests conducted by The National Physical Laboratory, Teddington.[24]

Co-incidentally with development of the funnel arrangements, Thornycroft came up with its own ideas, outlining a proposed destroyer based on the 'Weapon' class. The parentage could be seen in that it adopted the long forecastle form seen in the 'Hunt' class escort destroyers *Brecon* and *Brissenden*. The stated aim was to give nearly double the number of torpedoes, 50 per cent more small anti aircraft guns plus about 25 per cent more endurance. The design was to have the fore-funnel incorporated in the mast, although no detail was drawn as clearly knowledge of this development had only just reached the firm. The firm's ideas were taken seriously by the DNC for preliminary effective horsepower curves were calculated by The Admiralty Experiment Works in May 1944. The Chairman of Thornycroft was very disappointed with the results and the scheme inevitably died away. The preliminary effective horse-power curves for the 1944 class were also conducted at this time.[25]

The Staff Requirements for the new class were drawn up in July 1944. They were identical to the 1943 class except for the omission of the need to provide support for combined operations, which was perhaps an oversight. The fitting of the Squid anti-submarine mortar in the 'Weapon' class was also considered in July 1944 but at this point in time the option was rejected due to the loss of armament. The idea did not die, as we shall see, and in November fitting was also considered for the 1944 class. Again the option was rejected as it would have meant the loss of half the main armament. The design of the 1944

'Weapon', class now designated the 'G' class, was not submitted to the Board of Admiralty until November 1944, indicating a distinct lack of urgency. The standard displacement had just been kept within the limit of 2000 tons, being recorded as 1995 tons. The provision of the Buster-controlled 40mm mountings had been abandoned and two twin 40mm STAAG mountings now specified. Also carried were two 20mm twin Oerlikons and 10–21in torpedo tubes in two Pentad mountings. Fire control consisted of the Type 275 Radar. It was hoped to carry an American Mark 37 director with computer but if this was not available a British mk VI director was to be fitted. A separate MRS 1 barrage director with predictor control was specified for local control of the aft 4.5in mounting. As in the case of the 1943 'Weapon' class design there were various other armament options available. The cost per vessel was £750,000. The Board of Admiralty duly approved the design on 22 November 1944.[26]

The Last Months of the War and the Aftermath

By October 1944 the Admiralty was considering ship-building policy in the light of developments in the war. It was decided that work should be confined, with few exceptions, to warships which could be completed earlier than 1 September 1946 and that some 27 shipbuilding slips currently allocated to warship production should be available by the end of 1945 for merchant ship building. Three 'Weapon' class destroyers, *Grenade*, *Halberd* and *Poniard* ordered from Scott's were cancelled whilst *Claymore*, *Dirk* and the *Gallant* class were to proceed in slow time. The end of the war inevitably produced a substantial cutback in the warship building programme and the Controller drew up a list dated 12 September 1945. He indicated that *Claymore*, *Dagger*, *Dirk*, *Howitzer*, *Longbow*, *Musket*, *Spear* and *Sword* were to be cancelled, a recommendation formally approved on 16 October 1945. At this point eight 'Weapon' class and eight *Gallant* class remained in the programme. It was not long however before further economies were being sought. This time, however, matters were not straight forward for there seemed considerable justification in retaining the remaining eight members of the 'Weapon' class. Four ships were however under threat viz: *Carronade*, *Culverin*, *Cutlass* and *Dagger*. Some £440,000 had been spent on *Cutlass* which was assessed as 63 per cent of her total cost whilst some £400,000 (57 per cent) had been expended on the other ships. The Controller made a valiant attempt to keep *Culverin* and *Cutlass* on the grounds that loss of the ships would dislocate work at Thornycroft and Yarrow but they were not to survive and the Board of Admiralty approved their cancellation on 21 December 1945 with the First Lord confirming all arrangements on 23 December 1945. The *Gallant* class were also abandoned at this time. Prior to their cancellation, the sale of these four 'Weapon' class destroyers to Norway was being discussed in November 1945. In the event Norway purchased four 'CR' class destroyers which were originally to be taken over by Canada. One small problem thrown up at the end of the war was which destroyer should be given the name *Scorpion*, a wish proffered by the First Sea Lord who had commanded the World War One destroyer of that name. The 'S' class destroyer of that name was promptly transferred to Holland so it was decided to give the name to one of the 'Weapon' class destroyers. The first choice of The Ships names Committee in July 1945 was *Dagger* but owing to the likelihood of cancellations and no knowledge of just where the axe would fall the committee decided to leave matters in abeyance. Once the final decisions had been made *Tomahawk* was renamed *Scorpion*; the First Sea Lord had his wish granted. The *Gallant* class were not just a paper project, for work had commenced on assembling material and building machinery for the vessels. When the contracts for *Guernsey* and *Gift* were cancelled, Denny received £45,310 for machinery costs and a further £5835 for work expended on the hulls.[27]

One problem faced with the *Gallant* class was the sensitivity of the design to any weight increase. By July 1945, two single Bofors were being substituted for two twin Oerlikons and had added 7¼ tons, a barrage director added a further 2½ tons whilst the STAAG system had come out four tons overweight, adding a further eight tons. The problem could only be overcome by eliminating one STAAG mounting and dispensing with the streamlined funnel casing. The weight of the STAAG mounting also caused problems in the 'Weapon' class. To overcome this difficulty the 44in searchlight had to be given up and it seemed possible that the number of depth charges carried would have to be considerably reduced.[28] The end of the war did not put an end to developments in the 'Weapon' class design. By the end of November there were proposals evolving to convert all the eight survivors then remaining into fleet anti-submarine escort vessels. There were also tentative thoughts of converting two ships into radar pickets. On 22 December there will still hopes that six ships would survive and all were to become fleet anti-submarine escorts. Another idea current in early 1946 was that Nightshirt, a device intended to mask noise generated by the propellers, should be fitted in the first available ship. This suggestion was implemented and the system went to sea in *Scorpion*.

Formal approval to convert the four remaining vessels to anti-submarine escort vessels was given in March 1946. The squid was mounted forward in *Battleaxe* and *Broadsword* in lieu of 'B' twin 4in mounting and aft in place of 'X' mounting in *Crossbow* and *Scorpion*, the variation in armament layout being made to in order to test effectiveness. The class went on to complete with these specifications. The first of the class to be accepted was *Scorpion* in September 1947. The final member to be accepted was *Broadsword* in October 1948. She ran a six-hour trial on 25 May 1948. She displaced 2440 tons at the start of the trial, her mean speed was 31.318kts and mean shaft hp=40,169. Fuel consumption was 73 tons in six hours, mean displacement being 2388 tons. She had lived up to expectations.[29]

Perspective

The concept behind the 'Weapon' class destroyers produced a very flexible design capable of mounting a wide variety of armaments. Alfred Vosper, the designer however commented that 'We (The Destroyer Section) were always struggling to put a quart into a pint pot and I think the 'Weapon' class was a prime example of this (problem)'. They also incorporated advances in machinery design which, although conservative by American standards, produced a sensible compromise from both production and operational points of view. One has to remember that shipbuilders were conservative beings and even Thornycroft, which had a penchant for advances in warship design, did not like the changes asked for when it came to manufacturing the machinery. Once in service the class performed well. Their flexibility enabled the vessels to become what were in effect the first fast anti-submarine frigates and later they became the first radar pickets in the Royal Navy when the Type 965 radar was mounted. Apart from *Battleaxe*, which suffered collision damage, they all survived for 20 years or more; another measure by which to judge their success.

The *Gallant* class are more difficult to assess for no examples were constructed. There is however one major question to consider: should they have been designed? The alternative would have been to continue with the 'Weapon' class, which was the original intention up until January 1944. At this time the war was far from won and speed of production was still an important factor when the new programme was considered and change was inevitably going to cause delay. The new First Sea Lord, Sir Andrew Cunningham, considered that far too much emphasis was being placed on anti-aircraft capability, a judgement that was soon to be proved wrong. The *Gallant* class design did retain a major anti-aircraft capability with a dual-purpose main armament but it was achieved at the expense of a cramped ship, a weakness which could only be overcome by designing a warship with 'Battle' class dimensions which was not an acceptable objective. One has to conclude that it was a mistake to order the *Gallant* class; more 'Weapon' class destroyers would have been a better investment.

One lastly has to question the waste that occurred at the end of the war when so many ships of the two classes were cancelled. The decisions were traumatic but at a time of rapid change in naval weapons and with no potential foe in sight it was right to complete just four vessels. They enabled the Royal Navy to gain its first experience in operating fairly advanced machinery in fast anti-submarine escorts, a type of warship which was to dominate the coming decades.

The 'Weapon' class made their mark in the post-war Royal Navy and they proved to be an important milestone in both destroyer and frigate development.

Acknowledgements

My thanks are due to David K Brown RCNC for reading the draft and providing ideas which have been incorporated in the text, also to Alfred Vosper, the designer for his recollections and to Len Crockford for producing the drawings. I would also like to thank the staff at The Naval Historical Branch, The Public Record Office (PRO), Cambridge University Library and Bob Todd and his team at the National Maritime Museum (NMM) for all their help and kindness.

References

[1] The War Cabinet decision is recorded in minute WM (53) 42 held in CAB 65/26. The full details of the Programme are recorded in WP (42) 172 held in CAB 66/24, (PRO).

[2] 'Q' and 'R' class Destroyers (Ships Cover), ADM 138/625, (NMM).

[3] The Memorandum by the Assistant Chief of Naval Staff (Weapons) and extracts from discussion documents are recorded in FB (42) 2 dated 29 August 1942, ADM 116/5150, (PRO).

[4] Minutes of the meeting held on 7 September 1942 are recorded in FB (42) 3rd Meeting which is held in ADM 116/5150, (PRO).

[5] Minutes of the meeting held on 21 September 1942 are recorded in FB (42) 5th Meeting which is held in ADM 116/5150, (PRO).

[6] Minutes of the meeting held on 5 October 1942 are recorded in FB(42) 7th Meeting which is held in ADM 116/5150, (PRO).

[7] 1942 Prime Ministers questions of building of 'Hunt' class Destroyers; Answers from the Admiralty, ADM 1/11985, (PRO).

[8] 'Weapon' class Destroyers, (Ships Cover), ADM 138/697, (NMM).

[9] Department of the Director of Naval Construction – Papers, August 1942 – December 1942, ADM 229/27, (PRO).

[10] Engineer in Chief: Papers, ADM 265/2; there is a copy of the letter sent to the shipyards in Department of Naval Construction – Papers, March 1942 – August 1942, ADM 229/26, (PRO). The Prime Minister had asked the rate at which destroyers could be built in November 1941. The Admiralty reply indicated that on average it was taking 21 months to build an Emergency (Intermediate) Destroyer a figure which was later expected to reduce to 18 months. Admiralty Board Minutes and Memoranda 1942, ADM 167/112, (PRO). The Diary of Sir Stanley Goodall held at the British Library records Milne's commitment to welding. The very brief particulars of the three new sketch designs are quoted in the Ships Cover.

[11] First Sea Lord papers, ADM 205/20. The description of the class as being 'in effect a 'Hunt' class with increased endurance' is recorded in ADM 205/30, (PRO).

[12] First Sea Lord papers, ADM 205/21, (PRO).

[13] 'Weapon' Class Destroyers (Ships Cover), ADM 138/687, (NMM).

[14] Admiralty Experiment Works Reports, 1943, ADM 226/49, (PRO). The decision to eliminate fixed torpedo tubes is documented in (Ships Cover) ADM 138/697, (NMM). Agreement to eliminated fixed torpedo tubes and substitute two quadruple torpedo tubes is recorded in the diary of Sir Stanley Goodall, (British Library). The change in 4in Fire Control arrangements is recorded in ADM 138/697, (NMM). The 'Buster' fire control system was computer-based and under development at Vickers, Crayford for fitting in mountings produced at Vickers, Elswick. 102 systems were ordered but the project was cancelled after prolonged development delays. The one system delivered was finally produced in the last quarter of 1947, (Vickers Archives, Cambridge University Library).

[15] Drawing distribution is documented in ADM 138/697, (NMM). The planned laying down dates are recorded in the First Sea Lord papers, ADM 205/29, (PRO). The Programme as at mid April 1943 is set out in (Ships Cover) ADM 138/697, (NMM). The decision to build *Centaur* and *Celt* as units of the new class is recorded in an entry dated 13 March 1943 in the Diary of Sir Stanley Goodall, (BL).

[16] The Memorandum outlining the 1943 New Construction Programme dated 20 March 1943 WP (43)122 is held in CAB 66/33, (PRO). The minutes of the Cabinet meeting held on 1 April 1943 are recorded in WM(43)47 held in CAB 65/34, (PRO). 'Intermediate Fleet Type Destroyers 1943 Programme' details the orders placed on 2. 4. 1943, ADM 1/12581, (PRO). The memorandum 'Effect of replacing Fleet Destroyers by additional Frigates' dated 12 April 1943 WP (32) 145 is held CAB 66/33, (PRO). The final Cabinet approval of the 1943 New Construction Programme is recorded in WM (54) 43 held in CAB 65/34, (PRO).

[17] Warship Names are listed in the Minutes of the Ships Names Committee held at The Naval Library, MOD, Whitehall. London. The Staff Requirements are recorded in (Ships Cover) ADM 138/697, (NMM). The Memorandum for the Board of Admiralty dated 29 May 1943 is in ADM 167/118, (PRO) whilst the Minutes of the Board meeting held on 18 June 1943 are held in ADM 167/117, (PRO). Neither file contains any drawings.

[18] Report written by Sir Stanley Goodall following his visit to Scotts is dated 30 August 1943, ADM 229/31, (PRO). The LCT and Transport Ferry orders are in ADM 229/31 and ADM 229/32, (PRO). The report on progress in constructing the first boiler for the 'Weapon' class is dated 18 August 1943, ADM 229/30, (PRO).

[19] The discussion by the Future Building Committee is in FBC 43 28 held in ADM 116/5150, (PRO). The undated memorandum by the Director of Plans is in ADM 229/33, (PRO). The Prime Minister s comment was made on 31 January 1944, CAB 120/281, (PRO).

[20] The minutes of the meeting on 13 January 1944 called by The First Sea Lord are in ADM 205/57, (PRO); notes taken by Sir Stanley Goodall are in ADM 229/33, (PRO). The minutes of the Future Building Committee meetings are recorded on FB(44)2 and FB(44)3 and the report by the Director of Gunnery Division dated 5 February 1944 in FB(44)4 – Revised, ADM 116/5151, (PRO). Minutes of the Sea Lords meeting, 4 February 1944, ADM 205/40, (PRO). Minutes of the Future Building Committee meeting, 7 February 1944, FB(44) 4, (PRO).

[21] Memorandum to the Cabinet, 1 May 1944, WP(44)245 in CAB 66/49, (PRO). Minutes of the Cabinet discussion, WM(44) 65 are held in CAB 65/42, (PRO).

[22] 'Weapon' Class Destroyers, ADM 138/697 and *Gallant* class Destroyers, ADM 138/711, (NMM). The comments on use of aluminum and welding are contained in attachment to the Legend of the 1944 'Weapon' Destroyer contained in file NCD 24, (NMM).

[23] ADM 229/33, (PRO).

[24] Memorandum from Goodall to the Engineer in Chief is in ADM 229/32. Memorandum by the Director of Plans dated

Table 1:

Intermediate Destroyers 'Weapon' Class

Job Number	Yard Number	Name	Builder	Programme	Ordered	Laid Down	Launched	Completed
J 6235	1933	*Tomahawk*	White	1942	3. 2. 42	16.12. 44	15. 8. 46	17. 9. 47
J 6268	1934	*Sword*	White	1942	3. 2. 42	17. 9. 45		Can 15.10.45
J11006	1832	*Battleaxe*	Yarrow	1943	2. 4. 43	22. 4. 44	12. 6. 45	23. 10. 47
J11007	1833	*Broadsword*	Yarrow	1943	2. 4. 43	20. 7. 44	5. 2. 46	4. 10. 48
J 6113	4074	*Crossbow*	Thornycroft	1943	2. 4. 43	26. 8. 44	20.12. 45	4. 3. 48
J 6292	4075	*Culverin*	Thornycroft	1943	2. 4. 43	27. 4. 44	3. 46	Can 23.12.45
J11054	628	*Carronade*	Scotts	1943	2. 4. 43	26. 4. 44	4. 4. 46	Can 23.12.45
J11055	629	*Claymore*	Scotts	1943	2. 4. 43			Can 15.10.45
J11008	1834	*Cutlass*	Yarrow	1943	24. 4. 43	28. 9. 44	20. 3. 46	Can 23.12.45
J11009	1835	*Dagger*	Yarrow	1943	24. 4. 43	7. 3. 45		Can 15.10.45
J11056	630	*Dirk*	Scotts	1943	24. 4. 43			Can 15.10.45
J11057	631	*Grenade*	Scotts	1943	24. 4. 43			Can 23.12.44
J11058	632	*Halberd*	Scotts	1943	24. 4. 43			Can 23.12.44
J 6282	1935	*Musket*	White	1943	24. 4. 43			Can 15.10.45
J 6277	4076	*Howitzer*	Thornycroft	1943	24. 4. 43	26. 2. 45		Can 15.10.45
J 6231	4077	*Longbow*	Thornycroft	1943	27. 5. 43	11. 4. 45		Can 15.10.45
J11059	633	*Poniard*	Scotts	1943	27. 5. 43			Can 23.12.44
J 1286	1386	*Rifle*	Denny	1943	27. 5. 43	30. 6. 44		Can 23.12.45
J 1287	1387	*Spear*	Denny	1943	27. 5. 43	29. 9. 44		Can 15.10.45

Notes. *Tomahawk* renamed *Scorpion*. She was originally *Centaur* of the 'CE' group.
Sword was originally *Celt* of the 'CE' group.

1944 Weapon Class later *Gallant* Class.

Job Number	Yard Number	Name	Builder	Programme	Ordered	Laid down	Launched	Completed
J11010	1841	*Gallant*	Yarrow	1944	24. 7. 44			Can 13.12.45
J11011	1842	*Gael*	Yarrow	1944	24. 7. 44			Can 13.12.45
J 6271	4080	*Gauntlet*	Thornycroft	1944	30. 8. 44			Can 13.12.45
J 6302	4081	*Glowworm*	Thornycroft	1944	30. 8. 44			Can 13.12.45
J 1295	1395	*Guernsey*	Denny	1944	30. 8. 44			Can 13.12.45
J 1296	1396	*Gift*	Denny	1944	30. 8. 44			Can 13.12.45
J 6278	1937	*Grafton*	White	1944	30. 8. 44			Can 13.12.45
J 6312	1938	*Greyhound*	White	1944	30. 8. 44			Can 13.12.45

Note. Original names – *Glowworm* = *Gift*. *Gift* = *Gloworm* = *Guinevere*.

15 January 1944 outlining the effect of the transport ferry programme is in CAB 119/93, (PRO). Funnel arrangement details are in (Ships Cover) ADM 138/697, (NMM). The National Physical Laboratory report is in ADM 281/18, (PRO).

[25] Particulars of the Thornycroft design (T/1347), (NMM). Admiralty Experiment Works report, ADM 226/50, (PRO).

[26] Consideration of fitting Squid in both classes is recorded in (Ships Covers) ADM 138/697 and ADM 138/711, (PRO). The description of the 1944 'Weapon' design ('G' class) presented to the Board of Admiralty and the minutes of the Board meeting approving the project are in ADM 167/121, (PRO). The minutes of the Ships Names Committee records the suggested names.

[27] Shipbuilding policy notes prepared in October 1944 are in ADM 167/121, (PRO). Copy of the Controllers list dated 12 September 1945, ADM 138/730 (Ships Cover) Battleship New Design, (NMM). The documents containing the record relating to the December cancellations, ADM 1/19096, (PRO). Note concerning possible sale of 'Weapon' class to Norway, (Ships Cover) ADM 138/697, (NMM). The Canadian acquisition of 'CR' class, ADM 205/50, (PRO). The minutes of the Ships Names Committee record the quest for a ship to be named *Scorpion*. Compensation figures paid on the cancellation of *Guernsey* and *Gift* are recorded in the Denny list, (NMM). The figures for *Rifle* and *Spear* were £38,478 for the two hulls and £55,612 for both sets of machinery.

[28] Modifications to the *Gallant* design, (Ships Cover) ADM 138/711, (NMM).

[29] (Ships Covers) ADM 138/697, ADM 138/697A and ADM 138/711, (NMM).

Table 2:

	'Weapon' Class 29. 5. 1943	*Gallant* Class 14. 11. 1944
	(ADM 167 118)	(ADM 167 121)
Length between perpendiculars	341ft 6in	341ft 6in
Length on waterline	350ft	350ft
Length overall	365ft	365ft
Breadth, extreme	38ft	39ft 6in
STANDARD CONDITION.		
Displacement (tons)	1965	1995
Draught, forward	9ft 2in	9ft 1in
Draught, aft	10ft 2in	10ft 1in
DEEP CONDITION		
Draught, mean	12ft 2in (2700 tons)	12ft 1in (2740 tons)
Shaft Horse Power of Engines	40,000	40,000
Number of propelling shafts	2	2
Speed in Standard Condition (kts)	34	33.75
Speed in Deep Condition (kts)	30	29.75
Total Oil Fuel Capacity (tons)	620	630
Endurance at 20kts (miles)		
Clean Bottom Trial conditions	5000	5000
Complement of Officers and Men (as War)	230 (260 in Leader)	251 (279 in Leader)
GUNS		
4in Twin Mk. XIX Mountings (R.P.C.)	6 (400 Rounds per gun)	-
4.5in Twin Mk VI Mountings (R.P.C.)	-	4 (350 Rounds per gun)
40mm Twin Mountings (Radar Control)	4 (1440 Rounds per gun)	4 (1440 Rounds per gun)
20mm Twin Power Mountings	4 (2400 Rounds per gun)	4(2400 Rounds per gun)
TORPEDOES		
21in Torpedo Tubes in Q.R. mountings	8 (8 Torpedoes)	-
21in Torpedo Tubes in P. R. mountings	-	10 (10 Torpedoes Type 'D')
OTHER ARMAMENT		
Depth Charges	50	50
Throwers	2	2
Depth Charge Rails	2	1
DISPLACEMENT (Tons)		
General Equipment	103	103
Machinery	570	570
Electric Generators	30	30
Armament	241	290
Hull	1008	1002
Board Margin or disposable weight	13	-
Standard Displacement	1965	1995

Alternative Armaments

'A'	Normal Armament	Normal Armament
'B'	As 'A' but increase depth charge armament to 10 pattern 4 throwers 100 depth charges. Land one set torpedo tubes	As 'A' but increase depth charge armament to 10 pattern 4 throwers 2 rails 100 depth charges. Land one set torpedo tubes.
'C'	As 'A' but increase depth charge armament to 10 pattern 4 throwers 145 depth charges. Land both sets torpedo tubes.	As 'A' but increase depth charge armament to 10 pattern 4 throwers 2 rails 150 depth charges. Land both sets torpedo tubes.

'D'	As 'A' but fit Twin Speed Destroyer Sweep. Land one set torpedo tubes.	As 'A' but fit Twin Speed Destroyer Sweep. Land one set torpedo tubes.
'E'	As 'A' but fit ahead throwing anti submarine weapon. Land both sets torpedo tubes.	As 'A' except fit Squid Mounting Land both sets torpedo tubes.
'F'	As 'A' but fit a total of six 20 mm twin Oerlikons. Land one set torpedo tubes.	As 'A' but fit a total of six 20mm Oerlikon mountings (4 twin power operated and 2 either twin hand operated or singles) Land one set torpedo tubes.
FIRE CONTROL etc.	H.A/L.A stabilised director tower with Type 275 R.D.F. and a 15ft rangefinder. If available the Director will be the US type (computer). A separate barrage director is fitted for the after 4in mounting. The twin 40mm will be predictor controlled with Type 282 R.D.F.	H.A/L.A. stabilised director tower with Type 275 Radar and a 15ft If available the Director will be the US Mk 37 type (with computer). A MRS 1 barrage director with predictor gear is fitted for local control of the after 4.5in mounting. The twin 40mm are in twin STAAG mountings with self contained predictor control and Radar.
SEARCHLIGHTS	One 44in and one 20in.	Two 20in.
R.D.F. / RADAR.	One W.C. set, one G.A. set for main Armament, three G.C. sets for barrage director and 40mm predictors. R.D.F. beacon, I.F.F.	Two W.C. sets Types 293 and 291, one G.A. set for main armament Type 275, one G.B. set for barrage director, one G.C. set for STAAG, three Interrogator sets Type 242H, Transponder Type 253.

MODIFICATIONS 'Weapon' Class – March 1946. (ADM 138 697)

Armament.	4 – 4in one forward and one aft (*Battleaxe* and *Broadsword*) or two forward (*Crossbow* and *Scorpion*). 2 – 40mm Staag Mark II, 2 - 40mm Bofors Mark VII.
Torpedo Tubes.	10 - 21in, Pentad mountings.
Depth Charges	15
Rail	One.
Anti-Submarine Mortar	Double Squid and 20 salvoes fitted either forward or aft.
Fire Control	Mark VI tower forward. Radar target indicator 293M, gunnery 275 and 262.
Asdics	AS160X but one ship only to fit experimental dome and direction gear, the remainder to fit Types 144Q2 and 147F

NAVIES IN REVIEW 2000-2001

Antony Preston looks at current naval events.

Western European Navies

Belgium: Three new frigates are planned as replacements for the *Wielingen* class (E 71 type), after 2010-2012. A pair of *Kortenaer* class may be bought or leased from the Royal Netherlands Navy as an interim measure. Work starts on the first of four KMV type minesweepers in November 2000, and all are to be in service in 2003-2006.

Baltic Republics: The German Navy transferred three decommissioned *Lindau* class minehunters to the Estonian, Latvian and Lithuanian navies in 1999. Latvia took over the former *Völkingen* in October and renamed her *Namejs*. The former *Koblenz* went to Lithuania in December and was renamed *Süduvis*, while the former *Cuxhaven* was transferred to Estonia in January 2000 and renamed *Vambola*. The transfer is intended to help the three republics to establish their own mine clearance capability to clear their harbour approaches of German and Soviet mines.

Denmark: All three of the *Niels Juel* class corvettes have undergone modernisation, with the *Peter Tordenskjold* still in hand in July 2000. In the autumn of 1999 the Naval Materiel Command called for feasibility studies from DCN (France) and BAE Systems and DERA (UK) for the two command and support vessels approved under the 2000-2004 defence plan, with the intention of ordering them under the 2005-2009 defence plan. The length is likely to be 135 metres and displacement 5000-6000 tonnes. The patrol vessel variant will be smaller, about 115 metres and displacing some 4000 tonnes, and its basic design is expected to be completed by the end of 2000.

In March 2000 the Odense Staalskibsvaerft signed a Letter of Intent to join the Scandinavian 'Viking' joint submarine project. The joint venture company will submit proposals for the project-definition phase, ultimately leading (it is hoped) to four new diesel-electric submarines for the Royal Danish Navy.

Finland: The first *Rauma-2000* type fast attack craft (FAC), the *Hamina* (74), is in service. Three more were to be ordered in 2000, followed by four more, but to date only one has been ordered.

France: The aircraft carrier *Charles de Gaulle* will not be fully operational until 2001, when the first Rafale-M squadron is embarked, and will not be ready for full trials until October 2000 at the earliest. In 1999 the *Foch* spent a short time at sea, but she will be put on the disposal list as soon as the *Charles de Gaulle* enters service. The 35-year old helicopter carrier/training ship *Jeanne d'Arc* did useful relief work in Mozambique after the disastrous floods, and she will run on until 2006.

The submarine force now comprises six *Rubis* class nuclear attack submarines (SSNs), all modernised, and four nuclear strategic submarines (SSBNs), two *l'Inflexible* class and two *le Triomphant* class. A fifth SSBN, *le Vigilant*, is planned to enter service at the end of 2003, but *l'Inflexible* will be decommissioned in 2005, bringing the force back to four boats. Design work is in hand on Project 'Barracuda', six new 4000-tonne SSNs to replace the *Rubis* class in 2008-2018 (the first is to be ordered in 2001). The last of the *Agosta* class diesel-electric boats, *la Praya*, is a testbed for Project 'Barracuda' sub-systems.

The collapse of the 'Horizon' tri-national project to build an anti-air warfare 'frigate' in 1999 led the French Navy to propose a Franco-Italian 'Eurofrigate' to meet the requirement. This appears to be a derivative of the *Arriyad* design building for Saudi Arabia, an enlarged *La Fayette* design armed with the Principal Anti Air warfare Missile System (PAAMS). As a sop to the Italian partner the gun will be the Otobreda 76mm L/62 Super Rapid. The destroyer *Georges Leygues* will be decommissioned in 2000.

The fourth *La Fayette* class frigate, the *Aconit*, was to be fully operational by December 1999, but the fifth and last of class, the *Guépratte*, will not follow until early 2002. When it is recalled that the first three were ordered in 1988, a time-span of fourteen years for five ships seems too long for a Western European shipyard, but funding problems accounted for most of the delays. The total of *d'Estienne d'Orves* class A 69 type coastal escorts falls to ten in 2000 and nine in 2001, the remainder to be based at Toulon (three) and Brest (six).

The new emphasis on rapid-reaction forces is revitalising the French Navy's amphibious forces. Plans to build two more *Foudre* type amphibious dock transports (LPDs) have been replaced by a new design known

France's new CVN Charles de Gaulle with an E-2C Hawkeye AEW aircraft and Super Etendard strike aircraft at the forward end of the flight deck. (Chourgnon/ECPA).

as the *Nouveau Transport de Chalands de Debarquement* (NTCD), one to be ordered in 2000 for delivery in 2004, and a second to be ordered in 2002 for delivery in 2005. They will have command facilities and improved helicopter capability, and will be able to operate surface-effect ship (SES) landing craft. The second NTCD will replace the *Jeanne d'Arc*, and in an effort to stimulate competition it is hoped to build them at the commercial Chantiers de l'Atlantique yard in St Nazaire. The old LPD *Orage* will be decommissioned in 2004, and her sister *Ouragan* will follow in 2006.

The 4870-tonne landing ship *Bougainville* is no longer used to support nuclear testing at Mururoa Atoll in the Pacific. She returned from Papeete in November 1998, and was converted to an intelligence-gatherer (AGI) from December 1998 to July 1999. She retains her L pennant number, presumably to hide the fact that she is an AGI.

All 13 *Eridan* class Tripartite mine-hunters will be modernised, under a contract awarded to Thomson Marconi Sonar in November 1999. A

Three computer-generated images of the Royal Navy's new Daring *class (Type 45) air defence destroyers.* (BAE Systems).

new combat system will integrate the existing 2022 Mk 3 hull sonar with the Propelled Variable Depth Sonar (PVDS).

Germany: Work continues at Kiel and Emden on the Type 212 diesel-electric submarines, and all four are to be delivered in 2003-2006: *U.31* in September 2003, *U.32* at the end of May 2005, *U.33* at the end of January 6 and *U.34* a month later. They will replace four of the Type 206A boats, which will retired in 2002 (one), 2004 (one) and 2005 (one) but there is no hint of funding for replacing the remaining eight. Two of the older Type 205 boat, *U.11* and *U.12* are retained for trials.

The Type 124 air defence frigate programme is making progress, with the *Sachsen* launched in November 1999 and planned to be completed in November 2002. The Active Phased Array Radar (APAR) land-based test site was set up at Den Helder at the end of 1999, and deliveries of the production model will begin in 2001. The three ships are to come into service in 2002-2005. Only two Type 103B destroyers remain in service as the *Rommel* was decommissioned in October 1998 and partially 'canni-balised' to provide sub-systems for the *Sachsen*.

The FAC force is in decline, with 30 left and several of the Type 148 *Tiger* class already sold abroad. Their

replacements are the much larger Type 130 corvettes, and bids for the first five were submitted by Blohm+Voss and Howaldtswerke Deutsche Werft (HDW) late in 1999.

Great Britain: The aircraft carrier HMS *Invincible* started her sea trials in March 2000, following a year-long refit at Portsmouth. She has had a 'nose job' similar to her sister *Illustrious*. The GWS.30 Sea Dart missile launcher and magazine have been replaced by a starboard exten-sion to the flight deck for RAF GR.7 Harrier IIs. Both contenders for the

design of the Future Aircraft Carrier (CVF) are working on their propos-als, but the ultimate configuration will depend on the aircraft finally selected. If the Short Takeoff/Vertical Landing (STOVL) variant of the Joint Strike Fighter (JSF) is cancelled the alternatives would be a naval ver-sion of the Typhoon (Eurofighter) or the French Rafale-M. Either would require catapults and arrester gear, pushing up size and increasing com-plexity.

A greater priority is given to the Type 45 air defence destroyer, the successor to the cancelled 'Horizon' project. The main weapon system is

The 'Duke' class frigate St Albans *takes the water at BAE Systems' Scotstoun yard.* (BAE Systems).

Launch of the minehunter Blyth *at Vosper Thornycroft's Woolston yard.* (Vosper Thornycroft).

already selected as PAAMS, and a number of other decisions have been made. At the time of writing the ships will have electric drive, powered either by the Northrop Grumman/Rolls-Royce WR-21 intercooled gas turbine or a variant of the LM-2500. Baselines have been designated for the combat system (DNA) and the electronic warfare system (DLH and UAT); this does not mean a straight copy, but the parameters of performance will be the starting point for the new specifications. The main surveillance radar will be the BAE Systems SAMPSON multi-function active phased-array system, with Alenia-Marconi's S1820M surveillance radar (using the company's processor with the antenna array of the Dutch SMART-L). The in-service target for the first ship remains 2007, and the order may be placed late in 2000 with BAE Systems' Yarrow shipyard on the Clyde. They will be ordered in batches of three, and only Batch 1 will have the 4.5in Mk 8 Mod 1 gun. The rest will have a new 155mm weapon firing extended-range guided munitions (ERGMs); all will be fitted 'for but not with' land-attack missiles. According to Jane's Fighting Ships, names will be: *Daring, Dauntless, Decoy, Defender, Demon, Despatch, Diamond, Dorsetshire, Dover, Dragon,*

Dreadnought and *Duncan*, an odd mixture of old destroyers, capital ships, cruisers, submarines and frigates.

Only eleven of the Type 42 destroyers are still in service, as the *Birmingham* is to be scrapped. It is possible that the remaining three Batch 1 ships, the *Cardiff, Glasgow* and *Newcastle* (commissioned in 1978-79), may be laid up before the first Type 45 is delivered, or may have no more money spent on them.

Steel has been cut for the first *Astute* class SSN, and the new non-penetrating optronic mast contract has been awarded, following successful trials in HMS *Trenchant* in 1998. The older SSN HMS *Splendid* fired 30 Tomahawk land attack missiles against targets in Yugoslavia during the UN intervention, and all SSNs are now to receive Tomahawk instead of the seven planned. HMS *Vengeance*, the last Trident-armed SSBN, was delivered in December 1999.

The fourteenth 'Duke' class frigate HMS *Kent* was delivered a month early at the beginning of February 2000, and will become operational on 13 December the same year. She has a new bridge layout, which will presumably be common to her sisters *Portland* and *St Albans*, both currently fitting out at Yarrows (the latter

was launched on 6 May 2000). The *Kent* broke new ground by wearing the Blue Ensign defaced by a horizontal yellow Admiralty foul anchor, rather than the Red Ensign, while running trials. The projected sale of three *Boxer* class Batch 2 Type 22 frigates to Brazil in 1999 did not materialise, nor a similar offer to Chile, so they may be scrapped if another buyer cannot be found.

The ninth *Sandown* class minehunter, HMS *Bangor*, was completed in December 1999, leaving only *Ramsey* to follow in September 2000, and *Blyth* and *Shoreham* in 2001. Current plans are to sell HMS *Cromer* in 2001. Only ten of the older 'Hunt' class are still fitted for mine countermeasures (MCM), as the *Brecon, Cottesmore* and *Dulverton* are serving as Northern Ireland patrol vessels.

Amphibious forces are prospering, with the new helicopter carrier HMS *Ocean* proving a great success; she provided humanitarian relief in Honduras in the aftermath of Hurricane 'Mitch' and evacuated foreign nationals from Sierra Leone in May 2000. The dock transport (LPD) HMS *Fearless* is for disposal, but the new LPDs *Albion* and *Bulwark* are to be delivered in March and December 2003 respectively. The first pair of Mk 10 utility landing craft (LCUs) were to be delivered in December 1999, and eight more will follow between December 2001 and February 2003 when trials of the prototypes are completed.

To move the personnel and equipment of the Joint Rapid Deployment Force the Ministry of Defence requested bids early in 2000 for six roll-on/roll-off ferries. The most interesting proposal is from the Sealion Consortium, to build four at the former Kvaerner Govan yard (now part of BAE Systems) and to use two similar ships ordered by Stena from an overseas yard. The six ships would be managed by Sealion, including training for 'sponsored reserve' crews, maintenance and operation. If the bid is accepted the ships would be built in 2002-2003.

Only five of the 'Island' class offshore patrol vessels (OPVs) remain, HMS *Orkney* having been sold to Bangladesh in May 1999. Structural work on the trimaran demonstrator RV *Triton* was completed in March 2000, and she was launched on 6 May. She is to be commissioned in August 2000 for extended trials.

Greece: The Hellenic Navy has turned down an offer of the four ex-US Navy *Kidd* class destroyers, presumably because such big and complex ships would be very expensive to run. In their place it is possible that two 'stretched' MEKO 200 ships with Standard SM-2 missiles may be built in Greece. It remains to be seen what anti-air warfare capability is provided in the two missile-armed corvettes ordered from Ingalls, but it is likely to be only self-defence. The design is said to be an improved version of the *Sa'ar* V design produced by Ingalls for the Israelis.

Three Type 214 diesel-electric submarines were ordered from HDW in Germany in July 1999, one to be built at Kiel and two to be built by Hellenic Shipyards at Skaramanga. The first is to be delivered early in 2005, the second in March 2007, and the third in August 2007. The four Type 209/1200 *Poseidon* class boats are planned to start a modernisation programme in 2000, to bring them to the standard of the older Type 209/1100 *Glavkos* class.

The £200 million contract for three new 62-metre FACs was signed by Elefsis Shipbuilding & Industrial Enterprises and Vosper Thornycroft (UK) Ltd on 7 January 2000. The existing FAC force is being updated by the acquisition of second-hand craft from the German Navy. The four 56-metre *Pirpolitis* class large patrol craft ordered in February 1998 are to be equipped with Signaal's Tacticos combat systems, Variant target-indicating radars, Mirador electro-optical trackers and LIROD Mk 2 radar trackers. The first full system will be delivered to Hellenic Shipyards in 2001, with the remaining three to follow at four-month intervals. The main armament will be the Otobreda 76mm L/62 Compact gun.

Ireland: Details of the Irish Naval service's new OPV, LE *Roisin*, have finally been released after a prolonged and apparently pointless news

Launch of the trimaran demonstrator RV Triton *at Woolston. She is now running trials* (Vosper Thornycroft).

blackout. The short-list of October 1997 led to the selection of Appledore Shipbuilders, who used a modified design from Polar Designs of Vancouver, BC. This is unusual, flush-decked with a raked stem and transom stern, and is an enlarged version of an OPV built for Mauritius by ASMAR in Chile. Main armament is an Otobreda 76mm L/62 Compact gun, controlled by a Radamec 1500/2400 electro-optical tracker. The official delivery date was December 1999, and the order for No.2 was placed in April 2000.

Italy: The new air-capable LPD is to be named *Luigi Enardi* and is to be laid down in 2000, for completion in 2006. She will operate a mixed air group of Harrier Plus STOVL aircraft and EH101 helicopters.

The Italian Navy has surrendered its submarine design capability to Germany, with the acceptance of the Type 212A design, and in the wake of the cancellation of 'Horizon' has surrendered frigate design capability to France. The new 'Eurofrigate' will be a modified *La Fayette*, virtually identical to the French ships, with very little workshare, apart from PAAMS (already funded), the Otobreda 76mm gun and, presumably, some hardware for the electronics. Eight frigates are planned as replacements for the eight *Maestrale* class and eight *Lupo* class, with the first of class to

come into service in 2010.

The submarine force currently comprises four *Nazario Sauro* class and four *Salvatore Pelosi* class, an expansion of the original design. The *Nazario Sauro* herself is used for trials, with a reduced crew, and is not fully operational. Installation of the first ISUS 90-20 integrated sonar and command system in the *Primo Longobardo* at Muggiano was completed in 2000. The *Salvatore Pelosi* follows later in the year, while *Gianfranco Gazzana Priaroggia* and *Giulio Prini* follow in 2001.

In 1999 four *Aliscarfi* class 88.7-metre OPVs were ordered from Muggiano, for launch in 2000-2003 and completion in 2001-2004. Although funded by the Ministry of Transport they will be Navy-manned. The fourth *Esploratore* class 37.2-metre patrol craft, the *Staffetta*, was launched in October 1999 and completed in February 2000. The 13-year old former private-venture technology-demonstrator FAC *Saettia* was bought from her builders Fincantieri, and has been converted for service with the Guardia Costiera. Armament has been reduced to a single 25mm gun forward, twin funnels have been added, and a crane aft for handling an inflatable boat. She was delivered in July 1999.

The Netherlands: The new air defence frigate *de Zeven Provincien* was laid down at Flushing in December 1998 and launched in May 2000. The *de Ruyter* was laid down in 1999, followed by the *Tromp* in 2000, and the *Evertsen* will follow in 2001. They were to have had an American electronic warfare system, but this has been dropped in favour of the British Racal Sceptre system. A major modernisation is planned for the eight *Karel Doorman* class ('M' type), but the two *Jacob van Heemskerck* class air defence frigates will not be upgraded. Two of the surviving *Kortenaer* class ('S' type) are to be sold or scrapped.

The *Alkmaar* class tripartite mine-hunters are being modernised with an updated version of the German Troika triple drone system, a new navigation radar, a new hull sonar and a propelled variable-depth sonar (VDS), a new command system and a new mine identification and disposal system.

Norway: The Royal Norwegian Navy has finally made up its mind about the replacement frigate programme, announcing on 1 March 2000 that it has selected the proposals of Spanish builders Empresa Nacional Bazán and Lockheed Martin. Five frigates will be built, the first to be delivered in 2005. The combat system will be based on Lockheed Martin's Aegis associated with the SPY-1F phased-array radar. Norway is a member of the new 'Viking' submarine consortium, and hopes to build four of the joint design to replace the six *Kobben* class (IKL Type 207). Two of these 460-tonne boats were paid off in 1999.

Poland: The Polish Navy has a requirement for six Project 924 700-tonne missile-armed corvettes, and early in 2000 it was assumed that a bid from Blohm+Voss had been accepted, although no order has been announced. To improve training and to introduce relatively modern technology, the US Navy has agreed to transfer two *Oliver Hazard Perry* (FFG-7) class frigates. The former *Clark* (FFG-11) was handed over at Norfolk, VA on 15 March 2000, and has been renamed *General Plawski*. The *Sides* (FFG-14) is to be handed over in Fiscal Year 2003.

The two Russian-built Project 641 ('Foxtrot') submarines *Wilk* and *Dzik* will be deleted in 2002-2002, under present plans. Two Type 206A boats may be acquired from the German Navy.

Portugal: Although the Franco-Spanish 'Scorpène' submarine design was selected in 1998 no order has been placed. As the construction is intended to be co-ordinated with the Spanish programme, this must be assumed to be the cause of the delay.

Spain: Work on the first F-100 type Aegis frigate, the *Alvaro de Bazán*, is well advanced at Ferrol, with the launch planned for January 2001. A second LPD, the *Castilla*, was ordered in 1997 and is expected to join the fleet in July 2000. New medium landing craft (LCMs) have been ordered for the *Castilla* from the San Fernando shipyard.

Sweden: The Royal Swedish Navy's new corvette *Visby* was launched on 8 June 2000 at Karlskrona. The *Stockholm* class corvettes are to be upgraded at Karlskrona, with the same CETRIS combat system and sensors as the *Visby* class. They will also be modified to reduce their radar and heat signatures, and will receive and additional fuel and enhanced accommodation to allow them to take part in peacekeeping operations outside the Baltic. Both will return to service in 2002, and the four *Göteborg* class will follow.

As the driving force behind the 'Viking' submarine project, Sweden hopes to build two to replace the *Näcken* and *Najäd* afteer 2007, although eventually four more will be needed to replace the *Västergotland* class.

Turkey: The last of four Improved *Yavuz* class frigates, TCG *Kemalreis*, was to be handed over in August 1999, but severe earthquake damage to the Gölcük Naval Shipyard has delayed completion. Following the delivery of the fourth and fifth *Oliver Hazard Perry* (FFG-7) class frigates by the US Navy in February 1999, the Turkish Government has asked for a sixth. This was approved in May 2000, at a cost of US$60 million.

The as-yet unnamed frigate will be transferred as a 'hot ship', i.e. ready to go to sea, with all systems operational. The last Gearing FRAM I destroyer, TCG *Piyale Pasa*, was paid off at the end of 1999, releasing specialist ratings for the new frigate.

The fifth *Preveze* class submarine, the *Gür*, is under construction at Gölcük, and three more are planned. In addition to Tigerfish Mk 4 Mod 2 torpedoes, they are equipped with Sealion, Racal's export version of the Royal Navy's UAP electronic support measures system. A competition for a new heavyweight torpedo has been announced.

The third *Kiliç* class FAC, TCG *Mizrak* was commissioned in July 1999, bringing to an end this series. Three Type 332 steel-hulled mine-hunters have been ordered from Abeking & Rasmussen in Germany, equipped with the British Nautis-M command system and 2093 variable-depth sonar. The Coast Guard's first 'Seaguard' type large patrol craft is to be delivered by the Unuk Tasit Sanayii shipyard.

The United States, Canada and Latin America

United States: The nuclear-powered aircraft carrier *Ronald Reagan* (CVN-76) was to be launched in March 2000, and will join the fleet at the end of 2002. The unnamed CVN-77 is still at the planning stage (*United States* is the current favourite choice for a name, to commemorate the super-carrier cancelled before the Korean War). The only conventionally powered carriers left are the *Kitty Hawk* (CV-63), *Constellation* (CV-64) and *John F Kennedy* (CV-67), built in 1956-68. The older pair have received a service-life extension modernisation (SLEP), but the *Kitty Hawk* had only a 'complex overhaul' in the mid-1990s, and is in operational reserve.

In February 1999 the battleship *New Jersey* (BB-62) was replaced on the Naval Vessel Register by her sister *Iowa* (BB-61) as a Mobilisation Asset, and will become a museum at Camden, New Jersey. Her piping systems had deteriorated, and her 16in guns were wrecked during an overhasty demilitarisation. The *Iowa* is in much better condition, although her damaged turret has not been repaired (the materials are stored in her sister ship *Wisconsin* (BB-64). At the time of writing the Senate is debating the question of bringing the two back into service, as replacements for the ageing command ships *Blue Ridge* and *Mount Whitney*. By eliminating the 5inch gun mountings and automating more functions, considerable reductions can be made in manpower.

Modernisation of the first five *Ticonderoga* (CG-47) class Aegis cruisers has been dropped, and they may eventually be sold to a friendly navy. The *Lake Erie* (CG-70) and *Port Royal* (CG-70) have been used for trials of anti-ballistic missile defence systems and the Baseline 6 version of the Aegis weapon direction system.

All 28 of the original Flight I and Flight II *Arleigh Burke* (DDG-51) class Aegis destroyers were in service by the end of 1999, and work on he more advanced Flight IIA ships is progressing rapidly. The lead-ship, the USS *Oscar Austin* (DDG-79), is scheduled for delivery in July 2000. The latest names to be announced are *Mustin* (DDG-89) and *Pinckney* (DDG-91). DDGs 99-103 are to be ordered in 2002-3, bringing the programme to an end. During 1999 three Flight II *Arleigh Burkes* joined the fleet: the *Higgins* (DDG-76), *O'Kane* (DDG-77) and *Porter* (DDG-78).

Nine nuclear-powered surface ships and 43 submarines are listed for disposal and recycling of their nuclear plants. The third *Seawolf* class nuclear attack boat, the *Jimmy Carter* (SSN-23), was launched in June 2000 and will be commissioned at the end of 2001. The third Virginia class will be named *Hawaii* (SSN-776).

The last of the *Osprey* class minehunters, the USS *Shrike* (MHC-62), was commissioned in January 1999. No other warship was commissioned in 1999, although the Coast Guard took delivery of 19 assorted cutters and tenders, and the long-delayed icebreaker *Healy* (WAGB-20).

Amphibious forces are being replaced, with work in hand on the first of the *San Antonio* (LPD-17) class amphibious dock transports at Avondale Industries in New Orleans. An order has been placed for the second, *New Orleans* (LPD-18), and ten more planned. They will combine the roles of obsolete LPDs, dock landing ships (LSDs) and amphibious transports (AKAs), and will be the largest LPDs ever built. Very few of the older LPDs, LSDs and tank landing ships (LSTs) remain in service.

Canada: The first of four *Victoria* class diesel-electric submarines (formerly the Royal Navy's *Upholder* class), started training in April 2000 at Barrow in Furness. She is to be operational by August the same year, and her three sisters will follow at intervals of six months. The last Oberon, HMCS *Onondaga*, will be used for training until all four of the new boats are operational.

HMCS *Summerside*, the last of the twelve *Kingston* class combined minesweeper/patrol vessels (MCDVs), was completed in July 1999, but two of the class will be transferred to the Department of Fisheries & Oceans to reduce the defence budget. The Department of National Defence has revived plans to build four air defence ships to replace the modernised 'Tribal' class destroyers, instead of upgrading four of the existing 'City' class frigates. No design has been selected, but the new ships will be bigger than the 'City' class.

Argentina: The corvette *Gomez Roca* (46) is to be completed in 2000 or 2001, while her sister *Robinson* (45) was to be completed by the end of 1999 or early in 2000. Attempts to sell these two ships to other navies failed, and the improved state of national finances has finally brought this programme of six MEKO 140 type to a close.

The Argentine-built Type 42 destroyer *Santissima Trinidad* has apparently been refitting since 1999 to serve as a transport for marines. The former French oiler *Durance* was towed to Argentina in July 1999 and has since been renamed *Patagonia*.

Brazil: The IKL Type 1400 submarine *Tapajo* was delivered in December 1999, and her sister *Tikuna* is to be launched at Rio in 2002. The old British-built *Tonelero* is to come out of service in 2000.

The attempt to set up a surface combatant shipbuilding capability has proved only a partial success. The four *Inhaúma* class of light frigates proved very cramped and short on stability, and a Chilean evaluation showed poor seakeeping in southern waters. The *Barroso*, first of a group of four enlarged variants, was seen last year lying incomplete in a corner of the dockyard, presumably waiting for funds to continue work.

The funds were probably diverted to support the modernisation programme for the big *Niteroi* class frigates, built in Southampton and Rio to Vosper Thornycroft's Mk 10 design. The *Liberal*'s upgrading started in December 1996 and was completed at the end of 1999. The last of the four was scheduled for completion in June 2000 (two are excluded from the current plans, but may be brought to the same standard later).

Chile: The Chilean economy has been hit by a wave of inflation, and this has resulted in major cuts to the Navy's strength. The last Seaslug-armed destroyer, the *Prat*, will be paid off in 2000 or 2001, while the frigate *General Baquedano* has been laid up in reserve.

The submarine *Hyatt* was paid off in December 1999 to provide spares for her sister *O'Brien*. Both names are reported to be reserved for the new Franco-Spanish 'Scorpène' type boats building at DCN Cherbourg. The Italian Black Shark heavyweight torpedo has been selected for them, subject to successful trials in Chile.

The Navy has requested funding for Project 'Tridente', an ambitious plan to build a series of twelve warships to replace the existing second-hand destroyers and frigates. The ships would be built by ASMAR in three batches of four, starting off with a variant of the MEKO 100 to replace the ex-RN *Leander* class, and moving up to a class of four anti-air warfare (AAW) ships armed with US Standard SM-2 missiles, replacing the ex-RN 'County' class. The German MEKO 100 has been selected, but the Defence Minister is said to be very sceptical about the ability of local shipbuilders to run such a large programme within cost and time. The history of naval shipbuilding in Latin America is not impressive, notably the Argentine submarines, Brazil's light frigates and the Peruvian *Lupo* type frigates. The Minister is said to want the programme to be cut to a single prototype to demonstrate the capabilities of the shipyard, and in any case, no money has been voted.

Ecuador: The two ex-RN *Leanders*, *Presidente Eloy Alfaro* and *Moran Valverde*, have had Chilean SISDEF combat systems installed and twin Simbad short-range missiles have replaced the obsolete Seacat systems. Chilean shipbuilders ASMAR are reported to be offering to replace the steam turbines with diesel engines.

Peru: Despite their age, the two *Abtao* class submarines are still in commission as training boats. The ex-Dutch cruisers *Almirante Grau* and *Aguirre* are also in service, although laid down in 1939.

Venezuela: The *Lupo* type frigates *Mariscal Sucre* and *Almirante Brion* have completed their modernisation by Litton's Ingalls Shipyard at Pascagoula, MS. Work included replacing the Italian combat system with an Israeli Elbit system, and the *General Urdaneta* and *General Soublette* are to start similar modernisations in Venezuela in 2000.

The first of six 30kt fast attack craft was ordered in September 1999 from Empresa Nacional Bazan's San Fernando shipyard near Cadiz. She will be armed with Harpoon anti-ship missiles and a Spanish-made Otobreda 76mm L/62 Compact gun. The remaining five will be built locally.

The Russian Navy

Despite its appalling financial problems the Russian Navy is making heroic efforts to rebuild a credible force capable of defending the sea flanks. Progress on the Project 955 SSBN *Yuri Dolgoruky* is slow, with launch planned for 2005 and com-

missioning in 2008. Only two Project 941 'Typhoon' type SSBNs remain opeational, the *TK-17* and *TK-20*, but 16 assorted Project 667 'Delta Is, IIIs and IVs' are in service.

The first Project 885 *Yasen* class SSN, the *Severodvinsk*, is to be launched in 2003, and commissioned in 2005. Two of the much-hyped Project 971M 'Akula II' SSNs are in service, as well as eight of the older Project 971 'Akula Is', although a ninth unit, the *Gepard*, is not to be commissioned until 2000.

At the end of November 1999 a contract was awarded to the Zvezdochka shipyard for the refit of the Project 1144.1 nuclear-powered cruiser *Admiral Ushakov*. Launched in 1980 as the *Kirov*, she was renamed in 1992. She was the flagship of the Northern Fleet, but in recent years spent very little time at sea, leading *Jane's Fighting Ships* to claim that she was to be scrapped.

The Project 1164 cruiser *Moskva* has been refitted and started sea trials in the Spring of 2000. Only one of the Project 1134 cruisers is still in service, the lead-ship *Kerch*. Surprisingly, the 36-year old Project 58 cruiser *Admiral Golovko* is still in service, although she will probably be scrapped when the *Moskva* becomes operational.

Only seventeen destroyers are still operational, and it has been admitted officially that some will be offered for sale to foreign navies. The first such sale may be to China (see below). Seventeen frigates, mostly Project 1135 'Krivaks', remain, and thirty-eight light frigates.

A great swathe has been cut through the ranks of the older corvettes, FACs and coastal patrol craft, although some veterans survive. Similarly the amphibious forces have been cut back.

Middle East and Indian Ocean Navies

Bangladesh: The new frigate is to be delivered by South Korean builders Daewoo in 2001. Armament includes an Otobreda 76mm Compact gun, four anti-ship missiles and a helicopter. A 'Sapson-22100' frigate may

also be bought from the Ukraine Research-Design Shipbuilding Centre, adding to the already heavy burden of maintenance borne by this small navy.

Egypt: No decision has been made on the proposal to buy the Dutch 'Moray' diesel-electric submarine design as a replacement for the obsolescent 'Romeo' class supplied by China.

In March 2000 Alenia Marconi Systems annpunced a contract to modernise the combat systems of six 53-metrte *Ramadan* class FACs. The Egyptian Navy is slowly thinning out of its 'fleet of samples', but retains the ex-RN 'Z' class destroyer *El Fateh* in commission for harbour training.

India: The aircraft carrier *Viraat* (ex-HMS *Hermes*) is refitting at Cochin Shipyard, and doubts have been expressed about the likelihood of her ever decommissioning (she is planned to go out of service in 2006 or 2007). The Navy is publicly committed to building an Air Defence Ship at Cochin, and reports indicate that negotiations over repairing and refitting the former Russian *Admiral of the Fleet of the Soviet Union Gorshkov* are proceeding.

The modernisation of the submarine force proceeds at a rapid pace. The Russian-built Project 641 'Foxtrot' *Vagir* is to be paid off following a period in reserve. The Project 877 *Sindhushastra* was delivered from Russia in July 2000, bringing the total of 'Kilos' to ten. The 'missing' pair of IKL Type 1500 *Shishumar* class are reported to be planned for completion in 2004-2005, although Indian forecasts of building-times tend to be optimistic. These may be the Type 75 submarines, publicly described as an indigenous design.

The second Project 16A Delhi class destroyer, the *Mumbai* (ex-*Bombay*) is to be delivered in 2001, and three more are planned. The first Project 1135.6 Modifed 'Krivak III', the *Kashmir*, was launched at the Baltiisky Zavod shipyard in St Petersburg on 12 May 2000 and will be delivered in April 2002. The second and third of class will be named *Arunachal Pradesh* and *Sikkim*.

The new frigate INS *Brahmaputra* (F-23) was commissioned in April 2000 at Garden Reach Shipbuilders & Engineers (GRSE) in Calcutta. The first improved *Godavari* class lacked its main weapon system, the Trishul surface-to-air missile (SAM) developed by the Defence Research and Development Organisation (DRDO). The weapon is also touted as a prospective defence against anti-ship missiles, although it has yet to start Navy trials. The armament includes sixteen Russian *Uran* (SS-N-25) anti-ship missiles (SSMs) and the Sea King helicopter can carry two Sea Eagle air-to-surface missiles. The main gun is apparently the Russian 76.2mm L/59 AK-176. The ship also has a Russian close-in weapon system (CIWS), possibly the 30mm L/54 AK-630 'Gatling'.

The Navy has been putting great pressure on the DRDO to deliver Trishul on time and the Defence Minister has also condemned GRSE for taking twelve years to build *Brahmaputra*, which was laid down in 1989. GRSE will build two more of the class, the *Beas* (F-24) and *Betwa* (F-25).

The first of three Project 17 frigates was ordered from Mazagon Dock early in 1999, and names allocated are said to be *Talwar, Trishul* and *Toofan*. INS *Kora*, first of a new class of corvettes, was built by GRSE and commissioned on 15 August 2000. The *Kirch* is fitting out at GRSE and *Kulish* and *Kurmeek* are building.

Iran: Although still operating a number of elderly patrol and escort craft, the Navy of the Islamic Republic of Iran is trying to generate indigenous capability. Three 1200-tonne corvettes are reported to be building at Bandar Abbas. Described officially as frigates, they may be armed with Chinese anti-ship missiles. Two 65-metre training vessels were completed in 2000, the *Kilas-e-Qasem* class. At their commissioning, the Deputy Commander of the Navy announced that Iran has become the 'sixth largest exporter of submarine batteries in the world'. This raises intriguing questions about the design, for it seems unlikely that Iran would embark on battery-production

All three Israeli Dolphin *class submarines are now in service.*(HDW).

without technical support from an existing manufacturer.

Pakistan: The French-built submarine *Khalid* was commissioned in September 1999 and her sister *Saad* is to be launched at Karachi in 2001. On 18 April 2000 DCN Cherbourg passed a major milestone, when engineers installed the liquid oxygen (LOX) tank in a hull section of the *Ghazi*, the third of class. The air-independent propulsion (AIP) 'plug' comprises two modules, one for the LOX tank and one for the steam generator. In 2001 the complete AIP system will be put through its paces, using a shore test-facility. The AIP plug will then be integrated in the submarine at Karachi, creating the world's first MESMA AIP submarine.

PNS *Tariq* is the first of the ex-RN Type 21 frigates to recommission following a major modernisation. She now has an eight-cell launcher for Chinese LY 60N short-range air defence missiles in 'B' position, a French electro-optical director above the bridge, a Dutch DA-08 surveillance radar at the masthead and Mk 15 Phalanx 'Gatling' on the hangar roof.

Saudi Arabia: The first of three *Arriyad* class frigates was to be launched at DCN Lorient in Brittany in June 2000, for completion in 2002. No.2 will follow about a year later, but No.3 will not be delivered until 2005. The sailing for the frigate *Taif*

from DCN Toulon in March 2000 marked the end of the Mouette ('seagull') to overhaul the four *Madina* class. Virtually no changes have been made to the ships.

The Asia-Pacific Region

Australia: The Royal Australian Navy (RAN) has blown hot and cold over the US Navy's offer of the four *Kidd* class destroyers turned down by Greece, but finally abandoned the idea in June 2000. The dilemma is acute because only one of the American-built AAW destroyers, HMAS *Brisbane*, was in commission in 2000, and planned to pay off soon, and the over-ambitious plan to upgrade the eight *Anzac* class frigates to AAW ships proved unaffordable. The *Anzac* Warfighting Improvement Programme (WIP) was cancelled because the MEKO 200 design proved too cramped to allow the addition of a phased-array radar and Standard SM-2 missiles. BAE Defence Systems produced a solution for inserting a section amidships to accommodate the extra generators needed to run the additional weapons and sensors, but the cost was unacceptably high. In its place is a planned upgrade to anti-ship missile defence (ASMD), but options were still being looked at in June 2000.

Outweighing all the problems of replacing the AAW destroyers is the scandal surrounding the failure of the

The Japanese Maritime Self Defence Force training ship Katori *at Portsmouth.* (Portsmouth Naval Base).

combat system in the *Collins* class submarines. Following protracted discussions with contractors and a detailed government post-mortem in 1999, the RAN has decided to give priority to a programme to give full operational capability to the *Dechaineux* and *Sheean* at a cost of A$266 million. Consideration will then be given to bringing the remaining four boats to the same standard. The RAN's embarrassment was made worse by the prolonged rearguard action to stop the news of the shortcoming from becoming public knowledge.

In December 1999 HMAS *Hawkesbury*, the second *Huon* class minehunter, was handed over. Her sister *Norman*, started sea trials the following month, and three more are under construction. The conversion of the former US Navy LSTs *Kanimbla* and *Manoora* to assault helicopter carriers (LPAs) has proved very protracted, not least because of 'emergent work' such as hull corrosion.

Brunei: The three 'OPVs' ordered in January 1998 are well advanced at BAE Systems' Yarrow shipyard. First steel for No.2 was cut in November 1999 and it is hoped to launch the first in December 2000 or January 2001.

China: Yet again, rumours have circulated about an aircraft carrier for the People's Liberation Army-Navy (PLAN). According to the 'usual sources' a 48,000-tonne carrier will be built at Shanghai for completion in 2003(!) and full operational capability by 2005. Clearly the rumour-mongers have no idea how long it takes even the US Navy to build a carrier. The 30kt ship will, it is said, be driven by steam turbines of Russian design, and the air group will comprise twenty-four Sukhoi Su30MKK aircraft. Cost of the ship is claimed to be US$580 million, a modest figure by Western standards.

Submarine construction proceeds at a modest but steady pace. The first Project 039 'Song' type diesel-electric boat was completed in 1999 by Wuhan Shipyard, followed by the second in 2000. Two more are under construction, for delivery in 2001-2002, but there is no indication of more orders. Two more Project 636 Improved 'Kilo' type are on order from the Admiralty Yard in St Petersburg. Later purchases from Russia may switch to the smaller Project 1677 *Amur* design.

The second Project 956E *Sovremenny* type destroyer on order for the PLAN started trials in June 2000, out of the Severnaya Verf shipyard in St Petersburg. The as-yet unnamed ship, possibly to be numbered 137, was originally allocated the name *Vdumchivy* when laid down for the former Soviet Navy, but after the collapse of the Soviet Union was launched with the more traditional name *Aleksandr Nevsky*. Work on her and a sister were suspended until the PLAN shoed an interest in buying them, and both were ordered through the state-owned Rosvooruzheniye company.

The *Hangzhou* (136) sailed from St Petersburg for China early in January 2000. The second ship will be turned over to the PLAN in December 2000, and according to information released by the shipyard, consultations are under way between Chinese representatives, Rosvooruzheniye and the shipyard about selling two more of the type to the PLAN. One will be new-built and the other will be purchased from the Russian Navy and refitted by Severnaya Verf to meet PLAN requirements. Operating a squadron of four destroyers makes more sense, but the announcement puts in doubt earlier speculation about a building programme in a Chinese yard.

The first 'Luhai' type destroyer, the *Shenzhen*, was commissioned in January 1999. She shows some similarities to the earlier Project 053 'Luhu' design, but has two widely

The JMSDF destroyer Yamagiri *at Portsmouth.* (Portsmouth Naval Base)

spaced funnels, indicating a unit disposition of machinery. The electronics also show soma improvements. A second is planned, but had not been laid down at the start of 2000.

The sixth 'Jiangwei' type frigate was commissioned in March 2000, and two more are building. Like the new destroyers they are armed with the French lightweight Crotale Naval short-range air defence missile and the Ying-ji-1 ('Eagle Strike'). The PLAN is clearly trying to standardise to greater extent than before, as some of the older 'Jianghu' type have Ying-ji instead of the elderly HY-2 weapon.

Japan: The submarine *Uzushio*, third of the *Oyashio* class, was commissioned on 3 March 2000. Seven more are planned, four of which are fitting out or under construction. As usual three of the older *Yuushio* and *Harushio* classes have been relegated to training, to keep the numbers at sixteen.

Four more Aegis destroyers are projected, and the existing *Kongo* class will be upgraded to launch the US Navy's Standard SM-3 missile. This will give the Maritime Self Defence Force (MSDF) the ability to counter tactical ballistic missiles.

With six *Murasame* class destroyers in service by March 2000 and three more afloat, work has already started on an improved version. In the first half of 2000 the unnamed DD-110 and DD-111 were laid down, and a third is to follow in 2001. The major difference is the adoption of the Mk 41 vertical-launch system (VLS) rather than the less versatile Mk 48. This permits a change in the future from Sea Sparrow to the bigger Standard series.

Despite political repercussions, the MSDF is pressing ahead with two more *Osumi* class LPDs. Opposition parties in the Diet claimed that the full-length flight deck indicted an aircraft carrier capable of operating STOVL aircraft, and this would dive the MSDF the ability to wage 'offensive' warfare, contrary to the Constitution. In fact Japanese warship have already taken part in peacekeeping operations in Cambodia, and a ship capable of landing and refuelling helicopters is invaluable.

The minehunter *Tsunoshima* was commissioned in 2000, and the *Naoshima* is to be delivered in 2001. Three more are to be built by 2003, and another two are projected.

Malaysia: The new frigate *Lekiu* was commissioned on the Clyde on 9 October 1999, followed by her sister Jebat on 20 November.

The second pair of Italian-built corvettes, *Laksamana Muhammad Amin* (F-136) and *Laksamana Tan Pusmah* (F-137), were commissioned in Italy and arrived at Lumut in September 1999. Since being ordered for Iraq they have all been modernised, with Super Rapid guns replacing the original compacts, and Otomat Mk 2 anti-ship missiles mounted on the quarterdeck.

Work on the first six New Generation Patrol Vessels (NGPVs) has been delayed by the financial crisis in the region, and although a provisional order for two was placed in September 1998 and an option for four more was signed in August 1999, the first will not be completed until late 2004. Two more building at Hamburg by Blohm+Voss and the later ships will be built at Penang. Apart from the A100 design forming the basis of the hull, very lilt detail has been confirmed, but is likely that they will be fitted 'for but not with' anti-ship and air defence missiles.

New Zealand: The second *Anzac* type frigate, HMNZS *Te Mana*, was commissioned in December 1999. The only *Leander* remaining operational is HMNZS *Canterbury*, as her

sister *Waikato* is used for harbour training.

Full modernisation of the military sealift ship *Charles Upham* has been delayed because of funding problems, but it is expected to start in 2000 and run to 2002. She will receive a helicopter flight deck and accommodation for up to 150 troops.

Singapore: Two more *Challenger* class submarines, RSS *Centurion* and RSS *Conqueror*, were commissioned on 28 May 1999, and reached Singapore in July 2000. When all four are fully operational they will begin a modernisation programme to replace their combat systems.

RSS *Independence* (87), last of twelve *Fearless* class 55-metre patrol craft, was commissioned in August 1999. The plan to build up to six New Generation Patrol Vessels to an advanced Swedish stealthy design was dropped because the technical risk was thought to be too high, and in their place six modified *La Fayette* type 110-metre frigates were ordered from DCN International in France. The first will be built at DCN Lorient and is to be delivered in 2005. The remainder will be built locally by Singapore Technologies Marine, the last to be operational by 2009.

RSS *Endurance* and RSS *Resolution*, the first of the new class of LPDs, were both commissioned on 18 March 2000 at the Tuas naval base. Two more, the *Persistence* and *Endeavour*, are under construction. They will replace the last ex-US Navy LSTs.

Taiwan: The Republic of China Navy (RoCN) has been trying for some time to acquire four Aegis destroyers, to counter the missile threat from mainland China. The original attempt to develop the *Oliver Hazard Perry* design (the 'Kwang Hua II' project) proved over-ambitious, and it was to acquire variants of the *Arleigh Burke* design. The argument appeared to won, but on 14 April 2000 the Clinton administration decided to defer the decision for several months. Undoubtedly Mr Clinton has been subjected to intense lobbying by Peking, which is widely believed to have contributed to the expenses of his last election.

The last of eight *Cheng Kung* class frigates, the *Tientan* (1110), will be launched in 2002 and delivered in 2003. A class of ten 1500-tonne corvettes is projected as the 'Kwang Hua V' plan.

At the end of September 1999 the LSD *Pensacola* was acquired from the US Navy and renamed *Shiu Hai* when recommissioned. A second vessel is to be transferred at a later date. The LST *Schenectady* is also to be transferred in 2000, making a total of three.

Thailand: Despite the severe economic problems the Royal Thai Navy has kept its support carrier *Chakkrinaruebet* in service, although fixed-wing flying has been largely restricted to landing shore-based aircraft. Other plans for modernisation and acquisition have been deferred.

African Navies

South Africa: The first of two major procurement battles was won September 1999, when government approval was given to buy three Type 209/1400 submarines from the German Submarine Consortium. These will replace the long-lived *Daphné* class in 2005-2007. After a hard struggle the South African Navy (SAN) placed an order with the European-South African Corvette Consortium (ESACC) to build four MEKO A200 121-metre corvettes. ESACC includes African Defence Systems Ltd, Thomson-CSF NCS and the German Frigate Consortium. As previously planned, the bare hulls will be built in Hamburg and Kiel and sailed to Simon'stown for fitting of weapons and electronics, before commissioning in 2004-2005.

Umkhonto is a VLS variant of the French Crotale missile, incorporating improvements developed locally for the Cactus land-based version. It had been planned to re-use the combat systems from the FAC, but the latest information suggests that a new French system will be supplied. A dedicated sonar, the Kingklip, has been developed by Thomson-CSF for these ships.

NAVAL BOOKS OF THE YEAR

Andrew Lambert, Denis Griffiths and Fred Walker, Brunel's Ships. *London: Chatham Publishing, 1999, 160 pages, 118 illus., £30. ISBN 1 86176 102 3*

This book has its origin in a one-day Open Museum course at the National Maritime Museum when, over lunch, the three speakers agreed that their talks would form the basis for an interesting book. They are well qualified; a marine engineer, an historian and a naval architect, all of whom have written on the period. The work is not divided equal; Griffiths gets 7 chapters, Lambert 3 and Walker only one. The editor (Robert Gardiner) should, perhaps, be given some credit for welding these contributions into a homogeneous whole.

After the Introduction, Part I covers the formation of the Great Western Steamship Co (GWSS), Brunel and the Admiralty, iron ship-building (with a section on the little known *Vulcan*), the GWSS works and the *Great Britain*. Part II deals with the ships; *Great Western*, HMS *Rattler*, *Great Britain* and *Great Eastern*. All these chapters are fascinating with much material not readily available elsewhere. Rather surprisingly, *Great Eastern* gets much less coverage than the earlier ships and stops at the launch. Another chapter would have been welcome. Technically, Brunel's three 'Greats' all marked major advances and were successful but all were commercial failures.

Credit is given to the Admiralty for advice on the structure of the *Great Western* based on Seppings' diagonal style and the authors do much to dispel the notion of a feud between the Admiralty and Brunel.

Certainly there were ruffled feathers early in the design of *Rattler* but, quite soon, all concerned were working well together. Brunel seems to have realised that much of the heavy vibration associated with early screw ships was due to the action of a two-bladed propeller working behind a thick deadwood. He gave *Great Britain* a built-up, six bladed screw which failed and was replaced with a four-bladed solid unit.

The illustrations are both interesting and well produced and are an important feature of the book (thanks mainly to the National Maritime Museum). It is easy to read and well recommended.

Personally, I would not see Rattler as a 'Brunel ship' though he made an important contribution. She was a team effort, led by the Admiralty, with Thomas Lloyd, chief engineer at Woolwich as the driving force. I have read both the Brunel and Admiralty files on the subject for my own book *Before the Ironclad*, and it is not easy to be sure of the correct balance.

Eur Ing David K Brown, RCNC

Andrew Saunders, English Heritage Book of Channel Defences. *London: BT Batsford, 1997, 128 pages, 12 colour and 87 b/w illus., £15.99. ISBN 1 7134 7595 1*

Naval enthusiasts will probably not even have considered that an English Heritage book, ostensibly about land-based history and archaeology, would hold much information of interest to them. However, Andrew Saunders' book on Britain's Channel Defences should do just that.

From the reign of Henry VIII to the Cold War, the coastline of Britain has had its key strategic points fortified, as a back-up to the Royal Navy's defence at sea. Of special interest to *Warship* readers will be the chapters on 'The role of the navy', 'Invasion coasts' and 'Defence of the naval bases'. The book concludes with 'Times of danger' (an overview of Britain's wars when the Channel was in danger), 'Twentieth-century total war', and a very useful list of places to visit. Although the book covers the entire history of defending the Channel from the medieval period onwards, enough space is devoted to each period to prevent the information within from being too cursory, and the author has provided good commentary on the less well considered periods. For example, defences from the end of the Napoleonic period to the turn of the century, a period which saw a great perceived threat from across the Channel but no actual hostilities, is a subject where the author provides a particularly useful insight into Britain's defensive policy of the time.

Andrew Saunders is a renowned fortification expert; in *Channel Defences*, he not only considers the actual defences, but looks at the campaigns in which they were used, considers when Britain has most been at threat, demonstrates the role of the dockyards at Portsmouth, Chatham, Portland and Plymouth, and gives special consideration to the role of Dover in the two World Wars. Although the reader will perhaps not increase his or her knowledge of warships at sea in *Channel Defences*, the book does make the reader consider overall maritime defence strategy and exactly how effective coastal fortifications were in times of war.

Daniel Mersey

Walter Lord, The Miracle of Dunkirk. *Ware: Wordsworth Editions, 1998, 323pp., 7 maps, 12pp. b/w illus., £4.99.*
ISBN 1 85326 685 X

The evacuation of over 300,000 Allied forces from almost certain destruction during May and June 1940 was a turning point in the Second World War, The loss of these men would almost certainly have led to peace negotiations with Nazi Germany. Instead, Britain continued to fight and forced Hitler into ill-conceived invasion schemes, culminating in the unsuccessful air campaign of August and September 1940. In a coherent narrative Walter Lord examines the 'Miracle of Dunkirk' through the judicious use of eye witness accounts provided by survivors in addition to the existing secondary literature and the wealth of archive material contained in the PRO. First published in 1982 this affordable reprint remains an important contribution to the literature.

Martin Robson

Joseph Wheatley and Stephen Howarth, Historic Sail - The Glory of the Sailing Ship from the 13th to the 19th Century. *London: Greenhill Books, 2000, 208 pages, 91 colour plates (10 other illus.), £40.*
ISBN 1 85367 399 4

Joseph Wheatley has been drawing ships since he was a boy but later he began to produce carefully researched and very beautiful coloured drawings of sailing ships. Ninety one of the drawings are reproduced in this large format book (Page size 313 x 323mm - 14 x 15in). These are each faced by a short text written by the well-known historian Stephen Howarth.

The great majority of the drawings are profiles though there a few more spirited ones and some structural sections. References are given as to the source of the material used. A few are composite portrayals of a type rather than an individual ship. There is a reasonable distribution with date; all ships are European with a slight bias to British. Length and beam are the only particulars usually given though the armament is sometimes stated in full for warships. There is a useful glossary.

The price is not unreasonable for a handsome book with 91 large colour plates, I expect a number of copies will be dismembered and the pictures framed.

Eur Ing David K Brown, RCNC

John Terraine, Business in Great Waters. *Ware: Wordsworth Editions, 1999, 841pp., 19 maps, 28pp b/w illus., £4.99*
ISBN 1 84022 210 8

The German unrestricted submarine campaigns against principally Britain and the United States, in 1916-18 and again in 1939-45 were perhaps the greatest threat to Allied war making capability and are the subject of this study. Terraine combines the political, strategic and military context of the campaigns into a coherent narrative of operations while providing a full account of the human experience of this very dangerous mode of warfare. As he succinctly notes although often at the forefront of technical development the submarine and anti-submarine war was also a test of human determination, endurance and courage. With excellent maps and informative illustrations this work is an invaluable and affordable source.

Martin Robson

Richard Woodman. Malta Convoys. *London: John Murray, 2000, 552 pages, 33 b/w illus., 7 maps, £30.*
ISBN 1 7195 5753 4

Richard Woodman's latest work is a companion volume to his 1994 *Arctic Convoys* (reviewed in *Warship* 1994, pp 200-201). This very weighty, but well-written book represents a clever integration of historical overview, strategic summary, and personal reminisces from those who fought.

Covering the period 1940-43, the author first looks at the naval forces involved prior to the Malta campaign. He then goes on to consider the campaign in detail – looking at the different operations and convoys that comprised it, and taking in the personal accounts of those who served. The battles of Calabria, Matapan and the two battles of Sirte are also described.

Whilst dealing with the overall causes and events of each operation and convoy, the author has not trapped himself into writing history in 'the grand manner'. He provides more detailed accounts of the action, narrowing events down to the time of the day at which they took place and providing enough information to keep avid gunnery devotees happy.

As may be imagined in the light of *Arctic Convoys*, this volume is a comprehensive study of the ships and men involved in the Mediterranean during these three years; the author has managed to avoid regurgitating history in dull prose and presents his research in a logical and readable fashion. The 33 black and white pictures in the book show a variety of photos of some of the men involved in the campaign, shots of convoys at seas and in port, and a few 'action' shots of burning and sinking ships and the terrible damage caused by the bombing of Malta.

Overall, *Malta Convoys* is a useful companion volume to *Arctic Convoys*, and stands as an excellent read and resource in its own right.

Daniel Mersey

Ian Marshall, Ironclads and Paddlers. *Charlottesville: Howell Press, 1993, 108 pages, heavily illus., including colour images, £19.95.*
ISBN 0 943231 62 0

Concentrating on the development of the warship from ironclad to *Dreadnought* this book contains many fantastic colour images of paddlers and ironclads. The text, although functional, is not to be overlooked. This work also highlights the careers of two of the RN's most famous officers, Adm Lord Thomas Cochrane and Adm Lord John Fisher, whose careers encompassed this era of seemingly perpetual technological change.

Martin Robson

Gerhard Koop and Klaus-Peter Schmolke, Pocket Battleships of the *Deutschland* Class. *London: Greenhill books, 2000, 224 pages, 347 photographs, many line drawings and maps, £25. ISBN 1 85367 402 8*

This is a companion volume to the authors' *Battleships of the* Bismarck *Class* and the similar *Scharnhorst* class, previously reviewed, and has the same virtues and problems. The Treaty of Versailles allowed Germany to retain a few elderly pre-Dreadnought battleships and, in time, to replace them with ships of displacement not exceeding 10,000 tons. (It is not clear whether metric or Imperial tons was meant but after the Washington Treaty it was reasonable to accept Imperial tons giving the same limit as the cruisers of major powers). It was expected that this limit would lead to slow coast defence ships of limited capability and endurance.

By using advanced technology Germany attempted to produce potent warships within this limit. Weight saving involved the use of welding throughout which was to give problems as the steel used was not entirely suitable for welding and procedures were not fully developed (it is probable that the severe damage to the stern of *Lutzow* when torpedoed was exacerbated by poor welding, as with *Bismarck* and *Prince Eugen*). The authors claim 15 per cent reduction in structural weight which seems rather high, 10 per cent was more typical of early welded ships. Long endurance was achieved by the use of diesel engines, a very novel feature for their day.

Their actual displacement was greatly over the limit. The first, *Deutschland*, was 10,600 Imperial tons, perhaps an excusable error from a design team lacking recent experience and with so many novel features. The later ships at 11,550 tons and 12,340 tons were clearly a deliberate breach of the treaties. With six 11in guns and a speed of over 26 knots it was believed that they could run from any ship which could defeat them (except the three British battlecruisers) and sink anything which could catch them. They had an immense influence on naval thinking but, gradually, it was realised that their threat was over-rated. A DNC study of 1939 concluded that one could be defeated by two 'County' class cruisers; the battle of the River Plate had been 'won' many times in the tactical school before the war.

Their main machinery consisted of eight 9 cylinder two-stroke diesels with a maximum speed of 450 rpm in four engine rooms geared in two gear rooms to two shafts. (Maximum shaft speed 250 rpm) With one motor per shaft they could reach 13kts for 17,400 miles. There were a number of teething troubles which do not seem to have been entirely cured. They did generate severe vibration and, from other accounts, the authors may have under-stated this problem. Vibration of the director is said to have accounted for *Graf Spee*'s poor gunnery at the River Plate.

As with the earlier books, the photographs are superb. There are numerous photos of the ships under construction and in service with a fair number of internal views showing life on board. I particularly liked the photo of *Graf Spee* with a dummy B turret and a seecond funnel. The quality is generally high except for some of the action shots. There are fairly detailed accounts of the active service life of the three ships.

Eur Ing David K Brown, RCNC

Fred T Jane (introduction by Antony Preston), The British Battle Fleet: Its Inception and Growth Throughout the Centuries. *London: Conway Maritime Press, 1912, rp Conway Classic Reprint Series 1997, 424 pages, £14.99. ISBN 0 85177 723 6*

Fred Jane is now remembered as the eponymous founder of two annuals which, with many newer titles, continues to the present time. In is lifetime Jane was a man of many parts, an illustrator, a naval journalist and the author of a number of works of fiction, naval, romance and sci-fi, all now quite deservedly forgotten. In addition he introduced the general public to the history and some aspects of the work of the Royal Navy and two important foreign powers, Russia and Japan. His first book, *The Torpedo in Peace and War* appeared in 1898 and was reprinted in 1904. It gave a vivid account, based partly on Janes own experiences as a journalist in a torpedo gunboat during manoeuvres in 1894-1897, of the work of the torpedo flotillas ranging from 60-ton torpedo boats, the earliest destroyers, to the 800-ton torpedo gunboats, together with an account of what life was like on these frail craft. It deserves reprinting.

Jane's next production, *The Imperial Russian Navy*, appeared in 1898 giving some of the background of that navy but concentrating on its current state, and made more valuable by Jane being given access to dockyards and depots. It was followed by *The Imperial Japanese Navy* in 1904. *The Imperial Russian Navy* came out in a new edition in 1904 when it became clear that the two great empires were drifting towards war.

Jane's last important work *The British Battle Fleet* was published as one volume in 1912 with a two volume edition, incorporating a few additions to bring it up to date, appearing three years later. It is the one volume work that now features as the latest of the Conway Classics. There is a foreward by Antony Preston which tells us something about Janes all too brief life and then admirably sets the book in context, pointing out where Janes vision is, unavoidably, blinkered, but conversely, emphasising those prophesies, such as the importance of submarines and aircraft and the certainty that the war with Germany would be a long one.

The first half of the book is a general history of the fleet until the coming of the ironclad, with little detail of the ships but giving useful insights into the condition that the seamen experienced. The value of the second half, ranging from the first ironclads to the super-dreadnoughts, is much enhanced by Jane being, as Antony Preston points out, in close touch with those associated with this great revolution in warship design. Almost every ironclad receives a brief description and commentary, while the most important have a superb photograph from the collection of William Bieber. Jane also rescues the reputation of Sir Edward Reed's successor as Chief Constructor, Sir Nathaniel Barnaby, and heaps praise on Barnaby's successor, Sir William White.

One of the most attractive features of the original edition were 24 watercoulours by W L Wylie RA, apparently missing from an earlier reprint (not by Conway) in 1990, but here reproduced with perfect fidelity to the originals. Much of what Jane writes about is familiar to the naval enthusiast of today but not to the general reader and, although dated, is still a useful source of information.

Peter Brook

Keith Yates, Flawed Victory, Jutland 1916. *London: Chatham publishing, 2000. 332 pages, 23 photos, diagrams, £20.*
ISBN 1 86176 148 1

The battle of Jutland has been refought for the last 84 years, do we need another book? The answer has to be yes, partly because of the extent to which the facts were suppressed or distorted in the aftermath of the battle. The author of this very readable narrative has worked in the results of much recent research.

The book opens with a rather too conventional portrait of the navy at the opening of the century; reactionary in technical matters and over subservient to senior officers, saved by Sir John Fisher, the White Knight. Nicholas Lambert's book on Fisher paints a more credible picture of Fisher without diminishing his importance. The book continues with a brief but interesting account of naval action prior to Jutland. Failings are already apparent, particularly in the signals organisation of the battlecruisers.

The bulk of the book is a narrative of the battle. As far as I can tell it is accurate and fair. That said, Beatty and the battlecruisers come out badly. Beatty had failed to speak to Evan Thomas whose four powerful battleships had joined the battlecruisers a few days before Jutland. This meant that when the usual signal failures occurred, Evan Thomas had no basis on which to use his initiative. The gunnery of the battlecruisers was poor due to lack of practice, whereas the gunnery of the 3rd squadron was good thanks to recent practice at Scapa.

Perhaps the most interesting part of the book is the analysis of the performance of the four leading admirals – Jellicoe, Beatty, Scheer and Hipper. Jellicoe comes out as quietly competent. This was what was needed, as Churchill wrote, Jellicoe was the only man who could lose the war in one afternoon. In public, Fisher claimed that Jellicoe was the new Nelson, who could win a new Trafalgar. Professor Andrew Lambert has found an unpublished letter in which Fisher makes it clear that he no longer thought it possible for the Grand Fleet to defeat a High Seas Fleet bent on escape but it could lose; Jellicoe was therefore chosen as a safe pair of hands. Beatty comes out badly for signalling failures within his own force and for failing to keep Jellicoe informed of the German position. Even Goodenough, usually praised for his signals, comes in for criticism (rightly in my view).

Scheer and Hipper are blamed for their failure to realise that Beatty, running North from a superior force was clearly making for Jellicoe rather than home. Scheer's second and third turns merit the usual criticism. These reviews of performance seem fair, or at least match your reviewer's prejudices. Most if not all these admirals tried to distort the later accounts in their favour.

Defective shells were a major cause of the British failure to inflict more damage on the German ships. The author falls for Jellicoe's claim to have warned of the problem just prior to leaving the post of Controller. While this may be true, Jellicoe had been Director of Naval Ordnance and later Controller and he should have ensured that the shells were not defective. In these posts he should also have ensured that the cordite would not explode when ignited. Jellicoe's conscience may have pricked him as, when he became First Sea Lord, he recalled for destruction the DNO and DNC reports on the lessons of Jutland which he saw as criticising him and Beatty for encouraging unsafe procedures.

This book is welcome for those who know little about this, the only surface battle between dreadnought fleets. Even the more knowledgeable may find new ideas. For those who want the ultimate in technical detail, John Campbell's Jutland, has been re-published.

Eur Ing David K Brown, RCNC

Spencer C Tucker, Handbook of 19th Century Naval Warfare. *Stroud: Sutton Publishing, 2000. 288 pages, 158 illus., £25.*
ISBN 0 7509 2171 4

Until quite recently the navies of the nineteenth century have been badly served by historians with few books and many errors in fact. During the 1960's a small group, mainly working for the National Maritime Museum, including Tony Preston, David Lyon and this reviewer, met regularly vowing to correct the history of the period, with some success. Many of the old fallacies derive from a book Naval Administrations by a senior civil servant named Briggs and now recognised as a political tract rather than history.

Trucker avoids most of the pitfalls and has produced a short and readable account of the ships and naval operations of the period. Technical advances such as steam, screw propellers, iron hulls followed by the use of steel in construction and armaments are covered. The author seems a little confused over armour developments, particularly at the end of the period when developments were so rapid.

Operations, which were more numerous than usually recognised, are well covered. The author is American and there is a welcome input of USN (and Confederate) material, particularly from the Civil War ant the US war with Spain. The photographs are well selected and well reproduced.

There are a number of errors, mainly trivial, no author can avoid these, but one or two are more serious. He repeats the fallacy that the First Lord, Melville, wrote to the post office in 1827 advising against the purchase of steamships which might destroy Britain's naval supremacy. This has been shown in several of his sources to be a later fabrication, probably by Briggs, and can also be seen as unlikely as by that date Melville, himself had ordered a number of steamships for the RN. Tucker also defines the range of stability as the 'angle to which a ship could heel before it began to right itself'. It is the opposite, the angle at which the righting moment vanishes.

Tucker covers much the same ground as Hill's War at Sea in the Ironclad Age, and the choice is best seen as a matter of taste.

Eur Ing David K Brown, RCNC

Norman Friedman, Seapower and Space, From the Dawn of the Missile Age to Net-Cenrtric Warfare. *London: Chatham Publishing, 2000. 384 pages, 29 photographs, £25. ISBN 1 86176 004 3*

Much of the material in this book is appearing in open literature for the first time and many readers will be surprised how much is now de-classified. The first chapter is a simple guide to satellite mechanics and which orbits are possible. Following chapters deal with boosters, satellite navigation, communications, reconnaissance leading on to their influence on naval warfare. The Tomahawk missile led to the requirement and the solution for over the horizon targeting. The need to destroy attacking aircraft before they launched their missiles led to the so-called Outer Air Battle. The collapse of the Soviet Union meant that the role of the navy became increasingly concerned with coastal or littoral warfare, coastal meaning up to several hundred miles inland. The vast amount of information available demands

the highest standards of IT for it handling.

The background theme to this book is the struggle in the US between the navy and air force for control of space technology and, of course, Friedman has no doubts on this subject and makes it clear that the USN is the biggest user. He sees that space and missile technology has restored the (US) surface ship as the capital ship. A big missile strike can disable an enemy air defence system making it safe for an aircraft strike to follow. A missile strike involves no risk to one's own personnel, very important in the light of current popular opinion.

The book is very detailed and full of initials code names etc. For example, a Soviet era weapon will often have a Soviet name, a manufacturers designation and a NATO code name. It is not easy to remember them all. The even more detailed end notes fill a further 48 pages and in small print too. These comments are not meant as a criticism, but the reader should be aware that it is a book to work at and well worth the effort.

His lessons for the RN will be of particular interest. The increasing use of cruise missiles will demand over the horizon targeting and even if this is provided by an advanced helicopter it is likely that satellite communications will be needed and if such missiles are used in support of army operations further satellite communications will be needed. Since many of the allies of the US have already installed common communication equipment, the cost may not be as great as is often assumed.

Eur Ing David K Brown, RCNC

Nicholas Lambert, Sir John Fisher's Naval Revolution. *University of South Carolina Press, 1999. 426 pages, 15 maps and illus., £31.95. ISBN 03 02 01 00 99 54321*

In this important book the author re-examines Sir John Fisher's role in budgetary, strategic and technical changes in the RN prior to the First World War. Any book on Fisher's thinking and actions had the funda-

mental problem that Fisher 'fired for effect'. Even when he was telling the truth it was often a highly selective truth. For example, he wrote 'I had an excellent secretary. Whenever I asked him for the facts, he always asked me what I wanted to prove. There is no doubt that facts are most misleading'.

Some of Fisher's views are well known but the author often finds a new twist. It is clear that Fisher was not a great enthusiast for the *Dreadnought* battleship; he preferred the battlecruiser. Later writers have shown him as wrong, citing the loss of three battlecruisers at Jutland as disproving his views as summed up in the aphorism 'Speed is armour'. It is now clear that the losses were primarily due to defective ammunition whilst today's generation, familiar with totally unarmoured ships facing more powerful weapons, should be more sympathetic to Fisher's views. The rapid deployment of two battlecruisers to destroy Spee's squadron at the Falklands showed how Fisher intended them to be used (and the less well known deployment of *Princess Royal* to the West Indies as a long stop). The speed at which an overwhelming battlecruiser force could be deployed made it unnecessary to maintain small squadrons, usually of obsolete ships, all round the world.

The traditional view is that the navy, led by reactionary admirals was opposed to the introduction of the submarine and even as late as 1914 had failed to realise the threat posed by the submarine. This is clearly nonsense as the RN submarine force in 1914 was almost as large as that of the next two navies combined. What is surprising is the number of admirals who are on record as supporting submarine building and seeing submarines and mines as making at least the southern North Sea a no-go area for battleships.

The history of submarine building in this era is unclear and the author has clearly tried hard to unravel it. The problem was the contract with Vickers made it almost impossible to use other shipbuilders unless the designs came from abroad. This led to some very unsuccessful boats based on Italian designs, here I must disagree with Lambert who claims that DNC supported the Italian designs, my information is the exact opposite. He also says that the DNC form for a fast fleet submarine was poor. In fact the Haslar model tests show that this form (Model UR), used for the J and K classes was the best for its speed and length ratio ever tested, at least until 1988. I would also object to the statements that some classes were 'designed' by Roger Keyes.

Fisher also favoured 'Flotilla Defence' in which the North Sea was to be held by submarines, destroyers and by the use of minefields. The battlefleet could hold the northern approaches. Fisher saw the *Dreadnought* as cost saving, reducing the number of ships in commission. Lambert is incorrect in suggesting that commercial yards built faster than the Royal Dockyards; in fact the figures show that the Dockyards averaged about a year faster than commercial yards. From 1905 onwards the government was Liberal, not much interested in defence, dedicated to cutting spending whilst increasing social security payments. Fisher negotiated this situation with great skill, getting rid of older ships produced genuine savings whilst some exaggeration of the German threat helped maintain the budget.

The illustrations are familiar and poorly reproduced but this does not distract from a splendid book. In places it is controversial but the author supports his views with a very large number of references. Any student of the RN at the start of the 20th century should read this book, and then re-read it. It may also help in dealing with parsimonious problems.

Eur Ing David K Brown, RCNC

Norman Friedman, The Fifty-Year War. *London: Chatham Publishing, 2000. 640 pages, 16 photos, £25.*
ISBN 1 8716 140 6

The author dates the start of the fifty-year war of the title with the Soviet intervention in the Spanish Civil War and its end with the final lowering of the Soviet flag on Christmas Day 1991. He portrays it

as a real war though fought at a lower intensity that the two World Wars of the twentieth century.

The book is divided into six parts. Part one deals with Stalin's opening moves from the Spanish Civil War to the end of World War Two. The second section covers Stalin's moves into Eastern Europe and the perceived threat to Western Europe and the corresponding rise of nationalist feeling on both sides. The next part examines how relations between East and West began to change when both sides had access to atomic weapons, and highlights how few and complicated they were. Friedman reminds us how the Korean War was little affected by US nuclear superiority. Part four opens with the missile race and the Cuban Crisis. Part five describes the effects of the Vietnam war and the problems when Brezhnev's military build up coincided with a decline in US power. The final section of the book shows how the US under Ronald Reagan raised the stakes while the computer revolution both showed the Soviet weakness and began to give many Russians free access to 'information'.

The viewpoint is American (with a touch of Republican bias) but the author is at pains to show how the views of European allies and the UK in particular influenced US policy though these views are drawn almost entirely from American papers. The book is extremely well referenced.

Friedman is at pains to compare contemporary estimates of capability with what we now know. (I am not sure that all is yet disclosed). We are probably too close to the Cold War for a definitive history but this is an excellent early effort. Some time ago I reviewed David Miller's The Cold War and to two books are not contradictory though taking a different view in places, I am glad to have both. Freidman's earlier 'instant history' Desert Victory on the Gulf War has stood up quite well to later revelations, giving confidence in this new work.

The Fifty Year War is well written but it is so packed with facts that it requires some effort in reading, that effort is well worth while.

Eur Ing David K Brown, RCNC

Richard Hill, War at Sea in the Ironclad Age. *London: Cassell, 2000, 224 pages, 133 illus., 21 maps, £30.*
ISBN 0 304 35273 X

This book is part of Cassell's History of Warfare series and describes the strategy, tactics, technology and life at sea for the half century from 1855. It is a daunting task even for someone well known as the editor of Naval Review and author of several books.

The book opens with a brief account of the philosophical background to strategy and tactics. This is followed by a lengthy section on technology in the period from wooden sailing ship up to, but not including, the *Dreadnought*. The next section is about the people including the lowly status of the engineer. The second half of the book describes the numerous battles of the period, there were only two fleet encounters but many smaller battles and bombardments.

It is a very readable account of a very complex period and is generally accurate though there are signs that it was written in haste. For example, the first mastless battleship, *Devastation*, was designed by Edward Reed not Barnaby. She was based on his *Cerberus* whose remains may still be seen near Melbourne. *Monarch's* rigging was little obstruction to her arcs of fire as all but a pair of stays on each mast were removed in action. Also the RCNC was founded in 1883!

The illustrations form an important component of the book. There is extensive use of contemporary, highly coloured, in every sense of the word, drawings as well as photographs. The maps are superb, the clearest I have ever seen, and reflect great credit on Malcolm Swanston and his team.

At £20 it is good value for money and is recommended as a survey of the problems of an important but little known era.

Eur Ing David K Brown, RCNC

WARSHIP NOTES

This section comprises a number of short articles and notes, generally highlighting little known aspects of warship history.

REPERCUSSIONS OF THE KURSK SINKING

Antony Preston

The aftermath of the sinking of the Project 649A *Antey* class ('Oscar 2') nuclear-powered cruise missile submarine (SSGN) *Kursk* in August 2000 saw a continuation of the Russian Government's inability to tell the truth about the sinking, coupled with apparently related accusation of espionage. All 118 sailors onboard were killed, although about 25 survived for some days, and both Norwegian and British rescue teams were eventually sent, but to no avail. The British LR 5 rescue submersible was never used despite being available.

The explosions that sank the *Kursk* were detected by the USS *Memphis* (SSN-691) the attack submarine that put into a Norwegian port six days after the sinking on 12 August. Data collected by US Navy submarines and a surveillance ship in the area reportedly led US analysts to the theory that a weapon misfire was the likely cause of the two explosions that tore through the *Kursk* some two minutes apart. Russia also apparently asked the US Department of Defense to provide it with information about the disaster, a Pentagon official said.

The *Memphis*, which was in the area at the time, monitoring Russian naval exercises by means of her towed sonar array, immediately detected the back-to-back explosions on board the *Kursk*. A second, as yet unidentified, US submarine was also reported to be in the area. The *New York Times* reported that the first detailed record of what happened was delivered by the *Memphis*, which sailed into Bergen on 18 August. The newspaper said that the SSN unloaded sonar tapes and other recordings of the explosion.

A torpedo misfire had 'certainly been the leading speculation all along' as the cause of the explosions, a US official said. 'A weapon of some sort. Whether a torpedo or a rocket-assisted torpedo, but some sort of weapon most likely' caused the explosions, the official said. It was unclear whether the source of the explosion was a warhead detonation or rocket propellant that ignited, setting a fire that ignited other propellant, he said.

According to unofficial Russian sources the main suspect for the accident is an upgraded version of the rocket-powered torpedo *Shkval*, although informed US sources were sceptical. The explosion of a conventional thermal-fuelled torpedo is more likely to have caused the second, more powerful explosion which ripped through the submarine. Russian heavyweight torpedoes use a kerosene and high-test peroxide (HTP) thermal fuel which has caused problems in the past. It is also entirely possible that other weapons also exploded, such as the Type 65 650mm torpedoes and SS-N-19 cruise missiles on board. Safer thermal fuels are available but cost more than kerosene-HTP, and the cash-strapped Russian Navy is in no position to fund such an advanced fuel.

The businessman and former US naval intelligence officer Edmond Pope was meanwhile facing accusations of espionage, which apparently included an interest in the *Shkval*. Whether this accusation was merely part of the Russian Government's 'smoke and mirrors' tactics to distract Western observers (such as the unproven accusation of a collision between the *Kursk* and a Western vessel) was not clear. Another unofficial US suggestion was the possibility of the submarine being hit by an anti-submarine weapon fired accidentally by one of the accompanying surface warships.

The Russians want to begin efforts to recover the 118 bodies of the men who died aboard the sunken submarine by cutting holes in her hull, according to Deputy Prime Minister Ilya Klebanov, speaking on 29 August. He rejected reports that the *Kursk* was testing a new type of torpedo. Russian officials maintain that the *Kursk* collided with a large object such as a foreign submarine, or with a Second World War mine (hardly a 'large object'), but have also admitted the possibility of a torpedo misfire.

Klebanov said the investigating commission, after considering several methods of recovering the bodies, would recommend to President Vladimir Putin that the work be done by cutting holes in the submarine. If approved, the work could begin before the end of the month, and would be done by diving teams, two Russian and one Norwegian. Igor Spassky, head of the Rubin bureau, which designed the Project 949 boats, told the NTV television channel that the method would enable the divers to get into every compartment and remove the bodies.

Project 949 Antey *class ('Oscar 1') similar to the Project 949A* Kursk. *(NIP/Pavlov).*

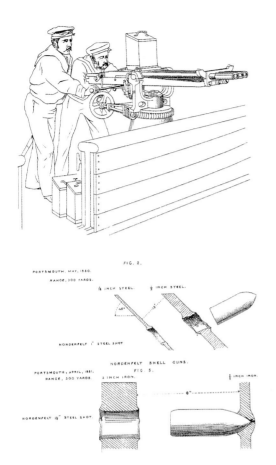

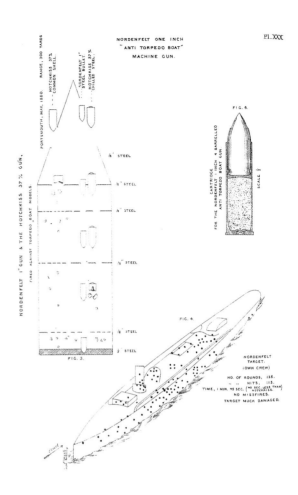

Nordenfelt One Inch anti torpedo boat gun. (BNA, 1886).

The Deputy Prime Minister also said the commission would give President Putin details of a proposal by 30 August for lifting the huge submarine to the surface, but he provided no details other than to say the project would take about a year and cost about US$100 million. Just removing the bodies would cost US$5-7 million, he said. Even that is a major burden for the government, but Putin was under strong public pressure to recover the remains for burial. Russian and Western officials said they had detected no radiation leaks. By the end of October four bodies had been recovered.

NORDENFELT ONE-INCH "ANTI-TORPEDO BOAT" MACHINE GUNS
Lord Brassey's Naval Annual of 1886 – the very first edition – contained a chapter on

'Machine and quick-firing guns'. Here, Daniel Mersey selects some details referring to Nordenfelt's 4-barrelled machine gun.

"In the competitive trial in 1881, Nordenfelt had a 5-barrel and a 10-barrel of 0.45in bore gun. These, however, are by no means the most important representatives of his system, but the 4-barrel 1-in bore which has long been in service. The 10-barrel Nordenfelt, according to the Committee, had the greatest absolute speed of fire though not the greatest per weight of gun. It also stood first in facility of laying. Nordenfelt guns, however, are best known from results obtained in perforation of steel and iron plates, such as might be used on torpedo boats. The 4-barrel 1-in gun above mentioned, which is shown in Fig 1 is termed by Nordenfelt an "Anti-Torpedo Boat Gun." ... The 4-

barrel 1-in gun was introduced into the Navy with a view to damaging the boiler of a torpedo boat at a distance of from 300 to 500 yds. Other essential conditions were required: (1) that the gun could be fired so rapidly that it would almost certainly score a sufficient number of hits on an approaching torpedo boat to ensure its being disabled during its run at full speed from the distance above named, before it could reach the vessel attacked; (2) that it could be fired so rapidly as to make it impossible for the boat to discharge a Whitehead torpedo at such range that the missile would have any reasonable chance of hitting its mark.

After various competitions, the Admiralty decided in favour of the Nordenfelt gun for reasons given in an official Admiralty Report of June 21, 1880. This report shows that (1) the penetrating power of the gun was proved to be sufficient, as the hardened steel bullet of 7 1/4 oz weight, at a range of 300 yds, penetrated at an angle of 45 deg the side and boiler of a torpedo boat, as represented by a 1/16-in steel plate, 18in in front of a second steel plate 1/2in thick (Fig 2). When firing directly end on at a torpedo boat, the bullet penetrated the steel bow plate 1/16in thick, at an angle of 10 deg, and four bulkheads at right angles; striking the boiler, the bullet then indented the 1/2in steel plate representing it, to a depth of half an inch (Fig 3). At a subsequent trial at Portsmouth, under similar conditions, the plate was perforated altogether.* (2) The accuracy was found most satisfactory, the mean deviation at 300 yds, of 10 rounds fired slowly, being 5.6in, while the mean deviation of 24 rounds fired in rapid volleys was 18.3in. (3) The rapidity of fire ashore at one trial was 108 shots in 30 seconds. During another the gun was fired at sea from HMS Medway when running at a speed of 9 knots. In this case the target was the bow of a model torpedo boat; during a run of 1 min 45 sec and over a range of from 500 yds to 100 yds, 115 hits were made out of 135 shots fired, equal to 65 hits per minute (Fig 4). In a subsequent trial at Spithead in July, 1880, the gun was placed on board HMS *Iris*. On this occasion two runs were made at a speed of 17.2 knots, directly against the bow of a torpedo boat model. Firing from 700 yds distance until close up, both runs occupying 2 min 19 sec, 110 shots hit the target out of 213 rounds fired, so that even at this high speed 48 hit per minute were recorded. Running past the torpedo boat at 200 yds range and at a speed of 17 knots, 58 rounds were fired in 22 sec, and of these, 38 shots hit the torpedo boat, being at the rate of 103 hits per minute.

The direct perforation is rather uncertain, and varies according to circumstances. Fig 5 shows the effect, not of an inch but of an inch and a half of steel bullet at 300 yds. The striking velocity was 1508ft, the weight of the shot 1.75lbs. This gives a calculated perforation of nearly 3in, which is rather better than the actual result The rule of thumb would give a little over 2 1/4in, which is too small, but may furnish a rough idea. The actual result lies

between the two estimates.

The only projectile fired by this gun is the steel bullet shown with its cartridge in Fig 6. The powder charge is 1.53 oz. The bullet weighs 7.2 oz. The case is solid drawn.

The Nordenfelt 4-barrel has fired about 150 to 200 rounds per minute. Under service conditions at Portland, in November, 1885, 400 rounds fired in 10 minutes.

* The fact of the Hotchkiss chilled and common shell failing to perforate as well as the Nordenfelt steel bullet is due to inferiority in the projectiles rather than the system. Beyond the fact of the calibre adopted in proportion to weight, a system imposes no conditions as to projectiles."

A 'THEME PORT' FOR TOULON?

Daniel Mersey reports on a proposed tourist development on the Mediterranean coast of France.

Under an £18.4 million redevelopment plan, the French navy is discussing handing over four of the forts that protect the anchorage of Toulon, to form the core of an historical 'theme park' celebrating the town and port's history. The sale of the aircraft carrier *Foch* to Brazil has cleared the way for the Defence Ministry to release her 870ft sister ship *Clemenceau* for use within the park as well.

The aim is to attract 500,000 visitors a year to Toulon, which is currently France's premier naval base yet also one of the Mediterranean's finest harbours. This would create a sizeable tourist industry to replace the 8000 jobs lost in the naval base over the past ten years.

However, the Navy, which owns 80 per cent of the Toulon waterfront, seems reluctant to surrender what it has held for centuries. Alain Richard, the French Defence Minister, may be asked to persuade the Navy that its symbols of power should be given over to teaching the country's maritime past and enlightening tourists on France's naval heritage.

BRASSEY'S NAVAL ANNUAL: A 100 YEAR PERSPECTIVE

This article, the first in a retrospective series, looks at naval developments reported a century ago, and will build into a useful record of Brassey's Naval Annual over its years of publication. Daniel Mersey of Brassey's looks at The Naval Annual, 1901.

The fifteenth year of *The Naval Annual's* publication in 1901 was edited by John Leyland (for the second time), and contained the usual variety of reports on recent developments and the strength of world navies.

Essays in 1901's annual included an overview of Naval Brigades in action

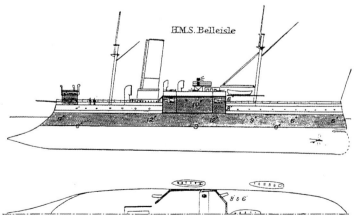

HMS Bellisle, *used as a target ship in 1900. (Brassey's Naval Annual, 1901).*

on land: 'It has been described as a characteristic of the reign of Queen Victoria that her Navy was never called upon to perform its function of defence upon its proper element; but, on the contrary, that there was hardly an occasion when the Army had been employed that it had not had the assistance of a naval brigade on shore'. Other contributions included a thoughtful piece on manning naval and mercantile ships, marine engineering, and a report on Royal Naval manoeuvres. This last contribution considered a mock engagement undertaken in 1900, 'to obtain information relative to the working of a fleet, which is composed of vessels of all classes and is fighting for the command of the sea'.

1901 saw British forces still involved in the Second Boer War, and John Leyland reports on 'The transport operations to South Africa'. Making the point that, at this time, 'No other nation has ever put into the field an army of a quarter of a million men, with lines of communications covering 7,000 miles of sea and land', Leyland goes on to outline the magnitude of the operation.

This year's extract is:

The Belleisle Experiments

During the early summer of 1900 it was announced that the Admiralty had determined to carry out certain experiments, using the old *Belleisle* as a target ship for various kinds of shell, the experiments having special reference to the risk of fire entailed on ships going into action without removing the multitudinous wood fittings with which every ship built before 1895, and most of those built since, have been only too liberally provided.

The account which follows is mainly taken from the pages of the *Engineer*, whose representative seems to have obtained a fuller history of what happened than most of the other representatives of the press. In some instances, however, information has been culled from other public prints, especially from the *Times*, and where two or more independent accounts agree in traversing the narrative as given in the *Engineer* or

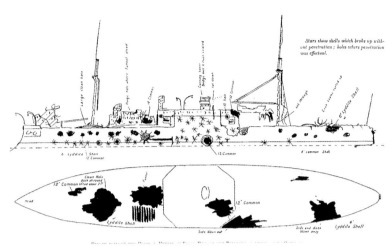

Sketch showing general effect of damage to Bellisle. (BNA, 1901).

Times, these independent accounts have been followed.

The general aspect of the Belleisle can be gathered from the sketches and photographs. She had a complete belt, with an armoured battery amidships, the armour (wrought iron) varying in thickness from 6 to 12 inches. The deck in line with the top of the belt had from 3 inches to 1 inch of armour. That covering in the battery was 1 inch thick. She carried four 12-inch RML guns in the battery, and six 6-pdr quick firers, and six machine guns on the top of battery.

The Belleisle was moored head and stern with some three or four feet of water under her bottom, and was attacked by the Majestic, which steamed in an elliptical course round the doomed ship. Fire was opened from the starboard broadside when the Majestic was right astern of the Belleisle and 1700 yards off on the port bow of the Belleisle at 1300 yards and was about 1700 yards off on the port bow of the Belleisle, when fire ceased after a period variously reported as being from six to eight minutes. The speed of the Majestic was about ten knots. The Majestic fired, as far as can be ascertained – eight rounds 12-in common shell, seven rounds 12-in AP shot, about 100 6-in lyddite at bow and battery, about 100 6-in common at stern, about 400 12-pdr common, and about 750 3-pdr AP shell. Full charges were used throughout for all guns.

Roughly speaking, about thirty or forty per cent of the projectiles fired were said to be effective, but there is no evidence to show that any of the 12-in armour piercers struck the armour. This projectile has a penetrating power of 30 inches of wrought iron, so that it should easily have gone in at one side and out at the other (see diagram showing thickness of armour). It is therefore pretty clear that either none were fired, or that if they did not miss altogether, they passed harmlessly through the light upper works. The projectiles that hit were, therefore, all shells. With regard to the condition of the ship for resisting the inflammatory effect of shells, not only was nothing removed in the way of splinter-making or inflammable material, but the men's kits, ham-

Mark of Lyddite shell on armour of Bellisle. (BNA, 1901).

mocks and mess gear, officers' bedding and furniture, and all the ordinary woodwork of cabins and living places, was left in situ. Boats were all in their places, some on the upper deck, others in crutches, some little height above the deck, and others again at the davits. Some spare spars were on deck stowed under the boats. On the other hand, the ordinary precautions against fire were taken as far as the circumstances allowed. The decks were well flooded beforehand, and the pumps were kept going, delivering a stream of water on to the various decks whilst the ship was being battered. In addition to the ordinary wood fittings, a crew of 130 wooden dummies were placed at the various guns and for passing ammunition. The guns' crews of the 6-pdrs were all exposed on the upper deck, those at the 12-in guns were protected by the battery armour. But, notwithstanding the numbers of shells that struck and burst, the Belleisle was not set on fire. It was stated by Mr Goschen in the House that there was only a little smouldering fire in one of the cabins amongst some clothes, and this notwithstanding that the woodwork was shattered in all directions, and the whole of the interior of the ship was filled with wreckage. But the *Times* and other reporters who gave account of the firing all believed that the ship was on fire, and spoke of the immense volumes of smoke that rose from the fated ship. This smoke must have been entirely due to the bursting shell. Nor is it remarkable that this should entirely hide the ship, and stream out at every orifice in dense clouds, seeing that the bursting charges of shells estimated to hit were about as under:-

	Bursting Charges (lbs)	
	Gunpowder	Lyddite
5 12-in shells	405	-
75 6-in	380	500
140 12-pdr shells	180	-
200 3-pdr	35	-
TOTAL	1,000	500

A battleship in the present day uses some 20 lb of powder for a twenty-one gun salute, and even in the old days of big smooth bores 100 lb suf-

Mark of 6-inch shell which grazed edge of port. (BNA, 1901).

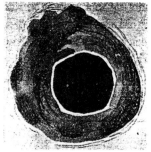
Hole punched by 6-inch shell, 10-inch in diameter. (BNA, 1901).

ficed. No wonder then that powder sufficient for some fifty salutes on the new scale, and for ten on the old scale, to say nothing of half as much lyddite, produced clouds of dense smoke, through which the gunners of the Majestic could scarcely perceive their target, and which must have considerably affected the accuracy of their fire.

As to the effect of the shells, the armour only seems to have been penetrated in three places, twice by 12-in shells and once by 6-in. One 12-in shell, described by the *Times* as a gallery shot, caught the upper corner of the citadel on the port after angle; checked by the massiveness of the target (6-in wrought iron), it exploded, wrecking the platform on which the conning tower stands, and doing immense damage inside the battery, though the guns themselves and heavier parts of mountings were uninjured. It seems to have been this shell which caused the wreckage of all the dummies, descried by the *Engineer*, inside the battery, where it is also said that the sights and "gear" of the guns sustained such damage that, though the guns themselves were uninjured, they could have been of no use. Several small shells, from 3-pdrs and 12-pdrs, may have passed through the ports and have contributed to this damage. Another 12-in shell struck on, or just below, the waterline amidships, where the plating varies from 12 inches to 8 inches in thickness. It made a large hole, and, though it did not send anything down into the engine room, was undoubtedly the cause of the sinking of the ship, which took place some minutes after the completion of the practice. Another entered the unarmoured lower deck forward, and

cut the spindle of the capstan, whilst a fourth is reported to have cut down the funnel and utterly wrecked the funnel casing.

With regard to the effect of the 6-in shells, only one punched its way through the armour; a sketch of the hole is reproduced from the *Engineer*. As is usual where an inferior projectile is used, the hole is much larger than the original diameter of the shell, showing that the head of the shell was crushed and the body expanded, but just succeeded in punching its way through, probably assisted by the lack of toughness of the plate, which was 6 inches thick at the spot struck. All the rest of the 6-in shells which struck the citadel or belt broke up harmlessly against the armour, with one exception – pointed out by the *Times* – that several lyddite shells which struck the plating forward, near the water-line, had so hammered it as to cause a dangerous leakage. A 6-in shell appears to have grazed the edge of one of the gun-ports of the battery, bursting as it did so, but the gun beside the burst was not damaged.

A writer in the *Engineer* argues from the slight effect of the 6-in common shell, notwithstanding their pointed heads, that, for efficiency, projectiles should either be made of hardened steel with strong tough heads, and if necessary reduced bursting charges, for dealing either with armoured or unarmoured parts, or should be made with the view of holding the largest possible bursting charge; and that the best shell exclusively for the attack of the unprotected structure is a nose-fuzed shell filled with lyddite.

The unarmoured parts of the ship before and abaft the central citadel

The only boat left on board the Bellisle. *(BNA, 1901).*

were simply riddled by the bursting shells, both 6-in, 12-pdrs, and 3-pdrs, but there was a marked difference between the effect of the powder-filled 6-in fired at the after part of the ship and that of the lyddite shell fired at the fore part. Between the damage done by one and the other there was no comparison. While the 6-in common destroyed as one might a wooden box with an axe, lyddite completely pulverised the wood, acting in a moment much as dry rot acts in a score or two of years. Moreover, where 6-in common shell burst between the decks, the deck above shewed no sign of it; but it was quite another thing with lyddite. Not only were huge holes blown upwards, but the entire deck was bulged up. These holes are well shown in the sketches taken from the *Engineer*.

Some claim that the funnel was cut down by 12-in common, others that a 6-in lyddite shell did the damage; possibly both contributed. One of these shells also cut a steam pipe down below, a fragment having passed through the gratings of the funnel. The 6-pdrs on the top of the battery were all disabled, and all the dummies stationed round them were "killed". Those on the port side were said to have been disabled by the upward radiating action of lyddite shell striking the armour below them, which radiating action is well shown in the sketch. The *Times* correspondent argues from this fact that light guns should be somewhat recessed back from the armoured side in order

to avoid this contingency. The lyddite shell smashed up ad overturned the unarmoured structure on the forecastle used as a seaman's head, but the masts, though riddled, stood although most of the rigging was shot away. The conning tower does not appear to have been hit, though the dummies inside it were broken by the concussion of one of the shells striking the boats and bridge close to it.

The only boat left was the steam pinnace, of which a sketch is given. It is not hard to understand from this sketch why the others disappeared.

The armoured deck does not appear to have been pierced. A correspondent of the *Engineer* states that several lyddite shells burst close to the deck where it was 2 inches thick without injuring it at all. At least one 12-in shell also burst close to the deck without causing serious injury, and generally the gas from the shells seems to have sought the line of least resistance, which in the case of the Belleisle was usually upwards.

In fact, there was nothing to show that a shell bursting between decks under the floor plates of a turret or barbette in ships like our Admiral class would do any damage on the other side of the plating. Moreover, the almost prohibitive difficulty of getting a shell to burst where required, namely, exactly under and close to the floor plating of a barbette, is sufficiently obvious.

The 12 and 3-pdrs did well as regards riddling all unprotected structures, but the difference of effect of the hard steel 3-pdr shell which pierced deeply into the armour, and the soft steel 12-pdrs which splashed harmlessly against it, was very noticeable. But the general

destruction of unarmoured parts was such as to make it impossible to identify the damage caused by each individual shell of small calibre. All was swallowed up in a general ruin, which is well shown in the sketches reproduced from the *Engineer*. It seems possible, if not probable, that the 3-pdrs and the 12-pdrs alone would have sufficed to wreck and destroy all the unarmoured parts of the ship, and to put out of action the unprotected guns, so that a large proportion of the 6-in guns might have advantageously fired armour-piercing projectiles for piercing the battery and waterline. But the object of the experiment being apparently to ascertain the effect of shell and not to sink or destroy the Belleisle, ordinary shells were naturally fired in lieu of armour piercers.

It was remarked by many observers that an attack by torpedo craft if supported by even half or a quarter of the shell fire directed against the Belleisle, would have considerable chance of success. The smoke alone which was poured out by the bursting shells in dense volumes would act as a screen for the torpedoists, and the fire of guns quite unprotected by armour would be very wild and slow under a shower of bursting shells. It certainly appears an open question, whether in our larger battleships and cruisers some protection should not be given to the men actually fighting the light quick-firing guns on which we must mainly rely to beat off a torpedo attack, and which might be assailed by the quick-firing guns of supporting ships.

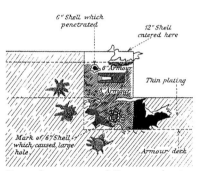

Port after corners of Battery, showing damage to thin plating. (BNA, 1901).

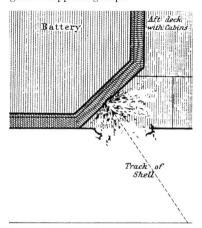

Section of Port aft corner of battery, showing damage to thin plating by 6"shell. (BNA, 1901).

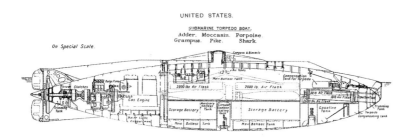

Inboard profile of US Submarine Torpedo boat. (BNA, 1901).

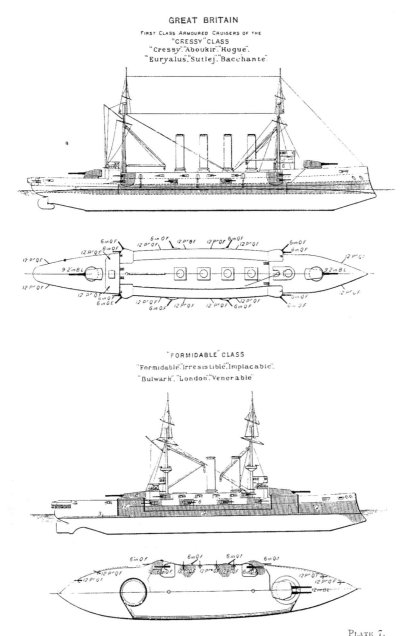

PLATE 7.

Plans of the Cressy and Formidable First Class armoured cruisers. (BNA, 1901).

No very exact information is to hand as to the destruction of the unarmoured side by lyddite shells. But judging by the photograph given in the *Engineer* showing the ship being towed into harbour, the damage must have been most extensive, and it bodes anything but well for the water-line of our very numerous protected cruisers. In this connection the effect of a single shell, apparently a 6-in, gives serious grounds for reflection. This shell blew away a large piece of plating, said by the *Engineer* to measure 10 ft square; which happened in this way.

The shell entered some feet abaft the junction between the thin plating of the lower deck and the armour of the casemate, passed through the outer plating, and burst against the casemate bulkhead. The gases caused by its explosion, unable to affect the casemate armour or unarmoured deck, rebounded and blew an enormous hole in the ship's side. If the rough sketch be looked at sideways it will be seen that the bulkhead might be taken to represent the sloping armoured deck in, say, the Diadem or Terrible. The object of this sloping armour is to stop shells which strike about the water-line. In doing this there seems a great liability that very large gaps will be blown in the ship's side. The only remedy would seem to be to give the gases free scope upwards inside the ship in some direction where they would be harmless, by no means a simple matter.

It is perfectly obvious that shells will burst after entering the unprotected parts of all ships, whether battleships or cruisers, but it seems extremely doubtful whether we are in the habit of so building our ships that the gases may do as little destruction as possible. Much might certainly be done to give shells which burst between decks, &c, a chance of discharging their gases comparatively innocuously. Large hatches, somewhat after the fashion of the old skids, might be made between main deck casemates; whilst on the other hand, in unarmoured cruisers, bulkheads or screens should be arranged so as to protect the men between decks from the blast of shells bursting before or abaft them.

Conclusion

The experiments demonstrated most forcibly that armour gives most efficient protection against shell fire, and that the unarmoured parts of a ship are hopelessly untenable under the fire of a number of quick-firing guns.

Contents of *The Naval Annual* 1901

HMS Cressy, First Class armoured cruiser. (BNA, 1901).

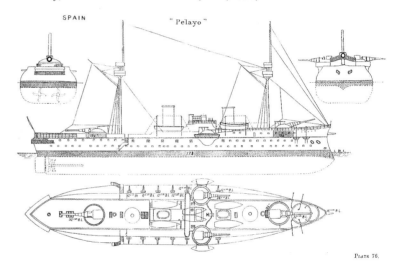

The Spanish ship Pelayo. *(BNA, 1901).*

Norge, *Norwegian coast defence ship. (BNA, 1901).*

French Navy Estimates
German Navy Estimates
Italian Navy Estimates
Russian Navy Estimates
United States Navy Estimates

LIST OF ILLUSTRATIONS
HMS *Cressy* (first-class armoured cruiser)
Hatsuse (Japanese first-class battleship)
Gromoboi (Russian first-class armoured cruiser)
Alabama (United States first-class battleship)
Mikasa (Japanese first-class battleship)
Norge (Norwegian coast-defence ship)
Idzumo (Japanese first-class armoured cruiser)

DIAGRAM
Diagram showing the Expenditure on the Construction of New Ships (British) in the financial years 1872-73 to 1900-1901

WHITEHEAD TORPEDO DRAWINGS

Denis Cahill replies to a query from Antony Preston regarding two unusual drawings from the Whitehead torpedo factory at Fiume.

The first of these drawings was simply identified as 'Torp Danese' and dated 8 August 1881. This drawing is one of the two second class torpedo boats (Numbers 4 & 5) built by John Isaac Thorhycroft for the Danish Navy in 1881-1882. References to these vessels can be found in:

R Chesneau and E M Kolesnik, *Conway's All The World's Fighting Ships, 1860-1905*, (London: Conway Maritime Press, 1979), p. 368.

K C Barnaby, *100 Years of Specialized Shipbuilding & Engineering*, (London: Hutchinson & Co. Ltd., 1964), p. 213.

H Fock, *Schwarze Gesellen Band 1 Torpedoboote bis 1914*, (Herford: Koehlers Verlagsgesellschaft, 1979), pp. 270-1, 318-9.

A more detailed description of these vessels can be found in David Lyon's

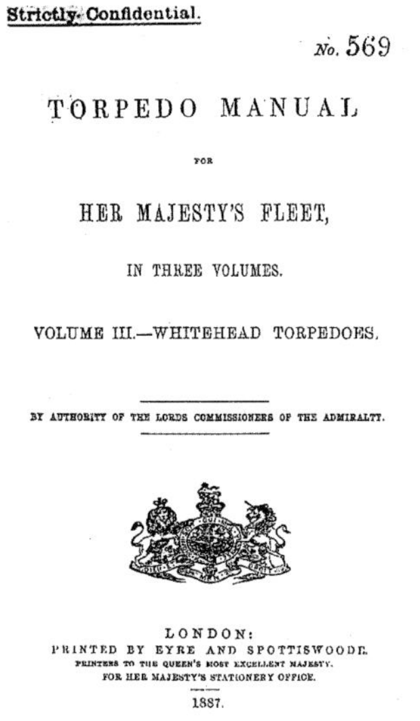
Strictly Confidential.
No. 569
TORPEDO MANUAL
FOR
HER MAJESTY'S FLEET,
IN THREE VOLUMES.
VOLUME III.—WHITEHEAD TORPEDOES.
BY AUTHORITY OF THE LORDS COMMISSIONERS OF THE ADMIRALTY.
LONDON:
PRINTED BY EYRE AND SPOTTISWOODE,
PRINTERS TO THE QUEEN'S MOST EXCELLENT MAJESTY.
FOR HER MAJESTY'S STATIONERY OFFICE.
1887.

Front cover of Torpedo Manual for Her Majesty's Fleet, Volume III – Whitehead Torpedoes, 1887. (WTM).

unpublished manuscript on the Thorhycroft papers held at the National Maritime Museum. The relevant section is here quoted:

"Yard Numbers: 153, 154, TB nos. 4, 5 1881-1882, Second class torpedo boats for the Royal Danish Navy. *Dimensions*: 63'oa x 7'6" x...+3'4". *Guns*: Hotchkiss multi-barrel revolving cannon. Torpedoes, etc: 2 fixed 14" bow tubes. *Machinery*: 8¼ inch x 13½ inch x 8inch. Loco boiler 130 pounds per square inch working pressure. Contract 15 knots on 2 hour trial.

Ordered: 31.10.1881 *Confirmed*: 1.12.1881 For delivery in 6 months [6½ months in pencil on contract]".

No 153 (TB4) was launched on 16.6.1882 and No 154 (TB5) on 21.6.1882. Both ran trials on the measured mile on 27.6.1882 and 2 hour trials on 28.6.1882, with results as follows:
No 153 - 16.98 kts at 616 rpm on the measured mile and 15.56 kts at 569 rpm on 2 hr trial; No 154 - 16.91 kts at 521 rpm on the measured mile and 15.94 kts at 588 rpm on 2 hr trial.

"*Weights*: (In hundredweight, quarters, pounds) (153) Hull 62.0.3¼, fittings 39.2.3, engines 36.1.20¼, boiler 49.3.16, spare gear 8.3.16¼, woodwork 2.2.21½ = 203.1.25¼, Costs: Contract price £6,000. Penalty of £20 per week late. Price reduced 10% if speed under 15 knots – boat rejected at 14 knots or below. *Notes*: Order on 10.2.1881 (D/1)". Thornycrofts wrote to Captain Johnke, RDN offering two second class boats similar to those supplied to the RN (to plan HO 1132) for £3,000 without torpedo gear. This finally led to the order for these two vessels. The contract is confusingly altered in pencil (presumably during the preparation for another design) to dimensions of 66' x 8' and a price of £6,050, but these alterations do not appear to concern the two boats described here. The load carried was to be 2½ tons including a ¼ inch thick conning tower whilst the lifting weight was not to exceed 10½ tons: "If during the construction of

REFERENCE TABLE SHOWING WEIGHTS, &C. OF FIUME AND BERLIN TORPEDOES.

Pattern.	Length.	Weight complete with Explosive and Air.	Approximate Speed of Torpedo for 600 Yards.	Air Pressure Engines, work at for 600 Yards.	Distance run by Torpedo for each Tooth of Counter.	Reduction of Pressure per Tooth.	Position of centre of gravity from nose of Torpedo.	Head. Weight of, with Charge complete, but without Pistol.	Weight of Explosive dry.	Weight of Explosive as supplied in Case or Warhead.	Position of centre of gravity of Explosive or Dummy.	Weight of Primer.	No. of Grains of Fulminate of Mercury.	Weight of Dummy Charge.
	Ft. In.	Lbs.	Knots.	Atmospheres.	Yards.	Lbs. per sq. inch.	Ft. In.	Lbs.	Lbs.	Lbs.	In. from large end.	Oz.	Grains.	Lbs.
14-in. Fiume Mark I. (various Nos.)	14 6	529	17 to 19§	21	60	75	6 6	51·5	26·5	37½	10	6	34 to 38	34¼
14-in. Fiume Mark II.	14 6	594	20	21	60	75	6 2¾	56	30	41	8	6	34 to 38	39
14-in. Fiume Mark III. (1338/9, 1357/8, 1442/3).	14 6	594	21 to 22	22	60	72	—	65	37·6	50	—	6	34 to 38	50
14-in. Fiume Mark I.* (2070/117, 1926/7)	13 3	550	21 to 22	22	50	60	5 11½	100	56·4	100	9·375	6	34 to 38	66
14-in. Fiume Mark IV.	14 6	660	23 to 24	28 to 30	60	65	6 8	114·4	58	114·4	8¾	6	34 to 38	70
12-in. Fiume, Baby (2223/8, 2453/6)	9 6	275	21†	25†	54†	150†	5 3½	46¼	25	46¼	7½	6	34 to 38	33
14-in. Berlin ‡	15 0	602	22 to24‡	28‖	65‖	130‖	6 6½	59	31	59	8¼	21	96	37½

(See also next page.)

§ Speed with tail stays about 17·5, without tail stays about 19·5; the Mark I. Fiume will go about 25 knots for 200 yards, with reducer set to 1", but it is not adjusted for this speed. ‡ The Berlin torpedo will go about 21 knots for 600 yards, with reducing valve set to ·63", but the torpedo is not adjusted for this speed. † For 300 yards. ‖ For about 430 yards (400 metres).
NOTE.—The charges for all Whitehead torpedoes contain 17 lbs. of water to 100 lbs. of dry guncotton.

Table illustrating weights of Fiume and Berlin Torpedoes. (WTM).

TORPEDOES SUPPLIED TO DIFFERENT NATIONS BY MESSRS. WHITEHEAD & CO.

Government	1874	1875	1876	1877	1878		1879	1880	1881	1882		1883											1884	
	Steel	Steel	Steel	Steel	Steel		Steel	Steel	Steel	Steel		Steel		C.	S.	Composite							Steel	
	16 in. by 14 ft.	15 in. by 19 ft.	15 in. by 19 ft.	15 in. by 19 ft.	14 in. by 14 ft. 6 in.	15 in. by 19 ft.	16 in. by 21 ft.	14 in. by 14 ft. 6 in.	15 in. by 19 ft.	14 in. by 14 ft. 6 in.	13 in. by 19 ft.	14 in. by 14 ft. 6 in.	15 in. by 19 ft.	14 in. by 14 ft. 6 in.	15 in. by 19 ft.	14 in. by 14 ft. 6 in.	14 in. by 14 ft. 4 in.	15 in. by 12 ft. 3 in.	14 in. by 14 ft. 6 in.	16 in. by 14 ft.	14 in. by 12 ft. 3 in.	14 in. by 11 ft.	15 in. by 19 ft.	14 in. by 14 ft. 6 in.
	B.	A.*	A.*	A.*	A.	A.*	C.	A.	B.	B.	B.	B.	C.	B.	C.	L.	C.	D.	E.	F.	D.	M.	O.	B.	C.
Argentine Rep.	—	—	—	—	—	—	—	—	—	40	—	—	—	—	—	—	—	—	—	—	—	—	—
Austria	5	—	—	—	—	20	—	30	—	50	—	—	8	—	—	—	—	—	—	—	—	—	—
Belgium	—	—	—	—	—	—	—	—	14	—	—	—	—	—	—	—	—	—	—	—	—	—	—
Brazil	—	—	—	—	—	—	—	—	—	—	12	—	58	—	—	—	—	—	—	—	—	—	—
Chili	—	—	—	—	—	—	—	—	—	—	—	—	—	—	—	—	—	—	—	—	—	—	—
Denmark	1	—	25	25	—	—	2	12	6	12	—	—	10	—	—	—	2	1	1	—	1	1	—	—
England	6	—	—	100	—	—	125	25	—	4	2	—	—	—	—	—	—	—	—	—	—	—	—
France	3	—	50	102	—	100	—	—	5	5	—	6	7	103	—	57	—	—	—	—	10	—	80	72
Germany	—	40	60	6	—	52	—	45	—	—	—	—	—	—	—	—	—	—	—	—	—	—	—
Greece	—	—	—	—	—	—	—	—	30	40	—	—	—	—	—	—	—	—	—	—	—	—	—
Holland	—	—	—	—	—	—	—	—	—	—	—	—	—	—	—	—	—	—	—	—	—	—	—
Italy	4	—	—	—	—	—	10	—	80	—	10	1	39	1	1	—	—	—	—	—	—	—	—
Norway	1	—	25	25	—	—	—	—	10	—	—	—	—	—	—	—	2	—	—	—	—	—	—
Portugal	—	—	—	5	—	10	—	20	—	15	—	—	—	—	—	—	—	—	—	—	—	—	—
Russia	—	—	20	30	—	82	25	—	90	10	—	—	—	—	—	—	—	—	—	—	—	—	—
Turkey	—	—	—	—	—	3	—	—	—	—	—	—	—	—	—	—	—	—	—	—	—	—	—
Victoria and S.A.	—	—	—	—	—	—	—	—	—	—	—	—	—	—	—	—	—	—	—	—	—	—	—

* Probably transformed to double screw, or about to be, in these countries.   † Transformed from 15″ A, not included in total.   ‡ Two in the hands of Turkey.

TORPEDOES SUPPLIED TO DIFFERENT NATIONS BY MESSRS. WHITEHEAD & CO.

Government	1884—cont.						1885														1886						Total number
	Composite						Steel		Composite												Steel	Composite					
	15 in. by 15 ft.	14 in. by 14 ft.	14 in. by 12 ft. 3 in.	14 in. by 12 ft. 3 in.	14 in. by 11 ft.	13 in. by 9 ft. 6 in.	15 in. by 19 ft.	14 in. by 14 ft. 6 in.	15 in. by 15 ft. 6 in.	15 in. by 15 ft.	15 in. by 10 ft. 6 in.	14 in. by 14 ft. 6 in.	14 in. by 14 ft. 6 in.	14 in. by 14 ft.	14 in. by 12 ft. 6 in.	14 in. by 11 ft.	14 in. by 9 ft. 6 in.	15 in. by 19 ft.	14 in. by 14 ft. 6 in.	14 in. by 14 ft. 6 in.	14 in. by 14 ft. 6 in.	13 in. by 9 ft. 6 in.					
	H.	H.	K.	L.	O.	P.	C.	C.	G.	K.	L.	E.	D.	F.	H.	N.	L.	O.	P.	C.	C.	D.	F.	G.	P.	R.	
Argentine Rep.	—	—	—	—	—	—	—	—	—	—	—	—	—	—	—	—	—	—	—	—	—	—	40
Austria	—	—	—	—	—	—	—	38	—	—	—	—	—	—	—	—	—	30	2	2	—	185
Belgium	—	—	—	—	—	—	—	—	—	—	—	—	—	—	—	—	—	—	—	—	—	14
Brazil	—	—	—	—	—	—	—	—	—	—	—	—	—	—	—	—	—	—	—	—	—	70
Chili	—	—	—	—	—	—	—	—	—	—	—	—	—	—	—	—	—	—	—	10	—	10
Denmark	4	—	6	—	—	—	1	—	—	—	1	—	—	—	—	—	—	—	—	—	111
England	—	—	50*	2	—	—	—	120	—	—	—	—	—	100	—	—	10	—	494
France	—	12†	—	—	—	2	2	—	—	—	—	—	2	70	30	—	—	—	712
Germany	—	—	—	—	—	—	—	—	—	—	—	—	—	—	—	—	—	203
Greece	—	—	—	—	—	—	—	—	—	—	—	—	—	—	—	—	—	70
Holland	—	—	—	—	—	—	—	—	10	30	—	—	—	—	—	—	—	40
Italy	—	—	50‡	—	—	—	—	—	—	—	50‡	—	—	—	—	—	—	196
Norway	—	—	2	—	—	4	—	—	—	—	—	—	—	—	—	—	—	69
Portugal	—	—	—	—	—	—	—	—	—	—	—	—	—	—	—	—	—	50
Russia	—	—	—	1	—	50	1	—	—	—	1	—	—	—	—	—	310
Turkey	—	—	—	—	—	—	1	—	1	—	1	1	—	—	—	—	7
Victoria and S.A.	—	—	—	—	—	—	—	—	30	—	—	—	—	—	—	—	—	—
																							Total 2611

*. Transformed from 14″ A, not included in total.   † Transformed 6 from 14″ A, not included in total, and 6 from their own air chambers.
‡ Transformed Italian air chambers.   April 19, 1886.

NOTE.—The term "composite" is applied to those torpedoes in which phosphor-bronze, or some other metal than steel, is used in conjunction with steel in the construction of the outside shell. Austria has made a few torpedoes at Pola. France has manufactured several 14-inch torpedoes in the country, probably 100 at least. Phosphor-bronze torpedoes are manufactured for Germany and other nations at Berlin. Italy manufactured 200 16-inch and attempted the manufacture of 14-inch torpedoes, but the speed was only seven knots, and several of the air chambers have been turned over to Whitehead to make use of in making torpedoes for the Italian Government. Russia has factories at Nicolaieff, Onboukoff, and Cronstadt for making torpedoes.

Tables showing torpedoes supplied to different nations by Whitehead & Co. (WTM).

---

the boats… [Thornycrofts]… should have any improvements to propose, the Danish Minister of the Navy expects they will do so in order to make the boat thoroughly efficient". The Danes were to deliver the torpedo gear to Chiswick 6 weeks before the completion date for fitting. History: On 30.4.1883 Thornycrofts suggested (D/2) fitting single barrelled Gardner machine guns on these vessels. Plans: Lines – GA & Section: 1416:½ inch. Charging doors – (Whitehead plan). Details of torpedo gear (3). Photos: none. Documents: Trial/Contract contract (K. p. 345)/ spare gear list (K. p. 845).

Unfortunately the scale given in the drawings (1/2in = 1 foot) cannot be used to confirm my conclusions (no reduction ratio for the plans reproduced in *Warship 1999-2000* is given). However, if we assume that the torpedo on the loading trough of the vessel to be a 14in by 14ft6in Fiume torpedo (see illustrations from *Torpedo Manual for Her Majesty's Fleet, Volume III – Whitehead Torpedoes*, 1887, p.146, or Edwyn Gray, *The Devil's Device*, Annapolis: Naval Institute Press, 1991, p.253), the vessel illustrated would have a beam of 7ft6in which is the same as tht of the second class torpedo boats Numbers 4 & 5 (Thornycroft Yard

nos. 153 & 154) built by John Isaac Thornycroft for the Danish Navy in 1881 and 1882.

WARGAMING: APPLIED HISTORY?
Paul French outlines the benefits wargaming can provide to the study of naval history.

Mention you are a war gamer to most people and you get a half smile and the comment 'so you play with toy soldiers?' The simple answer is yes, but in my case it's toy boats. But there is more to it than that. War gaming encompasses the recreation on the tabletop or screen of conflict from a Stone Age hunting party versus a mammoth to Science Fiction combats in space. At one end of the spectrum it can be simply a game based on but largely divorced from reality, to the other where it becomes a detailed simulation designed to recreate accurately real situations and to explore the myriad 'what ifs'. It can therefore range from a purely recreational activity to one which is used to train, test and explore different possibilities. It can involve large numbers of intricately painted miniatures or be largely a paper exercise; the combinations and medium, tabletop, board game or computer, are almost endless.

Naval war gaming breaks down into three broad groups: miniatures board and computer games. Often the boundaries are quite diffuse, with computer-moderated miniatures rules, and the use of board games to generate Grand Tactical or Strategic level contact, whilst combat is resolved in using miniatures or an abstracted method. If miniatures are used the choice of scale depends upon the number of vessels engaged; the range of weapons, type of engagement, eg a night action over short ranges allows a larger model-scale, and ultimately the playing area. The most common scales are 1:600, 1:700, 1:1200/1:1250, 1:2400, 1:3000, 1:6000, with 1:4800 perhaps the optimum for use at home but limited by the restricted number of manufacturers and ranges.

Whatever the medium, the key is the rule system. All games have rules and war games are no different. Rules come in a variety of forms from highly detailed with pages of small print backed up by copious data annexes, to simple single page systems and computer moderated systems, in the latter the computer does all the boring calculations and keeps a record of damage. The rules are the means to an end. They determine what may or may not be done, and define the mechanisms required to resolve the chance elements. The key components of any system, whatever the period or genre are the same; command level, time and distance. The three are inter-related. The first determines what forces are controlled by the player and what each model or playing piece represents. A ship model may represent a single ship or a division, flotilla, division or squadron. This in turn sets the level at which combat is resolved, the larger the action the less important an individual ship is, thus combat can be resolved between squadrons rather than individual ships. The second influences the turn length, hence what maybe accomplished in a given turn. Each turn may represent anything from 15 seconds to a number of hours or days. Many rules systems use two or more different turn lengths depending on the type of activity taking place. The final component, distance, is represented in the rules by the ground scale. In tactical rules, this is influenced by model scale, the speed of the combatants and their effective combat range. In grand tactical or strategic level games the emphasis is upon cruising speed and geography. In general the higher the level of command taken by the player, the longer the time period represented by each turn and commensurately larger ground scale. In Second World War based games the tactical turn is usually three to six minutes, with a ground scale of about 1in to 250yds. The key for rules designers is to pick the most appropriate combination.

Whilst, time, distance and levels of command are worthy concepts, the heart of any war game is combat. This requires detailed and explicit data, rate of fire, range, accuracy, armour thickness and armour penetration to name a few. In historical periods this data is generally available but often requires extensive research, combined with the ability to comprehend technical jargon. The information available is generally derived from various range tables or performance data. Despite this accounts are clear, the effect of a weapon on a target can be unpredictable. Therefore, data derived from tests carried out under optimum conditions need to be cross-referenced with contemporary accounts. In the post-war period the problem is twofold. Firstly, a lack of consistent information, and secondly, the volume, or lack thereof actual naval combat. Thus rule writers and gamers are left with the problem of interpreting conflicting information and conceptions. It is something of a paradox that a rule mechanism that allows the quick resolution of combat, which produces believable and broadly accurate results, is derived from complex data presented in a simple and often abstract fashion.

Take gunnery as an example. It is done by taking a particular weapons system, checking its hit probability at a given range against a given type of target and rolling a dice to establish the number of hits. This will vary according to rate of fire, target aspect, weather conditions and crew quality amongst others. Once the number of hits has been ascertained the amount of damage is calculated. This may vary according to the protection, strength of the target and location of the hit; usually this is based upon some points system ie a 15in shell does x points of damage, a ship is worth y points. Accumulated damage will eventually sink or destroy a target, it may also inflict 'critical hits', these include additional damage to systems, fires, flooding or catastrophic explosions.

One of the great virtues of naval war gaming is the ability to re-fight historical actions on a one-to-one basis. Relatively few models are required and expensive terrain may not be essential. There are of course, exceptions to every rule; Salamis and the Armada spring to mind, but in general the major actions are reproducible on the tabletop. Relatively little abstraction is required even for an action the size of Jutland. Combat prior to 1914 was conducted over relatively short distances, thus in most cases demands upon space are moderate. Even the climatic carrier actions of the Pacific War need surprisingly little space, essentially enough area to set up the Task Force under attack, the air searches are, typically, a paper exercise.

The greatest benefits a war game can give anyone interested in naval history are the practical application of ideas and the interaction between time and distance. Track charts give no comprehension of the time needed to cover the distance or the prevailing visibility; the fog of war is reduced to insignificant proportions. Jutland is one of the classic examples. In hindsight there have been many accounts and many suggestions as to how Jellicoe should have fought the battle. The simple test is try it. Using a system of 4-minute turns, and a scale of 1cm to 144 yards, the Grand Fleet Battle Squadrons cover something of the order of 100cm from front to back, they move at 20cm. It takes a minimum of four game turns to form the simplest line. Once in line the Grand Fleet is virtually impossible to manoeuvre. Experienced gamers, who had practised the action on numerous occasions, with the advantage of superior co-ordination and information, were unable to force a decisive action upon a relatively poorly handled High Sea Fleet on the tabletop. Conditions in the North Sea were considerably more difficult.

Whilst a well-written set of war games rules, interpreted by knowledgeable players, can reproduce the technical attributes of a period, they struggle to achieve the appropriate mindset. Player activity can be curbed by restrictive rules, or enlightened umpires manipulating the information available and preying upon the players fears and conceptions. However, there is no substitute for well-briefed players, with a good background of the history, role playing, in the broadest sense, the part of the historical commander. Picking the war games commander carefully can give remarkably accurate historical results, if the historical commander was bold, his gaming counterpart should be too. In a recent game based upon the relief of Wake Island in 1941, the US player with clear tactical and material superiority talked himself out of decisive action on the basis of intelligence reports and his assessment upon what the Japanese should have done. The parallels between his decisions and those of Admiral Pye and Admiral Fletcher were remarkable.

Whilst war gaming at the gaming end of the spectrum may serve only to entertain or to introduce young participants and to introduce basic concepts in an enjoyable way, towards the simulation end of the spectrum there is much to commend it to serious students. A good set of rules should 'teach' a player the problems and tactics of a period and provide some indication of the strengths and weaknesses of different fleets. To do this however the rules need to be based upon a firm understanding of the materials, principles and psychology of the time. All of which requires a broad knowledge base, particularly of the rules writers but also of the players and umpires. Whatever the emphasis of the simulation it is a game. The people participating are not at risk and often being naturally competitive try to win at all costs, up to and including suspending reality. One of my favourite anecdotes is of a gamer who was also an authority on English Civil War artillery. Despite researching the use of different types of ordnance and coming down conclusively against the use of heavy mortars in field operations, when confronted with the model on the table (for show) he insisted upon using it tactically. Care must also be taken to remember that the events depicted were far from a game to those involved and at times discretion is required.

The value of war games in illustrating history is becoming widely recognised by museums throughout the UK, with regular events at the Royal Navy Museum, Portsmouth, and the Tank Museum, Bovington to name two. In addition the National Maritime Museum has used war games in conjunction with special events. A well planned, researched and organised game can highlight the tactics and weapons of a period and

illuminate the theory of naval operations without the ultimate penalty if you get it wrong.

For further information on naval war gaming, contact the Naval Wargames Society (NWS). The Society was formed in the 1960's to promote naval war gaming. It produces a magazine entitled 'Battlefleet', which has articles of interest to gamers of all periods and lists of Traders offering a multitude of games and miniatures often with discounts to NWS members. The Society website maybe found at http://website.lineone.net/~swhite10 1/ alternatively write to

Hon. Sec. J Gorringe
The Naval Wargames Society
42, Simmonds Road
Ludgershall
Andover
Hants
SP11 8RH
United Kingdom

HAZE GRAY & UNDERWAY

Andrew Toppan reports on an website containing thousands of ship histories and images.

Haze Gray & Underway (www.haze gray.org) is a website dedicated to naval, maritime, and shipbuilding history and current affairs. The site offers a wide variety of resources related to these topics, including more than 7000 ship histories, over 3000 images, and hundreds of other documents. *Hazegray* has been in operation since 1994, and is a completely non-commercial site, operated and funded by a small group of volunteers. The site's popularity has grown over the years, and it now averages over 5500 visitors each day.

By far the most popular section of the site is *DANFS Online*. This is the 'unofficial' online home for the *Dictionary of American Naval Fighting Ships* (DANFS). The *DANFS Online* project is a long-term effort to put the entire contents of the nine DANFS books onto the web, so it will be easily accessible to all. A dedicated group of volunteers, whose numbers

have ranged from one to a dozen over the years, have completed over 7000 ship histories, with plans to add another 1000 histories by the end of the year 2000. The current *DANFS Online* database includes complete or nearly-complete coverage for most major warship classes, and selected coverage of other ship types.

Another major section of *Hazegray* is *World Navies Today*, a database of the world's current naval forces. *World Navies Today* was conceived as a readily-available and regularly-updated information source, primarily for people without need or budget for the expensive reference works. Currently *World Navies Today* includes listings for essentially all of the world's navies, along with some Coast Guards and non-naval forces. Each navy's list includes the basic specifications for all significant ship classes, along with ship listings by name and number. Many listings include representative photographs for each class. A major update and expansion currently underway will include additional photos, with a goal of providing at least one photo for each ship class throughout the world (contributions of photos are currently being solicited).

The third major section - and the original foundation of the website - is the *Naval History Information Center*. This section of the site features listings that combine design/technical and operational histories for major warship types. These listings currently include all the world's aircraft carriers, all US Navy battleships and cruisers, and other navies' battleships from the post-1906 era. The 'flagship' of these listings is the aircraft carriers section - a definitive listing of the world's naval aviation vessels from the start of naval aviation to the current day, featuring over 1000 photos.

Hazegray's fourth major component is the Photo Galleries section. Each photo gallery is constructed around a specific event, ship, topic, or theme, ranging from 19th century warships to maritime salvage, to modern warship construction and warship scrapping. Each photo gallery is made up of anywhere from six to 300 photos, often using materials contributed by website visitors.

The *Canadian Navy of Yesterday and Today* is the fifth major component of the *Hazegray* site. This section of the site features complete listings of major Canadian ships since the 1910 inception of the Canadian Navy, with photos of most ship classes, and several related photo galleries.

The final major section of the *Hazegray* site is the shipbuilding section, a relatively new and still-evolving project. This section features complete lists of ships built by several major US shipyards, and a growing section documenting the history of the now-defunct Quincy Fore River shipyards. Plans for future expansion of this section include histories of major US shipyards, and photo documentaries of interesting and unique shipbuilding operations, such as traditional ways launchings.

BATH IRON WORKS, MAINE
Andrew Toppan provides a variety of images of USN Arleigh Burke *class destroyers under construction.*

This group of photos illustrates the various *Arleigh Burke* (DDG 51) class guided missile destroyers under construction at Bath Iron Works, in Bath, Maine, during the summer of 2000. BIW is the lead designer and builder of the DDG 51 class ships, and will have delivered 18 of the class by year's end, with another nine DDGs on order. The photos represent a snapshot of BIW and the yard's major activities this year, and show the complete progression of warship construction from assembly on the building ways to launch, outfitting, sea trials, and final departure from the building yard. In addition to the ships shown here, *Chaffee* (DDG 90) and DDG 92 were in the early stages of construction within BIW's various fabrication, assembly, and preoutfitting buildings.

[Ed - Damage to the USS *Cole* (DDG-87) in Aden on 12 October 2000 showed how battleworthy these ships are.]

Howard (DDG 83) *fitting out at Bath Iron Works, August 2000. Howard was launched on 20 November 1999, and is scheduled for delivery in March, 2001. At this stage of her construction she is starting final completion, testing, and activation of her equipment, in preparation for sea trials scheduled for early 2001. (Andrew Toppan).*

McCampbell (DDG 85) *fitting out at BIW, August 2000. Just a month after her launching, she is only starting the long fitting-out process, which will culminate in sea trials during the summer of 2001, and delivery to the Navy late that year. A service barge and tugs are moored alongside. (Andrew Toppan).*

Tugs maneuver Winston S. Churchill *(DDG 81) to her berth on 16 August 2000, at the completion of her Acceptance Trials ("Charlie" Trials). Two brooms in the rigging indicate another successful trial. Churchill was launched 17 April 1999, and is scheduled for delivery 13 October 2000. She will be commissioned at Norfolk 10 March 2001. In honor of her famous namesake, she will fly the flags of both the United States and the United Kingdom, and her crew will always include a Royal Navy sailor. (Andrew Toppan).*

THE WORLD'S FIRST SUCCESSFUL SUBMARINE ATTACK
Martin Robson reports on plans to raise the CSS Hunley.

On the night of 17 February 1864, during the American Civil War, the Confederate warship *Hunley*, armed with a spar torpedo, attacked and sank the USS *Housatonic* blockading Charleston harbour. This historic event, the first successful submarine attack, was marred with tragedy as the *Hunley* was damaged in the subsequent blast and sank with the loss of her entire complement of eight or nine men. In fact 13 men had been previously killed testing the submersible, including Horace L Hunley, who had provided financial backing for the project and had the vessel named in his honour.

Now the 136 year-old submarine is to be raised and preserved, largely due to the perseverance of the writer, archaeologist, adventurer and discoverer Mark M Newell. The intention is to discover exactly why and how the *Hunley* sank, whether from damage inflicted in the blast or because of an alleged suicide pact between members of the crew. Marine archaeologists also intend to discover how the vessel actually performed under combat conditions. The bodies of the crew will receive a traditional Confederate funeral while it is hoped that the *Hunley* will be exhibited in the Charleston Museum.

Another view of Howard *(DDG 83) fitting out at BIW, August 2000. The two large rectangular openings in the aft deckhouse are the helicopter hangars, with their doors not yet installed. (Andrew Toppan).*

Oscar Austin *(DDG 79) departs Bath Iron Works on 20 July 2000. After an overnight stop at BIW's Portland facility,* Oscar Austin *got underway on 21 July en route to Norfolk, Virginia, where she was commissioned on 19 August.* Oscar Austin, *launched 7 November 1998 and delivered 11 May 2000, is the first Flight IIA version of the* Arleigh Burke *(DDG 51) class. The Flight IIA ships feature a number of improvements, mostly related to the addition of hangars and support facilities for two SH-60B Seahawk helicopters. Other changes include survivability and damage control improvements, such as additional blast-hardened bulkheads and a new electrical distribution system. The SQR-19 TACTAS towed array sonar and Harpoon missiles carried in previous ships have been removed, both to reduce costs and to make space for new equipment. (Andrew Toppan).*

McCampbell *(DDG 85) immediately prior to her 2 July 2000 launch at BIW. Secretary of State Madeline Albright served as the ship's sponsor, ceremonially christening the ship moments before* McCampbell *slid down the ways into the Kennebec River. At extreme right is the incomplete hull of* Mason *(DDG 87). (Andrew Toppan).*

WARSHIP GALLERY

In this section, we publish photographs of warships which are unusual, remarkable as images, mysterious or otherwise of special interest to readers. The section is not intended for standard ship portraits, but for out-of-the-ordinary pictures which illuminate aspects of warships not evident in the usual views. This year's special feature presents images of the US landings at Casablanca harbour on 8 November 1942 and was kindly contributed by **Robert P Largesse**. The images were taken by an officer on board the USS *Wilkes* (DD-441) who then passed them onto Robert's father, CDR George J Largesse USN. The editor would be happy to hear from readers with any other unusual pictures which might appear in future issues.

USS Murphy (DD-603), viewed from USS Wilkes, approaches Casablanca harbour on 8 November 1942 . (Robert P Largesse).

Landing craft passing Wilkes with a sister ship, either Swanson, Ludlow or Murphy, inshore. (Robert P Largesse).

USS Augusta (CA-31) under 15in fire from the Jean Bart. (Robert P Largesse).

Another view of USS Augusta (CA-31) under 15in fire from the Jean Bart. (Robert P Largesse).

Wilkes entering Casablanca harbour after the French capitulation, in the background is a sunken merchant ship. (Robert P Largesse).

Le Malin, with the battleship Jean Bart in the background, after her shelling by the USS Massachusetts. To the left, the American destroyer in drydock is probably either Ludlow or perhaps Murphy, both of whom were damaged by French fire during the assault. (Robert P Largesse).

Inboard of Le Malin is an older four-stacked contre-torpilleur, possibly the Albatross, the only one of this group of 18 ships to survive the war. (Robert P Largesse).

HMS Hermes pictured in July 1961 using her pre-wetting system, with her original Type 984 radar. Later this was replaced by Type 965, and before her sale to India in 1983 she was given a 'ski-jump'. (CPL).

HMS Sprat, one of four midget submarines built to replace worn-out wartime XE-craft, is pictured at King's Reach on River Thames, on 25 June 1957. At the helm is her commanding officer, Lieut. H H Brill. Note the Festival Hall in the background. (CPL).

With White Ensign and Tricolour flying, the 152 year old 'Wooden Wall' Implacable (ex-Duguay Trouin) sinks beneath the waves off the Isle of Wight. The last French ship of the line in the world, she was scuttled on on 2 December 1949. (CPL).

INDEX

Page references in *italics* refer to illustrations.